the president's agenda

domestic policy choice from Kennedy to Clinton

third edition

Paul C. Light

The Johns Hopkins University Press
Baltimore and London

© 1982, 1983, 1991, 1999 The Johns Hopkins University Press
All rights reserved. First edition 1982
Third edition 1999
Printed in the United States of America on acid-free paper
9 8 7 6 5 4 3 2 1

The Johns Hopkins University Press
2715 North Charles Street
Baltimore, Maryland 21218–4363
www.press.jhu.edu

Library of Congress Cataloging-in-Publication Data will be found
at the end of this book.

A catalog record for this book is available from the British Library.

ISBN 0-8018-6065-2
ISBN 0-8018-6066-0 (pbk.)

the president's agenda

To George Grassmuck

Mentor, Teacher, Colleague

contents

list of tables

preface to the
third edition

It has been almost twenty years since I first started the research for my dissertation on the President's agenda. Much has changed since then, not the least of which is my own perspective on time. The twenty years covered in the first edition of this book seemed like a very long time to me in 1980. My dissertation advisers rightly warned me not to expand the time lines for fear that I would never finish the project.

By doubling the number of years covered, this third edition provides a very different portrait of the agenda-setting process. As chapter 12 argues, the 1980s and 1990s have raised the barriers against new ideas, putting the 1960s and 1970s into clearer perspective. It is entirely possible, as I argue in the new chapter that caps this edition, that there is less room today for policy innovation as new party politics, budget pressures, and demographic destiny work their will in constraining presidential imagination.

Chapter 12 turns to this discussion of what I call the "derivative Presidency" only after a detailed assessment of the Bush and Clinton agendas. Although there has been a dramatic change in the policy content of the President's agenda in the wake of the Reagan Revolution, there is also considerable continuity over the years covered by the first and second editions of this book. Today's Presidents are still governed by the same two cycles of decreasing influence and increasing effectiveness that shaped the agenda-setting process in the 1960s and 1970s, and they are still forced to obey the simple rules of the No Win Presidency. "Move it or lose it" remains a rallying cry in each administration, despite the enormous risks involved in setting the course with limited knowledge.

What has changed is the content of the President's agenda. Even under similar political conditions, both Bush and Clinton had fewer proposals than their predecessors, and both tended to favor modifications of the status quo over bold breaks with the past. Although there are important differences between the two Presidents, not the least of which is Bush's high proportion of small-scale, old ideas, the two share a pronounced tendency to look backward for inspiration rather than forward. As I argue, that bridge to the twenty-first century that President Clinton talked about in his reelection campaign appears to be made of old boards and rusty nails.

acknowledgments

I wish to thank the entire range of scholars, friends, and reviewers who had a part in the research and writing of the original edition of this book. Special thanks go to John Kingdon, Jack Walker, and George Grassmuck, all of the University of Michigan, who gave their time and energy to the original project. Thanks go to the University of Michigan, the University of Virginia, and the National Science Foundation for their original support.

Portions of chapters 10 and 11 were presented at the Presidency Research Conference at the University of Pittsburgh in November 1990. I am grateful to the participants at the conference for their insights and suggestions. In particular, thanks go to Larry Berman, George Edwards, Fred Greenstein, Charles O. Jones, Robert Katzmann, John Kessel, Bert Rockman, and Norman Thomas for adding greater clarity to my ideas.

Special thanks also go to Elaine Casey, who did the core research updating the book to cover Bush and Clinton, and to my wife, Sharon, and our three children. Also thanks to Henry Tom of the Johns Hopkins University Press, who remains my steadfast supporter lo these many years after taking the risk to publish the first edition of the book.

introduction

Q: *Did you ever fight over the agenda?*
A: *When didn't we fight. The hostilities usually came to a head over the State of the Union address. We'd fight over the major programs and the laundry lists. We'd argue over the position of our pet projects and the President's emphasis. We'd fight over paragraphs, sentences, words, and even punctuation. I finally bought one of those pop-psychology marriage manuals to see if there wasn't some way to bring the staffs together.*
Q: *Did it work?*
A: *Hell no. You can't save a marriage like that.*

The President's agenda is a remarkable list. It is rarely written down. It constantly shifts and evolves. It is often in flux even for the President and the top staff. Items move onto the agenda one day and off the next. Because of its status in the policy process, the President's agenda is the subject of intense conflict. The infighting is resolved sometimes through mutual consent and "collegial" bargaining, sometimes through marked struggle and domination. It is not surprising that we know so little about it.

We do know that all Presidents make choices. Some of these choices are major, such as the selection of the Cabinet, strategic command under crisis. Others are minor, such as the assignment of White House tennis court privileges, the screening of dinner invitations. All Presidents face both the routine and the extraordinary.

We also know that the most important decisions of any administration may involve the choice of issues and alternatives for the political debate. Under intense pressure to limit the span of executive attention, the White House is often forced to choose between competing items for the President's agenda. These are the decisions that set the tone and direction of national policy-making for the term of office—and beyond.

1

If we are to understand these choices, we must understand how Presidents come to recognize certain issues as potential agenda topics; why some issues are accepted for the President's program and others are discarded and delayed; how issues are linked with alternatives; how Presidents eventually rank their priorities. In presidential agenda-building many are called, but few are chosen. It becomes our task to discover how the few emerge.

The President's agenda is far more than a simple list of topics for discussion. According to E. E. Schattschneider (1960), "The definition of the alternatives is the supreme instrument of power." Since participants in the policy struggle can rarely agree on what the issues are, "he who determines what politics is about runs the country, because the definition of alternatives is the choice of conflict, and the choice of conflict allocates power" (p. 68). The President's agenda is one product of the "definition of alternatives" and plays a central role in determining final outcomes, particularly when the administration is forced to exclude certain issues from potential consideration because of resource constraints or political pressure. By deciding what they will consider, policy-makers set the boundaries of the political debate, often defining the agenda in such a way that certain issues are never seriously discussed.

Thus, control of the agenda becomes a primary tool for securing and extending power. Presidents certainly view the agenda as such. According to one Kennedy aide, "We looked at the legislative program as a major weapon in our struggle for both reelection and national influence. No one in the Congress really felt that Kennedy was experienced enough to lead. We felt that the agenda would prove them wrong." A Johnson assistant echoed that view: "The President can't afford to fill his agenda with the requests of others. He has to know whether a proposal fits his needs, whether it will extend his influence or simply waste his time. For each decision he makes, there are a dozen other choices. He must find one that gives the maximum advantage at the least cost."

The President's domestic agenda also reflects the allocation of resources, which often are fixed and limited. As a President moves through the term, each agenda choice commits some White House resources—time, energy, information, expertise, political capital. Each agenda item also commits some policy options, whether federal funds or bureaucratic energy. The sheer number of participants in the policy process both inside and outside the White House has increased rapidly over the last two decades; interest groups and individuals have "discovered" Congress and the Presidency. This growing pressure has placed greater emphasis on the agenda as a topic of political conflict. Policy-makers increasingly turn to the agenda for the first battles over the distribution of scarce resources. Given the ever-tightening policy options, this pressure will not abate in the near future.

The President's agenda is perhaps best understood as a *signal*. It indicates what the President believes to be the most important issues facing his administration. It identifies what the President finds to be the most appropriate alternatives for solving the problems. It identifies what the President deems to be the highest priorities. Thus, every agenda item (1) addresses an issue; (2) involves a specific alternative; and (3) has some priority in the domestic queue.

Issues are the first component of any agenda item, involving the definition of the problems. The President asks which problems deserve national attention. In the presidential policy process, problems are defined in perceptual terms: the President and/or the staff recognize some political or social need that suggests a federal response. Thus, poverty, health care, highway beautification, education, and civil rights were all issues on the Johnson agenda in 1965, reflecting Johnson's perception of the most important problems.

Alternatives are the second agenda component, centering on the programs that address the issues. The President asks how the problems will be solved. In the White House, alternatives often take the form of detailed draft bills; however, alternatives also arise as informal outlines of potential solutions. According to one Johnson assistant, "There were many times when a program would be drafted following a bull session. We would sit around the table or the pool and shoot the breeze. A topic might come up, and LBJ would ask what the hell we ought to do. You'd be surprised how many programs moved up after one of those meetings." If the elimination of poverty is an objective, then manpower retraining might be one possible program acitivty; if pollution is the problem, air-quality standards might be one solution.

Priorities are the third agenda component, reflecting the level of presidential concern and interest. The President asks which proposals are most important and which can wait. If medical care for the aged was an issue and Medicare was an alternative, then Johnson's request for immediate action on Medicare following his landslide election in 1964 was a clear sign of the priority. The same holds true for Nixon's welfare reform. If the "welfare mess" was an issue and the Family Assistance Plan was an alternative, then Nixon's decision to call the program one of his Six Great Goals was an indication of the relative priorities. Any item on the agenda holds some priority. Yet, Presidents give certain items *higher* priority than others. Medicare was more important to Johnson than was highway beautification; welfare reform was more important to Nixon than was banking regulation.

It is not necessary to put into chronological order the process by which issues, alternatives, and priorities are set. Indeed, much of the contemporary confusion in the study of agenda-building stems from the attempt to define an ordered process where one does not necessarily exist. Presidents may set priorities long before alternatives are found. The promise of a top priority may be an essential incentive to drafting a major program; without that promise, the staff may be unwilling to devote the time and energy required. The Nixon administration designated welfare reform as the top domestic priority several months before the Family Assistance Plan was drafted. As one aide argued, "Without that knowledge, we wouldn't have been able to mobilize the staff. It was a complicated plan and demanded excessive amounts of staff effort." Presidents may also develop alternatives long before issues are selected—ideas "in good currency" often search for problems; alternatives may look for issues. Consider Carter's hospital-cost containment plan, introduced in 1977. According to the Carter staff, the program was completed before the issue was publicized. Though the staff agreed that hospital costs were a problem, they had not decided how to frame the issue. The plan could have been viewed as a first step toward national health insurance; it could have been viewed as a plan to control one facet of rampant inflation; or it could have been viewed as a program to reduce federal expenditures for Medicare and Medicaid. The choice of the issue had an important impact on potential support and passage. Viewed as a first step toward health insurance, the plan might have encountered less resistance. However, the Carter administration steadfastly refused to link cost containment to health insurance. Instead, the program was approached as a tool to reduce health care inflation; given the public concern for health care at any cost, it was an issue without a constituency.

Defining the President's Agenda

Technically, every legislative or administrative proposal originating in the executive branch belongs to the President. The number of items involved is staggering. The clearance process, located in the Office of Management and Budget (OMB), is designed to review all legislative proposals and reports leaving the executive branch en route to Congress. According to one OMB career official, by 1982 an estimated 25,000 executive branch items will move through the clearance process every two years, with roughly half of the draft bills surviving OMB scrutiny. In 1977 alone, OMB approved 2,360 congressional requests for information, 4,242 agency reports, and 552 draft bills. Is this what we mean by the *President's* agenda? It includes far too many items that could not be classified as presidential.

Within the tangle of executive branch proposals, there is a second group of requests that are in accord with the President's political commitments. How does OMB make the distinctions? One OMB assistant suggested that such reviews involve "the analysis of both the policy content and the budgetary demands of the specific draft. The emphasis varies with the Director's instructions. We try to evaluate each draft with the President's campaign commitments and current legislative slate." A second OMB assistant continued, "Carter made it much easier by compiling his promises into a succinct summary we called *Promises, Promises,* but his goals have changed since he first entered office. Obviously, all bills which have the President's endorsement are 'in accordance.'"

Once OMB completes a given review, the draft is labeled "in accordance," "consistent with," or "no objection." Still other items are rejected in toto. Though the original purpose of the clearance system was to give Congress some guidance on the executive program, OMB screens only formal proposals; there is no record of presidential telephone calls, letters, conversations, or informal suggestions. Johnson's poolside meetings with congressional leaders, for instance, were never recorded. Nor is there any record of the countless informal requests that originate in the bureaucracy and are transmitted through the "iron triangle." Do the "i/a" draft bills constitute the *President's* agenda? Once again, the list contains too many nonpresidential items.

Only a small percentage of the items accorded "i/a" status are presidential requests. Many never pass through the White House; few are ever recognized by the President as priorities. The administration simply cannot be aware of all the proposals moving through the clearance process, let alone the myriad requests for administrative action. Indeed, that is precisely why the OMB clearance mechanism was created (Neustadt 1954). The President needed some institutional framework to handle the less significant items; legislative clearance became the answer.

Within the nesting set of items both "in accordance" with the President's program and the subject of White House attention, there is a final set of items that are central presidential requests. These are the President's personal priorities, the ideas discussed and refined in the Oval Office. These are the items that absorb the President's time and expend the greatest resources. They are uniquely "presidential." An administration may choose to identify the agenda in a public statement, as Kennedy did in a press conference scarcely two weeks following his election. An administration may underscore its agenda in a major address to Congress, as Nixon did when he announced his Six Great Goals in his 1971 State of the Union message. In other years and other administrations, the agenda might not be openly publicized, but it is always known to the key participants. The executive staff knows, the press knows, and the Congress knows.

This agenda contains the items that belong to the President, those that receive maximum presidential support. These are the programs that are the top priorities of the administration. This is the *President's* agenda, comprising both formal and informal requests. Though I will talk about the domestic agenda in terms of specific legislative drafts, the agenda inevitably involves informal demands. However, our definition will remain rather restrictive; it includes only a small number of requests and focuses mainly on legislative proposals. Yet, it is a definition built from staff perceptions. Several aides argued that only one or two programs ever occupy the President's agenda at any single moment. A Kennedy assistant remarked that "Federal Aid to Education and Medicare were so dramatic compared to Kennedy's other requests. Those two programs have to be considered separately from unemployment, agriculture, or the tax reforms. Those two programs had such long-term impact that they were considered essential to the President's place in history."

How do we apply this definition to the presidential policy process? How do we find the specific programs? Most of the staff members interviewed suggested that we turn to the State of the Union address for the agenda items. Though the message often includes a "laundry list" of presidential requests, it is viewed by the Washington community as the vehicle for the President's agenda. According to the staffs, the President's top priorities will always appear in the message at some point during the term. Though my definition of the President's agenda places a premium on legislative priorities, it is useful for measuring the President's agenda across time. Coupled with the interview materials, it provides a variety of useful comparisons between the five executives.

Scope and Method

Though we are primarily interested in patterns of agenda-setting, we will also study recent changes that have altered the basic thrust of the domestic Presidency. Over the past decade, a number of changes have created what might be called a No Win Presidency. This No Win Presidency is marked by cross-pressures that allow little room for compromise. The President is often forced to choose between legislative success and "good policy," between short-term political influence and long-term policy effectiveness. Presidents increasingly are faced with severe restrictions on their internal resources, as well as a seeming decline in the impact of party in the congressional process. These declines, coupled with a growing fragmentation of the national policy process, affect the domestic agenda directly. The price of policy has increased dramatically, with little growth in the President's ability to absorb the "inflation"; the value of the presidential "dollar," however, has dropped.

This study has two purposes, then. First, we will search for comparisons across the Kennedy, Johnson, Nixon, Ford, and Carter administrations, adding some notes on the Reagan administration. How are domestic ideas selected? Why are programs adopted? How are agenda decisions made? Our emphasis will be on stable patterns over time. Second, we will examine changes in the domestic policy process over the past twenty years. The process has evolved since 1960, leading to the development of a No Win Presidency. We will be trying to discover how this No Win Presidency affects the domestic policy process.

But the first and foremost concern of this study is the President's agenda. It is not a policy history of the post-1960 era and should not be taken as such. Others have provided the beginnings of that research (e.g., Sundquist 1968) and continue in the effort.

This study is restricted to the President's *domestic* agenda. A distinction between foreign and domestic policy, though it is increasingly blurred, not only allows for the limitation of the research topic but emphasizes the differences that exist in the presidential policy process. Foreign and domestic staffs operate in separate environments; their decision chains move to different departments and agencies; their information contacts are separate, their calendars are incompatible, and Congress is more willing to grant presidential discretion in foreign policy than it is in domestic policy. Moreover, the distinction is made by presidential staffs, convention delegates, and the presidential literature. Within domestic policy, we will distinguish social policy from aggregate economic policy; this distinction, too, reflects both institutional and political reality. We will concentrate primarily on social policy. Though we will discuss economic policy—particularly unemployment and inflation—we will not systematically explore budgetary and tax decisions.

Some may find the emphasis on domestic affairs limiting. Why study domestic policy when Presidents prefer to spend their time on foreign affairs? The majority of legislation sent to Congress, however, still deals with domestic policy. Moreover, in both 1976 and 1980, domestic issues provided the cutting edge in presidential defeats. Presidents may spend the bulk of their personal energy in foreign policy, but the White House must allocate most of the total resources to domestic affairs.

Whether in foreign or domestic affairs, there have been a variety of problems in studying presidential policy. The familiar problem of $N = 1$ continues to haunt the research. As John Kessel argues, our knowledge of the office and its occupants rests on three central sources of data, all involving different executives at different times:

> First of all, there are some sensitive psychological studies which have offered interpretations of the style of given presidents. Second, we have generalizations extrapolated from analyses of particular sets of events in which a president has been involved. Third, there is the traditional understanding of the institution in terms of the formal and informal powers of the office. We have learned many things from these studies. A skilled narrator who draws examples from several administrations can tell much about the presidency. But there are limits set by the nature of the information we have. Our knowledge of the dynamics of presidential behavior rests upon particular presidents and particular instances (Kessel 1972, p. 1).

Scholars have used different means to handle the problem. Unfortunately, what each study brings toward solving the $N = 1$ dilemma, it loses in richness. As a focus for policy research, the Presidency is quite unlike Congress or the Supreme Court. We cannot isolate single moments when decisions take place. The Presidency does not render majority decisions, nor does it produce floor votes. Perhaps the most effective method of retaining the richness of the office while producing detailed analysis is to mix the best of both worlds. We are challenged to search for comparable data across a reasonable time frame and to review those records with an awareness of the complexities of the office.

This study represents one attempt to respond to that challenge. The research covers a twenty-year time span—not long by historical standards but certainly long for a presidential study. It also involves an attempt to identify a distinct sample of programs that make up the President's agenda. Aiming to isolate those variables that can be said to have an impact on agenda choices, the research concentrates on two primary sources of data—each with advantages and disadvantages.

The bulk of the research is based on interviews with 126 staff members from the five presidential administrations. The respondents were selected using three strategies. First, occupants of certain positions within the Executive Office of the President were automatically included as potential contacts. All past and present chiefs of staff, legislative liaison officers, heads of the Bureau of the Budget and OMB, domestic policy assistants, White House counsels, and press secretaries were contacted in this first sweep. Second, newspapers, magazines, journal reports, and biographies were scanned for names of potential respondents that might not have appeared on the personnel charts. Finally, all respondents were asked to recommend any other individuals who might be of use to the project.

In selecting potential respondents, I focused on five specific groups within the Executive Office: (1) legislative liaison, (2) the domestic policy staff, (3) the Bureau of the Budget/OMB, (4) the economic policy staff, and (5) the President's personal staff—counsels, public liaison, speech writers, personal secretaries, press assistants, and the top White House aides. (The specific figures on the sample of respondents are summarized in Appendix A.) Beyond these five groups of informants, I selected a small set of media contacts. These observers became particularly important in confirming the conclusions drawn from the staff interviews.

Though a semistructured questionnaire was used in each interview, the conversations covered a wide range of topics. Each respondent was asked five specific questions. (The interview schedule is presented in Appendix B.) However, the bulk of the interview time was spent discussing specific cases from the administration in which the respondent had served. The most important questions involved the respondent's impression of the factors and pressures surrounding particular agenda decisions. These responses are the major evidence supporting the study conclusions. Since the respondents were assured of complete confidentiality, no quotes are attributed directly.

The response rate varied from administration to administration. The Kennedy, Johnson, and Ford staffs were more willing to talk; I was able to reach a greater number of the top assistants from those staffs. The Nixon and Carter staffs were far less cooperative; the response rates were lower, and the top staff members were more reluctant to talk. Thus, the Nixon and Carter interviews involved a larger number of lower-level assistants. These differing response rates introduce some bias to the research. It is entirely possible that the lower-level staffs simply did not know as much about the Nixon and Carter administrations; it is also possible that the top aides from the Kennedy, Johnson, and Ford staffs may have overestimated their impact during their respective tenures in office. Moreover, for all respondents, there may have been a systematic overstatement of importance. In an effort to correct this interview bias, I searched for a second, independent source of data.

This second source of data came from OMB legislative clearance records, which included information on executive clearance requests and recorded the dates on which legislation moved to Congress. The figures were extremely valuable in the analysis of agenda timing and provide a useful confirmation of the interview results. The records were also important in identifying a specific group of programs that could be called the *President's* agenda.

Though the records are valuable, there are several problems with the data. The legislative clearance process keeps records only inasmuch as they serve an immediate purpose. Thus, the further back in time one goes, the softer the OMB records become. It has been only in the last five years that OMB has moved to a computer tracking system to keep control of the clearance records. The clearance records for the post-1974 period are readily available in the OMB "Status of Administration-Sponsored Legislation" report for each congressional session. Before 1974 the records were kept in a less than careful fashion. Though we can be confident that the pre-1974 records identify the bulk of the President's domestic program, caution must be exercised.

Nevertheless, the OMB data are an important source of information on the President's domestic decisions. As we shall see, the data present a variety of opportunities for both confirming and redirecting the basic conclusions from the interviews. The OMB clearance records, together with the State of the Union messages and assorted presidential documents, present a detailed guide to the President's domestic agenda. The multiple sources of data can only give added strength to the research findings. Finally, the OMB data help address the $N = 1$ problem. Using a simple definition of the President's agenda, we can develop a reasonably large data base. To be included in our sample, each item had to meet two criteria: (1) it had to have been cleared "i/a," that is, "in accordance" with the President's program, by OMB; and (2) it had to have been mentioned in at least one State of the Union address during the President's term. The result was a sample of 266 items culled directly from the OMB files.

Using this definition of the President's domestic agenda, there was no attempt to weight the items for importance—such efforts generally are crippled by bias. Johnson's request for highway beautification is counted along with Medicare and Model Cities; Carter's request for agricultural reform is tallied along with comprehensive energy and welfare reform. Since neither Nixon nor Carter presented a State of the Union message in the first year, we must find surrogate records. In Nixon's case, we can use his domestic priorities message of 14 April 1969. The address to Congress contains Nixon's major legislative requests for his first year in office. Since Carter did not present a similar message, we must turn to his press conferences of early and mid 1977. We can also use a series of documents that came to be known as the Mondale Executive Agenda. These documents were provided by members of the Carter staff and help reconstruct the top domestic priorities. A copy of the draft executive agenda for May 1977 is presented in chapter 8.

It is important to remember that both sources of data—the staff interviews and the OMB records—present potential problems. There was no effort to sample all White House personnel for the interviews, nor were the OMB records consistently reliable. Thus, the data should be viewed more as illustrations of a theory of agenda-setting than as absolute proof of specific hypotheses. Despite the problems, however, the data allow us to draw conclusions beyond what might emerge from a simple case-study approach.

A Preview of the Findings

This study hinges on a resource definition of presidential power. It is my argument that Presidents are constrained by the level of both internal and external resources. The internal resources involve at least four separate entities—time, information, expertise, and energy; the external resources flow from congressional support, public approval, and electoral margin. Without these requisite resources, presidential bargaining has no impact on domestic outcomes. Furthermore, these resources rise and fall over the term, creating two distinct policy cycles. The *cycle of decreasing influence* appears as time, energy, and congressional support drop. The *cycle of increasing effectiveness* enters as information and expertise grow. Both cycles have a dramatic influence on the President's agenda.

In the first chapter, my main concern will be with the basic parameters of the agenda. When is the agenda set? What does the agenda look like? It is important to recognize that the agenda changes substantively from administration to administration. However, the President's domestic agenda does have several stable characteristics. In chapter 2, I will suggest that the President's agenda is set very early in the term; that the timing of agenda requests affects ultimate legislative success; and that the size of the domestic agenda varies directly with what I will call presidential "capital."

This study of the President's agenda also asks why certain issues emerge from the domestic process but others do not. As noted above, agenda items can be separated into three distinct components—issues, alternatives, and priorities—and different pressures exist for each component. Accordingly, we will investigate the agenda issues separately from alternatives and priorities. In chapters 3 and 4, I will ask how Presidents choose from among competing issues? How much choice do Presidents actually have? What are the major sources of the agenda issues? In answering these questions, I will argue that issues are selected on the basis of perceived *benefits*; that Presidents are quite willing to coopt ideas from any available source; and that the campaign and primaries are not significant institutional constraints on the agenda ideas.

If agenda issues are selected on the basis of benefits, how are alternatives chosen? If alternatives constantly circulate throughout the White House, how do "preferred" solutions emerge? I am not immediately concerned with program formulation within the policy community; it is an important topic, but it constitutes a major task in itself. My main interest involves the President's choice of alternatives once specific programs enter the pool of options. Does the concept of ideas "in good currency" apply? Are Presidents restricted in the kinds of solutions they can choose? In chapters 5 and 6, I will suggest that alternatives are evaluated on the basis of *costs*. Moreover, chapter 5 pinpoints clear differences between Democrats and Republicans in terms of the kinds of alternatives that emerge from the policy process: presidential resources have a significant impact on the choice of alternatives.

If issues involve benefits, and alternatives involve costs, how are priorities determined? In chapter 7, I will suggest that Presidents do indeed rank their priorities; that certain agenda items reach what might be called a "must list" but others do not. Ford's energy corporation stands as a central example of a program that never moved onto the must list. Why do some issues receive high presidential priority? Why do some survive the early battles over costs and benefits only to fail at the President's must list? In specific, why do some agenda items move onto the must list and others move off? In this case, potentials for success aid the elevation to the must list, while changes in costs and problems in passage eventually force items off.

Finally, I ask *how* the agenda decisions are made. Do Presidents engage in what might be identified as comprehensive choice? Do Presidents fall into what might be called a garbage can? Decision style has an impact on agenda choice: it affects both the perception of benefits and the calculation of costs. In chapter 8, I will suggest that the agenda process closely resembles the behavioral model of the firm originally introduced by Richard Cyert and James March (1963). The process is characterized by internal conflict, staff coalition-building, standard operating procedures, and organizational learning.

In the final chapter, I will take a deeper look at recent changes which have altered the domestic agenda process. The Presidency of the 1980s is quite different from the Presidency of the 1960s. The political and economic costs of domestic programs have escalated, with no corresponding increase in the President's ability to absorb the "inflation." At least five explanations arise. First, Congress has become more competitive in the search for scarce agenda space—whether because of changes in congressional membership and norms or because of a steady growth in the institutional resources for program initiation. Second, Congress has become more complex. The evolution of subcommittee government during the late 1960s increased the sheer number of actors who wield influence in the domestic policy process and tangled the legislative road map. Though there are fewer single obstacles to passage of the President's program, there are many more potential dead ends and delays. Third, as Congress has become more competitive and complex, the congressional parties have weakened. The dispersion of congressional power has, in turn, reduced the President's potential influence over domestic legislation. As we shall see, party is no longer the "gold standard" of presidential influence. Unfortunately, Presidents must still cling to their party as the source of their political capital. Fourth, Presidents must now conduct domestic policy under increasing congressional and media surveillance. I will suggest that this atmosphere of suspicion has reduced the opportunities for effective presidential leadership in domestic policy. Finally, and perhaps most important, the basic issues that fuel the domestic policy process have changed since 1960. We have witnessed the rise of a new group of "constituentless" issues, issues that generate remarkably little congressional support and considerable single-interest-group opposition. Energy, social-security financing, welfare reform, and hospital-cost control are all examples of a new generation of constituentless issues. Separately these five trends have created difficult problems for the President's agenda. Together they have contributed to the rise of a No Win Presidency in domestic affairs. We will return to the concept of a No Win Presidency in chapter 9. For now, it is important to note that the domestic policy process continues to shift. In the few short years since Kennedy and Johnson occupied the Oval Office the Presidency has undergone a dramatic era of change. As one Johnson aide remarked, "This office is nothing like it used to be. It might look similar, but the relationships have all changed. Lyndon wouldn't like it one bit."

1 presidents and resources

You know, a president, in my opinion starts out with a bank full of good will and slowly checks are drawn on that, and it's very rare that it's replenished. It's a one-time deposit. And you have to be careful—the more you do to encourage public trust, the longer those reserves are there. And a president's power is not to be found much in the law or in the institutional strength of the president.
—Vice-President Walter Mondale, Washington Post, *20 January 1981*

In January 1965 Lyndon Johnson stood elected by the largest popular margin in recent history; he faced the Eighty-ninth Congress with a massive Democratic majority—with thirty-six seats more than in the Eighty-eighth. Yet, on the eve of his inauguration Johnson instructed his staff to move quickly. According to Harry McPherson, one of Johnson's top aides, the President told the staff:

> You've got to give it all you can that first year. Doesn't matter what kind of majority you come in with. You've got just one year when they treat you right and before they start worrying about themselves. The third year, you lose votes. . . . The fourth year's all politics. You can't put anything through when half of the Congress is thinking about how to beat you. So you've got one year (McPherson 1972, p. 268).

Perhaps Johnson knew that Vietnam would erode public confidence; perhaps he knew that challengers would arise from within his own party. He most certainly knew that the vast congressional majority would evaporate in the 1966 midterm elections. Johnson also recognized the limits of his political strength: the honeymoon would end; time would run out. "Johnson understood the gradual paralysis," one aide noted. "He knew the magic would wear off." As Johnson told McPherson, "That's why I tried. Well, we gave it a hell of a lick, didn't we?" (McPherson 1972, p. 268).

13

In his concern for his political strength, Johnson was not unique among recent Presidents. The first-year panic about dwindling resources affected all of them: Carter entered office with barely 50 percent of the vote, Kennedy and Nixon with less than half, Ford with none. Perhaps Ford represented the most extreme situation. According to one Ford official, "We began the term, such as it was, under the worst possible circumstances. We weren't elected; we had only two years left before the 1976 elections; the staff was in shock; the policy process was on the skids; and we faced a basically hostile Congress. The 'in'-baskets were full, and nothing was going out. Then Ford granted the pardon. We just didn't have enough political *push.*"

Presidential Power

Presidential scholars often overrate the President's "push," confusing the Chief Executive's literal powers with actual influence. Perhaps the most important source of this confusion is the failure to distinguish between *resources* and *prerogatives*. Formal prerogatives guarantee certain advantages, but they do not explain the vast differences between individual Presidents—they do not explain the success of a Johnson, the failure of a Nixon, or the frustrations of a Ford.

Resources have always occupied a prominent position in the presidential literature. Scholars have talked about personal resources—the sense of power, self-confidence, bargaining skills. They have talked about political resources—public approval, Washington reputation, congressional support. They have talked about institutional resources—the Office of Management and Budget, the staff, legislative liaison. However, the distinction between resources and the formal prerogatives of the office has often been blurred. As one OMB official remarked, "You ought to think of the Presidency as an engine. Each President enters office facing the same model—the horsepower is generally stable and the gears are all there. What differs is the *fuel.* Different Presidents enter with different fuel . . . Lyndon Johnson entered office with a full tank, while Ford entered on empty." Thus, it is not the system of checks and balances that determines agenda outcomes: it is resources that drive the presidential machinery; it is resources that shape the President's agenda. And these resources are frequently scarce.

If presidential scholars agree that resources are important, they rarely agree on the basic composition of the "fuel." Some believe that personality is the most important resource; others continue to confuse prerogatives with power. Richard Neustadt (1960) argues that professional reputation and public approval are critical; Peter Sperlich (1975) suggests that command has been underrated. Which formula is correct? According to the 126 White House staff members, at least two central packets of resources, at least two components of the presidential "fuel," have a bearing on the domestic agenda.

The first packet involves *internal* resources—time, information, expertise, and energy. Time refers to the duration of the President's term—how long he has to make his impact. Ford had two years, Nixon six. Information involves the amount of knowledge available on the particular issues under consideration, as well as the President's knowledge of program specifics. Expertise centers on the given administration's technical and political skills—how effective the President is in guiding the policy process, how competent the staff is. Finally, energy focuses on the amount of physical and emotional stamina available for domestic choice—how much the President can expend in the day-to-day conduct of business, how much stress the staff can handle.

The second packet involves *external* resources, the resources that have a bearing on the basic parameters of the agenda, as well as the perception of costs and benefits. These external resources create the President's congressional strength, what many respondents called presidential "capital." According to the staffs, the President's political capital rests on several external sources: party support in Congress, public approval, electoral margin, patronage. For the staffs, the term "presidential capital" reflected a specific view of status, authority, and influence. As one OMB assistant argued,

> Every President has a certain amount of capital—you know, power, push, "juice." It involves a number of factors—the President's past accomplishments, his campaign success, his legislative support. It's very hard to pin it down to a particular set of items, but capital is a very real presidential asset. Different administrations call it different things—I gather the Carter people like to call it "push." But it's always the same thing; it's the President's ability to get what he wants.

Capital must be distinguished from the internal resources time, information, expertise, and energy. Capital reflects the President's political strength, while the internal resources help to absorb decision-making costs. Though time, information, expertise, and energy have an impact on the agenda, they are generally expended in the decision-making process. This is not to argue that internal resources are unimportant; they have a significant role in the timing of agenda requests, as well as in the evolution of the domestic decision-making structure. However, according to the White House staffs, the President's political power is only marginally related to internal resources. As one Johnson aide remarked,

> We saw time as something we had to have to make the decisions. If we didn't have the time, we couldn't bring the staff together to make the choices. If we didn't have the time, we couldn't get the hearings scheduled or the liaison effort on track. We saw congressional support in an entirely different light. If we didn't have some basic support, it didn't matter how much time we had. We could have a twenty-year term and it wouldn't make a tinker's damn. Congress was the basic force in our *success;* time was important only inasmuch as it gave us the opportunity to get the

compromises nailed down. Bargaining takes time, but time does not give the President the power to win bargains.

Internal Resources

The White House staffs maintained that all Presidents, whatever their electoral margin, congressional support, or public approval, face structural limits on the domestic agenda. These constraints are intimately tied to the internal resources time, information, expertise, and energy. No matter how much of each a President starts with, during the term he will experience a decline in time and energy and an increase in information and expertise. This ebb and flow contributes to the creation of unique White House policy cycles, which ultimately shape the President's agenda.

By their very nature, presidential priorities demand heavy investments of internal resources. Presidential priorities are more complex and demand more time than does routine legislation. Consider Nixon's welfare reform. As Martin Anderson argues, "The bright, clear notions some of us had developed during the campaign about how a President and staff would make national policy soon tarnished and blurred. We had naively assumed that we would simply review whatever issue was a problem, identify the major areas of difficulty, consult leading experts, and with their help craft a solution." As Arthur Burns's top assistant for welfare reform, Anderson soon learned that the program "required many years before those involved felt any degree of confidence in what they were doing. The domestic side of the federal government had gotten so big that it was literally impossible to grasp it, intellectually, in its entirety" (Anderson 1978, p. 7). Nor was the welfare-reform quicksand restricted to the Nixon administration; it involved substantial commitments of time, information, expertise, and energy in the Ford and Carter administrations as well.

Presidential priorities also involve more conflict, both inside the administration and out. And the greater the conflict, the more time, information, expertise, and energy necessary to settle the disputes. "You'd be surprised how long it takes to iron out the differences," a Johnson legislative assistant argued. "Compromise doesn't usually happen overnight. It takes a hefty investment of presidential influence and effort." Once again, welfare reform serves as an example. One highly placed Nixon observer maintained that "the [Family Assistance] plan could have been announced much sooner if there hadn't been such a struggle. With Burns and Moynihan at odds, we couldn't move. When one would attack, the other would counterattack. Sure, the issue was intricate, but it could have been handled much faster without the in-fighting. As it was, there was a stalemate for three months."

These obstacles are complicated by the fact that presidential priorities tend to involve more participants. Few major programs can be drafted without the cooperation of a variety of agencies and actors. Moreover, presidential priorities demand greater follow-through once they move to Congress. The policy process does not end with the formal announcement of a program. There are hearings to staff, questions to answer, and amendments to draft. The decision to adopt a particular program for the President's agenda involves the commitment of a sizable amount of resources over the term. As one Nixon aide suggested, "Communications from the White House take so long to get out, and an equally long time in coming back. It is not uncommon for White House policy directives to take up to, or as long as, a year before they really get down to the action level in the departments . . . charged with carrying policy out" (Cronin 1974, p. 239). Thus the very factors that move an item to the President's must list also increase the amount of time, information, expertise, and energy needed to achieve results.

Time. Barring unforeseen tragedy or political scandal, the length of the President's term of office is constant, covering 1,460 days. In qualitative terms it is much shorter. According to one White House aide, "You should subtract one year for the reelection campaign, another six months for the midterms, six months for the start-up, six months for the closing, and another month or two for an occasional vacation. That leaves you with a two-year presidential term." If the President is reelected to a second term, the time passes even faster. Given the two-term limitation in the Twenty-second Amendment and the ever-increasing length of the primary campaigns, the President becomes a lame duck by the end of the second year. As a Nixon assistant argued,

> Even without Watergate, the term had started to wind down by mid-1974. Immediately after the inauguration, attention started to turn away from the President. The people began to speculate on the successor. Would the Democrats win in 1976? Could Congress afford to wait for a Democratic President? The spirit of cooperation that followed the first election was nonexistent. The Congress preferred to wait and see.

Time is essential in preparing the President's agenda. It takes time to organize task forces, to select issues, to draft alternatives, to pursue priorities. The amount of time needed will vary according to the particular issue—some items can be resolved quickly; others may take years. According to a Kennedy aide,

> There is never enough time to think profoundly about policy evaluation and the like at the White House. It is always in too much a rush, moving from one thing to the next. It is just about all you can do to get things started. The burden of the presidency is to get things started. The presidency is not an executive agency with clout to carry out the goals of the president. It perhaps ought to have been done, but we didn't have time for it, we just didn't work that way (in Cronin 1974, p. 237).

Moreover, the *quality* of time changes over the term, increasing the scarcity of the very kind of time needed for the President's agenda. According to Neustadt, "Trying to stop fires is what Presidents do first. It takes most of their time" (1960, p. 156). Firefighting often leaves little time for policy. According to former President Gerald Ford,

> There is a lot of wasted motion of course. The worst waste is that there are an awful lot of perfunctory, ceremonial things that have to be done. They take up about 15% to 20% of a President's time—more in election years. But I guess they have to be done. After all, if they are not done, the public gets the wrong perception of the President, that he is behind the walls of the West Wing of the White House and he does not want to meet the people. But if you look at it from a cost-benefit ratio of time spent, he ought to be spending his time on the business that just keeps flowing in and out of the Oval Office (in *Time,* 10 November 1980, p. 31).

At the start of the term, each day includes more time for planning. There is more opportunity for interaction and discussion. As the term moves inexorably on, calendars become filled with the routine—meetings begin to force out the free moments once used for creative policy-making. By the middle of the term, few have the time to engage in new frontiers. The President and the staff become mired in detail, entangled in the trivial. The more time an administration seems to need, the less it has. Eventually, the President and the staff simply cannot find the time needed for serious planning.

The very nature of time changes during the term: the days become shorter; the staff tires. As one Carter aide advised, "One day in the transition is equal to a week by the end of the first year, and two months by the end of the term." Carter was one of the first Presidents to use the campaign to the fullest as an opportunity for planning. Unfortunately, the Carter effort was lost through intense staff conflict following the election.

Information. Presidential scholars often argue that information is the key to good policy. Without information, careful planning is an elusive goal. The President needs a great deal of information on a wide range of topics to set the domestic agenda—information on the problem itself and on potential solutions; information on the political setting, public support, congressional acceptance, and bureaucratic resistance. As Theodore Sorensen, Kennedy's chief of staff, suggests, "To make informed decisions, the President must be at home with a staggering range of information. . . . He must cope with issues for which no previous experience on earth can equip him. For the essence of decision is choice; and, to choose, it is first necessary to know" (Sorensen 1963, pp. 38-39). Yet, despite the pressing need, information is a scarce resource. The White House staffs were willing to admit that many decisions are made with incomplete information.

This is not to argue that information is unavailable in the executive branch. Often there may be more raw data than it is humanly possible to absorb. Several recent Presidents have complained about the sheer weight of the paper that flows through information channels. Most questions can be answered somewhere in the federal system; the problem is to find the answers and use them. Moreover, even when the information exists, it is rarely tuned to the President's needs. The President and the staff generally are ill-equipped to convert most raw data into useful information; nor are they prepared to invest the time and energy necessary to locate specific details. "The executive branch just doesn't supply the right kind of answers," one Nixon aide reflected. "We need more than raw figures. How the hell are we to know if the data are correct or if the information fits our problem? We need accurate information, data we can trust. It's one thing to get a ream of data, another to figure out what it means. Most of the raw material is meant for internal use anyway."

Information is a scarce resource in the presidential policy process. In some cases, problems may arise so quickly that information is not readily available. There is generally a lag between the identification of a new issue and the development of a solid information base—experts may be unavailable and synthesis therefore impossible. Even when a substantial body of data exists, the President may be unable to absorb it fast enough. In 1973, the energy crisis caught the executive branch by surprise. This resulted in a near frantic effort to gather data on the problem and a heavy reliance on private industry. "We would have preferred public data on the problem," a Nixon expert reflected, "but it was simply not available. We knew the private data was bound to be biased, but we had no choice. That's how fast the problem arose and how little foresight there had been in the lead departments and agencies."

In other cases, the executive branch may deliberately withhold or distort information. It is a problem faced by all administrations, regardless of party. For the Nixon White House, however, it was acute. The conflict between the Nixon White House and the bureaucracy is well documented (see Nathan 1975). As one Nixon assistant complained, "We basically felt the bureaucracy was absolutely opposed to our programs and that we wouldn't get any straight answers. That hampered our efforts to implement our programs and restricted our supply of information. When we would initiate a search, we were never quite sure when we'd get the answers and if the answers were accurate. And, especially at HEW and HUD, we were often likely to face excessive delays and blatant refusals."

In most cases, however, the office itself is not prepared to generate and utilize information. Traditionally, Presidents have not been concerned with long-range planning; the emphasis has been on the "pass now/plan later" approach. Though this conventional ad hoc strategy has been under fire in recent years, Presidents characteristically have found little incentive in planning. Presidents are rewarded for presenting a full domestic agenda as quickly as possible, not for producing "good policy." "We felt that we could always change the program once it passed," one Johnson aide argued. "You can't wait for the perfect program. Pass it now, amend it later." (We will return to this question in chapter 2.)

What the President does not know can hurt him. According to William Carey, former assistant director of the Bureau of the Budget, "What a President does not know about the activities under way in Defense, State, and CIA, to say nothing of the Office of Education and the Bureau of Indian Affairs, is incalculable. There he sits, overworked and making the best of a bad situation, while all around him his princes and serfs are doing and undoing in thousands of actions the work of his administration without his having a clue" (Carey 1969, p. 453). Ultimately, the best defense against misinformation is the President's past experience with specific issues and alternatives—information is a product of not only the available base but also the President's ability to use it. A Kennedy aide summarized the equation as follows:

> When Kennedy was inaugurated, he had had detailed experience with a variety of programs. He had a sense of what was right, what would work. He understood the problem of parochial aid in the education bills; he understood the problem of area redevelopment in West Virginia; he most certainly understood the problem of the House Rules Committee. When the staff would give him advice, Kennedy had a good feel for the accuracy and value of the information. He knew where it would fit in the puzzle. The fact that he had had intimate contact with certain issues made him well prepared for the early decisions. The fact that he had very little experience with economics made him especially vulnerable to advisory pressure. He did not know how to choose among the economic options because he didn't know what they implied.

Presidents are free to make choices without adequate information; they are free to mistinterpret advice. However, those choices have the highest probability of failure. "If you shouldn't fire a pistol with a blindfold," one Johnson assistant argued, "you shouldn't propose a major program without some basic knowledge of what will happen. The Great Society was crippled by unanticipated consequences. We were driving at night without our headlights on."

Expertise. Most Presidents enter office with at least some experiences in common. Most have survived a primary campaign, a national convention, a general election, and hundreds of cold chicken dinners. Some have held appointive office; some have served in the House or Senate; some have worked behind a governor's desk. In recent years our Presidents frequently have been recruited from the Senate. In fact, Robert Peabody, Norman Ornstein, and David Rohde call the Senate a "Presidential incubator" (1976), arguing that the presidential nominating process caters to senatorial contenders. In both 1976 and 1980, however, governors became the final victors, perhaps signaling a new recruitment pattern. The Senate may still supply the bulk of candidates, but governors have become the survivors.*

Yet, despite candidates' common experience, each President enters office with a somewhat different package of skills. Thus, one congressional observer cautioned that "anyone can rate the Presidents on their experience or personality . . . the key is to recognize that nothing fully prepares a candidate for the office. It is unlike any position in the American system. Governors have trouble, senators have trouble. The only difference is that each has a different kind—they all have problems learning from each other." Hence, expertise does not equal experience alone. Rather, it rests on the President's ability to direct the federal machinery. As Emmet J. Hughes, former special assistant to Eisenhower, suggests, "The sheer size and intricacy of government conspire to taunt and thwart all brisk pretensions to set sensationally new directions. The vast machinery of national leadership—the tens of thousands of levers and switches and gears—simply do not respond to the impatient jab of a finger or the angry pounding of a fist (Hughes 1963, pp. 53-55). Expertise certainly is related to past experience, but they are not one in the same.

Do governors make the best Presidents? They are most likely to have the administrative skills to pull the levers. Do House members? They are most likely to understand the constituency pressure on the gears. Do senators? They are most likely to have long-term contact with national issues, to know which switches are most important. "It's not the position, but how much the President learned in the position that's important," one assistant noted. "It doesn't matter what the candidate did unless that experience is transferable to the White House. You would be better off reading the candidate's horoscopes than trying to guess how a President will behave solely from a resumé. Good God, Nixon had been a representative, senator, and Vice-President." Even individuals who served in the very same positions might be vastly different as President. Both Lyndon Johnson and Mike Mansfield served as Senate majority leader in the 1960s. Would they have been comparable Presidents? Both John Kennedy and his brother Ted represented Massachusetts in the Senate. Would they be similar executives? It is not the position but the performance and learning in the position that affect presidential expertise.

What kinds of expertise are most important for domestic choice? The staff members pinpointed two main areas. First, the President must know how the federal system works. Johnson and Carter offer a useful contrast. Whereas Johnson was considered to have no equal in legislative skill, Carter floundered in the congressional process. Johnson's experience as Senate majority leader was a clear advantage as his domestic agenda moved up Pennsylvania Avenue. "Johnson knew what he needed to do and when he had to do it," one media respondent noted. "He understood the process and the application. He had a good grasp of the institutional setup and a full appreciation of political influence. He knew exactly how hard to squeeze." Carter, however, came to Washington as a novice. "We spent a great deal of time simply learning how to do things," one aide admitted, "and even then we made more than our share of mistakes. The President told us that we should do things pretty much the same as we did in Georgia. But Washington isn't Georgia, and the White House isn't a governor's mansion." Nor did Carter have the requisite political skills. "He prefers to stand aloof when he should get involved," an OMB official remarked in 1979. "He wants to be alone when he ought to be surrounded by advocates. He wants to avoid conflict when an offensive would be the best approach. He just doesn't understand the need for political attack."

There are a number of channels for presidential influence. Some are obvious, such as OMB and the Congressional Liaison Office. Some are subtle—a telephone call at the right moment or a dinner invitation to a reluctant senator. To compete within the policy process, the President must be able to navigate the channels. That is Neustadt's argument. Experience in national politics may be the best opportunity for that learning.

Second, at least for domestic policy, the President must know how to guide the programming process. "Priorities don't spring full-blown from the executive branch," a Nixon assistant argued. "You have to know how to work the domestic process. One of Mr. Nixon's greatest liabilities was that he didn't know how to guide new programs; he didn't know how to direct the effort. He relied on the executive branch—and the executive branch represented the Democrats, not the Republicans." Drafting a major presidential program takes more than intent: it takes positive administrative direction. Kennedy's experience with education policy had a dramatic impact on his success in framing the domestic agenda early in his term. He had been exposed to a variety of ideas on the Senate Labor and Public Welfare Committee, and those ideas affected his performance in office. Carter's contact with reorganization in Georgia lifted that issue into prominence in Washington. "We didn't have that much trouble on that project," a Carter aide reflected. "Carter knew pretty much what he wanted and how to do it. We were familiar with the basic concepts and had plenty of practice. We eventually came up with twenty-one separate plans for Carter to review."

Presidents, like members of Congress, become specialists in certain areas. Nixon liked to think of himself as an expert in foreign affairs; Ford viewed himself as a specialist in budgetary policy. Staffs can be equally specialized. The degree to which the President and the staff understand the problems of policy formulation—including both obstacles and shortcuts —must be considered a resource for the President's agenda. According to one congressional observer, "The last thing a President needs is to relearn how to make policy once he is elected. He should know how bills are drafted, how the Congress works, how to implement policy. He should know what his specialties are, what the staff's are. But you'd be surprised about how much they don't know. Carter and Nixon didn't really know how the system worked when they entered office." That inexperience affected the speed with which they presented their domestic programs.

Once in office, Presidents can be expected to learn. The President and the staff become familiar with the executive machinery and develop strategies for effective choice. They become more confident over time; standard operating procedures are set, lines of communication are established, and decision loops are identified. In each of the five past administrations there was a clear attempt to develop a formal agenda procedure by the end of the first year. "By the end of six months, we felt the need for a more stable process," a Johnson assistant explained. "The first year had been too confused. By the end of that year, we knew we had to have some method for controlling the decisions. We were running out of time and had to conserve our options." In each case, the President acted to bring order to the domestic agenda process, to eliminate the waste of scarce resources and to control the increased conflict. That phenomenon should appear again under Reagan.

Energy. If the policy process demands time, information, and expertise, it also takes its toll in both physical and emotional energy. As Horace Busby, special assistant to Johnson, noted in 1968, "We are short of people, thin on experience, thinner on patience. . . . We are overworked, overburdened, overweight, and, on many things, overly anxious. . . . Increasingly, ours is a society slipping out of phase. In sector after sector—from the delivery of medical services to the delivery of the daily mail—we are barely able to do what we are doing, with no assurance of how long we can continue" (in Wood 1970, p. 39). According to Gerald Ford,

> It's a hard job being President—but despite all the talk about the heavy burdens, the job is not too big for any one man. I get sick and tired of hearing people say you ought to have two Presidents. I don't have any sympathy for that argument. Don't misunderstand me. It is a job that takes about twelve to 14 hours a day. But what is wrong with that? The President of the United States ought to be willing to spend that kind of time. Anybody who walks in there thinking he can punch a time clock at 9 in the morning and leave at 5 has got another thought coming. We do not elect Presidents who want that kind of a life (*Time*, 10 November 1980, p. 31).

One needs only to compare photographs of Presidents taken before their term with those taken after to note the impact of the pressure on aging over the term. The job is exhausting, even for those executives who prefer a more passive approach; and delegation rarely alleviates the stress. According to one former chief of staff, "Unless you can sit on the front porch during the campaign, every President enters office tired. Unless the program is ready and waiting, every President ends the transition exhausted. Once in office, we come to work at seven and don't leave until ten. There is no avoiding the exhaustion. In fact, if you're not tired, you're not doing the job." The impact of the tension can be found everywhere. As one Carter aide remarked,

Nobody ever talks about the fatigue, but it's very real. To admit it might imply dissatisfaction with your job. But toward the end of the first year, the staff really begins to suffer. It just doesn't let up. The major messages come up in January, so you don't spend the holidays with your family. The budget comes up in October, so you don't notice autumn. And the end of the first term looks like it is going to be hell. Four years is a long time to spend in that kind of a pressure cooker. I don't know if I'll be able to stay on.

The drain on energy arises from several sources. The schedule itself imposes broad limits on internal stamina. No matter how the President chooses to map his time, there is very little opportunity to relax. Nor do most Presidents want to slow down.

Presidents vary in the degree to which they can adjust to the schedule. Johnson became adept at brief catnaps during the day; Kennedy set aside specific segments of his schedule for recreation; Nixon was quite concerned about ill-health and made a special effort to remain rested. But while William Howard Taft could nap three hours each afternoon in 1910, contemporary executives cannot afford to rest. It is a potential problem for Reagan. His age may have a telling impact later in the term.

Staffs also vary in their ability to handle the stress of the White House calendar. Some aides are able to deal with even extreme pressure with little more than an increase in smoking; others do not cope. "This town is full of the remains of White House marriages," one aide admitted. "It is the first thing to go. The pressure was just too intense for my taste. I had a home, high blood pressure, and a low tolerance for stress. I decided to leave after two years as a matter of survival." The Johnson White House was no different:

> Lyndon Johnson demanded a great deal from his staff, and they received much in return: participation in great matters and an enormous arena for their talents, a relationship with a brilliant man who, though sometimes harsh, often honored them with benevolent intimacies. He exacted a precise account of how each staff member spent his time, whom he talked with, and where he went. Minutes became valuable, holidays a misfortune. Johnson considered it something dangerously close to treason for a staff member to spend Sunday afternoon with his family instead of at the office (Kearns 1976, p. 252).

As a result, the Johnson administration was littered with the resignations of staff members who could not tolerate the infamous "Johnson treatment." Other administrations have suffered similar crises in staff turnover, but rarely to the same extent. A Carter aide summarized the problem for all assistants: "You just don't stop moving. The days start early and don't end till late. You don't have time for lunch, and if you do get out, you work while you eat. There are always meetings to attend, and there are often a hundred calls to answer in a single day. If the President calls, you jump."

Does energy have an impact on the domestic agenda? After all, tired Presidents can still make choices. Beyond the loss of a few qualified aides who can't keep up, is energy an important resource? Clearly, program planning demands a great deal of what might be called "creative energy." It is not enough merely to be able to sustain attention, to keep one's eyes open. Planning involves a degree of activity and involvement not generally found in the final days of an administration. Creativity does not flow from exhaustion.

Stress also leads to errors in judgment and implementation. As the President and the staff begin to tire, there is a tendency not to follow through, to ignore the necessary cross-checks. The policy process demands energy. Thus, Sperlich criticizes the argument that all presidential behavior must be bargaining behavior: "The more a President opts for bargaining, the more he must do by himself. To strike the right bargains, a President must be 'his own executive assistant.' The President as a bargainer can really depend on no one. He cannot trust anybody but himself" (Sperlich 1975, p. 423). Presidents are not "superhumans," Sperlich continues.

> * A President who would always bargain and who would carry out by himself all the tasks associated with successful bargaining will not be a President for very long. An immense and consistent overloading of his physical and mental apparatus will produce a breakdown in short order. His search must be for alternative strategies and loyal help, and he must be alert to the ideological and personal biases upon which such strategies can be employed and upon which such help can be obtained (p. 426).

One Kennedy assistant offered the following tongue-in-cheek advice to all future executives: "Presidents should make an attempt to give the administration extended rest and relaxation periods, like in the armed forces. Top aides could be rotated to positions in other departments for brief rests. The President could move his chief of staff to Agriculture and the Director of the Budget to the postal service." Unfortunately, the demands for rest conflict with the White House calendar. Given the constraints on the President's term, it is to his advantage *not* to rest, but to drive on. At the start of the Carter term, for instance, the President specifically informed his staff: "I want you to spend an adequate amount of time with your husbands, wives, and children. We are going to be here a long time, and all of you will be more valuable to me and the country with rest and a stable home life." Both the President and the staff had ignored the order within the first month. It was an unrealistic expectation.

Presidential Capital

Call it push, pull, punch, juice, power, or clout—they all mean the same thing. The most basic and most important of all presidential resources is capital. Though the internal resources time, information, expertise, and energy all have an impact on the domestic agenda, the President is severely limited without capital. And capital is directly linked to the congressional parties. While there is little question that bargaining skills can affect both the composition and the success of the domestic agenda, without the necessary party support, no amount of expertise or charm can make a difference. Though bargaining is an important tool of presidential power, it does not take place in a neutral environment. Presidents bring certain advantages and disadvantages to the table.

Perhaps the best way to illustrate the impact of capital is to compare Kennedy's early legislative failures with Johnson's eventual victories. According to the *Congressional Quarterly Almanac,* Johnson secured passage of 60 percent of his legislative proposals in 1965, while Kennedy secured passage of only 27 percent of his in 1963. Was Johnson's success due to some change in the President's prerogatives? Was it due to his abilities as a legislative broker? The answer to both questions is no. Neither institutional prerogatives nor bargaining skills explain Johnson's dramatic success. Johnson's higher degree of success paralleled the increase in his political resources following the 1964 election. Johnson's greater impact was the result of the massive increase in House Democrats, particularly from Northern liberal districts. Johnson went from 263 Democrats in the Eighty-seventh Congress to 294 in the Eighty-eighth. Moreover, the Northern Democratic bloc, Johnson's base of support, grew from 152 seats in 1964 to 194 in 1965. Finally, whereas Kennedy was elected to office by 49.7 percent of the vote, Johnson returned to office in 1965 following a landslide. The increases in both electoral margin and congressional support assured a greater degree of success for Lyndon Johnson. Hence, Johnson's success stemmed from dramatic shifts in presidential capital. Though Johnson's skills might have stretched his scarce resources, the basic explanation for the change lies in his increased external resources, in his political "capital."

Though power may remain undefined in the presidential literature, among the presidential staffs it is generally understood to be equal to the President's party support in Congress. For most White House aides, capital is defined as the number of votes the President can generate in Congress at any one time on any given issue. As such, capital responds to the President's public approval and electoral margin. However, the base of presidential capital is always the number of party seats the President has in Congress. Throughout the following discussion, it should be remembered that *capital* is only a word—some aides used it frequently; others used a variety of other terms. Its attractiveness rests on the image of a fixed amount of influence expended over time. It should be remembered that this definition is restricted to the domestic agenda—a restriction with heavy legislative content; the definition would certainly change in foreign affairs.

Party Support. Party support is the chief ingredient in presidential capital; it is the "gold standard" of congressional support. Among the White House staffs, congressional parties are viewed as much more stable than public approval. Even if the President is slipping in the polls, he can count on support in Congress, particularly from his own party. Though congressional support does not guarantee victories on crucial votes, the President and the staff certainly believe that such support is a more consistent advantage than is public approval. Like public approval, congressional support usually drops over the term; however, it rarely drops as far or as fast. As one Carter assistant suggested, "We can always find support in Congress, even when we are under fire in the polls. The Congress is still a party institution, and we can count on a few votes by bringing out the party standard."

Further, Presidents and staffs tend to view party support as critical in the day-to-day conduct of domestic affairs. Public approval can be used to sway congressional votes, but with only limited success. "Everyone has a poll," one aide noted. "You can find any number of groups which can present a poll to support a given proposal. Depending upon how you word the questions and how you select the sample, you can get a positive result. Congress is fairly suspicious of polls as a bargaining tool, and public approval ratings are too general to be of much good." Public opinion is important over the term; it affects both midterm losses and the President's chances for re-election. Yet, public opinion is not easily converted into direct influence in the domestic policy process. Most often it is an indirect factor in the congressional struggle. Presidents cannot afford to ignore public opinion, but in the closed world of Washington politics, the party comes into play virtually every day of the term. Party support thereby becomes the central component of the President's capital.

In measuring potential legislative support, Presidents inevitably must return to the congressional parties. Though party seats do not guarantee automatic support, they are the primary basis for influence. According to one Johnson liaison assistant, "You can cajole Congress and try to buy the votes, but if you don't have your party on board, there isn't much hope. The President's legislative success starts with party. It's that simple." Members of Congress watch the opinion polls and gauge electoral mandates, but public approval and voter landslides rarely convert congressional minorities into majorities. Members of Congress work with the President because it is to their mutual advantage. Party sets up the basis of exchange. Thus, in Reagan's 1981 House budget victories, the most difficult challenge was keeping Republicans in line, not luring Southern Democrats to the fold. In the critical June battles over Reagan's substitute budget, for instance, liberal Republicans were actually more worrisome than conservative Democrats. As one Reagan observer noted in early July 1981, "the real problem was holding the 190 Republicans together. Had Reagan lost the northern wing of the party, his budget would have lost.

Twenty-nine Democrats don't help too much if you lose thirty Republicans. The liaison team started from the proposition that they had to hold the Republicans; only then could they think about courting conservative Democrats."

Public Approval and Electoral Margin. Public opinion is a valuable tool in fashioning congressional support. As noted above, seats do not guarantee support. Support comes only if both Congress and the President benefit. Though public approval cannot create vast gains in Congress, the *absence* of public approval eventually undercuts potentials for success. One Carter aide summarized the paradox as follows:

> When Eisenhower was on the top of the polls, he couldn't move. Even though he was one of our most popular Presidents, he just didn't have enough strength in Congress. Public opinion couldn't create what the electorate hadn't given him—party control of the House and Senate. In our case, we had the congressional seats. We had the potential support. But, where Eisenhower had the public approval, we had nothing. Our public ratings started to drop fairly quickly, and Congress started to back off. We had the seats, but we didn't have the public approval. Do you see the point? Public opinion can't help you, but it sure as hell can hurt you.

A second Carter aide concurred: "Public approval is mainly valuable as the well runs dry. When we reached the 30 percent level, it became paramount that we reverse the approval trends. We became small depositors in a big bank." Moreover, the impact of public approval seems to be contingent on party. Members of the President's party are more likely to view approval as a guide to support than are members of the opposition. Indeed, according to George Edwards (1980), the minority may actually intensify its opposition as the President's approval rating rises. Once again, party is the "gold standard" of influence.

Electoral margin may have a similar impact on presidential capital. If the President is elected by a slim percentage, congressional support may be undermined. Yet, a decisive victory may result in only limited advances. As before, the basis for political exchange is the key. If the President does not have the seats in Congress, electoral margin may have little effect. "Congress doesn't want to trade with someone who only made it by the skin of his teeth," one Kennedy assistant argued. "If the President runs behind in your district, he becomes a liability. If the President can't help you, why help him?" A Johnson aide agreed: "It is the coattail that is important. If the congressmen are indebted to you for pulling them in, you're bound to have greater support. Hell, we had a whole group of freshmen in 1965 who owed their seats to the President." Unless presidential coattails appear, electoral margin rarely creates capital. By itself, the President's electoral margin cannot turn a Democratic seat into a Republican seat or transform a minority coalition into a majority one. As one Nixon assistant lamented, "Nineteen seventy-two did not help us. It was similar to Eisenhower in 1956. We had tremendous public and electoral support. But that and a dime couldn't buy a cup of coffee. It was still a question of what we didn't have: what we didn't have was enough Republican congressmen."

Perhaps public opinion and electoral margin can be best understood in terms of a threshold effect. As long as the President remains at a specific level of approval—say, 50 percent or better—public support may have only a negligible effects on congressional success. As the President drops below the threshold, however, public opinion begins to have substantial impact in eroding legislative support. Public approval may not help the President, but lack of it can always hurt him. The threshold effect is more difficult to define for electoral margins. Since margins of victory often translate into gains for the congressional party, the relationship is clouded. We do know, however, that the lower the margin, the less the opportunity for coattails.

Reputation. How does reputation affect presidential capital? According to Neustadt, professional reputation is a "cardinal factor in the President's own power to persuade":

> When men in government consider their relationships with him it does them little good to scan the Constitution or remind themselves that Presidents possess potential vantage points in excess of enumerated powers. Their problem never is what abstract Presidents might do in theory but what an actual incumbent will try in fact. They must anticipate, as best they can, his *ability* and *will* to make use of the bargaining advantages he has. Out of what others think of him emerge his opportunities for influence with them. If he would maximize his prospects for effectiveness, he must concern himself with what they think (Neustadt 1960, p. 60).

For Neustadt, the "greatest danger to a President's potential influence with [Congress] is not the show of incapacity he makes today, but its apparent kinship to what happened yesterday, last month, last year. For if his failures seem to form a pattern, the consequence is bound to be a loss of faith in his effectiveness 'next time'" (p. 61).

Did the staffs agree? Only in a restricted sense. As one Nixon assistant argued, "The mistakes you make will always follow you, but they aren't that important in the long run. There is an air of anticipation at the beginning of the term, but that is quickly dispelled with the actual decisions. We made some mistakes on welfare reform, but I doubt that they affected the revenue sharing bills." A Carter assistant agreed:

> When we came in, I don't think there was any question that we were viewed as country bumpkins. I don't doubt that it affected Congress. But in comparison to what? Was that as important as the close election? Was that as critical as the drop in popularity? Or Bert Lance? Your reputation

is going to change over time. Our reputation today is much better than in our first year. Liaison is stronger, and the staff has learned. But have you looked at our success rates? They haven't increased that much. I know that anticipated reactions are important; I'm just not sure what they are based on.

There are several reasons why reputation was discounted. Some aides suggested that reputation is not a tangible resource but an abstract concept that often conflicts with the concrete world of presidential politics. Moreover, if Neustadt is correct, the impact of reputation is cumulative; we would expect to find its impact later in the term. Regardless of the President's preinaugural image, the impact of reputation snowballs over time. In the domestic policy process, however, the critical choices are made early. Reputation is often the product of these first choices. While it is true that Congress watches the President, reputation is likely to have a greater impact on capital toward the end of the first term and into the second. In 1980 Carter was still hampered by the impression of ineptness created in 1977. The question remains whether that reputation did as much damage as the steady slide in public approval or the initial absence of party cohesion.

Electoral Interaction. Party support, public approval, electoral margin, and reputation do not exist in an isolated system. There is ample evidence that the four variables interact. Electoral margin can create coattails, which in turn affect party seats. Public approval can increase legislative success, which in turn can mold reputation. Reputation can affect electoral margin, which in turn builds party seats. Though the presidential staffs emphasized the primacy of party seats in Congress, approval, electoral margin, and reputation have a play in what might be called an electoral interaction. In 1980, for instance, the Reagan election created a vastly different climate in Congress. Reagan ran well ahead of Carter in both Democratic and Republican districts and was able to fashion a new Senate majority. Though Republicans did not regain control of the House, the massive defeat of Senate Democratic liberals and the loss of thirty-three Democratic seats in the House inevitably predisposed some Democratic congressmen toward limited if not wholehearted support. In this sense, Reagan's electoral margin contributed directly to his party's seats on Capitol Hill and generated considerable uncertainty among the Democrats. As one Reagan aide remarked in early 1981, "We are going to push the mandate as far as possible. If you don't hear us say the people have spoken again and again, we won't be doing our job. The strategy is to keep the pressure on the Democrats, to keep jolting them back to November 4, 1980. It will play out pretty soon, but we're going to use it for all it's worth." House members are notorious for watching electoral trends, and the Reagan election created a climate of fear. The loss of the Democratic Senate majority, coupled with what Reagan often heralded as massive public support, had a pronounced impact on his early congressional victories. As

Reagan sought to trim the budgets of traditional "sacred cows," he was able to fashion repeated majorities with conservative Democrats and unified Republicans. Yet, even with his electoral margin and a burst of public sympathy following the March assassination attempt, Reagan's public approval had fallen by midsummer of his first year. Reagan aides openly predicted even further drops in a public backlash to spending cuts, and Reagan lost his first Republican House seat in a July 1981 election to fill a vacancy in Mississippi's Fourth Congressional District—an election where the Republican candidate campaigned on Reagan's program with Reagan's endorsement.

Measuring Capital. Different Presidents have used different measures of presidential capital. For Lyndon Johnson, capital rested on the number of votes in his margin of victory. As Doris Kearns argues, in the first months of 1965 "Johnson's optimism and energy were accompanied by an intense anxiety that his popular mandate might be swiftly eroded."

> In January, 1965, the congressional liaison men from all the executive departments were assembled in the Fish Room to hear Johnson explain his rationale for pushing forward on every front at once. "I was just elected President by the biggest popular margin in the history of the country—16 million votes. Just by the way people naturally think and because Barry Goldwater had simply scared the hell out of them, I've already lost about three of those sixteen. After a fight with Congress or something else, I'll lose another couple of million. I could be down to 8 million in a couple of months." (Kearns 1976, p. 226).

For the White House staffs, capital was referenced by three separate indicators: party seats in Congress, public approval, and margin of victory (the three measures are summarized for the past twenty years in table 1). Thus, without public approval and electoral strength, congressional support is only implied by seats. Yet, without seats, no amount of public approval or electoral strength will make an impact. As one Carter aide reflected, "The 292 Democrats in Congress were potential supporters—that was only three fewer than LBJ had. But with the close election and the drop in approval, they remained that way: potential. We couldn't force them to be active supporters." Or as a Nixon assistant remarked, "Any President's basic influence rests on his congressional strength—the actual votes in Congress. With only 190 Republicans in 1968, we were hamstrung. The President's electoral margin can give some extra juice. With only 44 percent of the vote in the '68 election, we were in serious trouble. Finally, the President's public approval can help—that was one area where we were strong. But one out of three just wasn't enough."

Can presidential capital be replenished over the term? If capital is expended with policy choice, can it be replaced? It is clear that capital declines over time—public approval consistently falls; midterm losses occur. Can the trends be reversed? Most of the staff suggested that capital can be

Table 1. Measures of Presidential Capital

President	Year	Senate Seats	House Seats	Public Approval[a]	Electoral Margin
Kennedy	1961	65	261	72%	49.7%
	1962			77	
	1963	67	258	76	
Johnson I	1964			79	
Johnson II	1965	67	295	80	61.1
	1966			61	
	1967	64	248	46	
	1968			48	
Nixon I	1969	43	192	59	43.4
	1970			61	
	1971	45	180	51	
	1972			49	
Nixon II	1973	42	192	65	60.7
	1974			27	
Ford	1974			71	0.0
	1975	37	144	39	
	1976			46	
Carter	1977	61	292	66	50.1
	1978			55	
	1979	59	287	43	
	1980			80	

[a] According to the *Gallup Opinion Index*. The figure represents the first approval rating of the year.

rebuilt, but only to a limited extent. The staffs generally subscribe to the rally-round-the-flag theme frequently found in the public opinion literature (Kernell, Sperlich, and Wildavsky, 1975). According to this concept, during periods of crisis in foreign affairs the President can expect support at a much higher level than during normal times. In the past, the rally-round phenomenon has frequently lifted public approval—the Cuban missile crisis and the Gulf of Tonkin crisis are two examples. In 1979 Jimmy Carter's public approval jumped fifty percentage points following the occupation of the U.S. embassy in Iran. The phenomenon also is not uncommon in domestic policy. It was a factor in Johnson's civil rights victories in 1964; it was the effect hoped for in Carter's energy package in 1979. In each case, the President turned to the rhetoric of crisis to replenish dwindling political capital. For Johnson it worked; in Carter's case the Congress continued to stall.

Though capital can be refreshed during the term, the pattern remains: *capital is expended with choice,* and can be replaced only to a limited extent. Even when there is a rally-round-the-flag crisis in foreign affairs, it is not clear how long the rise in public support will remain. Within two months of the 1979 Iran crisis, with hostages still in Teheran, Carter's public approval had dropped back from 80 percent to 50 percent. And scarcely two weeks before the 1980 Democratic national convention, a "dump Carter" movement gained momentary strength as party leaders sought a nominee who could win in the November election. Thus, it is difficult to predict just how much capital can be regenerated through national crisis. Furthermore, does public approval in a rally-round crisis affect decisions in the domestic arena? Did the hostage crisis help Carter's domestic agenda? Did domestic crisis increase capital? If the trends in public approval over the past twenty years serve as an indication of declining capital, declarations of war on energy or poverty create only moderate increases in support that rarely last.

Much like time, presidential capital does not keep. A Ford assistant compared it to the dollar: "Unless you spend it fast, it will fall in value."* No matter what their performance, Presidents can expect a midterm loss in the party ranks in Congress—it is a pattern across four decades. Thus, the best way to cash in on presidential capital is to present a program as quickly as possible. Presidents must be concerned about moving the domestic agenda immediately following inauguration. Not all Presidents have done this. Nixon spent his first months immersed in foreign affairs; he clearly wasted substantial amounts of already scarce capital by delaying his domestic agenda. Unless the President presents his agenda to Congress early, the congressional calendars will fill with competing business. Congress is willing to wait for the President's agenda, but only so long. With increased competition for congressional agenda space, the President is well advised to move quickly. Thus, capital is closely related to internal resources. Information and expertise may help the President stretch his capital through wise "investment"; time can give him additional opportunities; energy can sustain the effort. Conversely, capital can lead to more time and greater access to information; capital can also affect the recruitment of more expertise and energy. The greater the President's capital, the more he can tolerate waste in the commitment of his internal resources.

Conclusion

Resources are the key to the President's domestic agenda. According to the staffs, resources do exist. The presidential staffs tend to separate them into two separate groups: the internal resources time, information, expertise, and energy and the external resources congressional support, public approval, and electoral margin. According to the staffs, these resources are also scarce. Time, energy, and capital begin to decline from the moment of first election.

Presidents and staffs clearly *behave* as though resources exist. Perhaps this is the most important point. Even if resources did not exist in an objective sense, White House perceptions make them important. Lyndon Johnson's belief that his political influence would diminish over time had an important bearing on the timing and content of his domestic agenda.

In chapter 2, I will consider just how capital affects the basic parameters of the domestic agenda. Though the internal resources are important contributors to timing and size, capital remains the critical factor. That conlcusion will become essential in understanding the domestic agenda. Whatever the President's personal expertise, character, or skills, capital is the most important resource. In the past, presidential scholars have focused on individual factors in discussing White House decisions, personality being the dominant factor. Yet, given low levels in presidential capital, even the most positive and most active executive could make little impact. A President can be skilled, charming, charismatic, a veritable legislative wizard, but if he does not have the basic congressional strength, his domestic agenda will be severely restricted—capital affects both the number and the content of the President's priorities.

Thus, it is capital that determines whether the President will have the opportunity to offer a detailed domestic program, whether he will be restricted to a series of limited initiatives and vetoes. Capital sets the basic parameters of the agenda, determining the size of the agenda and guiding the criteria for choice. Regardless of the President's personality, capital is the central force behind the domestic agenda.

2 the opportunities for choice

Soon after the 1972 election the Nixon staff met to discuss the coming four years. They had reason to be confident. Nixon had been elected by over 60 percent of the popular vote and had carried every state except Massachusetts. His public approval had never been higher. The Cabinet would be cleaned, Nixon would proceed with the new China policy, and the domestic program would be redrawn. Yet, Nixon's legislative agenda remained quite limited. Nixon opted for administrative, not legislative, alternatives.

The basic problem for Nixon was presidential capital. Though he had an electoral mandate, he had very little congressional support. There were only 42 Republicans in the Senate and 192 in the House; even with Southern Democratic support, Nixon could not fashion a stable majority. As one Nixon aide argued, "We knew damn well that we weren't going to get any help from Congress. What the hell were we supposed to do—keep knocking on the door? We made the decision long before the 1972 election that if we won—and won big—we would change our approach. We had to avoid another close election. I suppose that was one reason behind the break-in." The Nixon administration did not renounce legislation altogether; rather, the President and the staff simply refused to invest heavy amounts of resources in the congressional struggle. Because of severe limits on his political resources, Nixon was unable to capitalize on his opportunities for domestic choice.

At least two basic dimensions for the domestic agenda limited Nixon's opportunities: (1) the timing of his agenda requests—his administration was remarkably slow in defining the issues, alternatives, and priorities for the 1969 and the 1973 domestic agendas; and (2) the size of his program—his administration was limited in the sheer number of items that could move to the agenda in both the first and the second terms.

35

Policy Cycles

All Presidents have opportunities to set the domestic agenda. They can pack the State of the Union message or reshape the annual budget. They can announce new initiatives almost at will, creating a separate media event for each announcement. Moreover, Presidents have access to the congressional agenda through the Office of Management and Budget, legislative liaison, and the departments. Presidents also shape bureaucratic agendas, whether through their appointments, executive orders, or the annual programming process. Yet, although all Presidents have the *potential* to set the national agenda, they vary greatly in their ability and willingness to use the opportunities for doing so.

The impact of resources on opportunities can be best described as a problem of policy cycles. Certain resources decline over the term, while others grow. "The more we seemed to learn about the domestic system," one Nixon aide complained, "the less we could do. We had our best shot at the start of the term but didn't have the organization to cash in. By the time we had the organization, the opportunity was closed." This ebb and flow of presidential resources creates two basic cycles within the domestic policy process.

The first pattern might be called the *cycle of decreasing influence.* It is based on declines in presidential capital, time, and energy. Presidents can usually anticipate a midterm loss of party seats in Congress and a steady erosion of public approval. At least for the past fifty years, all Presidents, whether Democratic or Republican, have faced a drop in House party seats at the midterm election. Johnson lost forty-seven Democrats in the House in 1966; Nixon lost twelve Republicans in 1970. And at least since George Gallup first began measuring public approval, all Presidents have experienced some decline in their public support over the term. In the last twenty years, however, the declines have been more severe. Today the President can expect a near-linear drop in his approval rating in the first three years of office, with a slight rebound at the end of the term. As one Ford aide remarked, "Each decision is bound to hurt somebody; each appointment is going to cut into support. There's really no way that the President can win. If he doesn't make choices, he will be attacked for being indecisive. If he does, he will satisfy one group but anger three others."

Declines in capital eventually bring the domestic process to a halt. Toward the end of each term, the President must spend increasing capital just trying to unclog the legislative calendar. Unless the President is highly successful with early requests, the agenda becomes dominated by the "old" business. Of the five most recent Presidents, excluding Reagan, only Lyndon Johnson was able to sustain a consistently high level of agenda activity into the second and third years. The other four Presidents were forced to begin repeating their domestic requests by the end of the first year in office. Even

Johnson recognized the problem. As one aide remarked, "You have to start backtracking almost from the first day. Unless the programs move off the agenda, you have to start investing your time trying to bump them off. You have to devote your energies to the old items before replacing them with your new ideas."

Time and energy also contribute to the cycle of declining influence. As the term winds down, the President simply does not have enough time to pursue major initiatives. Attention turns away from the domestic agenda and toward the coming election. In the first term, Presidents are forced to allocate their time between the domestic agenda and the campaign. In 1979 Jimmy Carter became the first sitting President to announce his reelection effort in the third year of office. In the second term, Presidents become lame ducks before the halfway point. As each term comes to a close, staff energy also touches bottom. There is less energy and creative stamina to draft major new initiatives. Though first-term Presidents inevitably present several major programs in the fourth year, there is little inclination toward massive revisions of the domestic agenda.

The second pattern in presidential resources might be called the *cycle of increasing effectiveness.* Presidents can be expected to learn over time. The presidential information base should expand; the President's personal expertise should increase. As the President and the staff become more familiar with the working of the office, there will be a learning effect. They will identify useful sources of information; they will produce effective strategies for domestic choice. Certainly, prolonged contact with specific policy issues will produce both specialization and knowledge.

Carter's first year is a prime example of the learning effect. According to the Carter staff and most informed observers, Carter's first year in office was characterized by a series of errors: the fifty-dollar tax rebate, the Bert Lance affair, legislative failure on hospital cost containment and welfare reform. Legislative liaison was among the first to change. At the start of the term, the Congressional Liaison Office was organized along issue lines. As Eric Davis notes, "Instead of having specialists for the Senate and for the various blocs within the House, there would be specialists for energy issues, foreign policy issues, health issues, environmental issues, and so on." The strategy caused considerable problems on the Hill and lasted less than six months. "At the beginning of the summer of 1977, a major shake-up occurred within the White House liaison office, involving personnel shifts as well as organizational changes" (Davis 1979, p. 289). According to the Carter staff, the change reflected increasing expertise:

> We recognized that liaison had to involve intimate contact with the members of Congress, not with the specific issues. We learned that liaison had to be much more sensitive to the needs of Congress and much less domineering. The issue-based system wasn't adequate for a liaison office that needed votes. We eventually learned that we had to shepherd

the members, that we had to give them our attention. They wanted to have someone they knew, someone they could call on whatever the problem. The issue system was designed for our needs. We found out that we had to have a system that was designed for their needs, too.

The Carter liaison staff learned; new aides were recruited, and expertise increased. The change was felt in other offices as well. The Domestic Policy Staff became more adept at formulation. Bills reflected tighter planning. "We definitely increased our understanding," one Carter assistant reflected. "Most of us had only limited experience before coming in. The longer we were here, the more we learned. We ironed out some of the kinks and smoothed out the system. You'll see the difference if we return for a second term." A media respondent confirmed the impression:

> I'd guess that Carter would be pretty effective in a second term. He's learned a lot in the first three years. I doubt that he would make the same kind of trivial miscalculations. I think that he would be much more deliberate with Congress, but not as aloof. I think that he's learned that the Presidency is a political office and needs a range of guidance. He's surely learned a great deal about political strategy. Look what he is going to do with transportation funds at the start of the campaign. He's going to give money to his friends. Screw the others. That's something he wouldn't have done in 1977. He just didn't know how.

Despite Carter's increased expertise, he was not noticeably more successful as the term progressed. As Carter's information and expertise grew, his influence dropped. The cycles of increasing effectiveness and decreasing influence were mutually incompatible. It is a pattern for all first-term administrations. As the President's time, energy, and capital decrease, his expertise and information expand. Hence, the staff complained about the absence of opportunity in the first two years. As one Carter Domestic Policy assistant argued, "Here we are with a great deal to say about specific programs. We have a national health plan which makes some sense for the future. We have a new urban policy which has some teeth. But Congress doesn't want much to do with it. We're coming up on an election year, and they would rather wait and see if Kennedy can win the nomination." Regardless of the President's initial expertise and information, the first year of the first term is characterized by a surprising level of confusion. As the President and the staff settle the chaos, the opportunities disappear. By the third and fourth years, the President and the staff are fully trained for domestic choice, but the agenda must be restricted.

The First and Second Terms. In the past, many presidential scholars have viewed the first and second terms as equal entities. Each term is of course four years long; each term begins and ends with a presidential election. However, the differences between the first and the second term have become more important since the Twenty-second Amendment. The two-term limitation and the two cycles of increasing effectiveness and decreasing influence force us to abandon the traditional view that all years are created equal. From a resource perspective, the second four years differ in at least three respects.

First, the second term is *qualitatively* shorter. With the ever-lengthening presidential campaigns and the reluctance of Congress to work with a lame-duck administration, the second term is clearly restricted. "President Nixon understood the need to act as quickly as possible in the second term," one OMB aide remarked. "He knew he didn't have that much time. There was already movement within the party to find the next candidate. Even during the inauguration there were rumors about the President's successor. President Nixon felt that the campaign for the '76 nomination would begin very early. The Democrats stopped working with him rather early." Indeed, several Nixon aides blamed the failure of national health insurance in 1974 at least partially on the two-term limitation. According to one assistant, "We had the compromises worked out; Kennedy was ready to go, and the compromises were set. But with only two years left until the next election, the coalition fell apart." What about Watergate? "Part of it was the scandal, but part was the coming election. Why work with a Republican when you can elect a Democrat? Why compromise if you don't have to?"

Second, there is rarely a honeymoon in the second term; the second term is often viewed as a continuation of the first. Presidents cannot expect the same deference in the first moments of the second administration. One former Eisenhower aide remembered that "the press and the public no longer looked on us as the hope and salvation. The faces remained the same, and the programs were essentially unchanged. There was no reason to grant the President any favors. He was going, going, gone."

Third, both the cycle of increasing effectiveness and the cycle of decreasing influence peak in the second term. Whereas the first days of the first term are characterized by inexperience and disorganization, the first days of the second term are marked by greater skill and organization. As we shall see, Nixon's expertise made a difference in the speed with which he presented his domestic program in the second term. As one aide suggested, "We knew much more about the system at the start of 1973. We were more prepared to move forward. We knew more about what we wanted, and we had a better grasp of how to get it." The first days of the second term offer the greatest opportunity for presidential effectiveness. The on-the-job training of the first four years has significant payoffs in the second term, a fact that figured prominently in Jimmy Carter's 1980 campaign rhetoric. However, even here the President cannot win. Though capital should be available, the cycle of decreasing influence accelerates in the second term. There is no honeymoon, and the two-term limitation cuts the President's capital in the second, third, and fourth years. The rapid decline in influence clearly accentuates the impact of timing: in both the first and second term, the sooner the President moves, the greater the chances of success.

The Timing of Domestic Choice

Timing is often considered a critical tool of presidential leadership. The timing of the announcement of a major program is believed to have a significant impact on its passage and implementation. Moving the most controversial legislation early is viewed sometimes as a dramatic maneuver, sometimes as a grave mistake. Moving the divisive issues last is often seen as a strategic waste of resources. Presidents are expected to recognize the moment of greatest impact; to hold the agenda like a poker hand, revealing the cards at the moment of maximum effect. According to Lyndon Johnson,

> Congress is like a dangerous animal that you're trying to make work for you. You push a little bit and he may go just as you want but you push him too much and he may balk and turn on you. You've got to sense just how much he'll take and what kind of mood he's in every day. For if you don't have a feel for him, he's liable to turn around and go wild. And it all depends on your sense of timing (in Kearns 1976, p. 238).

Presidents are expected to have that sixth "sense of timing," an uncanny knowledge of the precise moment to act. Unfortunately, that sense is more myth than reality.

Our analysis of presidential timing will concentrate on two basic questions: First, when are the agenda decisions made? Is there substantial variation that would reflect the sense of timing? Second, if most agenda activity falls in the first year of office, do Presidents move early in the year or late? That choice can have a significant impact on success. As one Nixon assistant argued, "The later you are with the program, the less successful you are. We would have had a better shot at welfare reform if we could have presented it in May 1969 instead of August. By the time we actually moved the plan, the congressional calendars were booked for the year, and we had to wait for a vacancy. We lost the momentum, and it cost us a possible victory."

According to Neustadt, there is a "certain rhythm in the modern Presidency." The first year in office is a "learning time for the new President who has to learn—or unlearn—many things about his job." This "intensive learning time . . . dominates the first two years." Neustadt argues that if the President is to achieve any results in the first term, it must be in the third year, for in the fourth year the President must turn to reelection. If the President captures a second term, the fifth and sixth years hold the keys to success. Thus, the "seventh year is the beginning of the end—now guaranteed by constitutional amendment—as all eyes turn toward the coming nominations and the *next* administration" (1960, pp. 198-99).

If the first two years of the first term are for learning, they are also the most important focus for agenda activity. According to both the OMB legislative clearance records and the 126 White House respondents, the bulk of agenda activity occurs in Neustadt's "learning time." The conclusions were clear: if the President spends the first year only learning, he will lose major opportunities for impact. Whereas Neustadt argues that the first year must be for learning, the White House staffs emphasized that it must be for *action:* the first year determines outcomes well into the final days of the term. Whatever the President's party or term, the first year is the most important, and the first year of the first term is critical. Although information and expertise are at a general low in the first year, nevertheless Presidents select the dominant themes and directions in the early moments. Those choices tend to follow the administration throughout the remaining years of both terms. They guide decisions at the start of the second term and haunt the administration until the end. As one legislative assistant argued, "The President gets a second chance to set the program in the second term. But most of those choices are predetermined by the first. The failures of the first term are often the failures of the second."

The OMB legislative clearance records confirm this argument. By counting the number of legislative drafts that were both cleared "in accordance" with the President's program and mentioned in one of the President's State of the Union messages, we can create a tally of agenda requests. The coding rule is simple: each specific request that is both cleared "i/a" and presented in the State of the Union message is counted as one single item on the President's agenda. Table 2 summarizes the number of requests for legislation made each year by each presidential administration, as well as the simple number of repetitions from the previous year's State of the Union message. The number of repetitions indicates how much of each President's agenda remained from earlier years.

Examining the OMB data by year, table 2 indicates that all Presidents experience a drop in agenda requests following the first year in office. The number of requests always falls in the second year of office, while the number of repeats in the State of the Union messages steadily grows. *Presidents set their domestic agendas early and repeat them often.* Yet, Presidents do vary in the rate of decline of their agenda requests. Of the five executives, Nixon faced the greatest drop, falling from twenty requests in 1973 to five in 1974. Johnson sustained his level of agenda activity the longest. Though most Presidents decline at roughly the same rate, Nixon's dramatic slip was related to the Watergate crisis: as the crisis expanded, Nixon's agenda contracted.

The First Year. Why is the first year so important for the President's agenda? The answer rests on the cycle of decreasing influence. Presidents and staffs are painfully aware that their most valuable resources dwindle

Table 2. Requests for Legislation, All Years

President	Year	Total Requests	Total Repeats[a]
Kennedy	1961	25	0
	1962	16	8
	1963	6	12
Johnson I	1964	6	11
Johnson II	1965	34	4
	1966	24	7
	1967	19	8
	1968	14	12
Nixon I	1969	17	0
	1970	12	9
	1971	8	12
	1972	3	14
Nixon II	1973	20	3
	1974	5	11
Ford	1975	10	3
	1976	6	7
Carter	1977	21	0
	1978	8	3
	1979	8	5
	1980	4	7

Source: OMB Legislative Reference Division clearance record.
[a] From the previous year's State of the Union address.

over the term. They understand that the essential resource, capital, evaporates over time, that the first year offers the greatest opportunity for establishing the domestic program. Though information and expertise are rarely at a peak in the first year, capital does not keep, and Presidents must take advantage of whatever momentum they have; to wait is to squander the most important advantage.

Thus, the domestic agenda is often seen as a race against time. Consider the views of a Kennedy aide: "We didn't spend as much time as we needed on program development. If we didn't get a good jump in 1961, we would be stuck for four years. We hadn't exactly been swept into office. We had to get off the mark fast and make a good showing. Otherwise, who would take us seriously?" A Nixon assistant echoed the attitude: "Some of us were very concerned that the President was so relaxed in December 1968. Those of us who had been in Washington knew that Congress would give us six months of air time. I'm not sure that the President understood the need to move quickly. He'd been with Eisenhower, and God knows, Eisenhower didn't set the land speed record." The concern for early action is reflected across administrations. In the words of a Carter official, "It's definitely a race. The first months are the starting line. If you don't get off the blocks fast, you'll lose the race. Congress will come in first. You might say we had a false start."

The first year presents the greatest opportunity for programmatic impact. Regardless of the President's policy intent—whether to expand or restrict the federal role—major initiatives demand time. As a Kennedy aide argued, "It just makes sense to move as fast as humanly possible. A major program like Medicare takes a good year just to pass through the Congress. It will take at least two to implement. By that time, you'll want to make some changes—increase the funding, rewrite some regulations. That may take another two years. If you don't get going early, you'll be out of office before you get the program set." All programs will have enemies. The earlier the President moves, the better the opportunity to defend the program and ensure its survival. Even the budget demands speed. According to a former Nixon OMB staffer, "It will be two years before the President can have any impact on the budget. But if he moves quickly, he can ask for some revisions on his predecessor's budget. If you are not ready to move by the end of the first six months, you can lose a full year of budgeting."

Ultimately, first-year pressure is the result of competition. The President is only one actor among many. As Carter quickly discovered, there is considerable competition for scarce congressional agenda space; there is competition for media coverage; there is even competition on the bureaucratic agendas. If the President is to compete for the scarce space, it is to his advantage to move early. Presidents must also be concerned about opposition. The longer a program must wait for introduction, the greater the potential for organized opposition. As one Nixon aide suggested, "We gave our opponents a great deal of time to fight the Family Assistance Plan. They had at least six months to prepare for the initial announcement. Then, because we were late, the program bogged down in committee. We gave them too many chances to hit us." The growth of congressional independence has definitely increased this first-year pressure, giving future administrations an even greater stake in the first moments of the term. The rise in congressional competition and the coinciding increase in complexity have led to a scramble for scarce agenda space. Presidents cannot afford to waste the few opportunities they have.

The First Months. If Presidents are advised to act in the first year, they are are also encouraged to move as early as possible *within* that year. In many respects, each year of the term is similar. According to Kessel, all Presidents face an annual program cycle which begins sometime "after Labor Day when programs to be proposed to Congress in the coming year are readied. Fall is probably the time of the heaviest work load for the policy-staffer in the White House, because work is still progressing on Capitol Hill on the present year's program at the same time preparations for the next year are being made." The annual cycle continues with basic decisions about the budget in December, major messages in January and February, lobbying in the spring, a relaxation of pressure in June, and a return to planning in August. For Kessel, "in election years, major bills will be on the floor just before adjournment, following which there will be a rapid shift of focus onto the campaign, so any real attention to the legislative program for the coming year gets deferred until November and December" (Kessel 1975, p. 9).

Though Kessel's description is accurate for the second, third, and fourth years of the term, it is not as appropriate for the first. Although the President has a variety of planning tools at his disposal once in office—OMB, the Domestic Policy Staff, departments, and agencies—the first year generally is mapped out during the transition. The program is detailed as the staff is moving in—as phones are installed, offices found, desks exchanged. The first-year agenda is a product of considerable confusion, and the degree to which the President succeeds in battling that confusion determines the speed with which the program is presented.

Presidents vary in their ability to set the agenda early. We can compare the relative efficiency of the five most recent executives by returning to the OMB data. Recall that the President's domestic agenda is defined as any item that is both cleared "i/a" by OMB and mentioned in at least one State of the Union address. The OMB data pinpoint the exact date when clearance occurred. In the 1965 State of the Union message, Lyndon Johnson asked for a wild-rivers system; the legislation was cleared on February 2. In 1969 Nixon asked for general revenue sharing; the draft was sent on August 13. We can divide the first-year requests into quarters: January-March, April-June, July-September, and October-December. The first-year records for Kennedy, Johnson, Nixon, and Carter are presented in table 3 (Ford is excluded because of the unusual circumstances surrounding his inauguration).

Table 3 indicates that Kennedy and Johnson were far more successful than either Nixon or Carter in moving programs early. Whereas the bulk of the Kennedy and Johnson programs moved in January-March, the Nixon and Carter domestic agendas were delayed until summer. When Kennedy 1961 is compared with Nixon 1969 and Carter 1977, the disparity is dramatic. All three entered office following opposition party control; all three were elected by a slim margin. However, whereas 71 percent of Kennedy's program had moved to Congress by the end of March, only 11 percent of Nixon's had been introduced, and 38 percent of Carter's. The difference between Johnson's 1965 experience and Nixon's 1973 record also is distinct. Both Johnson and Nixon were continuing previous terms, but Johnson was significantly more effective than Nixon. Johnson's program was in the hands of Congress by the end of the first quarter.

Is it important that Nixon was six months later in 1973 than Johnson was in 1965; that revenue sharing came in August 1969 instead of March? Timing certainly has an impact on legislative success. For items

Table 3. Requests for Legislation, First Year

President	Year	Percentage of Requests in			
		January-March	April-June	July-September	October-December
Kennedy	1961	76%	24%	0%	0%
Johnson	1965	94	6	0	0
Nixon	1969	12	41	41	6
Nixon	1973	40	30	15	15
Carter	1977	33	57	10	0

Source: OMB Legislative Reference Division clearance record.

introduced in January-March of the first year, 72 percent eventually are enacted; for items introduced in April-June, the success rate drops to 39 percent; by July-September, it falls to 25 percent, remaining stable through October-December. This pattern does not seem to reflect an effort to present the "easier" items first. Though these success rates reflect a number of separate variables, the date of introduction does seem to have a bearing on eventual congressional success.

Much of this initial success involves the honeymoon, the early period of grace and good temper. Presidents can always expect at least a limited honeymoon. However, by the middle of the first summer the euphoria wears off, leaving the Washington community less willing to support the President's requests. Although public approval remains at a peak over the first six months, it begins to drop as the first year ends. Even if the administration fails to offer a single proposal the President's capital begins to dissipate. When a program is presented in January-March, it will be considered under the most favorable conditions. If its presentation is delayed until summer, it will enter the congressional process just as the President begins to slide. Presidents and staffs may recognize the need to draft a program as quickly as possible, but their success in doing so varies. As one Carter aide put it, "We knew that we were losing time, but no matter how hard some of us pushed, it was impossible to get action. Welfare reform got gummed up in the works, and even a presidential deadline couldn't get it out. We weren't really that slow, but we weren't that fast either."

The need for speed was no less important for Reagan, particularly in dealing with the economy. According to David Stockman, Reagan's budget director, early action was essential in avoiding a "GOP Economic Dunkirk":

> Things could go very badly during the first year, resulting in incalculable erosion of GOP momentum, unity and public confidence. If bold policies are not swiftly, deftly and courageously implemented in the first six months, Washington will quickly become engulfed in political disorder commensurate with the surrounding economic disarray. A golden opportunity for permanent conservative policy revision and political realign-

ment could be thoroughly dissipated before the Reagan administration is even up to speed (*Washington Post,* 14 December 1980).

With recent changes in the political environment, neither Congress nor the public is quite so willing to wait for the President's agenda. Individual members have pet projects and constituent demands; study groups have separate programs and objectives; future candidates have competing agendas; the public is impatient for results. There is no shortage of competing ideas on the Hill. According to Robert Shogan, the Carter administration was aware of the fact:

> Under the last two Republican Presidents, the White House had blockaded most of the social and economic legislation offered by the Democratic Congresses. "It's impossible to exaggerate how much legislative backlog there is on the Hill because of the Ford vetoes," Eizenstat told [a] staff meeting in Mondale's office [in early 1977]. "For eight years, for God's sake, you've had essentially negative Presidents in the sense of not having strong legislative programs that a Democratic Congress could buy. And so they developed their own legislative packages. And now that they have a Democratic President they're gung-ho to go straight forward on it." As a result, while Carter was still putting his own program together, he was being pressured to deal with congressional initiatives, such as farm price supports and the minimum wage, which threatened his priorities (Shogan 1977, p. 205).

Given this awareness, why was Carter so slow? Why were Kennedy and Johnson so fast? Two explanations arise from this study.

Expertise. One explanation rests on the President's expertise. Both Kennedy and Johnson entered office well prepared. Both had considerable contact with the legislative process before assuming office; both understood the need for dispatch in announcing the domestic agenda. Not only did they recognize the need for speed but they were well prepared to achieve the results. According to their respective White House staffs, both Presidents put heavy pressure on the domestic process in the first months. Kennedy began his planning effort immediately following the 1960 election. "We worked our tails off," one aide remarked, "and worked overtime doing it. There was very little rest during December and January. Kennedy wanted a full slate of programs ready for the State of the Union address. Kennedy just didn't want to waste any time." Despite the usual exhaustion following the campaign, Kennedy pressed his staff to devote full time and energy to the domestic agenda. He delivered his first State of the Union address ten days after his inauguration—Nixon and Carter waited over a year.

Johnson faced a very different situation as he began his first full term in 1965. Johnson did not enter the transition as a novice—he had been President for a year, and he had a well-staffed Executive Office. There was less confusion and less uncertainty than usually accompanies a new adminis-tration. Though the bulk of Johnson's agenda emerged from the unfulfilled Kennedy program, Johnson took full advantage of the domestic planning process to draft the elements of the Great Society. As one Johnson assistant suggested, "We were very effective in presenting the program following the inauguration. We had been planning it for over six months. Once Goldwater became the certain nominee, Johnson started drafting the 1965 program. We all felt we were going to win and wanted to move as soon as possible."

Nixon and Carter were not as prepared for the rigors of the presi-dential transition as were Kennedy and Johnson. In fact, Nixon's post-election planning was somewhat haphazard. Though he appointed a number of post-election task forces, he was not particularly interested in the findings. Nixon preferred to concentrate his energies on foreign policy. The problem was partly the complexity of the domestic issues—welfare reform was a very intricate problem demanding considerable attention—and partly the absence of an interested hand in the Oval Office. According to one disenchanted aide, "We spent a great deal of time running in place. The President was not interested in the domestic agenda and did not participate in the early de-cisions. As the White House staff took form, he did nothing to reduce the conflict between competing factions. If anything, Nixon's lack of involvement increased the feuding." Nixon's disinterest contributed to staff conflict and confusion. Much of this confusion stemmed from the appointments of Arthur Burns and Daniel Moynihan. Each was told that he alone would direct the domestic program; each assumed that the agenda would be under his ex-clusive control. Nixon did little to referee the conflict. Indeed, Nixon once argued that "this country could run itself domestically—without a President; all you need is a competent Cabinet to run the country at home." By 1973 Nixon's expertise had grown; he had learned that the President has to inter-vene in domestic affairs, if only to coordinate the staffs. Nixon's increased understanding was reflected in a sizable jump in his effectiveness in moving the agenda early in the second term.

Nixon's first hundred days may also have reflected a deliberate decision to slow down the domestic process. That is the opinion of several former aides. According to Ray Price, chief speech writer in 1969, Nixon decided to strike a balance between those who wanted immediate action and those who cautioned restraint. In an early memo to Nixon, Price joined those who advised restraint:

> For a third of a century, the fashionable critics have been measuring progress according to the standards established by Roosevelt in his first 100 days. If we're going to change the pattern of government, we've got to change the standards of measurement. This is central. . . .
>
> The fact of the matter is that the nation still is suffering from the first 100 days of Johnson, from the first 100 days of Kennedy, and even, lingeringly, from the first 100 days of Roosevelt. It should be neither our

plan nor our style to repeat those 100 day stunts—and we should present this not defensively, but as a positive virtue (Price 1977, p. 77).

What about Carter's first year? According to media reports, Carter's transition planning was the best in recent history; however, the actual record suggests that several major problems complicated the transition effort. Carter was certainly less effective than his two Democratic predecessors in presenting his agenda. Like Kennedy, Carter entered office following eight years of Republican rule. Like Kennedy, Carter placed heavy emphasis on transition planning. However, Carter's transition, unlike Kennedy's, was marked by conflict, not consensus. As Shogan notes, Carter should have been better equipped than any of his contemporaries to minimize the transition turmoil.

> A few days after his election [Carter] was presented with a 20-foot stack of briefing books intended to lay the groundwork for a successful transition. By contrast, after his election, John Kennedy was provided only with a handful of memoranda prepared by Clark Clifford and Richard Neustadt. Richard Nixon, according to one chronicle of his Presidency, had little more than a "short list of notions" when he set up his transition headquarters in New York's Pierre Hotel. Moreover, Carter knew that the planning could continue with plenty of financial support. Congress had set aside $2 million to pay for the postelection transition, more than four times what had been available to President-elect Nixon (Shogan 1977, p. 75).

Unfortunately, Carter's transition effort was beset by intense conflict between Jack Watson, head of the campaign policy team, and Hamilton Jordan, Carter's chief political advisor. During the campaign, Jordan's staff complained that far too much energy was being diverted by the midsummer planning effort, that too much effort was being expended on nonpolitical needs. Watson's staff retorted that too little attention was being focused on the post-election agenda. The arguments reflected the personal struggle for power between Jordan and Watson. By late October the battle lines were drawn. The conflict had its most damaging effect early in the transition. According to Shogan,

> The shuffling for position was a delay and a distraction, a period of about ten days during which, as one transition staffer conceded, "basically nothing was happening." Even after the original plans had been re-ordered, an atmosphere of tension and uncertainty prevailed among those charged with carrying on the process. It is hard to tell how much more might have been accomplished under other circumstances, but the bumpy beginning robbed the incoming administration of some of the early impetus its leaders had hoped to build (Shogan 1977, pp. 80-81).

The problem was compounded by Carter's lack of experience. Whereas Kennedy entered office with a detailed knowledge of the federal process,

Carter was a novice. According to one Carter aide recruited from Congress, "It was like a maze to them. Most of the staff kept bumping against unfamiliar obstacles. They didn't have the kind of background necessary for effective choice. Before you can present a program to Congress, you have to know how to do it. That's not to say Carter was completely uninformed, but he didn't really grasp the needs of the Washington system." Nor did Carter express a desire to become involved in the "nitty-gritty" of presidential politics. Observers characterized him as aloof, detached, and isolated. Whatever his reasons, Carter did not enter the political fray with the same energy as either Kennedy or Johnson. As one media respondent commented, "I don't think Carter actually perceived the error until Mondale became more involved. I think Carter was accustomed to a different legislative style, one where you have time to think things out. It just didn't fit with the congressional mood. Carter might have been more comfortable at the turn of the century." For Carter, the delays were critical. Congress was simply not willing to wait.

The Availability of Alternatives. A second, possibly more attractive explanation for presidential timing rests on the availability of program alternatives. Though programs may be relatively straightforward, most presidential draft requests involve some detail and length. There is no doubt that the development of certain alternatives takes time. The degree to which the President's programs are available upon election will influence the speed with which they are presented. In Carter's case, many of the top priorities involved considerable delays at the drafting stage. While hospital cost containment was rather simple and moved in April 1977, welfare reform was quite complex and was not ready until August. According to the Carter staff, there was some consensus on the major agenda *issues* early in the transition, but the *alternatives* took time:

> Even though we set the agenda early, we didn't have the proposals ready for several months. In part, it just took time for us to start moving. But primarily, the delays were from the nature of our agenda goals. We chose some very complicated issues. Welfare reform and energy tended to dominate both the presidential and staff time. They were highly technical issues and needed considerable work. And hospital cost containment was a very recent issue. The community of experts had not agreed on the alternatives.

The linkage between timing and readiness affected other administrations as well. In Kennedy's first year the agenda was ready to move early. As James Sundquist notes, "The Democratic program that was presented to the country in 1960 was truly a party program. The platform writers and the presidential nominee contributed emphasis, style, and form, but the substance of the program had been written with unusual precision and clarity during the eight years out of power—eight years that at the time seemed endlessly frustrating but that were, it is clear in retrospect, extraordinarily fruitful" (Sundquist 1968, p. 415). In short, Kennedy's program was ready to go at the time of his election. Aid to Education, Area Redevelopment, the Youth Conservation Corps, Medicare, Wilderness Preservation, and civil rights had all been refined by the Democratic party during the 1953-60 period. When Kennedy entered office, he did not have to commit large blocks of time drafting proposals. "We changed some bills, altered the specifics," one aide maintained, "but the basic content was there even before the campaign. Our problem was in choosing among the items. We couldn't do everything."

That was not the case for Nixon: he did not choose a ready-made program; one simply did not exist. Though Nixon assumed office after eight years of Democratic control, the Republican party had not been as active in developing an agenda as their Democratic colleagues of a decade before. Part of the reason was ideological: the Republicans were not inclined to draft a competing agenda for social policy. However, as the minority party, the Republican party had been concerned with resisting the Democratic initiatives. According to one Nixon aide, "The party was of little use to us in the early stages of the administration, at least for policy. They had not created that many new ideas during the Johnson years. They had not been notoriously successful in building any new programs in the period. Theirs was a problem of countering Johnson's huge majority." Thus when Nixon called for new ideas on welfare reform, several answers came from Democrats. As Martin Anderson suggests, "When Nixon made clear his intent to push welfare reform, Moynihan was quickly provided with a detailed plan by fellow Democrats in the federal bureaucracy. The welfare reform plan that had been brusquely dismissed by President Johnson was hauled out and dusted off. The plan was rewritten, numbers were updated, and a few new ideas were added" (Anderson 1978, p. 8). It happened again with revenue sharing: Nixon turned to a proposal first supported by Walter Heller, a top economic assistant from the Kennedy and Johnson administrations. As the minority party, the Republican party simply did not have a slate of fully drafted programs. There was little incentive for the party to create such an agenda. The primary need was to organize a solid front against Johnson's Great Society. As a result, Nixon was at a distinct disadvantage at the start of his term. Similar problems returned to haunt Reagan's first days in office. Though Reagan had campaigned on a pledge to cut government spending, congressional Republicans were unable to offer a substitute budget for the incoming President. As the minority party during the 1970s, the Republicans had resisted the Democrats only on the margins. Now, with a Republican in the White House, the party scurried to cope with its new found political status. Neither the House nor the Senate party could offer the new administration much help. Instead, OMB director Stockman had to begin the budget review from scratch, collecting estimates on hundreds of programs. Though Stockman finished in remarkable short-order, he made a variety of miscalculations, forcing a second round of budget revisions in mid-March.

What about Carter in 1977? After all, Carter entered office following eight years of Democratic control in Congress. Had Congress been less active in generating programs? One problem was that Carter did not come from the Democratic mainstream. Unlike Kennedy or Johnson, Carter did not have extensive Washington exposure. As one aide argued, "We just didn't know what was on the stove." Nor did Carter naturally identify with the Democratic program in Congress. Carter had not been involved in the long struggle for national health insurance; he had not been present for the battles over Ford's vetoes. Carter was regarded as an outsider, and his inexperience with federal policy created problems in office. He certainly was not cut from the same populist cloth as were Kennedy or Johnson; he did not identify with what little party program existed. Thus, Carter's staff suggested that Congress was less important as a source of ideas in 1977 than in 1961. "We had run against Washington," one aide remarked. "It should not have come as a surprise that we didn't automatically adopt the standard Democratic program. In several areas we had to start from scratch."

Carter's second problem came from the lack of consensus in the Democratic party. Did the Democratic party have a national program in 1977? Unlike the 1950s, the Congress had not shown consistent support for any single body of policy, nor was there agreement on national needs. Did the Democrats want national health insurance or tax limitation? Whereas Kennedy faced a focused set of party proposals, Carter faced a set of loosely connected, often confusing party plans.

The Sense of Timing. Does the sense of timing exist? In the case of the domestic agenda, it exists perhaps only inasmuch as Presidents respond to the pressure to move quickly. This is not to suggest that Presidents have no control over timing. They will certainly delay some agenda requests over the term; they may hope to find a more supportive Congress or fashion a stronger proposal, or they may be forced to wait until the legislative calendars clear. Johnson's domestic style as interpreted by Kearns is one example.

> Johnson's decision to push for health and education legislation ahead of housing proposals and the granting of home rule to the District of Columbia resulted from his carefully considered judgment as to the amount of time each of the bills would consume and which measures were most likely to provoke the kind of debate and controversy that would drain valuable energy. Recognizing that John Kennedy had lost a full legislative year in pursuit of federal aid to education, Lyndon Johnson refused to let the education bill go to the Congress until administration officials had secured the agreement of two major lobbying groups (Kearns 1976, p. 236).

In talking with Kearns, Johnson summarized his view of legislative timing:

A measure must be sent to the Hill at exactly the right moment and that moment depends on three things: first, on the momentum; second, on the availability of sponsors in the right place at the right time; and, third, on the opportunities for neutralizing the opposition. Timing is essential. Momentum is not a mysterious mistress. It is a controllable fact of political life that depends on nothing more exotic than preparation (p. 238).

Yet Johnson recognized the importance of the first year. Though the President could affect the timing of legislation in terms of weeks and days, the first year held the secret of legislative impact. Johnson believed in "maximum attention in minimum time." Though bills for housing and home rule could be held back for health and education legislation they had to move before the summer. Indeed, housing and home rule bills followed their more prestigious predecessors in less than two months. As Lyndon Johnson argued, "I keep hitting hard because I know this honeymoon won't last. Every day I lose a little more political capital. That's why we have to keep at it, never letting up. One day soon, I don't know when, the critics and the snipers will move in and we will be at stalemate. We have to get all we can, now, before the roof comes down" (in Valenti 1975, p. 144). Though Johnson varied the timing of important bills in 1965, he was keenly aware of the need to get all the bills to the Hill before the end of the year. Thus when aides questioned Johnson's decision to pursue District home rule on the heels of Medicare and Aid to Education, the President refused to wait: "[The congressmen will] all be thinking about their reelection. I'll have made my mistakes, my polls will be down, and they'll be trying to put some distance between themselves and me. They won't want to go into the fall with their opponents calling 'em Lyndon Johnson's rubber stamp" (in McPherson 1972, pp. 105-6). Johnson understood the cycle of decreasing influence, and in that understanding lay his sense of timing.

Presidents are encouraged to set the agenda as early as possible. It is not surprising that most presidential priorities are announced as soon as they are ready. There is little incentive to wait. According to a Johnson aide, "Congress won't wait for anyone. If you don't get going early, you will be out of the running fast. There are times when the President has to slow down, when he is even required to stop. But when the openings appear, you have got to move." Thus the sense of timing may be little more than the President's ability to react early instead of late, which is grounded in the President's expertise and punctuated by the sheer availability of alternatives.

Agenda Size

In addition to timing his domestic requests, each President must decide on the number of requests to be presented. We must assume that Presidents are at least quasi-rational, that they want to maximize success. In that effort, Presidents must often limit agenda size.

Agenda size is the absolute number of items on the President's agenda. Though Presidents can ask for everything they want, Congress rarely grants all presidential requests. Thus, if the President and the staff hope for some measure of success, they must limit the number of items they send to the Hill. When Nixon entered office in 1969, his staff was acutely aware of the constraints on the domestic agenda: "No one felt we could send a large number of programs to the Congress. We had to pick among the best ideas and concentrate our energies. Congress was not likely to give us much freedom, so each choice had to count."

Kennedy, Carter, and Ford faced similar limits. According to one Ford assistant, "We couldn't label our program the great this or the new that. There wasn't enough there. We spent most of our time reviewing then-current federal programs and drafting modifications. Once the President imposed the no new spending rule, we turned toward 1977 as the first available opportunity. We all hoped that Mr. Ford could be elected, that we would have a chance to present a complete agenda at some point in the term." Or as a Carter aide argued, "It makes no sense whatsoever to throw up a group of programs you are sure to lose. The President has to say no even if the programs represent everything he stands for. It's worse in the long run to send up proposals that are sure losers than to hold back for a couple of years or until the next election." It is often to the President's advantage to restrict the agenda size; sometimes it is a necessity. As one Johnson assistant reflected, "Even LBJ recognized the need to limit his requests. Congress can only handle so much at one time. The calendars can't react that fast. If most of the programs are headed to the same committees, the President has to hold up. You don't want the committees to start to bitch, but you don't want them to twiddle their thumbs either."

Congressional Limits. Presidents face several structural limits on agenda size, but the congressional calendar involves the greatest institutional restrictions. Though Congress can act quickly during a crisis, most legislation must pass through a series of decision points en route to enactment. According to John Kennedy, the process contains a number of hurdles:

> It is very easy to defeat a bill in the Congress. It is much more difficult to pass one. To go through a subcommittee . . . and get a majority vote, the full committee and get a majority vote, go to the Rules Committee and get a rule, go to the Floor of the House and get a majority, start all over again in the Senate, subcommittee and full committee, and in the Senate there is unlimited debate, so you can never bring a matter to a vote if there is enough determination on the part of the opponents, even if they are a minority, to go through the Senate with the bill. And then unanimously get a conference between the House and Senate to adjust the bill, or if one member objects, to have it go back through the Rules Committee, back through the Congress, and have this done on a controversial piece of legislation where powerful groups are opposing it, that is an ex-

tremely difficult task (transcript of television interview, in *Public Papers of The Presidents, 1963*, pp. 892, 894).

Kennedy's complaint came long before the rise of subcommittee government and the increased complexity within the legislative process. Past Presidents and their staffs generally have been sensitive to the demands of the congressional process. "The liaison office always walks a tight line," one Nixon officer suggested. "If you press too hard, you're likely to anger the committees. They have a heavy work load and won't take too much White House pressure. But if you don't press hard enough, the Congress will put your agenda on the back burner."

Yet, if Presidents understand the problems of overloading, they also recognize the dangers of waiting. Regardless of the President's legislative strategy, Congress will accommodate only so many requests at one time. Accordingly, in past decades the House Rules and Ways and Means committees have emerged as bottlenecks for presidential priorities. Kennedy, for instance, repeatedly battled the Rules Committee. Despite his successful 1961 effort to expand its membership to include more liberals, the committee still set stringent limits on the number of Kennedy programs under consideration at any given moment. Why did Kennedy invest so much capital in packing the committee? One aide answered that it was "because we wouldn't have been able to move anything to the floor. We had to give ourselves a fighting chance. We saw the Rules Committee as a key obstacle to our success, and felt that we had to deal with them first."

Has the structural limit increased since 1961? The Carter staff firmly believed so. Though Carter repeatedly has been accused of overloading Congress, in reality he proposed not much more than Kennedy and much less than Johnson. However, Congress has become more sensitive to competition for agenda space. As one congressional observer suggested, "The legislative system has become much more competitive since 1960. The system is more interrelated with the bureaucracy; there are more proposals up for consideration. Congress is less willing to squeeze the President in. You have to be much more careful about sending up clear signals." Carter did not ask for much in absolute terms; as we shall see, his agenda was relatively small. Rather, Congress was simply more inclined to view the requests as competition, especially since Carter's agenda moved so late. One frustrated assistant summarized the Carter trouble:

> The staff honestly didn't believe they were flooding Congress. They felt they were making some choices and moving the legislation in an orderly fashion. But the Congress was scheduled up before most of the items arrived. Congress was already working on tax reform; [Edward] Kennedy was moving on national health insurance; there was an effort on unemployment. About the only thing Congress wasn't doing was energy, and that was because it was so unpopular. I think some of them expected Carter just to sit back and wait for the Congress to act. For once, the

President would be the rubber stamp. Congress proposes, the President disposes.

Presidential Limits. Even if Congress could handle every item, the White House policy process itself places certain limits on the domestic agenda. Though recent scholars have complained about the size of the presidential staff, the White House policy process can accept only a limited number of items at a time. The President needs time to make decisions; the staff needs information to draft specific proposals. Basically, the President's internal resources demand limits on choice. According to a Nixon domestic aide, "Nothing ever happens overnight. When you enter office, if looks as if the sky's the limit. After a month, you find that the gears don't mesh. We could only concentrate on a couple of problems at a time. There were a lot of bodies, but only a few could be involved in the critical decisions."

Though the White House staff hit a peak size of 632 in 1970, the number of staff directly involved in policy choice is quite restricted. The bulk of the staff is usually engaged in "firefighting," while the rest are forced to tackle one or two problems at a time. One Ford assistant suggested that "it's easy to criticize the office for its size, but you have to know that size doesn't mean a damn. Most of the staff is clerical; a third is on loan from the departments." According to staff records for 1977, Carter had approximately twenty-eight individuals on his Domestic Policy Staff. Two aides were directly involved in health policy; three in energy policy; two in urban affairs. Though all Presidents have access to departmental support, the number of White House aides directly involved in policy is rather limited. Yet, despite the small numbers, the staff tends to specialize, which in turn limits the ability of aides to cover several problems at once. "Even if we had all the time in the world," one Carter assistant maintained, "we couldn't move any faster. Most of these problems must be worked out in the departments. If there isn't a solution handy, it takes some time to develop one."

In the White House, a presidential proposal must cross a variety of obstacles to reach the agenda. In the Carter White House, for instance, potential programs were reviewed by OMB, the Domestic Policy Staff, the Council of Economic Advisors, the Office of the Vice-President, the Office of the Assistant to the President for Public Liaison, the Office of the Secretary to the Cabinet and Assistant to the President for Intergovernmental Affairs, the Office of the Counsel to the President, the Office of the Assistant to the President for Political Affairs and Personnel, the Office of the Assistant to the President for Communications, the Office of the Assistant to the President, and the Office of the Assistant to the President for Congressional Liaison. Any one of these offices could slow the process—and the list does not even include the agencies or departments that had to be involved. The Carter decision loop covered well over a dozen separate offices within the White House; the process could take several weeks to complete, and it often generated considerable conflict. As a result of these problems and the tendency of the staff to specialize, Carter faced a significant institutional drag on agenda size.

Political Limits. Agenda size and content vary directly with the President's capital. Of the five presidential agendas, Johnson's must certainly be regarded as the most extensive, and Ford's as the most limited. According to a former Bureau of the Budget official:

> Johnson's program was certainly the broadest of the four that I watched. In the first months of 1965 Johnson presented more than Nixon did during his entire first term. It was a massive amount of legislation which won't be matched for some time. There's no doubt that Johnson's program was the most extensive of the 1956-1974 period. Much of the program had originated in the Kennedy term but had been delayed by Congress. Johnson had considerable leverage in 1965 and made the most of it. Neither Kennedy, Nixon, nor Ford had the same political opportunities. Johnson's legislative agenda was the fullest and the most detailed. The main programs were all presented in the first and second year; the rest were logical extensions of Johnson's successes.

How did Johnson's agenda compare with those of Kennedy, Nixon, and Ford?

> Kennedy, Nixon, and Ford were all frustrated at one point or another. They had to restrict their programs to fit the political situation. Still, Kennedy was far more successful in scheduling his program than Nixon or Ford. Kennedy hit some serious roadblocks, but he still presented a substantial amount of legislation—not as much as Johnson, but still up there. Nixon, of course, was stopped by Congress. He was also unsure of what he wanted. Not much needs to be said of Ford. He was just starting when I left. Even then, it was obvious that he wasn't going to be able to charge forward. There wasn't much he could do given the circumstances of his inauguration.

The OMB data support the conclusions. Table 4 gives the total number of requests in each administration, as well as the number of "new" and "old" proposals. The distinction between new and old is quite valuable for this research, particularly when we turn to the discussion of policy content in chapter 5. Here, it helps us evaluate the impact of capital on agenda size. New proposals involve requests for innovations in federal policy; old focus on the modification and amendment of past programs. Kennedy's request for Medicare, Johnson's proposal for Model Cities, Nixon's revenue sharing, Ford's energy-independence program, and Carter's hospital cost containment are examples of new agenda items. Each involved significant changes in the government's relationship to society (Campbell 1978). Most social security increases, minimum wage expansions, unemployment extensions, and food stamp extensions are examples of old agenda requests. Each involves simple changes in the existing framework.

Table 4. Agenda Size

President	Requests		New Requests		Old Requests	
	Total	Average per year	Total	Average per year	Total	Average per year
Kennedy-Johnson	53	13	33	8	20	5
Johnson	91	23	55	14	36	9
Nixon I	40	10	25	6	15	4
Nixon II	25	13	21	10	4	2
Ford	16	8	6	3	10	5
Carter	41	10	25	6	16	4

Source: OMB Legislative Reference Division clearance record.
Note: Content coding is discussed in Appendix C.

Two conclusions emerge from table 4. First, Presidents vary in their agenda activity. Johnson is at the top in both the number of total requests and the number of new proposals. As one observer noted, "It makes sense that LBJ would look so strong. That's nothing new. Johnson had all the advantages; he had all the momentum. It would be very surprising if he didn't come first among the recent Presidents—if Ford had somehow come out first." Second, Ford leads all five Presidents in the average number of old agenda items. In fact, he is the only executive to have more old proposals than new. The Ford staff did not dispute the finding. "We were well aware of our position in Congress, and the problems following the resignation," one Ford assistant noted. "That's not to say we didn't want our share of new initiatives. We were working on comprehensive welfare reform and national health insurance. We just read the Congress, looked at the budget, and decided to hold off. We knew that the new programs would have to wait at least until 1977."

Variations in Agenda Size. The main factor contributing to variations in agenda size is capital; as presidential capital contracts, so does the President's domestic agenda. That is certainly the explanation offered by the five White House staffs. The Johnson respondents pointed directly to the heavy congressional majority. "Congress expected us to send a large program. Some of the leaders even asked for it. It was assumed that Johnson would present a dramatic program and introduce it with some fanfare. That was his style, and that's exactly what he did." The interviews with Johnson staff members are punctuated with references to that first year as the time of great opportunity. By Johnson's second year, the capital had begun to dissipate—the cycle of decreasing influence had started. According to Sundquist, "The inconclusive war in Vietnam preempted public attention. Consumer prices rose 4 percent in a year's time. The summer's riots—thirty-eight separate disturbances were counted—cast a pall over the very concept of the Great

Society. President Johnson suffered his most crushing legislative defeat with the loss of the 1966 civil rights bill" (Sundquist 1968, p. 496). Johnson eventually decided to stop using the term "Great Society." Califano strengthened his hold on the agenda process. Whereas Johnson requested thirty-four separate measures in 1965, by 1967 the total dropped to twenty-one. According to one assistant, "Johnson lowered his sights. The 1967 program was reduced to a series of battles for funding and amendments. The drama was gone; the program started to drift to minor requests and a defense of the early victories."

The impact of capital on agenda size is best illustrated in the Ford administration. Ford was not elected to office; following the September pardon of Nixon, his popularity dwindled rapidly, and his veto activity jumped dramatically. According to Gallup figures, Ford's public approval dropped thirty points between 19 August and 12 December 1974—the fastest decline since the poll began measuring public approval of the President's performance. By the end of that same three-month period, Ford had already vetoed a stunning twenty-seven bills. Though Ford was certainly respected in the Congress, there were only 144 Republicans in the House, the lowest level of support for a sitting President in this century. Whereas Johnson, Kennedy, and Carter each held some congressional leverage at the start of their term, Ford was forced to fashion a veto strategy to maximize his limited opportunities. As one Ford aide reflected, "There was no sense in presenting a full legislative agenda. Economic conditions did not permit any increase in federal spending; political conditions did not permit any flexibility in Congress. It was better to wait for Congress to act, and see what we could do with a one third-plus-one approach."

Initial legislative success has an impact on agenda size. If the President's program is enacted quickly, there is a limited opportunity to replace the enacted requests, to fill the empty space. Once again, Johnson was able to take advantage of the opportunity to a far greater extent than any other recent executive. He was simply more successful in his early months. To a limit, the faster Johnson's programs were passed, the faster the agenda could be replenished. As congressional calendars reopened, Johnson had the opportunity to move more legislation. This relationship was accentuated by the cycle of increasing effectiveness. Johnson's staff was more prepared to send a second wave of proposals than were the staffs of most first-term Presidents. The Johnson domestic process was in full swing at the start of the Eighty-ninth Congress. As programs moved through the legislative process, Johnson's staff was able to supply limited replacements.

That was not the case for Nixon. Even had Nixon enjoyed similar legislative success in 1969, the administration was not prepared to offer major replacements. The Nixon domestic process had already spent eight months producing the Family Assistance Plan; it did not have a set of programs in the agenda queue. As a first-term President, Nixon simply was not as effective.

Nor was Carter. As hospital cost containment entered the congressional struggle, Carter was only beginning the serious discussion of welfare reform. According to internal documents secured for this study, Carter budgeted six months for welfare reform planning, beginning in March 1977, exactly one month after hospital cost containment. Had hospital cost containment passed quickly, Carter could not have filled the empty agenda space.

The Impact of Ideology. Do ideology and partisanship affect agenda size? After all, Eisenhower entered office in 1953 with a solid Republican majority in Congress and strong public approval. His activity certainly did not rise to his available capital. Are Republican Presidents naturally disposed to a passive approach? Does the recruitment of Republican executives lead to a natural bias toward a smaller legislative "plate"? The traditional passive stereotype does not fit Nixon or Ford; both were "active" in all senses of the word. According to the two staffs, both Nixon and Ford felt that the emergence of the Great Society demanded a Republican counterresponse. Both Presidents had extensive hopes for legislative impact upon inauguration; both were frustrated by congressional resistance; *both wanted to act.* Although Eisenhower could be passive and still accomplish his policy goals, Nixon and Ford could not. In 1953 the federal role was still relatively small; by 1969 it had vastly expanded. The New Frontier and the Great Society had completed much of FDR's New Deal. In order to restructure the government toward a New Federalism, Nixon had to offer a competing slate of ideas and programs. As one Nixon assistant argued, "There were many things we wanted to do across the term. Some were undermined by the executive branch; others were destroyed by staff conflict. Some turned out to be too ambitious; others were technically impossible. But it is not true that we didn't want to act. We had a set of ideas, and we were angry that Congress would not cooperate. We wanted to move."

Thus, Nixon's "administrative Presidency" was more a reaction to political circumstance than presidential ideology. "We could have accomplished much more through legislative channels," one aide argued. "If you want some lasting impact, it has to come through statutes. We could tighten welfare rules, but we couldn't change the basic thrust. We could rearrange agencies, but we couldn't alter the basic framework." Similar sentiments were expressed by the Ford staff:

> Things have changed for Republican Presidents. I doubt very much that Eisenhower could survive in the 1970s. You can't sit back and hope the country goes your direction. You've got to get in there and fight like hell. If you can't get a program passed, you have to adopt a different tactic. Try the veto, use an executive order, work the budget. There aren't many Republicans around today who don't have elaborate legislative programs and who wouldn't work to get them passed. That includes Ronald Reagan and Phillip Crane.

This is not to suggest that ideology and partisanship are unimportant in the domestic agenda; they are significant factors in the choice of specific issues and alternatives. But it is evident from interviews with former Nixon and Ford staff members that neither administration consciously restricted agenda size in accordance with a passive Republican style. Both had programs they wanted but couldn't pass; both had goals they couldn't reach. Their goals were obviously different from those of the Democrats. Yet, in pursuit of those goals, Nixon and Ford were as active as the Democratic Presidents; they simply had less capital to fuel their programs. As one Nixon-Ford liaison assistant stressed, "I reject the idea that we were somehow less active than Johnson or the other Democrats. Our legislative program was as ambitious, but we weren't given the opportunity. If we had faced a Republican Congress, it would be much more apparent." The Reagan administration has demonstrated a similar activism, albeit conservative in nature. No Republican President currently can afford to adopt a passive style as a mainstay in solving national problems. In the six weeks following the inauguration, the Reagan administration was able to complete a full review of the fiscal 1981 and 1982 budgets, which normally would have involved at least twelve to fourteen months.

Conclusion

The basic parameters of the domestic agenda are intimately tied to the President's resources. Both the timing and the size of the President's program respond to the ebb and flow of time, information, expertise, energy, and most important, capital. The dual cycles of decreasing influence and increasing effectiveness create the pressures on the President to move the agenda as early in the term as possible, as well as the need to restrict the sheer number of items under consideration at any one time. The impact of these cycles depends, of course, on several factors, including the level of resources at the start of each term. The decline in time was far more important for Ford, given his two-year term. The increase in effectiveness was more significant for Carter, given his early inexperience.

Ultimately, the cycles produce countervailing pressures. The cycle of decreasing influence encourages the President to move the agenda quickly; the cycle of increasing effectiveness cautions restraint. If there is any point in the presidential term when the cycles are at the best blend, it is in the first moments of the second term. The President and the staff have had four years of on-the-job training; time, energy, and capital are at the highest point since the first-term inauguration. Yet, the cycle of decreasing influence accelerates as the two-term limitation takes effect. The Twenty-second Amendment limits the President's ability to use that greater effectiveness gained in the first four years. As one Kennedy aide argued, "The President can't win. If he moves too slow, nothing will pass. If he waits for the second term, it will be too short. If he goes too fast in the first term, the mistakes may cost him the re-election. Damn if I know why anyone would want the job."

3 selecting the issues

Immediately following the Kennedy assassination in 1963, Lyndon Johnson met with a small group of advisors to discuss the national agenda. The talks covered a wide variety of issues and alternatives but concentrated on the domestic program. Would the tax cut proceed? Would civil rights legislation move forward? According to those involved, there was no question that Johnson would adopt the Kennedy agenda. Though Johnson elevated the importance of both civil rights and the poverty program, the Kennedy agenda remained intact.

Johnson's decision reflected both his personality and the immediate climate of expectations. Johnson believed he was the "trustee and custodian of the Kennedy administration":

> Rightly or wrongly, I felt from the very first day in office that I had to carry on for President Kennedy. I considered myself the caretaker of both his people and his policies. He knew when he selected me as his running mate that I would be the man required to carry on if anything happened to him. I did what I believed he would have wanted me to do. I never wavered from that sense of responsibility, even after I was elected in my own right, up to my last day in office (Johnson 1971, p. 19).

Johnson's decision reflected his own personal and political goals. Indeed, for all Presidents, the choice of issues involves the search for benefits, benefits directly linked to presidential policy goals. As Presidents go about the business of selecting domestic issues, their behavior is purposive. Nothing compels a President to choose one issue over another unless the incentives exist.

Johnson's decision to continue the Kennedy agenda involved at least three specific goals. Johnson certainly wanted some programmatic impact; he had a set of personal beliefs which directed his choice of domestic programs. Johnson also wanted to be elected President in his own right.

Whether because of partisanship or ambition, he fully intended to campaign for the Democratic nomination. Finally, according to the White House staff, Johnson viewed the transition as an opportunity to secure a place in history. Throughout the transition, Johnson's behavior was designed to provide electoral success, historical achievement, and good policy. Johnson's goals upon entering office affected his choice of domestic policy.

Presidential Goals

Presidents have a degree of choice in selecting agenda issues. Whether their goal is reelection, historical achievement, or good policy, Presidents choose issues in a purposive manner. Though the political environment may elevate some issues and discard others, we assume that Presidents are not controlled by a hidden hand.

Although new topics will surface throughout the term, the President retains considerable discretion. Although the President must present an annual State of the Union message, he is not required to propose any new legislation; and although he must submit an annual budget, he is not required to assert control. *Presidents choose to act.* Just as congressmen are motivated by electoral considerations (Mayhew 1974), Presidents concentrate on issues that match their personal and political goals—not because of statutory requirements or abstract responsibilities. The critical component of each choice thereby becomes the specific configuration of *incentives.* In an extreme sense, nothing forces the President to devote more than passing attention to any issue; Presidents are free to succeed and fail on their own. Granted, if the President chooses to ignore the economy, he will probably fail; if the President ignores ever-lengthening gas lines, reelection may be impossible. Still, nothing mandates presidential attention unless the incentives surface. From this perspective, Presidents are left with a great deal of discretion in framing the domestic agenda; and an understanding of presidential goals becomes necessary in order to understand the selection of issues. Political "necessity" thereby becomes a problem of motivation: Presidents decide to act lest certain goals be lost.

The proposition that goals affect behavior is not new to the presidential literature. However, in the past, presidential scholars have focused on power as the primary motive. Yet, if power is important we must also ask, Power for what? It is also essential to distinguish between the President's *activities* (for example, power-maximizing behavior) and his *goals* (reelection, good policy). In this discussion, we are primarily interested in the President's policy goals. Unfortunately, past research on the Presidency has devoted considerable energy to underlying personality traits without asking how personality affects the President's goals and how these goals in turn are translated into specific outcomes. The President's personal goals and beliefs have a dramatic impact on domestic choice, yet they have received only fleeting attention in the literature.

The connection between goals and benefits is implicit. Goals belong to the individual; benefits are connected to the issues. If the President seeks reelection as a goal, a stable economy may provide the benefit hoped for. If the President seeks good policy as a goal, national health insurance may produce the desired benefit. Goals thereby color the perception of benefits. Some issues help attain the President's goals; others do not. As Presidents and staffs evaluate potential agenda topics, they actively pursue the issues that provide the greatest incentives. As Presidents choose among competing issues, they allocate their attention on the basis of potential benefits. In the following discussion, we will concentrate on three main goals that prompt the presidential search for *benefits:* (1) reelection, (2) historical achievement, and (3) good policy.

Reelection. Every first-term President is interested in reelection. A desire for reelection is a side-effect of the very first campaign—whether for President, governor, or mayor. According to one Ford assistant, "Some candidates will say they aren't interested in campaign politics. Don't believe it. Every candidate for office wants it. That's why they are willing to give up their freedom and their private lives. Any candidate who says he is interested in some broader purpose is only giving part of the story. Candidates have to be elected first."

Nor does the goal of electoral success abate with the first inaugural. Though Presidents have been known to renounce their intentions for a second term, reelection remains a critical goal through much of the first term. Both the President and the staff have considerable energy invested in returning for a second term. As Jack Valenti, one of Johnson's top aides, said,

> I don't think there is any doubt that the principal goal of the president, any president, is to win enough votes in November of an election year to have a second four-year term. I believe the reelection process has become blubber, a national waste that is burdening the presidency. The point is no sooner does the president get elected, he starts his reelection process. The reelection caravan is provisioned every day. Anybody who tells you differently tells you wrong (Valenti 1980, p. 4).

How does the search for electoral success affect policy outcomes? It has an effect primarily because the President and the staff *believe* that certain issues determine public response. Whether that belief is rooted in a rational view of the electorate or not, they are convinced of the impact of issues on electoral success. Even if issues account for only a small percentage of all ballots cast, the President is inclined to perceive the impact as dramatic. Congress provides a useful example:

> No matter what the objective measures of political scientists may tell us about their electoral safety, members of Congress feel uncertain and

vulnerable—if not today then yesterday, if not yesterday then tomorrow. A congressman who describes his or her seat as "safe," will implicitly add, "because and so long as I work actively to keep it safe." Furthermore, many a House retirement decision is made in anticipation of electoral difficulty (Fenno 1978, pp. 233-34).

This attitude also permeates presidential politics. Though the selection of agenda issues involves more than a simple calculus of public support, the "electoral connection" keeps many ideas afloat in the early moments of the term. Though the White House staffs recognized the limits of the campaign as a source of ideas, they perceived certain issues as critical components of electoral success. As one Johnson aide reflected,

> Every President has a set of issues which he believes holds the key to the first victory. Whether because of opinion polls or intuition, the President may believe that this item or that promise was the central factor in the vote. Now, political scientists might not be able to prove it, but that doesn't make a difference to the President. The President has been trained to accept it as an article of faith. And that faith propels the issue to the agenda. Even when the President wins a second term, he may feel obligated to the issues which gave him the White House the first time around.

This search for electoral benefits stems from several sources.

Presidents and their staffs believe that the electoral coalition decays over time. This "coalition of minorities" theme surfaces frequently among White House aides. As one Johnson assistant noted, "By the end of the first six months, the President generally loses his momentum in Congress. By the end of the first year, the dissatisfaction spreads to the public. If you don't start rebuilding at that point, you won't make it to a second term." Promises are the glue that holds the coalition together.

The calculation of electoral benefits rests on presidential perceptions. Presidents and staffs often subscribe to a critical promise theory. According to this theory, certain issues are essential in building and maintaining the electoral coalition. As candidates draft the campaign platform, these perceptions influence choice. As one Carter aide argued, "We understood which issues were primary to the election. We knew what the bread-and-butter issues were. When the term started, we felt a certain need to cash in on the campaign agenda. We worked on unemployment and the tax rebate. But it didn't take long to recognize that the basic constituency was changing, that the liberal program was failing. Proposition 13 would have an impact on any administration." Often the President and the staff will define a critical promise on the basis of personal intuition. In recent years, however, the White House staff has turned increasingly to opinion polls. In the Carter administration, these polls took on a new dimension in shaping presidential choice. Patrick Caddell, Carter's chief campaign pollster in 1976, was able to swing several key decisions once he was entrenched as the administration's key public opinion analyst. Caddell's reading of public malaise in early 1979 led to the midsummer Cabinet crisis. According to one Carter public liaison aide, "This President has been quite willing to look at public opinion in a very realistic way. If the trends are there in the data, Carter will more often than not react."

Despite the importance of reelection in the first term, we would expect the goal to dissipate in the second four years. Theoretically, the search for electoral success should decline. However, old habits are difficult to change. Presidents may continue to court the public simply because it is what they were trained to do. Since only one of the five administrations studied survived to a second term, and since that administration fell after one year, there is very little hard data to draw on. Interviews with a handful of Nixon aides who had worked for Eisenhower indicated that the pressure on reelection predictably fades in the second and final term. One former Eisenhower assistant said, "We felt a definite freedom from pressure after 1956, a freedom to take a little more time and a freedom to take on the high rollers. The speech on the military-industrial complex was one example. You can do things in a second term that you could never attempt in the first. I like to think we were a bit more courageous."

Historical Achievement. Presidents are obviously concerned with historical achievement. They are generally aware of the historical rankings of past executives; they are interested in the paths to "greatness." As one Nixon aide argued, "When the public opinion polls go sour and Congress slows down, the President can always fall back on history. President Nixon spent a great deal of time wondering how his decisions would fare in twenty or thirty years. That was the original intent behind the [secret White House] tape system. He wanted a detailed record so he could write his memoirs with the utmost historical accuracy." Though Presidents vary in the degree to which they emphasize competing domestic goals, most of the staffs agreed that historical achievement was a central presidential motive. Just as Presidents measure potential policies against electoral reaction, they also consider the "judgment of history." It is a very powerful influence on policy choice. As one Johnson assistant noted,

> You think Johnson didn't read the historical polls? Hell, Schlesinger's poll of "greatness" was a topic for six months. Everyone wondered how the hell we would get into the top ten. Part of it was a joke—you know, how to get the historians to vote for us—but part of it was serious. Johnson wanted to be remembered as a "great" President. That may have been why the Johnson library opened so early. I think Johnson believed that if the historians could see the record, particularly in social welfare and education, they might view the administration differently.

Why is history so important to Presidents? First, it surrounds the office. It would be difficult for a President not to be preoccupied with history.

Every corridor in the White House contains reminders of the President's potential place in history; every portrait suggests the impact of historical judgment. According to George Reedy, former assistant to Lyndon Johnson,

> The atmosphere of the White House is calculated to instill in any man a sense of destiny. He literally walks in the footsteps of hallowed figures—of Jefferson, of Jackson, of Lincoln. The almost sanctified relics of a distant, semi-mythical past surround him as ordinary household objects to be used by his family. From the moment he enters the halls he is made aware that he has become enshrined in a pantheon of semi-divine mortals who have shaken the world, and that he has taken from their hands the heritage of American dreams and aspirations. Unfortunately for him divinity is a better basis for inspiration than it is for government (1970, pp. 14-15).

Second, the Washington community openly encourages the historical orientation. Comparisons of one President with another are common in the press. How does Johnson compare with Kennedy? How does Reagan compare with Carter? The Washington community often draws historical comparisons between Presidents. And these comparisons are not lost on the White House staffs. "When a column comes out showing your President to be second-rate to Franklin Roosevelt," a Carter assistant said, "the automatic response is to ask how FDR got to be so good. The reaction is to ask how to make your President look better."

Historical benefits are easily the most abstract of the three presidential incentives. Unlike electoral benefits, which are realized in actual ballots, or programmatic benefits, which are cashed in the policies themselves, historical benefits must await the passage of time. The President must be willing to wait for the eventual judgment. But that wait does not reduce the value of the benefits to the President and the staff. Carter summarized the importance of history in his acceptance of the 1980 Democratic nomination:

> I have learned something else—something that I have come to see with extraordinary clarity. Above all, I must look ahead—because the president of the United States is the steward of the nation's destiny.
> He must protect our children—and the children they will have—and the children of generations to follow. He must speak and act for them. That is his burden—and his glory.
> And that is why a president cannot yield to the short-sighted demands of special interests, no matter how rich or powerful they are. That is why the president cannot bend to the passions of the moment, however popular they may be. That is why the president must sometimes ask for sacrifice when his listeners would rather hear the promise of comfort.
> The president is the servant of today. But his true constituency is the future. That is why this election of 1980 is so important (*Washington Post,* 15 August 1980).

References to historical achievement often may reflect reactions to temporary failure. A President who cannot secure passage of a critical bill may argue that history will judge him right. Yet, historical impact is more than an explanation for current trouble. Some Presidents enter office with historical achievement as the primary goal. "Some Presidents react to office by trying to get the biggest margin of victory or the greatest amount of legislation," a veteran media observer remarked. "However, most eventually take the approach that it is not important what the contemporary pundits say, but what the long-term critics find. They look ahead and ask how they will compare in the future."

Thus, all Presidents single out issues which will "mark" their administrations. For Kennedy, the program was Aid to Education; for Johnson, the issues were civil rights, health care for the elderly, and poverty; for Nixon, revenue sharing and welfare reform. In pursuing these issues, these Presidents were interested in more than immediate success. They searched for historical recognition. In justifying their actions on these issues, they often asked that history be the final arbiter. Energy, hospital cost containment, welfare reform, and civil rights are all examples of issues that lacked strong constituencies in the first weeks of consideration. In each case, the President turned to historical achievement as a primary goal. "Energy was never a very popular program," one Ford aide remembered. "It never really caught on. Still, we felt that it had to be done. Twenty years up the line we would look back and see that our decisions were right, but in an immediate sense, it didn't mean much."

Good Policy. There is little doubt that all Presidents enter office with ideological concerns. Whether the President wishes simply to defend the status quo against further encroachment or wishes to propose expansion of federal programs, each President has personal commitments. Regardless of public pressure, congressional hostility, or bureaucratic resistance, the President can be expected to support certain policies simply because of his personal beliefs. Presidents' personal ideologies influence their selection of issues. According to one OMB career assistant, "Not everything in the Executive Office can be explained by electoral pressure. There are some issues that emerge just because the President believes them to be right. Presidents are often willing to go out on a limb for those kinds of issues." A Johnson aide agreed: "There comes a point in any administration when the President must say to hell with Congress, when the President has to proceed because he is right. Even if Congress tears his program to bits, it is important to do what the President believes to be correct."

Regardless of the precise definition of presidential ideology, it is evident that Presidents do search for programmatic benefits. Whether these beliefs are constrained by the liberal-conservative continuum is only secondary to the issue of domestic choice. It is not enough to state that the President is liberal or conservative, Democrat or Republican. We have to look at specific positions on specific issues. We also have to measure the President's intensity and commitment. The Great Society under Lyndon Johnson is one example. One cannot read Johnson's speeches on the Great Society without being struck by the intensely personal nature of his commitment:

> Somehow you never forget what poverty and hatred can do when you see its scars on the hopeful face of a young child. I never thought then, in 1928, that I would be standing here in 1965. It never occurred to me in my fondest dreams that I might have the chance to help the sons and daughters of those students and to help people like them all over this country. But now I do have that chance—I'll let you in on a secret—I mean to use it. . . . I do not want to be the President who built empires, or sought grandeur, or extended dominion. I want to be the President who educated young children . . . who helped to feed the hungry . . . who helped the poor to find their own way and who protected the right of every citizen to vote in every election. . . . God will not favor everything we do. It is rather our duty to divine His will. But I cannot help believing that He truly understands and that He really favors the undertaking that we begin tonight (1965 State of the Union address, in *Public Papers of the Presidents, 1965*).

Obviously, Presidents do not have ideological positions on all the issues. "When energy came up," a Nixon aide remembered, "we were not sure of which direction to take. There were no clear-cut positions to occupy. It was not a question of liberals versus conservatives." Yet, there can be little question that Presidents do engage in the search for programmatic benefits. Presidents do have notions of what constitutes good policy. According to a Ford aide, "In anticipating the President's reaction to an idea, we looked at a variety of factors. We looked at Congress, the public, the departments, and most importantly, the budget. However, the final consideration was whether Ford would agree on principle, whether the idea would fit with Ford's personal and political beliefs. If it did, we could go from there." Or as a Kennedy aide reflected, "We all had certain ideas on how the world should have looked —you know, pictures of how people should act, how the system should work. When we took a specific idea, we always applied that view of how things should be. We never weighed the pros and cons on any abstract scale. Instead, it was more of an automatic response. An idea would appeal to us because it struck a familiar chord."

The Search for Benefits

Do presidential goals affect the actual selection of domestic issues? Thus far, I have talked in rather general terms about the relationship between the three presidential goals and agenda issues. In more specific terms, the staff indicated that goals are a central factor in the choice of issues. As one aide argued, "Choosing the problems is the easiest part of the process.

Table 5. The Most Important Domestic Programs

President	Program	Percentage of Staff Mentioning Program
Kennedy	Aid to Education	91%
	Medicare	77
	Unemployment	45
	Area Redevelopment	18
	Civil Rights	18
Johnson	Poverty	86
	Civil Rights	79
	Medicare	64
	Aid to Education	32
	Model Cities	29
	Wilderness Preservation	11
	Environmental Protection	4
Nixon	Welfare Reform	75
	Revenue Sharing	65
	Crime	40
	Energy	35
	Environmental Protection	15
Ford	Energy	79
	Inflation	50
	Regulatory Reform	8
Carter	Energy	84
	Inflation	63
	Welfare Reform	59
	Hospital Cost Containment	28
	Economic Stimulus	19
	Reorganization	9

Note: White House staff members were asked to name the most important domestic programs of their respective administrations. Respondents could give more than one reply. The number of respondents was 126.

There is relatively little conflict; the President and staff develop a consensus on the most valuable issues. We all have goals which lead us toward given issues. The trouble comes when you have to talk about specific solutions."

The importance of reelection, historical achievement, and good policy was very evident when the White House staffs were asked to explain specific decisions. Each respondent was first asked to identify the most important domestic programs in his or her administration. Most aides from the Kennedy administration mentioned unemployment, Aid to Education, Medicare, and Area Redevelopment; most Nixon aides focused on welfare reform, revenue sharing, environmental protection, crime, and energy. Each respondent was allowed to give multiple answers. Each respondent was then asked to explain the choices. The most important programs, as identified by the White House staffs, are summarized in table 5.

Two brief observations can be made about table 5. First, as noted in chapter 2, Presidents indeed have a limited number of top priorities. One Kennedy assistant who emphasized only Aid to Education and Medicare argued that "the President has only enough time to concentrate on one or two top issues during the term. Everything else is icing on the cake." The small number of programs may also be an artifact of selective perceptions or poor memories. The staffs may have been unable to recall more than a handful of top priorities, or they may have chosen to remember only the most successful items. However, it is far more likely that the table reflects presidential reality—that only a small number of programs fall into the President's agenda. There are very real limits on the number of issues that can be included on the President's agenda at any one time.

Second, the lists vary in content. We can witness the decline and virtual disappearance of certain issues and the rise of others. Further, there is some evidence of disagreement on just what the most important programs were. In the Kennedy administration, for instance, 91 percent of the staff identified aid to education as a top priority; in the Nixon staff, 75 percent selected welfare reform. As one Nixon aide remarked, "Welfare reform was the only program we produced in those first six months. It was a high priority and received maximum staff support. It is also one of the few programs that people remember when they look back." Yet, although there is consensus on the top one or two items from each Presidency, there is some variety in the staff responses. The variety is due in part to specialization; Ford aides who worked solely on deregulation were more likely to mention it as an important program.

What were the main incentives behind the domestic programs? Why did Johnson adopt the War on Poverty? Why did Ford concentrate on energy? Immediately after identifying the most important programs, each respondent was asked to explain the main reasons why each issue was selected (the staff responses are summarized in table 6). The bulk of the reasons given fall into specific categories:
1. *Electoral benefits.* Respondents referred to the attractiveness of an issue to past or future campaigns; the importance of the issue to the electoral coalition; opposition candidates, public opinion, party pressure.
2. *Historical benefits.* Respondents referred to the potential impact of an issue on historical images of "greatness"; the importance of an issue to the President's long-term record.
3. *Programmatic benefits.* Respondents referred to the attractiveness of an issue to the President's personal or political beliefs; ideology; the importance of an issue as a pressing problem and the need to act.

Though the bulk of the interview material fell into the three benefit categories, approximately 5 percent of the answers contained references to luck, accidents, and political pressures. Once again, there may be a problem with selective perceptions. All staff members have a natural ten-

Table 6. Benefits Sought in Domestic Program Selection

President	Benefits		
	Electoral	Historical	Programmatic
Kennedy	54%	25%	42%
Johnson	44	37	52
Nixon	70	43	22
Ford	60	22	44
Carter	57	23	39

Note: White House staff members were asked to name the benefits hoped for in the selection of the top domestic programs of their respective administrations (only the first two programs for each Presidency, as given in table 5, were pursued). The percentages for each administration total more than 100 because respondents could give more than one reply. The number of respondents was 126.

dency to see their respective Presidents in the best possible light. Carter aides, for instance, spoke at length about the need to convert campaign promises into actual policy—not necessarily for reelection but because of the need for democratic accountability. Nixon aides seemed to be more willing to talk directly about the linkage between policy and reelection; few felt the need to explain their decisions in abstract, normative terms. Regardless of the different rationales, however, both sets of campaign references were placed in the electoral benefits category. Thus, as with any coding, these data have rough edges and serve more to illustrate a general theory of agenda-setting than to provide absolute proof of each President's motives. The major finding here is simply that the staff explanations fit into the coding scheme, thereby supporting a goal model of domestic choice.

Electoral Benefits. Electoral benefits constitute the most frequent explanation offered by the staffs for the choice of domestic programs. Reelection is the primary goal behind most domestic decisions. As one former Nixon campaign aide argued, "Every President has to be reelected. That becomes the primary motive for decisions, particularly toward the end of the first term. It determines travel plans, press contacts, foreign affairs, and the State of the Union. Presidents know that four years is not enough to get much done." A Carter domestic policy assistant echoed this conclusion: "How can the President expect to make an impact in just four years? It just isn't enough time. The programs are barely in place; Congress is still at work. A President has to have a second term to make an impression. He has to protect his programs; he has to have time to build on his success and correct his failures." Thus, the high percentage of electoral benefits may be an artifact of the first term. Kennedy, Johnson, Ford, and Carter were all first-term Presidents only; all four originally intended to run for a second term. The emphasis on electoral incentives may also reflect the limited second-term experience. "We didn't have time to be thinking into the future," a Kennedy assistant reflected. "We had to stay firmly planted in the present. History was not that important to us as we moved toward the second term. It might have been more important if the President had won a second term."

Programmatic Benefits. Good policy emerges as the second most important explanation for issue choice. Presidents enter office with specific social concerns; they search for programmatic impact. As one Johnson assistant argued, "We tend to underestimate the importance of the President's personal beliefs. In part, that is a problem of the Nixon experience. We have become so cynical that we refuse to see Presidents as interested in making positive changes. We have shifted our focus to the negative." Whatever the reason, presidential scholars have underplayed the impact of ideology. When we have considered individual factors, we have looked to quasi-stable personality traits.

Personality may have some effect on the President's goals and ideology. Perhaps Nixon's concern for historical achievement evolved from his "negative" view of life; perhaps Johnson's concern for programmatic impact emerged from his childhood poverty. There is very little research on the linkage between presidential "character" and policy goals. Though Barber (1972) briefly addresses the concept of "world view," ideology remains a forgotten category in presidential research. We have been far more interested in personality and power as the two primary variables in presidential behavior and have neglected ideology.

The staffs differed in their emphasis of the three benefits. The Nixon administration's emphasis on programmatic benefits was the lowest, and on historical benefits the highest; the Johnson administration's emphasis on programmatic benefits was the highest, and on electoral benefits the lowest. Though the differences often are slight, Nixon emerges with the most unusual package of goals. According to one OMB official, "Nixon was certainly the least ideological of the last three Presidents. I think that he was so concerned with reelection that he didn't pay much attention to what needed to be done. Everything he did seemed to be leading up to a landslide in 1972." This is not to argue that Nixon was apolitical. Rather, Nixon's decisions may have reflected his precarious political situation. Though the Nixon staff did not use ideology to explain the most important programs, Nixon had legitimate social concerns. The fact that Nixon entered office with a very slim plurality and an opposition Congress contributed to the emphasis on reelection. In short, Nixon's initial resource base created pressure on the drive for reelection.

Why do some Presidents strive for electoral success, while others search for historical achievement? The main answer rests on presidential capital. As Presidents rank their personal and political goals, capital becomes a critical factor. Presidents with lower capital tend to emphasize electoral rewards first; the effort to generate greater capital takes precedence. "Every President has to make choices based on the situation," a Nixon aide reported. "When a program will hurt the President's standing in the polls, he has to decide if that is important; when a program will run counter to the President's ideology, he has to ask if that's important. It all depends on the person and the situation." A second Nixon aide continued: "If the President is low in the polls, that makes the political problems much more important, doesn't it? At the beginning of the term, when the President is in the honeymoon, the polls may not matter. It is a lot easier to think in ideological terms when you aren't fighting for your political life." Thus, Johnson did not have to stress reelection to the same degree that Nixon did. As one Johnson aide suggested, "We had so much support that first year that we didn't spend much time worrying about the second term. We felt the reelection campaign could wait. We had enough influence to buy whatever we wanted. We definitely didn't have to go to the bargain basement."

Three Case Studies

One way to illustrate the impact of goals on issue selection is to examine specific cases. Here, three brief case studies may help to illuminate the influence of goals on policy.

Carter and National Health Insurance. Carter's pursuit of national health insurance in 1978 is one of the most recent examples of the search for electoral benefits. Though Carter believed in the issue, the primary force behind adoption rested on electoral considerations. According to the Carter staff, national health insurance was put "on hold" in the first year of office. As one domestic aide argued,

> Most of us recognized that health insurance wouldn't make it. The money just wasn't available; the costs were astronomical. Hell, we couldn't even get a fix on the exact dollar estimates. Instead of going ahead with national health insurance, we decided to opt for cost containment. We felt that cost containment had to come first—the government couldn't undertake financing for health insurance if the costs continued to rise at 14 percent per year.

For 1977 at least, national health insurance was dead; it was not part of the Carter agenda, and most outside observers expected it to remain dormant until the second term.

Two factors contributed to the reemergence. First, Carter's labor allies increased their pressure for a commitment on national health insurance. From the very beginning of the battle for a comprehensive health plan, labor had been at the forefront. As early as 1935, labor had backed some form of federal health insurance. Labor support was critical in Truman's decision to request medical care for the aged in 1949; labor pressure was essential in the Medicare effort in 1961 and 1965. Labor continued to press for national health insurance in 1974 but decided not to compromise with then-President Nixon. Instead, labor decided to gamble on the election of a Democratic President in 1977. Carter recognized the importance of labor in his electoral coalition. "We knew that the UAW and AFL-CIO had to stay with us," one Carter aide remarked. "Labor was important to us in our first election, and it was going to be important in 1980. We couldn't afford to lose their support." When Carter continued to delay introduction of national health insurance, labor stepped up the pressure. Indeed, in late 1978 Douglas Fraser, head of the United Auto Workers, threatened to throw his support behind Ted Kennedy for the 1980 Democratic presidential nomination.

Fraser's action raised the second reason for Carter's reversal: Ted Kennedy. Interviews with the Carter staff in 1979 revealed substantial concern about Kennedy's candidacy. According to one Carter assistant, "We don't think Ted Kennedy can win the nomination, but he could cost us the election. He could so divide the party that it would be impossible to win against any legitimate Republican candidate." For Carter, the major policy issue in the Kennedy effort was national health insurance. The staff believed that labor would stay with Carter under most conditions; they also knew that national health insurance was a key to holding labor in. Thus, by spring 1978 Carter had decided to present a set of national health insurance "principles." The principles outlined Carter's main requirements for any draft bill: cost containment, catastrophic coverage, phased-in administration. "We felt that was one way to keep labor in the fold," a Carter assistant argued, "but it didn't work very well. The labor people just weren't satisfied with a statement of principles. They wanted a bill."

As Carter's popularity continued to slip in 1979, the Kennedy candidacy became more prominent. Labor leaders began to consider a switch, and the Carter staff became more concerned. According to members of the Carter staff, the threat of a Kennedy-labor alliance forced national health insurance onto the agenda. On 12 June 1979 Carter presented his proposal for a national health plan. Though the plan was a substantial retreat from Carter's promise for comprehensive and universal insurance, it was a major step toward breaking the Kennedy-labor coalition. Clearly, Carter's decision was intimately related to his search for electoral benefits.

Nixon and Welfare Reform. Nixon's decision to present radical welfare reform in 1969 is an excellent example of the search for historical achievement. Indeed, according to the Nixon staff, that is precisely how the program was "sold" to the President. Nixon was looking for a major social program as he entered office. He was also convinced that the welfare system needed reform; that was his primary reason for appointing a transition task force on the issue. However, the decision to adopt welfare reform involved a very different set of factors. Granted, there was a problem, but it was not need that elevated welfare reform to the top of the Nixon domestic agenda.

The early battle on welfare reform involved Arthur Burns and Daniel Moynihan. Burns opposed the expansion of welfare benefits; Moynihan supported a system of family allowances that would provide every American family with a guaranteed minimum income. Initially the debate was centered on whether there would be any welfare reform at all.

There were several reasons why Nixon moved ahead. First, he believed that a problem existed; welfare reform was an idea "in good currency." Second, there were available alternatives. Nixon did not have to invest several years developing a consensus on a program. Third, and most important, Nixon was persuaded of the impact of the issue on his historical image. Though the first two reasons were important, the Nixon staff consistently pinpointed *persuasion* as the source of Nixon's decision, persuasion that focused on history. As one Nixon aide argued, "The President had a weakness for Moynihan's brand of argument. Moynihan kept telling the President that welfare reform would make him a great President; that years from now people would look back and applaud him for the bold ventures. The President bought it." A memo from Moynihan to Nixon dated 6 June 1969 summarizes the argument:

. . . This Congress is almost certainly going to begin the discussion of a major change in our welfare system. The 1970's will almost certainly see such a change instituted.

It is open to you to dominate and direct this social transformation. . . .

Thus I would argue that if you move now, you will dominate the discussion. Congress will be discussing *your* proposal. It hardly matters what final form it takes, or how many times we change our position in the process. The end result—if you wish it to be—will be *your* change.

This is a time to be ahead of the Congress and even the country. For they will follow. This is an idea whose time has come. . . .

I am really pretty discouraged about the budget situation in the coming three to five years. I fear you will see nothing like the options I am sure you hoped for. Even more, I fear that the pressure from Congress will be nigh irresistible to use up what extra resources you have on a sort of ten percent across-the-board increase in all the Great Society programs each year. This is the natural instinct of the Congress, and it is hard for the President to resist.

If your extra money goes down that drain, I fear that in four years' time you really won't have a single distinctive Nixon program to show for it all.

Therefore I am doubly interested in seeing you go up now with a genuinely new, unmistakably Nixon, unmistakably needed program, which would attract the attention of the world, far less the United States. . . .

> This way, in 1972 we will have a record of solid, unprecedented accomplishment in a vital area of social policy, and not just an explanation as to how complicated it all was (in Burke and Burke 1974, p. 82).

We will return to the topic of persuasion in chapter 8. For now, it is important to recognize that welfare reform represented a major program in Nixon's search for historical benefits. As one disenchanted Nixon aide suggested, "Welfare reform was going to get the President in the record books. It was all part of his interest in the long bomb. He wanted dramatic achievements, not minor changes; he wanted a fifty-yard pass, not four yards up the middle."

Kennedy and Area Redevelopment. Kennedy's decision to adopt Area Redevelopment reflected both political and congressional pressures, but clearly it referenced Kennedy's search for programmatic benefits. Area Redevelopment had been part of the congressional struggle several years before Kennedy became President. As Sundquist notes, "As early as 1954, legislation designed to assist 'depressed areas' was introduced in Congress. During the next dozen years, a series of measures were developed, introduced, refined, and enacted to deal with structural unemployment—progressively bolder, broader, and involving greater federal expenditures" (Sundquist 1968, p. 60). As Kennedy drafted his first legislative agenda, Area Redevelopment was guaranteed a position. However, as the agenda took shape, Area Redevelopment became the first priority; it was designated as Senate Resolution No. 1 of the Eighty-seventh Congress and was introduced even before inauguration.

The importance of Area Redevelopment reflected several pressures. Certainly, the program was a cornerstone of the Democratic party platform. It had first been adopted in 1956. The program also addressed critical campaign commitments. It was one way to secure electoral benefits. Yet, beyond these factors, Kennedy was deeply committed to the measure. According to several Kennedy assistants, that personal dedication flowed from the West Virginia primary. These aides argued that Kennedy was "educated" by West Virginia. As one aide remarked,

> Here you have a rich kid, someone who has never really seen poverty. Take that person to West Virginia and into the Appalachian range and he'll find a kind of poverty that just doesn't exist in the cities. I believe that Jack Kennedy was touched by West Virginia; I believe he saw things there that he had never known before. I remember talking with him during the primary and noting his surprise. He had no idea of how devastating poverty could be.

According to Kennedy's staff, his commitment was both sincere and intense. "Any number of items could have gone first," one legislative assistant remarked, "but Area Redevelopment was somehow most important to the President. He seemed to feel a certain responsibility to the program."

Goal Conflict and the Search for Issues

Thus far, we have ignored the potential for conflict among the three presidential goals. We have assumed that the goal of reelection is compatible with the dual goals of historical achievement and good policy. That assumption is not always justified. Programs that benefit reelection may hinder historical achievement—Presidents may be labeled as short-sighted or over-ambitious. Programs that lead to programmatic impact may undermine reelection—calls for national sacrifice may fall on deaf ears. Kennedy's decision to exclude parochial schools from his 1961 aid to education proposal reflected electoral concerns, while his hesitation on civil rights involved the climate of public acceptance. As Presidents seek to resolve goal conflict, they inevitably weigh benefits. Presidents with slim electoral margins may turn to reelection as the primary first-term goal, as Kennedy did in 1961. Presidents with massive congressional support may emphasize historical achievement or good policy, as Johnson did in 1965.

Goal conflict is not new. All Presidents face a degree of dissonance. However, with the emergence of a new set of domestic issues, goal conflict has increased dramatically. During the 1960s a wide range of domestic issues involved compatible goals; the poverty program, for example, satisfied both Johnson's drive for reelection and his goal of good policy. For both Kennedy and Johnson, there was potential linkage between competing goals; a single program could provide more than one benefit. As we enter the 1980s, however, the bulk of domestic issues involve at least some element of goal conflict. Energy, welfare reform, hospital cost containment, and social security financing are all examples of the rise of "constituentless" issues. Presidents who select these kinds of issues for the domestic agenda are exposed to a greater degree of goal conflict. They do not necessarily promote reelection, yet they have come to dominate the pool of available ideas. The question is whether any President—Democrat or Republican—can balance the goal of reelection against either historical achievement or good policy.

Have the issues changed so dramatically that presidential goals are no longer compatible? Two answers arise. First, goal conflict seems to be more pervasive for Democratic Presidents. Given the traditional Democratic agenda, future "New Deal" Presidents must walk a tightrope when concentrating on the new domestic issues. The rise of inflation as a primary economic problem tends to accentuate these pressures. Accepting the conventional balanced-budget wisdom as a cure for inflation, Democratic Presidents put themselves in a precarious position when they try to balance the budget while standing for reelection. A massive jobs program might spur reelection, but would it also heighten inflation? Urban assistance might enhance electoral support, but would it affect prices? Democratic Presidents were happier when they were asked only to solve recessions, when government spending was the obvious solution. The rise of stagflation and the decline in budget flexibility over the past decade may have foreclosed pump-priming as a tool of Democratic policy.

Second, for both Democrats and Republicans goal conflict is increased by the the seeming inability to convert constituentless issues into winnable programs. Carter might have succeeded with hospital cost containment had he linked it to national health insurance, thereby tying a constituentless program to a popular Democratic ideal. Carter eventually took note of this strategy in promoting his windfall profits tax, promising increased domestic spending from the sizable windfall revenues. Unfortunately, such linkage requires considerable skill, expertise, and luck. Moreover, there is some doubt that the new domestic issues actually provide the opportunity for linkage. Can gas rationing be acceptable under any circumstances? Can cuts in social security benefits be linked to a more popular rider?

Republicans are not immune to the increased goal conflict. Assuming that goal conflict arises from the growth in competition for scarce national resources, Republicans face many of the same cross-pressures that Democrats face. In this regard, President Reagan might take note of Jimmy Carter's remarks on the rise of special interest groups. Only nine months before his defeat, Carter argued that one of his biggest surprises in coming to Washington was the "extraordinary and excessive influence of special interest groups."

> There is no lobbying effort, there is no interest group, that has any influence in Washington for a calm, measured, long-range, moderate solution to an extremely complicated question. But there are plenty of interest groups on the radical right or the radical left, or the extreme positions, who are fighting for some selfish advantage. And a President has to remember that he himself represents the breadth of America and the best interest of our people. But the demands by special interest groups who are powerful politically are extraordinary, and a president has to say no. And when you say no against massive give-away programs, massive government programs, it doesn't benefit a president politically. And I think that's why the attrition rate among presidents has been so great in the last 20-25 years (PBS, "Every Four Years," transcript, January-February 1980, p. 34).

The conflict between good policy and reelection was evident in the first moments of the Reagan administration. In the very first meeting between the President-elect and his Cabinet nominees, Reagan offered one rule for policy decision: choices were not to be made on the basis of politics. According to James Brady, Reagan's newly appointed press secretary, the President-elect told his Cabinet there was only one "no-no": "The no-no is to discuss the political ramifications of anything. We are to operate as if there is no next election. Decisions should be made on the basis of what is good for the nation, not their political ramifications" (*Washington Post,* 9 January 1981). It was a sign of just how far the domestic issues had evolved. Reagan openly instructed his staff to ignore the pressures of reelection in favor of the national interest. He believed that both goals could not be satisfied at the same time; what was in the national interest was not necessarily in the President's political interest. Whereas Johnson chose the War on Poverty in 1964 for reelection and good policy, Reagan felt compelled to choose between goals. Whether symbolically or not, reelection was to be ignored in the search for solutions to national problems.

Conclusion

Goals affect the President's choice of domestic issues. Both in specific case studies and in interview responses, the search for benefits emerges as a significant factor. Moreover, the goals of reelection, historical achievement, and good policy often interact in the presidential policy process. Issue selection is neither comprehensive nor careful. Presidents rarely sit down and review each program in direct contrast to the others. The process is much more fluid; most decisions involve *sequential* attention to separate issues, a problem we will discuss in chapter 8.

If the President and the staff do not engage in a formal, comprehensive comparison of issues, how are the agenda issues selected? According to a Carter domestic policy aide,

> The President has to look at a number of ideas in the first moments of the term, and there is often agreement on which issues offer the greatest payoffs. But we don't sit around a table and rank each item. There is a sense of comparison, but it is not systematic by any means. In this administration, we talked to the President about each item separately and received a decision. Each of those choices involved elements of our perceptions and the President's goals.

The President's analysis of the issues is often inseparable from the discussion of alternatives. Most issues arrive in the Oval Office already attached to potential solutions; some may arrive with specific drafts. However, the decision to pursue a given issue, regardless of the alternative, reflects the assessment of benefits. Before turning to the discussion of alternatives, we will focus briefly on the sources of domestic ideas. Though Presidents have much discretion in selecting domestic issues, they are constrained by what might be called the pool of available ideas.

4 the source of ideas

Shortly following the 1976 election, the Carter transition team began compiling the President's campaign pledges. The list was eventually published and became known by the title *Promises, Promises*. The main purpose of the document was to guide policy decisions; it reflected Carter's belief that candidates are obliged to convert campaign promises into action. Yet, even as the book took shape, Carter aides began to discount its value. According to one domestic policy assistant,

> Most of us felt that the book would be of little value in making the actual choices. We already understood the issues and recognized which ones were important. We knew that we couldn't pursue every item, that we had to make some choices. The promises document was of very little long-run use to us, but it sure helped the media keep track of what we weren't doing. The book was just too long and covered too much ground. It didn't tell us enough about the specific pledges; it didn't contain specific drafts; it didn't anticipate congressional reactions.

Though the document was 111 pages long, covering ten major policy areas, it had marginal impact on the President's priorities. Like his predecessors, Carter soon learned that his campaign promises constituted an overwhelming pool of ideas. From among the two-hundred-odd promises made in the heat of the presidential contest, Carter could choose only a few top priorities. Though Carter had promised a national health insurance plan, he soon discovered that it had to wait; though he had opposed deregulation of domestic crude oil, in his second energy plan he supported it. As one Carter assistant suggested, "We all recognized that there would be issues that would have to wait. We understood that there would be issues that would have to be ignored. We were all committed to most of the campaign promises, but the realities of office forced us to choose. Health insurance had to wait until welfare reform passed; energy had to be at the top." Or as a second Carter

81

aide argued, "The promises book simply misled the press and the public. The campaign was actually quite limited as a source of ideas."

The Impact of Ideas

The campaign was not the only source of ideas for the Carter domestic program. Carter looked to the executive branch and followed events, the Congress, and the press. According to one Carter aide, "The President has to canvass as many sources as possible in building the presidential program. He can't rely only on the party or the bureaucracy. He has to use the press, the Cabinet, OMB, and Congress. And he can't restrict himself only to Democrats. There are good ideas on both sides."

Is the source of issues important? Does it matter whether the President draws ideas from the Congress or the press, the public or special interest groups? The answer is yes, it does make a difference.

First, overreliance on certain sources limits innovation. Consider Lyndon Johnson's analysis of the executive branch in *The Vantage Point:*

> I have watched this process for years, and I was convinced that it did not encourage enough fresh or creative ideas. The bureaucracy of the government is too preoccupied with day-to-day operations, and there is strong bureaucratic inertia dedicated to preserving the status quo. As a result, only the most powerful ideas can survive. Moreover, the cumbersome organization of government is simply not equipped to solve complex problems that cut across departmental jurisdictions (1971, pp. 326-27).

According to one Nixon aide, "Nothing ever comes from the bureaucracy that hasn't been hashed and rehashed for years. The career civil servant simply isn't interested in new ideas. It is much safer to keep trumpeting the old."

Though the executive branch is the most frequent target of such criticism, it is not alone. "We found that Congress, especially the House, was a constant source of frustration," a Ford energy expert argued. "There is little incentive for Congress to produce new ideas, particularly in the most difficult areas. The constituents and interest groups force too much attention on the old issues." Despite recent increases in both staff and technical resources, the Ford and Carter staffs maintained that Congress has declined as a source of new ideas. "The consensus has disappeared," one Ford aide reflected. "The Congress is working on hundreds of specialized projects, nursing constituents, and fighting for reelection. There is no longer any sense of a party program. Ideas are harder to come by."

Second, concentration on single sources of issues can restrict representation for certain groups. As Presidents emphasize certain sources and ignore others, they participate in the mobilization of bias. Groups that do not have access to the sources of ideas have only limited access to the President's agenda. According to a Kennedy aide, "You have a whole set of people out there who have virtually no representation in Washington. Now, if you keep your eyes only on the Capitol, you'll never see their problems. You have to broaden your scope and look for problems outside of Washington. If you just ask Congress what's important, you'll get a very restricted set of answers, most of which will ignore some pretty important segments of the country." Unfortunately, as Presidents enter office, there is very little incentive for that kind of extensive problem search. The agenda must be prepared early and pressed forward to passage. At least at the start of the term, the President must rely on the institutional sources of ideas. If those sources have ignored or suppressed certain problems over time, that is a necessary hazard of the presidential policy process.

Do Presidents have to abandon the traditional sources of ideas in the search for political change? According to one media observer, "Carter's greatest advantage in 1976 was that he came from outside Washington. He hadn't grown up hearing the same ideas over and over again. Unfortunately, Carter didn't stay with it. Once he arrived, he turned to the age-old sources. He looked to Congress and the executive branch. Carter had some very creative ideas before he became President, but he had to give them up after the election." According to Hamilton Jordan, Carter's chief of staff,

> There are a lot of things about this city that are interesting and attractive, but you won't find the answers to most of this nation's problems by gaining a consensus of what people think inside the Beltway. There's a very cautious attitude politically, there's a compromising attitude politically and there's a terrible tendency to procrastinate in terms of dealing with the country's problems. If you look at the things that I would say are the hallmarks of the Carter years, they are examples of where Carter has gone against the grain and gone against conventional wisdom (*Washington Post,* 2 December 1980).

In searching for the source of domestic issues, we must remember that the President's domestic agenda is a product of the pool of available ideas. If a given issue is not in the pool, it will not rise to the domestic agenda. As one Nixon aide suggested, "We all read the newspapers and watched the news. We took the proper journals and scanned the congressional record. We used telephones and went to parties. It was not as if you had to search for the issues. *They searched for us.* The problem was to select from the hundreds of available issues." All Presidents face a pool of issues upon election, a pool that shifts and evolves during the term. The question of how items reach this pool has been tackled by others and will not be covered here.

Issue Patterns

As Presidents pull items from the available pool, they have considerable discretion. In 1977 Carter opted for energy and welfare reform but not for national health insurance. In 1969 Nixon selected crime and revenue sharing but not civil rights. Yet, Presidents are also limited by the range of available ideas. The domestic agenda is affected by patterns in the available issues. Some ideas are "hot"; others are not.

Issues move through the pool with differing speed and support. Medical care for the elderly was a prominent issue for at least two decades before Kennedy adopted it in 1961; welfare reform had been circulating for ten years before Carter adopted it in 1977. For Jack Walker, the surge of issues responds to "entrepreneurial" activity. At least in the Senate, once an issue breaks in a policy area formerly ignored, there may be a period of intense interest lasting several years:

> Activist senators are joined by lobbyists, ambitious agency chiefs, crusading journalists and policy professionals of all kinds in a rush to exploit the newly discovered political pay dirt. The sometimes frantic burst of activity that follows an initial political breakthrough may bring proposals on to the Senate's discretionary agenda that do not necessarily have broad appeal, where little evidence of a problem exists and where no feasible solutions are anywhere in sight. Legislation of this kind may not only be debated but often passes into law because the pressure on the Senate to act in such circumstances is nearly overwhelming. Once a topic like pollution control or mass transit has achieved the status of a chosen problem and it becomes clear that the votes are there for passage of bills on the subject, powerful forces are unleashed that press for action. As the surge progresses, the relative importance of succeeding legislative proposals tends to decline and the case for their passage becomes weaker. Although efforts are made to sustain the momentum created by initial legislative successes, the vein of interest and support is rapidly played out (Walker 1977, p. 15).

Issues have a certain momentum of their own. As Presidents scan the pool of available items, some issues may have greater support than others; some issues may have greater visibility.

One way to estimate the impact of these issue patterns on the domestic program is to look at the five presidential agendas. Have certain issues remained stable topics of concern? Have others disappeared from the available pool? Return to the 266 items culled from the OMB clearance records. Table 7 summarizes the policy content of the five domestic agendas. The percentages reflect the number of domestic programs in each issue area. Thus, 17 percent of the Kennedy agenda involved urban affairs, while 19 percent focused on education.

Two conclusions emerge from table 7. First, certain issues seem to get hot and then cool off. Civil rights has virtually vanished from the President's domestic agenda; education has consistently declined. As one Carter aide remarked, "There are some ideas that have tremendous local support. Every time you turn around, there will be someone telling you to act. It's damn hard not to notice those issues." Ideas may become hot for a variety of

Table 7. Issue Patterns

Issue Area	Domestic Agenda of					
	Kennedy-Johnson	Johnson	Nixon I	Nixon II	Ford	Carter
Agriculture	4%	2%	3%	0%	0%	2%
Civil rights	7	4	3	0	0	0
Consumer affairs	4	10	5	4	0	10
Crime	4	9	13	4	19	0
Education	19	13	8	4	0	4
Energy	0	0	0	40	31	24
Government affairs	4	10	18	8	6	15
Health[a]	9	8	13	12	12	13
Labor/Employment	19	5	5	0	6	9
Natural resources	13	17	18	20	6	7
Transportation	4	7	8	0	0	5
Urban affairs/Welfare	17	18	10	8	19	11

Source: OMB Legislative Reference Division clearance record.
[a] Includes medical education, e.g., nurses training, medical-school construction.

reasons. An external event may focus attention, or the campaign may generate support. Regardless of the cause, some ideas enter the pool with greater momentum than others.

Energy is a specific case of the rapid rise of an issue. Energy had not been an issue during the 1960s, but it came to dominate the Nixon, Ford, and Carter agendas. As one Nixon aide remarked, "It was a shock to most of us. We had not anticipated the oil embargo and the gas shortages. The problem simply exploded, and we were engulfed." A second Nixon aide concurred: "Energy came on so fast that we were caught by surprise. That tells you something about the government's ability to plan for the unforeseen future." Energy remains a central theme of presidential politics.

Second, certain issues seem to exhaust themselves over time. Education is a prime example. According to table 7, education dropped from 19 percent of the Kennedy agenda to 4 percent of the Carter program. One powerful explanation is that the issue simply "played out." Kennedy and Johnson were so successful in drafting education policy that it was no longer considered a problem. Thus, from 1961 to 1968 there was a long string of logically related education programs: Aid to Primary and Secondary Education, Aid to Higher Education, Headstart, school construction, teacher-training, the Teacher Corps, library aid, transportation, and school lunches. As one Johnson aide remarked, "I don't think there was that much left to do in education after we left. We had the programs in place, and education was accepted as a federal responsibility. What remained was proper funding and implementation." Indeed, the main component of Carter's policy was the establishment of a separate Department of Education, a tool more of implementation than of new policy.

Table 8. Sources of Ideas

Source	Percentage of Respondents Mentioning
External sources	
Congress	52%
Events and crisis	51
Executive branch	46
Public opinion	27
Party	11
Interest groups	7
Media	4
Internal sources	
Campaign and platform	20
President	17
Staff	16
Task forces	6

Note: Respondents were asked the following question: Generally speaking, what would you say were the most important sources of ideas for the domestic agenda? The number of respondents was 118.

The impact of issue patterns rests on the President's exposure to ideas. If an issue is not in the pool, it is highly unlikely that it will reach the President's agenda. Although Presidents have considerable discretion in drawing items from the pool, they are limited by the range of available ideas "in the water."

Issue Sources

Presidents look to both institutional and informal sources for domestic issues. As with resources, the 126 respondents separated issue sources into two clusters. When asked about the sources of ideas, the staffs talked about internal and external channels (these responses are summarized in table 8). Before we examine each source separately, one conclusion should be stressed. It seems clear from table 8 that Presidents react to *external* sources much more than they do to *internal* sources. The bulk of the domestic issues enter the agenda from outside the White House. According to one Kennedy aide, "The classic idea of the President as a competing source of programs is only partially correct. When you think about it, most of the programs originate in other institutions and in the public. The White House just isn't equipped to create that many new ideas." A Nixon assistant concurred: "Most of our time was spent looking at proposals coming from the executive branch and Congress. I'd characterize the process as a funnel. We were quite prepared to winnow the incoming ideas, but I don't recall that we generated that much from inside. Our job was to select from the available proposals, not to be the starting point."

The major explanation for the reliance on external channels rests on resources. Presidents do not have the internal resources to generate new ideas. The pressures to move the domestic program early in the term force a heavy emphasis on the pool of available issues. The President simply does not have enough time, energy, information, or expertise to move into vastly new endeavors. Though Presidents do produce new ideas—Johnson's poverty program, for example—the majority come from external sources.

Democrats and Republicans. Though all Presidents face a relatively fixed set of issue sources, the attention they pay them varies. The most significant differences are between the Democrats and the Republicans. The Democratic staffs—of Kennedy, Johnson, and Carter—were far more likely than were the Republicans to identify the legislative branch as a major source of issues. Of the Democratic staff members interviewed for this study, 62 percent mentioned Congress as an important source of domestic ideas. One Kennedy aide summarized that reliance as "the logical result of eight years of Republican rule. The Democratic party in Congress had been laboring under Eisenhower for two full terms—six in the majority. The party had a clear platform and had hammered out the substance of a legislative program."

The Carter staff generally agreed about the importance of Congress. However, as one assistant remarked, Congress was not always cooperative.

> We obviously had to look to Congress for some of the issues. The Democratic Caucus was willing to trade their support on some issues for our support on others. Still, we found that there was much less consensus on the program than might have been expected following the Nixon and Ford years. The party was more disorganized. One of the reasons why liaison had so much trouble was that we couldn't find a unified structure to deal with.

Though Congress had increased its staff, technical expertise, and information base, the process had also become more diffused and decentralized. Leadership was more difficult, and policy fragmentation had increased. Thus, the Carter staff seemed less enthusiastic about Congress as a source of ideas. The traditional advantages of congressional programs were no longer automatic, and the traditional incentives for adopting congressional ideas no longer evident.

Of the Republican staff members contacted, only 30 percent pinpointed Congress as a major source of ideas—32 percent less than the Democrats. Both the Nixon and Ford staffs placed the blame directly on the minority-party problem in Congress. "We seriously looked for the Republican programs," one Nixon aide argued. "We had a great need for fully developed programs in the early months. We were so wrapped up in welfare reform and foreign affairs that we would have jumped at a strong congressional program. When we looked, we couldn't find one." Basically, the Nixon staff agreed that the problem began in the Eighty-ninth Congress, in 1965-66, when Republicans were outnumbered 295 to 140 in the House. "The entire planning effort was destroyed," one Nixon aide noted. "We lost committee seniority; we lost several major seats." When the party recaptured 47 seats in 1966, the problem remained.

The problem persisted into the Ford administration. One Ford liaison officer suggested that "staying in the minority for twenty years will eventually cripple any party. Members become more involved with staying alive than with drafting a unique platform." Nor does the minority party have the same resources to compete. As the minority party, the Republicans had less staff, less money, and less support in the planning agencies.

Where did Nixon and Ford turn to pick up the slack? Only one other source shows any significant difference between the Democrats and Republicans: the executive branch. Whereas 28 percent of the Democratic staffs identified the executive branch as an important source, it was mentioned by 50 percent of the Republican staffs. Ironically, the two Republican Presidents may have turned to the very source that would be least representative of the Republican coalition. This is not to argue that Nixon and Ford were forced to swallow hostile ideas. Rather, it is a sign of the increased influence of the executive branch in setting the broad parameters of the agenda, particularly when the President cannot use Congress. Nixon and Ford had to form an uneasy alliance with the executive branch, an alliance that led to considerable frustration and conflict.

Sources of Pressure. The sources of ideas are often the sources of political pressure. As Presidents set the domestic agenda, they face considerable lobbying from outside interests. As one Carter aide reflected, "Everyone in Washington has some opinion on almost every issue. They may not be able to tell you anything new, but they are always ready to give you their opinion. When you start out developing a new program, the White House can be pretty lonely. But when the wind starts to carry the message, the opinions start to come out of the woodwork." A second Carter aide agreed: "You don't just sit up here and pick and choose. There are any number of people and organizations who want to get a hold of the President and lay on a little pressure. Our job is not so much to guide opinion, but to deflect the onslaught of interests."

Ideas do not enter the White House under neutral conditions. The vast majority of ideas enter the domestic policy process with some pressure attached. Moreover, the pressure is not restricted to the original "parent." Interest groups, executive agencies, even White House staff may add to the clamor for a specific idea. Although interest groups, the parties, and the media are only a limited source of new ideas, they are formidable sources of pressure. Thus, the White House staffs talked of limited sources of ideas but multiple sources of pressure. As one Johnson aide remarked, "We used to feel that we had a pretty free hand in choosing programs. That was probably true. When it came down to working up specific programs and making a run for enactment, we had a different problem. There were groups who never gave a god-damn about the original problem but who wanted to get a piece of the legislative action."

External Sources

From a resource perspective, the emphasis on external sources is to be expected. Indeed, there are ample incentives to turn to Congress, events, public opinion, and the executive branch. Issues that originate in these sources are more likely to reduce presidential decision costs. Many of the issues arrive with alternatives already attached; others have received substantial public attention and acceptance. We will consider each of the external sources in turn.

Congress. Congress is the most frequently mentioned source of domestic ideas. Clearly, the staffs regard the Congress as a primary hunting ground. The staffs were quite willing to admit that Congress serves as an important supplier of presidential policy; it is an accepted seedbed for White House domestic initiatives. "Obviously, Congress is the first place to look for issues," a Kennedy liaison assistant reflected, "particulary in social policy. If an issue has anything to do with distributive policy, you can bet Congress will be the most helpful source." A Kennedy domestic policy aide put it more bluntly: "We were willing to take everything we could from Congress. We had been there during the last years of the Eisenhower administration and had worked on many of the issues. But even if we hadn't been involved, we felt it was our right to take the congressional programs for our own. We didn't rob Congress of any programs, but we sure did borrow. We turned a number of congressional ideas into presidential priorities."

For the presidential staffs, the "President Proposes, Congress Disposes" issue was irrelevant. "What difference does it make?" one Johnson aide asked. "A program is a program. We felt no embarrassment at taking congressional initiatives. It is all part of the game." The argument between Congress and the President is unimportant for the program staffs; they are more than willing to borrow, steal, coopt, redraft, rename, and modify any proposal that fits their policy goals. "It was never our concern who the original author was except to find a sponsor," a Johnson aide noted. "We took everything we could and tried to fashion a legislative program. Who cares about the first claim? We were the final owners."

Congress is a wholesaler of presidential issues, in part because of the availability of tested ideas. For Kennedy, the bulk of the congressional agenda had been passed and repassed long before his inauguration. This reliance is reinforced by the President's internal resources—the White House is simply not as able to produce detailed programs. Finally, as noted above, many of the domestic ideas arrive already matched to a specific alternative, which increases the attractiveness of the congressional source to the presidential staffs. According to one Nixon aide, "We simply didn't have the time to search out new ideas. The fact that Congress was interested in a particular idea made it a logical candidate for discussion. If a congressional program existed that appealed to the President and had already been ironed out, why not take it?" The White House staffs certainly recognize that Congress is very much in the "legislative business," and they are fully prepared to reap the profits.

The impact of Congress as a source of ideas obviously increases if the President is from the majority party. However, it is not enough for the President's party to sweep into control of Congress upon inauguration day. The impact of Congress seems to be contingent on the majority party's having been in power *before* the given President's term; the program must be ready for the President's first year. A minority party is not as capable of developing a legislative platform as is the majority party. The minority party is restricted by both resources and incentives; the primary emphasis is on defense, not offense. Even when the party gains the White House, the program opportunities are still constrained in Congress. Thus, when Nixon became President in 1969, the Congress did not represent a potent source of agenda ideas. During the eight-year Republican absence from the White House, the party was unable to draft a full legislative package. The Republicans had been on the defensive and in the distinct minority.

Events. The President and the staff have ample incentives to watch events. Presidents interested in reelection must be concerned about the potential impact of crises; Presidents are also invited to capitalize on the possible gains from effective response. Oil embargoes, urban riots, price spirals, plant closings, embassy occupations—all constitute opportunities for electoral, historical, and programmatic benefits. Events also have an impact on potential enactment. According to Gerald Ford, it often takes a crisis to produce change.

> How much more can a President do than to recommend legislation, have his people do their very best to talk to committee members, to chairmen, to the leadership?
>
> I have talked to them. I have met with the leadership. There are just roadblocks up there that are apparently unbreakable until we get a real crisis.
>
> And I am being very practical now. I do not think you are going to get a breakthrough in legislation in the field of energy until you get a brownout or a blackout. I think it is just that pragmatic.
>
> You won't get deregulation on natural gas until the cutbacks in natural gas in Washington and New York and New England start to hurt people

or hurt jobs. That is a bad commentary on our system, perhaps, but that is the way we act, right or wrong (*Newsweek,* 9 December 1974, pp. 33-34).

According to the presidential staffs, events fall into three categories. First, the staffs talked about *crisis.* Over the term, Presidents will inevitably encounter flare-ups. Issues may heat up very quickly in response to crises—the oil embargo, for example. Second, the staffs emphasized what might be called *focusing events.* Under certain conditions, an event will occur that is directly relevant to a previous presidential commitment. An issue may bubble along unnoticed for several years and then, without warning, explode onto the agenda. The long gas lines in the summer of 1979 are one instance where a focusing event pushed an agenda item further up the list. Finally, the staffs touched briefly on the *expiration of past legislation* as an important event in the domestic process. The staff pays some attention to the renewal of key statutes; both OMB and the departments provide semi-regular lists of expiring legislation. Immediately upon entering office, for instance, Reagan faced a long list of difficult renewals, including the Clean Air Act, the Clean Water Act, oil-price deregulation, the food-stamp program, the saccharin ban, the Economic Opportunity Act, the omnibus farm bill, and the Consumer Product Safety Commission. All came up for some form of renewal or reauthorization in 1981. All forced at least some consideration within the domestic policy process.

Presidents are free to ignore events only if they also wish to ignore the structure of incentives. Thus, presidential goals often lead to a marked concern with crisis. As a Kennedy aide suggested, "A President must keep in touch with what's going on outside of Washington. This is an isolated city, with a separate sense of what is important. The President has to look beyond the District of Columbia; he has to set up a system which constantly scans the 'real' world."

The concern about crisis rests on the staff's belief that events are at the forefront of political pressure. According to a Johnson aide, "Our entire domestic system was oriented to hold the initiative in the Executive Office. We felt that events were at the root of most of the President's political problems, and we wanted to spot the major crises before any damage. We wanted to avoid the impression that the President was forced to take action because he was late; we wanted to convey the image that the President was first on the scene." If "firefighting" occupies the bulk of presidential time and energy, it is because unanticipated events spark the tinder.

The Executive Branch. Presidents and staffs repeatedly complain that the bureaucracy is unresponsive; that information is distorted; that the civil service is more concerned with protecting jobs than with new programs. Yet, when they are asked about the major sources of domestic ideas, the executive branch emerges as quite important.

The reason rests squarely on resources. Despite all the complaints, the executive branch fills the gaps created by scarce presidential resources. Departmental liaison is involved in the lobbying process; departmental research is involved in formulation; departmental aides are often on loan to the White House itself. The executive branch is involved at virtually every step of the policy cycle; the departments are asked for ideas at the start and implementation at the end. "We are dealing with a system that places a premium on bureaucratic initiatives," one Carter assistant suggested. "The executive branch has all the advantages. . . . the information, the manpower, the congressional support, and the expertise. Instead of fighting the bureaucracy, the President should get some kind of control. But only God knows how." Given constraints on the President's resources, the executive branch is guaranteed as a source of ideas.

Aides who critized the executive branch in one breath were more than willing to acknowledge the impact of bureaucratic ideas on the agenda in the next. As one Nixon aide argued, "The White House has to give up control of the bulk of the programs and issues to the departments. Cabinet government makes a great deal of operational sense if only because the White House cannot do it all. Unfortunately, Cabinet government does not have a notable history of political success." In some cases the President can retain some influence by setting the broad outlines of policy and leaving the substance to the departments. In other cases issues bubble up from within the depths of the bureaucracy regardless of presidential intent. In most cases, however, the White House openly invites bureaucratic involvement, whether through the programming process or task forces. The budgetary system is a prime example. Whatever the budgetary model, whether the Planning, Programming, Budgeting System (PPBS), Management by Objective (MBO), or Zero-Based Budgeting (ZBB), the executive branch is encouraged to present new ideas. Though departments often concentrate on protecting the base, the budgetary process clearly emphasizes the creation of new justifications for old programs. One OMB official argued that "in justifying the base, an agency will often develop a new rationale. The departments are continually searching for new problems to soak up old money." That search for new issues eventually climbs the bureaucratic ladder to the President.

Public Opinion. Whereas Presidents complain that they are forced to seek issues from the executive branch, they actively cultivate issues from the public. The search for public concerns has even become an institutionalized process. Starting with Nixon, and continuing with Ford, Carter, and Reagan, the White House has maintained a formal effort to scan public opinion. The analysis of opinion surveys reached its peak in the Carter administration. Under the guidance of Patrick Caddell, the presidential polling operation became a feature of the planning process. "Carter has now elevated polling to a new plane," an outside observer argued. "Presidents are now in the polling business and are likely to remain active for some time." In 1981, for instance, the Republican National Committee spent over two million dollars on public opinion surveys for the Reagan economic program.

There are, of course, limits to the impact of public opinion on the domestic agenda. Public opinion is generally too ambiguous to be of help in framing specific programs, and the levels of public awareness are often low. According to Gerald Ford,

> On any specific issue the President needs to know the facts, get the best information, so that he can make the decision and then lead from there. I do not think a President should run the country on the basis of the polls. The public in so many cases does not have a full comprehension of a problem. A President ought to listen to the people, but he cannot make hard decisions just by reading the polls once a week. It just does not work, and what the President ought to do is make the hard decisions and then go out and educate the people on why a decision that was necessarily unpopular was made (*Time,* 10 November 1980, p. 31).

Yet, given the limits of individual opinion, the staffs argued that public opinion is important. Its importance varies with intensity. According to a Ford aide, "Public opinion usually doesn't make much difference. Occasionally, however, an issue will reach such an extent that it can't be ignored. It doesn't happen often, but when an issue gets that hot, you have to do something. The closest we came to that kind of heat was inflation." A Carter aide agreed:

> I'm not sure whether we would have been so concerned about the tax-cutters if Proposition 13 hadn't been so popular. Normally, the tax-cutters would have been considered part of the fringe. But when the issue started to spread, there was no way to get out from under. Christ, even Jerry Brown reacted. Imagine a balanced-budget amendment under Brown. That's how strong the public opinion was.

As intensity grows, Presidents begin to anticipate potential electoral rewards or punishments. Though such issues arise sporadically, Presidents listen; indeed, their rarity may increase their impact.

Parties, Interest Groups, and the Media. Why do parties, interest groups, and the media fall at the bottom of external sources? Why did the staff discount these three sources? The Democratic staffs' lack of enthusiasm for the *parties* may reflect their opinion of past occupants of key congressional positions. Neither Mike Mansfield in the Senate nor Carl Albert in the House was viewed as a strong legislative leader; their offices were not considered a significant source of domestic issues. "We did not view Senator Mansfield with the same awe as Johnson," a Kennedy assistant remarked. "Mansfield was not willing to exercise the same kind of power; he did not bring his ideas to us with the same kind of pressure." With the replacement of

Carl Albert by "Tip" O'Neill in the House, the Democratic leadership has grown stronger. Yet, even with the tighter leadership, the Carter staff played down the leaders' impact on the domestic agenda.

> We listen to the leaders; we ask them to present their ideas. But more often than not they tend to repeat what we have already proposed. In many respects, it is not their role to bring new ideas to the President. Instead, they should guide him on the potential for passage. The leader's office is not the source of ideas to the same extent as the executive branch or the congressional committees. Ordinarily, the leaders echo the same ideas that we have already tapped.

Both Democrats and Republicans view the leadership more as a conduit to and from Congress than as an independent source of ideas.

The same attitude pertains to the party elite, whether the national chairman or convention delegates. For the staffs, the causal path moves *from* the White House *to* the party elite, not vice versa. As one Nixon aide argued, "Let's face it, the party is for the President. He picks the chairman, the executive committee; he runs the convention and guides the platform. The parties meet only once or twice every four years; the President is the party when it is not in session."

Interest groups are approached in a somewhat different light. Whereas the President attempts to maintain contact with party leaders, there is a conscious effort to avoid interaction with most interest groups. Unless the interest group is a key member of the President's electoral coalition, there is only limited contact. The absence of contact rests in part on the sheer number of interest groups in Washington. In 1945 only two thousand lobbies were registered with Congress; by 1980 there were fifteen thousand. Given the restrictions on the President's calendar, the lobbies clearly are encouraged to spend their energies elsewhere. Though interest-group influence has certainly increased with the emergence of the issue networks, interest groups generally concentrate on the Congress and executive agencies, not on the White House. "We didn't receive that much pressure from the lobbies," a Ford aide reflected. "They preferred to work the Hill instead. It's a problem of limited access. Only the largest groups have any openings—labor, the AMA. But even there, they prefer to work the Congress." As one Johnson assistant argued, "There are 535 opportunities in Congress and only one in the White House. You can get an hour to present your case before each representative; you get fifteen minutes once a year with the President. Where would you put your effort?"

Ultimately, interest groups have a greater impact on the pool of ideas through indirect channels. They supply information to both Congress and the executive branch, each of which is a significant source of issues according to the presidential staffs. Yet, interest groups operate most effectively at the subterranean levels of government. They are rarely the direct source of domestic ideas.

This pattern has changed somewhat in recent years, particularly with the institutionalization of an office of public liaison within the White House. Though the office existed under both Nixon and Ford, Carter used it extensively for building grass-roots support for his legislative agenda. Under the guidance of Anne Wexler, the Public Liaison Office (PLO) was remarkably effective in building issue coalitions among interest groups. Indeed, according to one member of the Carter legislative liaison staff, "The public liaison folks had a pretty sophisticated operation for pinpointing potential interest-group allies. When they pulled together a coalition, it could be quite valuable on the Hill. I'd guess they had about thirty thousand names and contacts on their computer for mobilization." Yet, despite its intent to manage interest groups to the President's advantage, the PLO obviously permitted greater access to the White House. Interest-group representatives were invited to participate in formulating and lobbying for presidential programs. As the PLO reached out to interest groups for help, interest groups inevitably reached further in. By the end of Carter's term, the PLO had established itself as a key participant in the White House policy process. It became involved in the drafting of programs from the very beginning of an idea to the final bill signing. One by-product of the public liaison operation was to legitimize interest-group involvement in presidential decisions. Whether the operation will remain as powerful in the Reagan administration is still unclear. However, Reagan's appointment of Elizabeth Dole as PLO director was a signal of his interest in maintaining a channel for interest-group contact.

One final note on interest groups. It is possible that the percentages in table 8 reflect the staffs' perception of the President as immune to special interest influence, a perception intimately tied to the White House value system. Staffs may consistently underestimate the importance of interest groups to protect that image of presidential immunity. According to one Kennedy assistant, "The President cannot admit that the interest groups have that much influence. The Presidency is not supposed to be that kind of office. It is supposed to represent the nation, not special interests. If the staff looked hard, they would see a lot more interest-group activity than they could imagine. The interest groups are in the woodwork, under the floors, in the hallways, and in the rose garden."

One is perhaps most surprised to find the *media* among the three bottom sources. The media is usually viewed as a critical participant in the agenda process. In Cobb and Elder's model of outside initiation, the media has "a very important role in elevating issues to the sytemic agenda and increasing their chances of receiving formal agenda consideration. Certain personages in the media can act as opinion leaders in bringing publicity to a particular issue. . . . Individuals who have acquired an audience simply by constantly appearing in the news can also publicize an issue" (Cobb and Elder 1972, pp. 91-92). Yet, for the White House staffs, the media is not a source of new ideas; it is at best a bridge to the political environment.

Thus, the media acts as an indirect channel to the White House. Indeed, the staffs viewed the media more as a source of pressure than as a supplier of ideas. As one Carter aide remarked, "We all read the papers and we notice if an event is causing a reaction. We watch the evening broadcasts and recognize the lead stories. If an item makes a stir and we haven't noticed it, we are in trouble." Thus, Presidents generally attempt to follow events through the media. Kennedy scanned a dozen major papers each morning; both Nixon and Carter received a full news summary each day; Johnson had three televisions installed side by side so he could watch the three networks simultaneously.

Why is the media so important as an indirect source? First, we know that Presidents pay attention to it. Issues that appear in either print or the electronic media are accorded some status on that basis alone. Second, newspapers and television often provide useful summaries of activities in Congress, the bureaucracy, and the public; ideas that originate in these sources often reach the President through the media. There are a variety of incentives for watching the press. However, as a separate source of new ideas, the media was consistently discounted. It was viewed as a vehicle for issues, not as an originator. In this respect, the media falls into the same category as the congressional leadership: it is a major conduit for ideas, a major catalyst.

Internal Sources

There are a number of reasons why most domestic issues do not originate within the White House. It is more convenient to draw issues from external sources. External sources are more likely to supply ideas with alternatives already attached. External sources can also substantially cut White House decision costs. Given restrictions on time, information, expertise, and energy, the President is well advised to concentrate on external sources. This is not to argue that the Presidency is devoid of new ideas; however, according to the staffs, we may have overestimated the impact of several time-honored internal channels to the agenda.

The Campaign and Platform: A Reassessment. Over the past two decades campaign promises and party platforms have been the subject of considerable attention in the presidential literature. The concern rests on the argument that the President must be accountable, that the domestic agenda must reflect the candidate's promises. The linkage between campaign promises and actual performance becomes a key characteristic of "responsible parties." According to this concept, political officials must be responsive to their campaign commitments. Unless promises are converted to specific actions, there is no connection between the public and the government. But does this goal fit the presidential policy process? Should a promise made in the heat of a campaign become a priority in office? Here we are concerned with the campaign and platform not only as a source of ideas but also as a source of pressure on the President's domestic agenda.

Past research by Gerald Pomper (1968), Fred Grogan (1977), and Jeffrey Fishel (1979) suggests that the campaign is a major guide to policy choice. Yet, when we look at the specific figures, the campaign does not seem as strong. When Fishel compares campaign promises with in-office response for the last twenty years, he finds that a "predictable chasm always exists between presidential proposal and actual policy, as every president in the twentieth century has learned. The complications and frustration of the [Carter] administration with and in Congress are hardly unique in the late 1970s even if they seem more intense" (1979, p. 53). Using coding categories originally proposed by Pomper, Fishel discovered that the actual percentage of programs that reached the President's domestic agenda "fully comparable" to the original promises was 36 percent for Kennedy, 41 percent for Johnson, 34 percent for Nixon, and 42 percent for Carter. Less than half of the 1960, 1964, 1968, 1972, and 1976 campaign promises reached the agenda. Though Fishel interprets the relationship as strong, it seems evident that *mere mention in the campaign does not guarantee agenda status in office.* When Fishel adds in the number of promises "partially comparable"—that is, somewhat similar to the original pledge—the figures rise substantially. Kennedy's promise-to-performance percentage rises to 67, Johnson's to 63, Nixon's to 60, and Carter's to 57. In short, the President can be expected to convert roughly three out of every five campaign promises into actual policy. The prediction rate is only slightly higher than the toss of a coin, leaving room for considerable presidential discretion.

In addressing that discretion, Grogan suggests that presidential performance varies "according to whether campaign promises required congressional action or could be achieved on the President's own authority. While Johnson acted most fully on those promises requiring congressional action, Nixon, facing a relatively unfriendly Congress, acted more fully on those he could achieve on his own." Yet, the main incentive for campaign accountability seems to be the importance of the pledge to the candidate, not the prominence of the pledge in the campaign. As Grogan continues, "Knowledge of those promises most 'salient' to the candidate himself would appear to provide the best feasible indicator of which promises a President will pursue. For both Johnson and Nixon this general knowledge would have been the best indicator of what the two men would do in office" (Grogan 1977, pp. 20-21). If you uncover the President's goals, you will discover the President's agenda.

This conclusion presents a problem for democratic theory. Added to the staff comments in table 8, it seems that neither the campaign nor the platform is a particularly powerful constraint on eventual outcomes. According to one Nixon aide, "The campaign should be seen as a set of options. The

President has the opportunity to explore a number of different proposals. Once the ballots are in, the program can change radically. As the task forces come in, the President comes down to earth." A Carter assistant concurred: "Even with the list of promises, most of the staff recognized that the realities of office would make the biggest impact. Once you're in office, the perspective changes. The promises are too simple to be of much use." Though most aides admitted that the campaign is an important learning period, few were willing to argue that the campaign constitutes a driving force behind the domestic agenda.

Perhaps the most important complaint about the campaign was the sheer number of promises. According the Fishel, Carter made at least 186 separate pledges, Kennedy 136, Nixon 114, and Johnson 63. "When you look at the number of items in the platform and promises book, you can't help but be staggered by the amount that Carter proposed," a media respondent argued. "There was no chance that Carter could do that much. He was creating a problem by promising so much. He certainly shouldn't have published a book for record-keeping." In absolute terms, Carter converted more promises to policy than did any of his contemporaries—to begin with, he made more promises. Yet, of those 186 pledges, Carter acted on approximately 57 percent, a figure lower than those for Kennedy, Johnson, and Nixon. Which is more important to presidential accountability—the actual number of conversions or the percentage? According to a Ford campaign aide, "It is the general impression that is essential in the long run. Carter promised more and delivered less. He may have hit half his promises, and that may be, as you say, more in real terms than Nixon or LBJ. But he has that much more left to be done. And that will be an issue in 1980. It is a problem of rising expectations."

Beyond the sheer number of promises involved in an election season, the staffs discounted the impact of the campaign and platform sources for several additional reasons. First, the staff argued, the bulk of the major issues are selected long before the campaign starts. The influence of the campaign may be negligible once the original themes are presented. Accordingly, Carter's 1976 campaign began with a set of thirteen issue statements, each with a series of subitems. These statements, released in December 1975, emphasized what Carter and his staff believed were the top issues in the campaign: health policy, economic stimulus, reorganization. The statements set the tone for the presidential contest. "Once the thirteen planks were set," one Carter aide suggested, "the campaign was in place. We didn't go into New Hampshire looking for new ideas. We knew what the major issues would be long before the first leaflet was distributed. We ran on the President's *image* as an honest outsider and attacked Ford's record as an incumbent. I'm just not sure how much policy content there was."

In the search for issue sources, the *pre-campaign* period becomes a critical focus. It is in these very first moments that the candidate and his staff choose the basic issues; these are the issues that generally receive the greatest attention. Even if an issue must be abandoned during the campaign, it may return after inauguration.

Second, the campaign and platform rarely focus on more than a handful of high-intensity items. "Beyond the Vietnam War and unemployment, what was the 1968 campaign about?" a Nixon aide asked. "There are only two or three top issues in any campaign. That gives the President a lot of leeway once in office. How many of the campaign promises does the public actually remember? How many will return in the next election?" Several assistants echoed that argument, saying that the campaign is limited because of the concentrated nature of presidential politics. "We made a series of what we felt were key statements on the American system," a Johnson aide remarked, "but I'm not sure how many really sank into the electorate. We couldn't tell if any made a difference. That's one reason why LBJ didn't feel particularly bound to follow through on everything. If we had been sure that an issue had been important, however, you can be sure of our reaction."

In evaluating campaign promises, the staff returned to the intensity of public opinion as a barometer of importance. Though the staff emphasized the importance of the public as a source of issues, they also discounted the public's understanding and awareness. Though the staff acknowledged the public's concern on certain pervasive issues, few granted the public such credit in evaluating the campaign pledges. "Do they understand the oil depletion allowance?" a Nixon aide asked. "Do they recognize the difference between welfare and a guaranteed income?" The questions returned throughout the interviews. If the public cannot recognize the issues, why should the President be honor-bound by past promises? The staffs clearly did not believe that the bulk of the issues touched the public. Yet, even though public opinion is often ambiguous, the staffs listened when it was clear that opinion had crystallized.

What about the party platform? After all, the platform is drafted by the party elites, not the general public. The staffs agreed that the platform had some influence on the President's agenda, but they disputed the causal flow. As one Ford aide suggested, "Unless the President is truly inept, the platform is his. The platform belongs to the President. There are times when an issue will arise that must be adopted, but the platform does not carry much force. The President can pick and choose among the items." The influence flows from the President to the platform. Despite delegate assurances to the contrary, the candidate is the arbiter of the platform. At least for the past twenty years, the party nominee has been given considerable say on the platform.

Just what is the impact of the campaign and the platform? Even with the limits, does the campaign act as a source of ideas? Certainly the campaign exposes the candidate to a variety of problems and issues. Though the issues may have been tapped in the pre-campaign period, the long drive to office constitutes an important part of the President's learning. Kennedy's exposure to West Virginia poverty, Nixon's contact with welfare reform, Carter's problem with "ethnic purity"—each sensitized the candidate to a particular issue. Regardless of the promise-to-performance ratio, the campaign and the platform have an impact on the President's perception of the intensity of public opinion. A candidate may have a firm commitment to national health insurance long before the election year, but the campaign might move the issue from the bottom to the top of the agenda. Candidates also inevitably discover new ideas during the primary and general election campaigns; hence, the two sources receive a fair number of mentions in table 8. Though there is ample criticism of the campaign and platform as a constraint on domestic choice, the staffs still pinpointed each as a potential source of agenda issues.

The President and the Staff. The President's personal experiences have a dramatic impact on the domestic agenda. Over a lifetime, a President will be exposed to a variety of issues and problems. It is natural that once he is in office, those ideas will influence his framing of the foreign and domestic agendas.

Though we might agree on the importance of the President's personal experiences as a source of domestic issues, there is considerable confusion over the staff's impact. In the past, the presidential literature has not viewed the staff as particularly important. The staff has been seen as simply an extension of the President, as a single entity comprising similar individuals with similar thoughts. According to this view, the President usually recruits like-minded assistants. Moreover, the staff is often seen as a group of ambitious yesmen, each scrambling to tell the President just what he wants to hear. It does not matter what the individual assistant actually believes, since he or she will try to anticipate the President's reactions. Both views are only partially correct. It is true that the staff tend to be recruited from similar streams; it is also true that there is a definite effort among aides to second-guess the President. However, the two viewpoints neglect the potential impact of individual assistants on presidential choice.

Take Daniel Moynihan. Recruited by Nixon in 1969, Moynihan was not from the Republican mainstream. Though Moynihan has changed his views on welfare since joining the Senate in 1977, he was among the most liberal members of the Nixon staff. Thus, Moynihan was not recruited as a like-minded aide; nor was he interested in selling the President on traditional Republican reforms. Moynihan attempted to persuade Nixon that welfare reform was a necessity. According to Martin Anderson, Moynihan's adversary in the struggle, Moynihan had considerable advantages.

> He was one of the very few people on the White House staff who had operated in the Washington bureaucracy and understood it. He had an extensive network of contacts throughout HEW and OEO, many of them Democrats shocked at Humphrey's defeat, who flooded him with research data and other information. And he had great persuasive resources. In the

sea of dark gray and blue that surrounded Nixon, Moynihan, in his cream-colored suit and red bow tie, gleamed like a playful porpoise. He was a charming Irish rogue, a delightful dinner companion, a fascinating teller of tales. His presence lighted the gloom of national policy deliberations, and even his opponents liked to have him around. The President liked to read his memoranda, sometimes even searching through the pile on his desk to find them (Anderson 1978, p. 6).

The staff cannot be discounted as a source of domestic ideas. Moynihan was not alone in trying to persuade Nixon that a particular idea belonged on the agenda; Arthur Burns, Erhlichman, and Haldeman all tried, with varying degrees of success. Nor were these efforts unusual compared with other administrations. Kennedy, Johnson, Ford, and Carter faced their share of internal pressure.

The domestic staffs serve as both a direct and an indirect source of ideas. Assistants will always enter office with pet projects and interests. According to one Nixon assistant, "If you had worked on education before, you focused on the issue again. That is where your contacts were; that's where your specialties were. It was in your best interest to see that education was on the agenda. It would increase your influence." A Carter assistant concurred: "We were all brought in for one job or another. Some of us fit our positions, others did not. Once we knew where we were going, we started looking for ideas. That was our job: canvass the area and see what could be done." Assistants also serve as conduits for departments and Congress. The very structure of the domestic policy process ensures that aides will carry ideas from external sources. The annual programming process is a prime example. Established by Truman in 1947, the process involves a canvass for ideas. But though the staff controls the canvass, it is rarely the original source. Traditionally, Presidents ask the executive branch for new ideas and suggestions for the legislative program; however, it is the President's staff that digests the information and determines what issues are of interest. According to Clark Clifford, special counsel to Truman, the purpose of the annual process was to

> have the needs and also the opinions of the departments and agencies of government so that we would be able to extract from that voluminous source of information a legislative program. While much of it was self-serving, at least we felt that we had tapped knowledgeable and experienced people in government. Sometimes in that general request a real pearl would appear. It is like a diver swimming around and all of a sudden there would appear a pearl as large as a hen's egg. In my opinion, that alone would justify the effort (in Wayne 1978, p. 104).

Past Presidents have received a great deal of substantive advice from task forces, yet, according to the staffs, task forces are not a significant source either of new ideas or of pressure. Carter's experience with his post-campaign task forces may explain the finding. According to his staff, Carter received over 130 policy statements, including reports on the budget, health, education, staffing, and executive reorganization. Yet, the task forces were rarely the source of new ideas. According to one Carter assistant, "The ideas for the task forces came from a small group of advisors, including Jody Powell, Pat Caddell, Ham Jordan, and Jimmy Carter himself. They sat down on several occasions and talked about the issues that might be important after the election." The decision to appoint a task force reflected the earlier adoption of an issue; task forces are a *product* of the issue-selection process. As a Nixon aide argued, "Who had the ideas for the task forces? Where did they come from? We had the ideas. We were exposed to the concepts. After a while, some sink in. The decision to form a task force involved our assessment of the issues. You don't push a task force until you know where it is going." Thus, task forces become valuable tools for the analysis of alternatives and priorities, but they rarely generate new issues; indeed, it is new ideas that tend to generate task forces.

Conclusion

The source of ideas is important. The emphasis of one channel to the exclusion of others can restrict both representation and change. Presidential reliance on Congress and the executive branch may inhibit the potential for dramatic departures from past experience. Given the President's resource constraints, however, there is little opportunity for the exploration of new ideas. As a Kennedy aide remarked, "We didn't have the time to look too far beyond the Congress. We had to move our program fast; we didn't have the opportunity to develop that many novel programs. We had to stick with the basics." If an idea does not reach the pool of available items, it has little chance for adoption. Presidents have few openings for new ideas; if the issue has not moved into the pool by the start of the term—indeed, if the idea is not available by the start of the campaign—it may lie untouched for the full four years.

Perhaps the most important recent change in the source of ideas is the relative decline of Congress as a supplier to the President's agenda. Ever-increasing legislative complexity and internal dispersion have limited the congressional channel to the President's program. This decline has occurred at the very time that Congress wants greater influence. As one Carter aide argued, "Congress is not as important to the President as it used to be. There is a great deal of activity on the Hill. I'm just not sure they are producing much of value anymore." Whereas Kennedy faced a refined national agenda ripe for presidential picking, Carter faced a highly fragmented legislative process. Though Congress continues to innovate, there is considerably less cohesion among the legislative entrepreneurs. Presidents find themselves in the unenviable position of searching for ideas in an increasingly diffuse system. Presidents still need reliable sources of issues; indeed, they need more help today than ever before. Unfortunately, Congress is no longer the best source of ideas. Congress still produces policy, but it is of less value to the President. According to a Carter liaison aide, "Congress has become a Pandora's box. We were almost afraid to ask Congress what it wanted for fear of the answer."

Thus far, I have talked of the President's search for issues. I have looked at presidential goals and the sources of ideas. In chapter 5, I will turn to a discussion of alternatives. Where the selection of issues involves the search for benefits, the choice of alternatives rests on the perception of costs.

5 defining
the alternatives

As Kennedy drafted his domestic agenda in January 1961 there was no question about his commitment to civil rights. Though he had been less than enthusiastic in the 1957 Senate fight for title III of the civil rights bill, the issue was a cornerstone of his presidential campaign. Kennedy had specifically pledged full action to "obtain consideration of a civil rights bill by the Senate early next session that will implement the pledges of the Democratic platform." Yet, despite the promise, there was no action in that first session nor in the second. Kennedy was decidedly passive on the issue. According to Arthur Schlesinger, Jr., the decision to abandon the legislative route rested on Kennedy's assessment of his political capital:

> While he did not doubt the depth of the injustice or the need for remedy, he had read the arithmetic of the new Congress and concluded that there was no possible chance of passing a civil rights bill. Moreover, he had a wide range of presidential responsibilities; and a fight for civil rights would alienate southern support he needed for other purposes (including bills like those for education and the increased minimum wage, of direct benefit to the Negro). And he feared that the inevitable defeat of a civil rights bill after debate and filibuster would heighten Negro resentment, drive the civil rights revolution to more drastic resorts and place a perhaps intolerable strain on the already weak social fabric. He therefore settled on the strategy of executive action. No doubt wishing to avoid argument and disappointment, he did not even establish a interregnum task force on civil rights (Schlesinger 1965, pp. 849-850).

In short, Kennedy could not "afford" a major civil rights bill. As one Kennedy aide argued, "We believed that civil rights had to wait until we could strengthen our hold in Congress. For the first two years at least, we had to concentrate on executive orders. It was simpler, more direct, and certainly more successful." Even in 1963, when the civil rights bill finally moved to Congress, Kennedy was still worried about its impact on the rest of the

104

domestic agenda. "We knew that there were several senators who might hold our program hostage," a Kennedy aide noted. "That was a primary consideration in delaying the bill for as long as we did. We didn't want to sacrifice the entire program for a single bill."

Initial Choices

Selecting alternatives is perhaps the single most important step in the presidential policy process. It is the point where the programmatic content is framed, where the political benefits are set. More than any other choice, the choice of alternatives determines who gets what when, where, and how. Though Presidents are granted considerable flexibility in choosing the domestic issues, the definition of alternatives is fraught with conflict. Indeed, my argument is that the search for acceptable alternatives has become more difficult over the past decade, that the kinds of programs that can survive the legislative process are increasingly limited. The search for alternatives may now be the most difficult task in the domestic agenda process. As Lyndon Johnson reflected, "Legislative drafting is a political art. The President is continually faced with a number of tough choices: how to strike a balance between the bill he really wants and the bill he's got a good chance of getting; how to choose between a single-purpose or omnibus bill; how to package the bill for the Hill, when to send it up" (in Kearns 1976, p. 232).

For some, the following discussion may seem reminiscent of Theodore Lowi's (1964) effort to develop a policy typology. In Lowi's framework, policies were separated into three categories: distributive, redistributive, and regulatory. Though Lowi's work is interesting and provocative, I am not concerned with building such typologies. Rather, I am concerned with examining specific presidential decisions in the hope of finding differences among the domestic programs. In most cases these differences involve a continuum between distinct packets of alternatives—from large-scale to small-scale, from spending policy to nonspending, from legislative proposals to vetoes. In choosing among these program alternatives, Presidents evaluate both their political resources and personal goals; these evaluations affect the selection of specific alternatives. Thus, the following discussion should be taken less as an effort to develop a new policy typology and more as an attempt to make better sense out of the President's agenda.

Initially, the President must decide whether to act. As simple as it seems, this is a critical first choice. Just as Presidents have discretion in selecting the original issues, the decision not to act is a legitimate alternative. According to an OMB official,

> Let's say that the President finds the welfare system to be a mess. Well, the first thing to do is to decide whether the President is going to do anything about it. Does he want to act? The welfare system is pretty bad,

but it could be worse. How much can reform accomplish anyway? The history of welfare reform has been dismal. There has been little positive progress in Congress. Even if the President thinks there is a problem, he might not want to invest the time in an extensive reform. He might choose to wait. It is always a reasonable alternative.

The choice between doing something and doing nothing involves both goals and resources. Presidents rarely are forced to foreclose action until at least some alternatives are in. "The staff had a good idea that welfare reform could not be a top priority," one Ford aide reflected, "but the President was still interested in the proposals. The President took the items under consideration but decided we couldn't do much along those lines." In most cases, Presidents do decide to act. The policy process is oriented toward action. Once an issue is selected, the President and the staff move toward some discussion of potential alternatives. Under other circumstances, however, inaction may be the only available option. According to a Carter aide, "Believe it or not, it is a legitimate solution to do nothing. To demand that Presidents always come up with detailed programs creates an overload. Presidents can solve some problems by simply leaving them alone." Yet, according to a second Carter assistant, "If the President decides that hospital costs are a problem, the staff is obliged to present some set of options. Doing nothing will be one of the options, but it will be far down the list. The President's choice of an issue implies that he will act."

The search for domestic agenda alternatives is also oriented toward substantive programs, not symbolic ones. This assumption reflects the President's need to reserve scarce resources for substantive proposals. In the past, scholars often argued that Presidents should engage in at least some effort to educate the public about new ideas. Presidents were encouraged to send symbolic legislation to Congress even if there was virtually no chance of passage. Kennedy's 1961 requests for Medicare and Aid to Education were viewed in just this light. Since Kennedy could not hope for passage, the legislation must have been to educate. According to Schlesinger,

> Kennedy used to quote Jefferson: "Great innovations should not be forced on slender majorities." Nor was he one to see great virtue in losing. "There is no sense," he once said, "in raising hell, and then not being successful. There is no sense in putting the office of the Presidency on the line on an issue, and then being defeated." Yet, despite such aphorisms, he did, in fact, submit to Congress an astonishing number of innovations, doing so less perhaps in the expectation of immediate enactment than in the knowledge they would never be enacted without a long campaign of congressional and national education (Schlesinger 1965, p. 651).

There is, of course, a fine line between symbol and substance. In the following pages, however, we will assume that most presidential proposals are intended as substance. President's rarely spend capital on impossible dreams. Moreover, as one Kennedy aide argued, even the symbolic programs are expensive: "Medicare and Aid to Education cost us just as much as anything else. We didn't send them up to be ignored. We pushed them despite the congressional resistance. You can't educate the public without using some of the same resources you'd use lobbying for immediate enactment."

The opportunities for educating the public seem to have dropped in the past decade. Given restrictions on competition and resources, Presidents cannot afford to send symbolic proposals to Congress if substantive requests are available. Given limits on the amount of congressional agenda space, Presidents are advised to concentrate their energies on the "doable" legislation. As one Carter aide suggested, "There is so little room to begin with. Why should we spend our time working on unattainable goals? Maybe that was a mistake, but we didn't intend to lay back on any of the programs." The days when the President can go out into the country and light a fire under Congress are increasingly limited. The effort takes both time and energy from the more pragmatic programs.

Setting Directions. The search for domestic alternatives generally starts with decisions on basic directions. As Presidents begin the discussion of potential alternatives, they must set initial guidelines along broad political and philosophical lines. The President's search for programs is not a blind process. The White House looks for alternatives that fit the President's perceptions of the original issues. Ronald Reagan was no more willing to approve vast expansions of the federal government than John Kennedy was to rescind the New Deal. Thus, at the very start of any search for alternatives, the President must set directions. As we shall see in chapter 6, the President evaluates the specific alternatives with respect to policy costs—whether the costs of congressional passage, the costs to the economy, or the costs of workability. At the start of the search process, the President must decide how the search will proceed; he must evaluate the potential benefits of each given issue and set an appropriate search in motion. When Reagan began the search for domestic alternatives in 1981, for instance, he set a series of natural boundaries. Reagan did not want programs that expanded the federal role, that increased spending, that buttressed the Great Society; rather, he wanted programs that would help him achieve electoral, historical, and programmatic benefits. He wanted legislation that would cut spending in domestic policy and raise spending in defense. In this sense, Reagan's search for alternatives was directly tied to his selection of issues. In evaluating specific programs, every President turns to the cost criteria, but in setting the search in motion, each President focuses on his personal and political goals. In this sense, alternatives are the product of what Cyert and March (1963) call "problemistic search." The search for alternatives reflects the effort to solve a perceived problem; the selection of a "preferred" alternative is biased by presidential goals. Thus, in looking at Reagan's political capital—his Senate majority and public support—and his political goals—reelection, historical achievement, and good policy—we could have predicted an agenda made up of large-scale legislative proposals, involving departures from past Democratic policies, and renewing the importance of the budget as a policy tool.

Five Programmatic Choices. The domestic agenda generally is geared toward both action and substance. As one Kennedy aide remarked, "There is so little the President can do during the term. He can't afford to waste the opportunities. The domestic agenda is a vehicle for the tangible programs." In searching for specific alternatives to fit the domestic issues, however, Presidents face at least five additional choices.

First, the President must decide whether to offer a specific program to Congress or to oppose and veto a competing initiative within the legislative process. It is a question of legislative strategy. Depending upon the President's policy goals, the legislative agenda may focus on opposition to congressional action or requests for specific programs.

Second, the President must decide between legislative and administrative action. If the legislative channel is foreclosed, executive action may be the only acceptable alternative. The use of the executive order, for instance, responds to several criteria. The President may issue an executive order when administrative action is the logical alternative, when it is the simplest and most direct route. He may issue one in order to prevent a given program's being involved in congressional controversy. He may use it when the risk of congressional defeat is too great. Finally, the President may issue an executive order after testing the congressional path and finding failure. Executive action is not limited to orders. Presidents can and do influence bureaucratic practices and regulations; Presidents can and do have an impact on appointments and dismissals. Regardless of the specific executive tool, the staffs are aware of the distinction between executive and legislative alternatives.

Third, at some point, the President must decide on the size of the program. Using John Campbell's distinction, is the proposal to be *large* or *small?* For Campbell, the decision rests on both the budgetary impact of the individual program and the level of national attention.

> Large-new decisions are the sort one reads about in case studies and the agenda setting literature; a good example for the aging policy area in America is Medicare. . . . At the extreme, these decisions have a large fiscal impact and they significantly alter the relationships among social groups or between state and society. Accordingly, they are controversial and receive considerable publicity; participation is relatively broad (interest groups, political parties or subgroups, chief executive, perhaps several agencies); and the outcome in some sense will represent the political balance of power for the society as a whole.
>
> Small-new decisions do not have as broad an impact and probably will receive little publicity; participation is often confined within a "subgovernment" of officials, interest groups, representatives, and the few

politicians directly and routinely concerned with a specific policy area; outcomes often depend on the balance of power or views within the sub-government (Campbell 1978, p. 3).

Compared with the majority of programs that circulate through Congress, most presidential priorities would be classified as large. However, the large/small distinction is a continuum. Programs on the President's agenda differ. Contrast Kennedy's request for Medicare and his proposal for oceanographic research; Johnson's demand for federal aid to education and his land-conservation fund; Nixon's interest in revenue sharing and in airport development; Ford's proposal for energy independence and his expansion of law-enforcement assistance; Carter's comprehensive energy plan and strip-mining reclamation. In each case, the President and the staff recognized the qualitative difference between the competing programs.

Fourth, the President must often choose between "new" and "old" programs. The new programs reflect departures in domestic policy; the old programs involve modifications of established programs. There are advantages to both. This distinction between new and old was briefly examined in chapter 2, but it deserves further clarification here. Like the distinction between large and small above, it involves a continuum: programs often introduce a new idea or involve variations on past initiatives. Though we are dealing with a continuum, the new programs can be distinguished by several characteristics. The staffs viewed modification of old programs as the simplest of initiatives, but only if such modification runs in the same direction as the original intent. The old programs evoke patterned images; the coalitions remain stable. There is an implicit link between the large/small and the new/old distinctions; Campbell (1978) consciously combines the two. For the presidential staffs, the large-new programs are the most difficult and time-consuming of all the presidential priorities; they demand the greatest commitments of presidential resources.

Fifth, the President must choose between competing "strategies of intervention." For the domestic process, the choice often rests on spending versus nonspending policy. Though the distinction hides considerable variance, it is often used by the staffs to describe policy decisions. Spending policy centers on federal expenditures as the primary tool to achieve policy goals. Though spending involves a variety of options—categorical grants, block grants, tax cuts—the staffs tended to view spending policy as a single entity. The staffs did not seem preoccupied with the distributive or redistributive nature of spending programs, despite the increasing pressure on the federal budget. Rather, they tended to view programs in simple terms. The preference for spending over nonspending varies with the tightening of the federal budget; the preference for spending policy has dropped dramatically since the mid-1960s. According to one congressional observer, "There has been a definite shift in the kinds of policies we see. In the early 1960s the bulk of the programs centered on expenditures of one kind or another. In many respects, we had concluded that economic conditions demanded substantial federal spending. That is no longer the case. We now measure our spending programs with extreme care. The well has run dry." I will return to the rise and fall of spending policy, while addressing the increased importance of the budget as a domestic battleground.

Domestic Alternatives

Using these five policy dimensions, it is possible to compare the Kennedy, Johnson, Nixon, Ford, and Carter agendas, to search for stable patterns across time. Returning to the set of 266 items pulled from the OMB clearance records, we can test for differences between the five Presidents.

A Theory of Legislative Expense. The following discussion is linked to what might be called a theory of legislative expense. In choosing among domestic alternatives, Presidents must evaluate potential costs—whether political, economic, or technical—against available political capital. In chapter 6 I will examine the impact of costs in detail. For now, it is important to frame our findings in a theory of legislative expense. Given each President's initial resource base, the choice between different kinds of alternatives reflects the potential for congressional passage. Our basic assumption is that each presidential program has a specific cost and that some programs are more expensive than others. Legislative proposals are more "expensive" than vetoes; passing a bill requires a majority vote, but sustaining a veto requires only a third plus one. Large-scale programs demand more congressional support than do small-scale programs; new programs demand more capital than do old ones. And with recent increases in fiscal pressure, spending programs are now more "expensive" than nonspending programs.

Presidents and staffs openly subscribe to a theory of legislative expense; they believe that programs have specific political and economic price tags. Whether Congress actually restricts the President is not as important as the fact that the President and staff perceive certain programs as more expensive than others. In examining differences between recent Presidents, I will often return to the concept of legislative expense. The programs that Johnson could "afford" were different from those that Nixon or Ford could afford; the programs that Reagan can afford are different from those that Kennedy could afford. In defining the alternatives, Presidents pay attention to the impact of costs; yet, they are sometimes willing to spend more for certain programs. Despite the cost, Carter wanted a comprehensive energy program instead of a limited research-and-development package; Kennedy wanted Medicare instead of a more restricted expansion of social security benefits. Thus, the selection of specific alternatives reflects the impact of the

President's *resources* and his *goals*. As Presidents measure alternatives against the potential for congressional adoption, they also evaluate their personal and political goals. Goals affect the substance of the domestic agenda, while resources restrict both the size and the scope of the programs that each President can afford.

The theory of legislative expense inevitably involves an interaction between resources and goals. On one hand, costs affect how much each President can propose and the choice of specific alternatives. Ford could not afford to spend his limited political capital on a series of legislative proposals, so he concentrated on the veto. Nixon could not afford to request large-scale retrenchment from a Democratic Congress, so he focused on smaller initiatives. On the other hand, goals affect each President's view of the status quo. Since both Nixon and Ford viewed the federal status quo as large and unresponsive, and since both faced democratic majorities in Congress, they turned to policies that either rescinded or modified previous New Deal and Great Society programs. But since both also had limited political capital, they had to stick with small-scale programs to accomplish those ends. Goals and resources thus have a combined impact on alternatives: goals set the general directions; costs limit the range of potential options.

Proposals versus Vetoes. Presidents vary in the degree to which they propose specific legislative programs or oppose competing congressional ideas. However, since the set of 266 requests includes only proposals, some surrogate measure of opposition must be created. Vetoes emerge as the logical candidate. The veto is the most visible method for the President to emphasize his opposition to congressional initiatives. Despite other, informal channels for opposition, the veto is the most convenient measure. Here, we are concerned with public and private bills. The contrast between the number of vetoes and OMB proposals is summarized in table 9. We are interested in the number of vetoes as a percentage of the total domestic agenda and in the average number of vetoes per year. The average number of vetoes per year helps us to compare the domestic agendas across time; the percentages help us to explore the texture of each agenda on its own. Whereas Nixon's *number* of vetoes is roughly average when compared with those of his Democratic colleagues, his vetoes represent a higher than average *proportion* of the agenda.

Several trends emerge from table 9. Most important, there is considerable variation in the proportional amount of presidential opposition. All Presidents oppose congressional action at one time or another, but few use the veto as an exclusive tool of policy. According to one Johnson assistant, "It is inevitable that the President will use the veto at some point. It's the best method to show the Congress he means business." Yet, the veto also engenders congressional hostility; for that reason, it is not the most effective means to accomplish policy goals. Consider the reaction of a Ford assistant: "The veto

Table 9. Proposals versus Vetoes

President	Proposals		Vetoes		Proposals as Percentage of Totals
	Total	Average per year	Total	Average per year	
Kennedy-Johnson	53	13	29	7	65%
Johnson	91	23	22	5	81
Nixon	65	11	43	7	58
Ford	16	8	66	33	20
Carter	41	10	29	7	59

Sources: OMB Legislative Reference Division clearance record; and *Public Papers of the Presidents of the United States,* 1961-80.

strategy had certain costs. Each veto crippled future opportunities for success; each veto eroded the President's already limited base of support. No President can afford to veto twenty-five bills a year, not in the 1970s at least. It's too damn much, and Congress won't stand for it."

Of the five recent executives, Ford exercised the veto most frequently; he is the only President to have had more vetoes than agenda proposals. The explanation does not rest entirely on the Democratic Congress. Though Nixon faced a hostile Congress throughout his tenure, his proposals still outnumbered his vetoes. Ford was the only recent President consciously to design a "veto strategy." Though there was no explicit decision to pursue the veto in lieu of legislation, the pattern evolved early in the Ford Presidency. "By March 1975 we knew that we were going to be using the veto frequently," a liaison officer remembered. "We never deliberately sat down and made the decision that we would veto sixty bills in two years. Each one came in separately and was reviewed separately. We knew that the veto was the best possible option. Given the composition of Congress and Ford's concern about inflation, it was the only alternative." Indeed, the liaison staff frequently pointed to their record. Of the sixty-six vetoes, fifty-four were sustained. "Do you know how difficult that was?" one aide asked. "We had to build a new bloc on each item. We were damn proud of the success."

For Kennedy, Johnson, Nixon, and Carter the proposals consistently outnumbered the vetoes. All four staffs viewed legislative proposals as the best route for reaching the President's policy goals. According to one Kennedy aide, "There is always some pressure to attack Congress when you are losing; always some advice to bring the veto down hard. However, if the President wants to accomplish anything, he has to present positive proposals. He has to make a mark on the legislative calendar." Even the Nixon and Ford staffs recognized the problems of opposition. Despite Democratic strength in Congress, the Nixon administration used the veto sparingly until 1972, when Nixon vetoed seventeen bills in six months; these vetoes constituted Nixon's attack on excessive congressional spending. Nixon's veto of the 1973 Labor-

Health, Education, and Welfare (HEW) appropriations bill was one of nine vetoes contained in a single package. Though the vetoes forestalled the spending problem, they were unsuccessful in the long run. As before, vetoes were a substitute for legislative compromise, a last resort in congressional stalemate. According to members of the Nixon liaison team, the President and top domestic assistants understood the need to present competing programs.

The Ford staff also knew the inherent problems of the veto strategy. In the short run, it helped Ford deal with his limited capital; in the long run, it decreased his opportunities and alienated potential members of the legislative coalition. According to one Ford assistant, the cumulative impact would have surfaced had Ford been elected in 1976: "Congress wouldn't have listened to Ford. The constant flood of vetoes had angered too many potential allies. We weren't able to offer anything substantial in place of the vetoed items either. We would send up the veto message and fight to sustain it. What we didn't do was send the message and present an alternative package. . . . it would have crippled us in 1977." Thus, the staff did not view the veto as a positive policy tool. Most emphasized the limits. The staffs did not discount the veto as a tactic in the legislative struggle; they believed, however, that proposals held the key to long-term policy impact. Vetoes are not interchangeable with solid legislative proposals. Ford's veto strategy was a poor substitute for solid legislative success. According to one Ford assistant,

> Why did we adopt the tactic? What choice did we have? We had virtually no support in Congress. We had lost forty seats in the mid-term elections. Public approval dropped thirty points between August and October. The pardon had angered a large group of liberal Democrats. There was no other alternative. We went to the veto strategy because it was the best method we had. It was never the best method possible. Besides, where would we have been if Ford had signed all the bills? Reagan would have made it into a major campaign issue.

The decision to pursue a veto strategy reflected Ford's assessment of his political resources. Given his congressional support, Ford and his staff agreed that the veto was the strongest alternative. Ford would not create an impressive record of success with Congress, but he would stand tall among Republicans. Certainly, there was little opportunity to present a competing platform. The policy machinery was incapable of producing a full legislative agenda in the shortened term; nor was Ford committed to a legislative offensive. As one aide argued, "We felt that we had to spend at least the first year restoring confidence. Remember what the resignation did. The President had to spend the first months rebuilding the Presidency and the public trust. It was not the time to present a full slate of programs."

Proposals involve a greater commitment of presidential resources than do vetoes. Since vetoes span a very limited time period, the President can concentrate what little capital he has on the specific battle. Proposals, however, involve a much larger investment; the commitment may last several years. According to one Nixon assistant, "It is much easier to turn to the veto. You don't have to devote too much energy over too long a time. At the most, the battle will last two weeks." Coalitions for vetoes are easier to build. As one Ford aide noted, "Putting together 34 like-minded senators or 147 representatives isn't as difficult as it may seem. It is a hell of a lot easier than pulling a majority into place. All you have to win is one House." Nor does the veto require a number of successive tests. It demands a single coalition for a single vote. Whereas a proposal often demands multiple coalitions across multiple decisions, the veto requires only an intensely focused effort at a specific moment. It is a very "cheap" alternative with temporary impact.

Presidents are keenly aware of the differing costs associated with proposals and vetoes. According to a Nixon domestic policy aide, "A veto is the least expensive of any choice, short of doing nothing. Depending upon the original legislation, all a veto requires is a signature. The burden is on the proponents. If the bill squeaked by in the first place, the President doesn't have to commit much at all." If the original bill was quite popular, however, the costs of opposition increase. Nixon's veto of the 1970 Hill-Burton Hospital Construction Act is an example. The veto was overriden, despite significant investments of presidential capital. The cumulative impact of vetoes may also affect the costs of proposals. Vetoes alter the climate in Congress, creating greater hostility and resistance. If the President finally presents a proposal after a period of intense veto activity, the costs may be greater than anticipated. As one Ford assistant argued, "Once we began to use the veto regularly, the Congress never came back to the mood for passage. In part, we lost the energy package because of the vetoes. Why should they have listened to us after sixty vetoes?"

If opposition reflects low levels of presidential capital, it also involves presidential goals. If Ford did not endear himself to the Democratic Congress, he did not alienate the Republican party. Though Ford wanted a measure of legislative success, he also wanted to run for election in 1976; Ford had to be nominated by Republicans, not Democrats. The veto offered one way to demonstrate his ideological commitment. Moreover, the veto was the only avenue to accomplish Ford's policy goals. According to James Reichley, a staff consultant in the Ford administration,

> The administration had positive legislative objectives in areas like defense, energy, deregulation of the economy, and tax policy, for which it sought majority support in Congress. But Ford's main legislative effort was devoted to achieving what he viewed as the highest governmental priority of the age: restraint of the growth of federal spending. . . . To secure these objectives, while spending more for defense, which he also believed was necessary, Ford called for more drastic cuts in the growth of domestic social programs than had ever been attempted by Nixon, even

during the budgetary offensive of 1973. In the battle that followed, Ford's chief legislative weapon was the presidential veto, which gave him formidable power so long as he held the support of one-third plus one in either the House or the Senate (Reichley 1981, p. 323).

Once Ford selected fiscal restraint as a prime domestic issue, he had few other alternatives beyond the veto. Thus, both Nixon and Ford had goals that were consistent with a greater level of veto activity. The movement toward opposition was affected by dwindling presidential capital, reinforced by Nixon and Ford's political goals.

In both administrations, the increased use of the veto coincided with growing concern with federal spending. Ford, in particular, saw the veto as a central weapon in the fight against an expanding federal budget. "We had to use the veto to protect the budget," a Ford OMB aide recalled. "Dealing with a Democratic Congress, more importantly a liberal Congress, forced us to use the veto to hold down spending." Yet, even in this case the veto was the result of low levels of congressional support. Both the Nixon and Ford administrations would have preferred to influence the budget through legislative compromise—as Reagan did early in 1981. Given the absence of party support and rapidly falling public approval, neither President could secure the congressional backing to head off potential budgetary expansion. The veto was an avenue of last resort.*

Legislation versus Administration. Presidents who limit their legislative programs might be expected to spend more resources on administrative alternatives. By Nixon's third year in office, for instance, he had openly switched to an administrative Presidency, with a domestic program characterized by efforts to control social service expenditures, appointments, regulations, and reorganization. For our purposes, it is extremely difficult to measure such administrative activity. One useful measure of executive action rests on the numbered series of executive orders. A frequent source of executive action, the orders reflect clear presidential intent. The series allows us to count the exact number of executive orders in each administration (see table 10). However, it is important to remember that executive orders constitute only one channel of executive action.

Perhaps the most interesting finding in table 10 is the absence of significant variation across administrations. For Kennedy, Johnson, Nixon,

*The emphasis on opposition led in late 1970 to the institutionalization of an OMB monitoring effort called the "legislative watchlist." OMB budget analysts were instructed to track potentially difficult bills and to identify possible veto candidates. If a bill violated either the President's budget or the legislative program, it would be placed on the watchlist. This watchlist was then circulated to the White House and interested departments. Started sometime in late 1970 at the request of the Nixon staff, it was continued and expanded under Ford and remained in effect under Carter. It is a prime example of OMB's effort to respond to the needs of the President. However, the watchlist was less important to Carter than it had been to both Nixon and Ford.

Table 10. Executive Orders

President	Orders	
	Total	Average per year
Kennedy-Johnson	278	70
Johnson	255	64
Nixon	375	63
Ford	121	61
Carter	318	79

Source: *Federal Register,* 1961-80.

and Ford there is only a marginal difference in the average number of orders per year. If Nixon pursued an "administrative Presidency" (Nathan 1975), it is not evident in his absolute number of executive orders. Only Carter stands out in terms of the level of executive orders, in part because he used orders for a higher degree of "administrative tinkering" and in part because he needed them to implement several complicated domestic and foreign programs. The implementation of the Iranian hostage agreement in 1981, for instance, required ten separate executive orders.

Executive action involves far more than the issuance of executive orders, however. Nixon's "administrative Presidency" used a variety of executive tactics, including selective appointments, impoundment of appropriated funds, reorganization, and tightening of regulations. Why did Nixon opt for the administrative approach? According to the Nixon staff, the decision reflected the frustrations of dealing with a Democratic Congress. "We simply could not get passage of the kinds of programs we wanted," one Nixon aide argued. "The only choice was to focus on administration. We started to catalogue a list of programs that could be tightened from the White House. It was an unpleasant option when compared to our original hopes, but it was about all we could do." Despite reports to the contrary, Nixon's effort to control domestic policy was limited. It is doubtful whether the strategy would have produced long-term impact even without Watergate. The administrative Presidency was at best a very temporary approach, subject to increasing congressional and judicial surveillance.

Ultimately, the Nixon effort failed on two counts. Initially, Watergate intervened. As Richard Nathan notes,

> On April 30, 1973, John Ehrlichman, the driving force behind all of these preparations, was gone. Soon, too, the designations of the super secretaries were removed. As the new White House staff was assembled in the late spring and summer of 1973, it came into being in a far different setting. The mandate of 1972 was dissipated. Decisive action, including unneeded fights with program bureaucracies and congressional committees, could not be undertaken now (Nathan 1975, p. 76).

More important, Congress began to limit the President's administrative discretion. A decade of congressional backlash has created severe restrictions on administration as a future domestic alternative. Congress refused, for instance, to renew the President's reorganization authority in 1973, and when Carter finally succeeded in winning restoration in 1977, the power was limited. Presidents could no longer easily eliminate statutory programs, nor could they press for more than three reorganization plans at any one time. Congress also passed the Budget and Impoundment Control Act of 1974. Coupled with changes in the congressional budget process, the bill severely limited the President's ability to impound or defer federal funds. Congress now demands strict accounting of impoundment and reserves the right to approve or disapprove major rescissions. The era of massive impoundment is over. Presidents have to cooperate with Congress if they wish to rework the budget. Moreover, Congress has increased its oversight of executive implementation and has begun to use the legislative veto quite frequently. Indeed, the rise of the legislative veto signals a dramatic change in the President's rule-making discretion. Congress has restricted the impact of executive action, while demanding a greater legislative role.

Regardless of the administrative channel—whether executive orders, impoundment, or reorganization—the White House staffs discounted the impact of executive action. Though Presidents can achieve policy ends through administrative means, legislation still remained the preferred alternative, at least among the 126 respondents. As one media observer remarked, "I doubt very much if Nixon's administrative Presidency would have succeeded with or without Watergate. It was a very narrow-sighted strategy, as evidenced by its failure as soon as Ehrlichman left. Any program that falters as soon as the key figures leave isn't worth its weight. It is the programs that survive long *after* they leave that are important." The White House staffs offered several explanations for the lukewarm acceptance of the administrative alternatives.

First, the executive option is generally reserved for routine decisions; it is not perceived as a suitable alternative for major initiatives. Executive orders, for example, offer a very limited and temporary alternative for policy initiatives. According to one study of over eleven thousand orders (Schramm 1977), less than 7 percent could be classified as having a discretionary impact; but 70 percent dealt with routine problems in an "ordinary problem context." Moreover, nearly three-fifths of all orders focused on the civil service or the Department of the Interior land policies—rarely topics of concern for the White House staff. This is not to argue that all orders are minor; rather, the bulk of executive orders have only limited policy impact. As one OMB officer observed,

> Nixon's administrative strategy was quite limited, and the media's response remarkable. The Democrats were very concerned about Nixon's adminis-

trative maneuvers, but most of us believed that the approach was both short-sighted and temporary. Executive orders and rule-making do not lead to the same results as legislation. Nixon's administrative strategy was very limited in the long run. It was like a temporary filling.

At best, most administrative options involve "executive tinkering." Though orders, regulations, and reorganization have an impact on the distribution of political benefits, they lack the glamor of legislative programs. Executive orders took on a slightly greater prominence in the early moments of the Reagan administration, as the new President searched for ways to make early impact. Given the delays involved in moving legislation through a split Congress, Reagan sought to issue a series of executive orders, of which the most prominent was a freeze on federal hiring. Yet, once again, executive action was a substitute for legislation. It was precisely because Congress could not act fast enough that Reagan opted for the orders—they were a temporary tool.

Second, executive action is often viewed as a short-term solution. Even when Presidents use executive orders to accomplish major policy goals—Kennedy's equal opportunity orders, for example—the staff recognized the need for eventual legislative action. The Kennedy staff interpreted the civil rights orders as a product of the legislative stalemate. According to one assistant, "The President had to issue the orders. We just could not justify moving a major bill in 1961. We understood that we couldn't make any long-term impact with the orders, but that was about all we could do." The White House staffs viewed legislative action as having greater impact and legitimacy. Once again, Nixon's "administrative Presidency" serves as an example. As one HEW officer suggested, "The President's decision to dismantle the OEO [the Office of Economic Opportunity] and tighten welfare regulations simply didn't have the same force as legislation. Executive action is easier to fight and easier to undermine. The career civil service is not inclined to agree with executive action if the executive action doesn't agree with them."

There is a glimmer of hope for administrative alternatives in the recently created Senior Executive Service (SES), an elite group of former civil service supergrades who now occupy some 8,500 positions within the executive branch. Members of the SES gave up much of their traditional civil service protection in exchange for greater mobility, status, and pay. There is also the potential for very sizable bonuses for exemplary service in the SES. Moreover, each President can add noncareer appointees to the SES, thereby creating a more politicized senior talent pool. Theoretically, the President can shuffle members of the SES into and out of jobs that are particularly important. At the start of the Reagan administration, the SES received considerable attention. Reagan aides dreamed of seizing control of the executive branch through replacement of hostile bureaucrats. Unfortunately, like many other administrative alternatives, the SES is highly limited as a tool of policy. First, no member of the SES can be reassigned within 120 days of the inauguration of a new President. Further, no member can be reassigned within 120 days of the appointment of a new department head or agency supervisor. No member of the SES can be involuntarily moved to another agency—a provision which restricts movement even within an executive department. Though each new President is allowed to appoint a group of noncareerists to the SES, at least 40 percent of all SES positions are specifically reserved for careerists. Finally, the appeal process for SES removal or transfer is both intricate and time-consuming. Given these restrictions, the Reagan enthusiasm for the SES may be short-lived. The advantage of the SES, however, may rest not in its formal structure but in the ability of the President or a department head to make an example of one reluctant bureaucrat in the hopes of frightening the rest. Yet, even here, the specific rules of the SES limit removal or reassignment. President Reagan is likely to be much more successful by working through Congress or by gentle persuasion. Frontal attacks on the executive branch have not been notably successful. Though the legislative channel is the most expensive, it is also the most effective.

Large Programs versus Small Programs. Presidents have a degree of discretion to select either large or small programs for the domestic agenda. Our problem is to distinguish between the large and the small. One method is to ask how many people are affected by the given program—the more people, the larger the program. Another is to ask how much each program costs—the more money, the larger the initiative. Still another method is to look for controversy—the greater the controversy, the larger the program. In the following analysis, the distinction between large and small will be based on a combination of all three definitions. However, we will be interested more in the *perceptions* of size within Congress and the Presidency than in any absolute measure of largeness or smallness. As such, size is often a function of controversy and perceived importance. For convenience, the large programs are defined simply as all presidential requests listed in the *Congressional Quarterly*'s "Legislative Boxscore." The boxscore focuses on what the *Quarterly* views as the top 10-15 issues on the legislative agenda and should not be confused with the now defunct "Presidential Boxscore." The "Legislative Boxscore," which reflects the assessment of the major issues under consideration during the given session, can be found in the *Congressional Quarterly Almanacs.* Unfortunately, since the *Quarterly* abandoned the boxscore in 1979, a careful reading of the legislative record must suffice for coding the last two years of the Carter administration. The number of large and small programs for the 1961-80 period is summarized in table 11.

There is considerable variation among the five Presidents in the sheer number of large and small agenda programs. Johnson leads recent executives in the average number of large programs per year. As one LBJ assistant remarked, "Johnson didn't want the programs unless they were big. His entire concept of the legislative process was to go for the dramatic; he wanted a War on Poverty and a Great Society. It was a Texan's dream." A

Table 11. Large Programs versus Small Programs

| President | Large Programs | | Small Programs | | Large Programs as Percentage of Total Programs |
	Total	Average per year	Total	Average per year	
Kennedy-Johnson	28	7	25	6	53%
Johnson	50	12	41	10	55
Nixon	23	4	42	7	35
Ford	8	4	8	4	50
Carter	22	6	19	5	54

Sources: OMB Legislative Reference Division clearance record; and *Congressional Quarterly Almanac*, 1961-78.

second Johnson aide agreed: "Once he declared war on poverty, he had to have a major program. War involved a major assault. A series of small interventions didn't fit with his concept of war." One OMB official noted half-jokingly that Johnson's problem was insomnia:

> He'd wake up in the middle of the night and have nothing to do. He might read for a while or get a drink, but finally he would wander down to the Oval Office. He'd sit down and start rummaging through the memos and drafts. By morning, what were small programs were major commitments. Johnson would spend his sleepless hours redrafting the programs. We might not have had such a "great" society if he had been able to sleep eight hours a night.

Both Kennedy and Carter also emphasized large initiatives, but to a lesser extent than Johnson. Carter, in contrast to contemporary press accounts, tried to limit the number of large programs moving to Congress in 1977. "We saw what the Great Society had done," one aide remarked. "We were dealing with its aftermath. Look at welfare reform. It was designed to correct some of the problems with the War on Poverty. That was the purpose of regulatory reform as well." Carter may have felt that he didn't have the political strength to carry a full slate of large initiatives. It was a problem echoed by the Kennedy staff. As one Kennedy assistant argued, "The President has two choices when he doesn't have enough congressional support: he can send up everything and blame Congress for the failures or he can tone down the program. We didn't feel that the first choice was reasonable. It's damn hard to blame your own party for the failures. We had to cut some of our programs down to size. That's part of the reason why Kennedy scaled down aid to education."

Both Nixon and Ford pursued a greater percentage of small programs than did their Democratic colleagues. "We had several critical items," a Nixon legislative aide argued, "but our preference was to start with a smaller intervention and see how it worked. Our orientation was to present the first draft as a limited program and build on it later." That was the case with revenue sharing. Originally, the revenue-sharing program called for a rather limited federal investment of $50 million. By 1970 the program had to be "sweetened" to generate greater state and local support. As one Domestic Council member remarked, "The governors didn't come on board until we increased the funding level. We couldn't get their support until the dollar amounts made the fight worthwhile." For Ford, the problem in developing large-scale policy rested on political capital. "We didn't feel the time was right for a series of broad initiatives," one aide argued. "That is not to say we didn't have them. We were looking at national health insurance and another version of welfare reform. However, we didn't feel that we could get much progress with the items. We thought the President could be elected in 1976 and decided to wait."

Given their prior party experience, both Nixon and Ford may have had a natural Republican preference for smaller programs. However, capital remains the most powerful explanation for variation in large and small programs. Capital definitely influenced Ford's decision to pursue more limited programs. "There was no point in presenting a full set of compre- hensive items," a Ford legislative liaison officer argued. "Congress would not have acted. Even if we had moved a series of heavy measures, we wouldn't have won. After the 1974 midterms, we only had 144 Republicans in the House. How could we hope for any major success?" Nor was the Ford adminis- tration equipped to produce a full slate of large items. Once again, resources are the key. With only two years remaining in the term and the policy process in ruins, there were limits on the capability to generate new programs. Most of the large items introduced in early 1975 had been in the works before the Nixon resignation. Ford had very little time or staff energy to produce a major agenda effort. Instead, the administration chose to concentrate on inflation as the top priority. That choice eventually produced a "no new spending" rule. Unless the specific issue focused on energy, Ford would not consider any new commitments of federal funds.

Presidential capital affected all five presidential agendas. Not only did Johnson express an ideological commitment to large-scale programs but he could afford to pursue their passage. "I suppose that was a major reason behind the Great Society," one Johnson aide admitted. "We had the votes in Congress to present that kind of agenda. We had the support to get it through committee and onto the floor; we had the power to secure some semblance of implementation." The percentages of large versus small programs match the measures of presidential capital for all but Ford. Johnson has the highest proportion of large initiatives, Nixon the lowest. As one media observer suggested, "The Ford and Nixon people knew what was happening. They understood the problems with Congress. That is why they moved toward the administrative strategy. Even then, they couldn't make massive alterations in the federal system." This is not to argue that small programs are insignificant; according to Campbell (1978), small programs may have the greatest long-term impact. It is true that Nixon's effort to alter welfare policy through adjustment of administrative rules was temporarily successful. Yet, while Nixon could tighten regulations, shift personnel, impound funds, and rewrite rules, he could not alter the major thrust of welfare policy. That demanded a large-scale legislative effort.

It might also be argued that the President's preference for large or small programs is shaped by an interaction between goals and capital. Ford's natural preference for small-scale programs fits closely with his lack of political support; Johnson's predisposition toward large-scale initiatives paralleled his political opportunities in Congress. Yet, even here, the interaction is dominated by capital. That is one finding from the first weeks of the Reagan administration. Faced with a Republican majority in the Senate and a viable conservative majority in the House, Reagan presented a series of large-scale budget revisions. Totaling over $67 billion for fiscal 1982 alone and over $400 billion for the 1982-86 period, Reagan's requests demonstrated the impact of capital on program size. Though Reagan's requests were conservative in substance, they were large in scope. Both Nixon and Ford had expressed a similar desire to cut federal spending: that was the goal of Nixon's impoundments in 1971 and 1972 and of Ford's "no new spending" rule in 1974-76. Unlike Reagan, however, neither Nixon nor Ford had the political capital to pursue large-scale revisions. Given the same congressional support, Nixon and Ford would have made similar large-scale reductions in the federal budget. Indeed, many former Nixon and Ford aides joined the Reagan White House staff in 1981 to participate in just those decisions. Though goals have an important impact in guiding the search for alternatives, capital remains the determining factor in the size of specific requests.

New Programs versus Old Programs. Presidents also vary with regard to new programs versus old programs. In measuring the number of new and old programs, each of the 266 agenda items was reviewed with respect to a very simple question: Did the program involve a new departure in domestic policy or a modification of a past initiative? Medicare is a good example of a new program; expansion of the minimum wage is an equally valid example of an old program. The number of new and old programs is presented in table 12.

In table 12 Nixon emerges as the President with the greatest proportion of new programs, an unexpected result given Nixon's capital. If we remove Nixon from the table, the results are in line with the distribution of capital: Johnson leads in new proposals, followed by Carter, Kennedy, and Ford. Yet, the Nixon agenda remains an anomaly. According to the Nixon staff, there are several potential explanations for the figures. One may rest on Nixon's drive for reelection. Recall that Nixon led all five Presidents in his emphasis of electoral benefits (table 6). According to one Nixon aide, "The President was clearly worried about both Kennedy and Muskie. He wanted to

Table 12. New Programs versus Old Programs

President	New Programs		Old Programs		New Programs as Percentage of Total Programs
	Total	Average per year	Total	Average per year	
Kennedy-Johnson	33	8	20	5	62%
Johnson	55	14	36	9	60
Nixon	46	12	19	5	71
Ford	6	3	10	5	44
Carter	25	6	16	4	61

Source: OMB Legislative Reference Division clearance record.

make sure that he was viewed as a different kind of Republican. He wanted to present new ideas and carve a legislative record to match his opponents. He wanted to show that Republicans weren't passive, that Republicans could present new ideas."

A second answer may rest on Nixon's reliance on the executive branch for ideas. Recall that Nixon believed that the country could run itself domestically. As an OMB aide remembered, "Once Nixon turned control over to the Domestic Council and the departments, we received a flood of ideas that had failed in the Johnson administration. Nixon offered a second chance. He wanted a dramatic program, and the agencies provided plenty of material." A third reason may rest on Nixon's concept of the "New Federalism." The very nature of the program meant a restructuring of the federal purpose. Programs had to be not only modified but redirected. In order to make an impact on federal policy, Nixon had to concentrate on fundamental departures from past programs. Johnson's success with the Great Society forced Nixon toward an agenda composed of new programs.

The most persuasive explanation rests on this description of the status quo; Nixon had little choice but to present new initiatives. To adopt modifications of old Democratic programs would have been contrary to his political goals. One way to explore the Nixon paradox is to ask the inverse question, Why did Kennedy, Johnson, and Carter concentrate on more old programs than Nixon? Simply stated, given the legislative success of Roosevelt's New Deal, Kennedy, Johnson, and Carter experienced less pressure to produce new programs. As one Kennedy aide noted, "Our job was to extend the New Deal into the 1960s. We wanted to expand the programs and revise their impact. We wanted to complete some of the unfinished business." The answer also involves the Democrats' greater success in Congress. In 1968, most of Johnson's "old" requests focused on programs he had initiated, so he could focus on amending his previous successes. The Democrats did not have to present a full set of new programs to accomplish their program ends. Given the nature of the federal system, most Democratic suggestions for change could be easily tied to past initiatives; most Republican requests for change would be for substantial redirections of the status quo. The Republican Presidents were in the unenviable position of trying to change the system while dealing with an opposition Congress. By the early 1970s the status quo had become increasingly a Democratic animal.

Perhaps the most viable method for reconciling Nixon's emphasis on the new programs is to compare the new/old content with the large/small. How much of the Nixon agenda comprised *large*-new departures? How much concentrated on *small*-new proposals? By blending the two categories, we can generate a much richer picture of the domestic alternatives. The two dimensions are combined for each President in table 13.

Table 13 contains several important findings. First, though Nixon has the greatest percentage of new proposals, the bulk of the items rest on small-scale initiatives. Of Nixon's forty-six new requests, twenty-eight were small. Though Nixon could present a substantial number of new proposals, he could not sustain action on a similar number of large items; he simply did not have the necessary capital.

Moreover, contrary to the expectations of the civics book image of the Presidency, for all Presidents the majority of presidential requests do not involve large-new programs. On the domestic level, only one-third of agenda requests can be classified as large-new initiatives. If the requests of the five presidents are combined, less than 34 percent of the domestic agenda centers on what might be called major items. Presidents do not have the necessary internal resources to generate that many comprehensive items. From a decision-making perspective, Presidents do not have enough time, information, expertise, or energy to pursue that many large-new items. From a legislative perspective, Presidents do not have enough capital to secure passage of an agenda comprising only large-new items. Presidents spend a great deal of time dealing with routine domestic policy.

In the mixture of large/small and new/old programs, there is considerable variation in the content of the five agendas. Once again, Johnson and Ford serve as counterpoints: Johnson stressed large-new proposals in roughly 39 percent of his agenda requests, but Ford in only 25 percent. Ford's emphasis is one more example of the impact of both restricted capital and conservative ideology. According to the staff, Ford actively encouraged the small items. The effort stemmed from Ford's attempt to regain control of the federal budget, as well as the "no new spending" rule. That led the staff to remove the large-scale items from the pool of potential alternatives—national health insurance and welfare reform were ruled out long before they could reach the agenda. It also led the staff to search for small-scale items. Since the large-new items could not pass, the staff concentrated its energy on the smaller initiatives. The Ford staff lowered its expectations in the short term, hoping for a second chance in the winter of 1977. As one media observer suggested, "It would have been very interesting to see what Ford would have done had he been elected in 1976. My impression is that he would have

Table 13. Large/Small Programs versus New/Old Programs

President	Large-new		Large-old		Small-new		Small-old	
	Number	Percent	Number	Percent	Number	Percent	Number	Percent
Kennedy-Johnson	19	36%	14	26%	9	17%	11	21%
Johnson	35	39	20	22	15	17	21	23
Nixon	18	28	5	8	28	43	14	22
Ford	4	25	4	25	2	13	6	39
Carter	16	39	6	15	9	22	10	24

Source: OMB Legislative Reference Division clearance record.
Note: This table includes combined information from tables 11 and 12.

produced some very interesting programs. I know they were preparing a new surge on welfare reform and more deregulation. My feeling is that Ford would have followed Nixon's path—a lot of new ideas toward expansion of the New Federalism."

Finally, table 13 helps settle a longstanding question about the Carter administration. Throughout 1977 and 1978 the Carter administration was repeatedly accused of sending too much legislation to Congress. We have already seen that in absolute terms Carter presented no more than Kennedy or Johnson had. Carter exceeded neither Kennedy nor Johnson in his requests for large-new items; indeed, Carter's pattern is fairly consistent with those of his predecessors. But Carter faced a dramatically different congressional atmosphere. The competition for agenda space had increased. As we shall see, Carter's problem was compounded by the absence of explicit priorities. He did not rank his top agenda items, leaving Congress to guess which programs came first.

Spending versus Nonspending. Beyond the choice of large programs versus small, new versus old, Presidents must decide on a "strategy of intervention," that is, the specific tool of policy impact—allocation of federal funds or regulation. There are at least two ways to tap the distinction. First, we can compare the absolute number of spending requests with that of nonspending requests. Here, the 266 agenda items serve as a guide to programmatic content. A second method to measure spending policy rests on the calculation of actual program costs. Ford may have selected only a handful of spending programs, but the few could have committed a great deal of money; Johnson may have presented a wide range of spending requests, but the many could have expended very litte. Unfortunately, it is very difficult to measure long-term program costs, and it is often impossible to estimate the actual expense. Some programs may be more efficient than others in spending funds; others may be more effective in finding recipients. Thus, we will use estimates of each program's first-year costs as a guide to spending policy. These first-year figures give us an insight into the President's thinking, and more importantly, they are obtainable. Adjusting these first-year costs for inflation, we can generate a very simple measure of spending commitments. The number of spending requests and the total first-year costs are summarized in table 14. The first-year costs given are only ball-park estimates, based on the available public record. The figures do not represent the total costs involved in each long-range spending request, but only the anticipated funding in the first year of each program. Nor does the spending figure include guarantees for loans such as the Chrysler loan, Ford's energy corporation, or Carter's Synfuels program.

Table 14 demonstrates the decreasing preference for spending policy in the past decade. Starting with the Nixon administration, there was a steady drop in the number of spending requests until Carter entered office.

Table 14. Spending versus Nonspending

| President | Spending Programs[a] | | Nonspending Programs | | Spending Programs as Percentage of Total Programs | First-year Costs[b] (billions of dollars) |
	Total	Average per year	Total	Average per year		
Kennedy-Johnson	33	8	20	5	62%	8.8
Johnson	49	12	44	11	53	5.1
Nixon I	13	3	27	7	34	3.4
Nixon II	7	3	18	9	28	1.4
Ford	5	2	11	5	31	2.0
Carter	16	4	25	6	39	4.5

Source: OMB Legislative Reference Division clearance record.
[a] Programs that required federal funds.
[b] First-year costs as estimated by the White House, expressed in 1972 dollars; these figures should be viewed as approximate.

According to the Johnson staff, the decline began as early as 1966. "The economy was definitely starting to turn," one economic advisor noted. "Inflation was beginning to heat up. You have to remember that in 1966 an inflation rate of 4 percent was considered unacceptable. As the war stepped up, the economy turned down." Some economists blamed the price spiral on the tax cut of 1964; it had been late and was characterized by one aide as "like pouring gasoline on a fire." Others emphasized the heavy expenditure levels of the first and second quarters of 1965. Yet, whatever the precise explanation, by December 1965 Johnson received the first of many warnings on the need for a tax increase to slow unrestrained economic growth. Until 1966 Johnson was unwilling to tone down plans for the Great Society. Economic pressure eventually forced Johnson to accept the steadily growing advice for a tax surcharge to cool the economy and a tightening of spending policy. According to the Johnson staff, the fall of 1966 was the turning point. From that point on, Johnson pursued a more restrictive spending stance. "We began to tone down the programs," one Johnson legislative assistant remarked. "We did not ask for as much in total dollars. We also lengthened the program life to spread the expenditures over a longer time frame. We received the message to cut back, and we did."

That message was not lost on the Nixon administration. Nixon's first term reflected the growing preference for nonspending alternatives and tighter budgetary control. Yet, even in 1969 the economic pressure had not reached its peak. Legislative aides still talked of the "peace dividend" that would come with the end of the war; Nixon produced the first balanced budget in two decades. From the anticipated surplus, Nixon fashioned three major expenditure programs: welfare reform, revenue sharing, and expanded public transit. According to a Nixon aide, "The economic crunch didn't hit until the third and fourth years, 1971-72. Up to that point, we were cutting back certain programs to meet the balanced budget, but we still had several large items ourselves. People sometimes forget that the welfare plan was a huge commitment in terms of federal dollars." There were budgetary skirmishes in the first term, but nothing that resembled the coming war. At least in 1969, Nixon's New Federalism involved a degree of allocative policy. By 1973 that was no longer true.

By the start of Nixon's second term, cuts in spending policy became a domestic priority. Inflation was increasing rapidly, and there was a consensus within the program staffs that a "no new spending" rule was in effect. Welfare reform dropped from the agenda, to be replaced by an attempt to reduce fraud. Revenue sharing continued, but without commitments of new federal funds. Whereas Nixon had proposed a moderate increase in spending commitments between 1969 and 1972, he cut back sharply in his second term. As one Nixon aide argued,

> There was heavy pressure to bring expenditure items in line. It was our job to see where we could cut funds, not where we could spend them. The President's top economic advisors pushed hard for a tight money policy, both at the Federal Reserve and in the legislative program. Money definitely dropped as a solution for problems. There was in infusion of regulatory expertise into the domestic process.

A second assistant agreed: "The Council of Economic Advisers had most of the influence. Nixon was convinced that a restrictive policy was critical. We did not bring too many expenditure items forward in the second term. They would not have received a hearing."

The drop in spending policy was reflected in Nixon's changing budget policy. Starting in 1970 and culminating with Nixon's 1972 demand for a $250 billion spending ceiling, the budget emerged as a battleground for domestic policy. Whereas Nixon had flirted with impoundment of appropriated funds in his first term, the tactic became a primary weapon in 1973. Following his second inaugural, Nixon impounded $6 billion in pollution-control funds, $225 million in the rural environmental assistance program, $10 million from the water bank program, and more than $10 billion from other domestic commitments. As Allen Schick argues,

> After he lost the spending limitation battle in 1972 but won the election, President Nixon embarked on a large-scale effort to overturn the priorities established by Congress. Far from the administrative routine, Nixon's impoundments in late 1972 and 1973 were designed to rewrite national policy at the expense of congressional power and intent. Rather than the deferment of expenses, Nixon's aim was the cancellation of unwanted programs (Schick 1980, p. 46).

Nixon's actions eventually prompted increased congressional surveillance in the form of the 1974 Budget and Impoundment Control Act, thereby limiting future presidential budget impact *outside* of the legislative channel. As before,

Nixon's budgetary strategy—whether in the form of vetoes or impoundment —was a poor substitute for legislative cooperation. Moreover, the strategy is no longer available to contemporary Presidents. Under the Budget and Impoundment Control Act, the President must receive approval for even the simplest rescission.

Yet, just as inflation was beginning its greatest acceleration, in 1974, Nixon presented a plan for comprehensive national health insurance, with an estimated first-year cost of two billion dollars. According to many observers, the decision was part of an effort to salvage Nixon's crippled Presidency. As one Ford Domestic Council assistant reflected, national health insurance was introduced to direct attention away from Watergate: "Nixon was obviously concerned with the impeachment proceedings. National health insurance was something to refocus the congressional agenda back onto substantive policy. I don't think the President gave a damn about costs at that point. He wanted to save his administration and thought health insurance might appease the Democrats."

Immediately upon assuming office, Ford repeated that request for a national health plan, calling for immediate action in Congress. Scarcely six months later he had dropped the proposal. According to the Ford staff, economic pressures led to the reversal. Originally, the Ford administration had expected major problems with unemployment in 1975, lending support to a more flexible spending program. Moreover, Ford did not want to alienate an already hostile Congress. However, as the economic forecasts cleared, inflation became the dominant concern and led to Ford's spending moratorium. "The President felt it was his first priority to reduce inflation," an assistant remarked. "The President was unwilling to consider any new spending programs and was reluctant to review even requests for minor increases. He was fundamentally committed to reducing the deficit."

Carter's agenda involves some confusion. Like Nixon and Ford, Carter continued the effort to restrict the absolute number of spending requests. Whereas Carter's Democratic predecessors' spending programs had constituted about 50 percent of their total agendas, for Carter they constituted only 39 percent. Yet, whereas Nixon and Ford had reduced their total first-year figures, Carter jumped to $4.5 billion (adjusted for inflation). On one hand Carter expressed a preference for nonspending solutions; on the other he endorsed the traditional Democratic spending program. Carter had fewer absolute spending requests than did Kennedy and Johnson, but those few requests cost a considerable amount.

Carter's domestic agenda reflects two basic pressures. Much of Carter's $4.5 billion came from his 1980 agenda. Up to that point Carter had limited his total budget increases. With the coming of the 1980 election, Carter may have decided to use spending as an electoral advantage. Though Carter refused to propose the traditional election-year tax cut, he did request both national health insurance and a youth training program. We have already noted that Carter's decision on national health insurance was closely tied to the drive for reelection. Here, we might argue that Carter's increased spending in 1979-80 also is related to electoral pressure. By mid-summer 1980 Carter's agenda had jumped back onto the roller-coaster ride. National health insurance was off again; Carter steadfastly refused to accept a Kennedy-sponsored twelve-billion-dollar jobs program; youth training was dead. This dramatic shift was intimately linked to the worsening of inflation and the impending Reagan nomination. Once Carter had disposed of Edward Kennedy in the primaries, he changed directions to meet Reagan's challenge from the conservative right. Budget-cutting was once more a priority.

Carter's early spending policy focused on his perception of unemployment as the most important economic priority. The main sources of spending in the 1977-78 period were welfare reform, youth employment, public-service employment, business incentives for the poor, and expanded urban assistance. In all but one case—welfare reform—Carter's allocative policies focused on unemployment. Thus, Carter's first major legislative request focused on the ill-fated fifty-dollar tax rebate, a proposal designed to stimulate economic growth. Several aides blamed the early decisions on economic advice that failed to predict the rapidly accelerating inflation. Carter had been much more of a traditional Democrat than most believed, entering office with a standard slate of employment programs. Ford had left office with some success in cutting inflation; Carter may have expected a continued decline. By the end of the first three months, inflation reappeared as the top economic concern. The fifty-dollar tax rebate was quickly dropped. The resulting economic pressure steadily increased until 1979 when Carter announced his "real wage insurance," a program initially designed to reward workers who settled for wage increases below the inflation rate. According to the Carter staff, there was considerable internal pressure to restrict both the number and the amount of spending policies. Carter clearly wanted to convey both the image and the substance of a tight economic policy.

The Budget and Domestic Alternatives. A decade of increasing pressure and competition have raised the federal budget to a new level of importance within the domestic policy process. The 1980 Republican demand for increased defense spending, coupled with pressure for tax cuts, leaves the budget as a new battleground for domestic policy. The Ford, Carter, and Reagan administrations have focused on the battle for scarce federal funds to a far greater extent than did their 1960 predecessors. The budget has become the embodiment of both foreign and domestic priorities. With Reagan's commitment to cuts in both spending and taxes, the budget has become a significant tool for achieving domestic goals.

Much of the renewed pressure on the budget comes from the steady drop in spending flexibility. Over the past two decades, the budget has been increasingly restricted by "uncontrollable" commitments. Yet, as the available dollars have dropped, the number of claimants has risen. There is less money available but more demand. In the first moments of the Reagan administration, for instance, the federal budget was caught in a squeeze between proponents of expanded defense spending and advocates of massive tax cuts. Eventually, the Reagan administration opted for both, leaving domestic policy to absorb the shortfall. We will return to the problem of uncontrollables in chapter 6. For now, it is important to note that a decade of steadily rising inflation has placed increased focus on the budget as a means to policy ends. This pressure on scarce federal funds will not decline in the near future; there will be fewer dollars to spend but ever-burgeoning demands.

Changing public attitudes also have contributed to the rise of the budget as a political symbol. A renewed public interest in the size of federal spending has added to pressures on scarce federal resources. As in the early 1960s, Presidents must now be concerned with the symbolic impact of budget policy. The pressure is particularly reminiscent to Kennedy aides, specifically those who fought to keep the 1963 budget from topping the hundred-billion-dollar level. As one Kennedy aide remembered, "We were so cautious not to step over that line. As long as we kept below the $100 [billion] threshold, we were fine. But even if we only hit $100.01 [billion], we thought we'd be in trouble." Today as in 1961, Presidents must be careful to avoid the spending label. Regardless of the objective impact, Presidents must watch the budget for its political effect. This symbolic pressure is compounded by the prevailing wisdom that federal spending has an important bearing on inflation. With inflation as the number one public concern, Presidents cannot gamble with high-expenditure programs. The current political and economic climates have eliminated allocative policy as a viable domestic alternative.

Budgeting thus takes on an increased visibility in the domestic policy process. As programs are weighed for costs and benefits, Presidents will need to spend more time and energy on the budget. As one Johnson aide said, "In the Great Society, the actual costs were just about the last thing you looked at. It wasn't that important. We wanted to know if the programs would pass and if Lyndon would be happy. Money—or the lack of it—was never a problem, at least until the war heated up." Today, money is the most important factor; estimates of potential costs have become critical hurdles in the policy debate.

Democrats versus Republicans

To this point, we have considered differences between individual Presidents. It is also important to examine differences between the parties. Such differences are one guide to "responsible parties." If the Democrats and Republicans differ in their choice of domestic alternatives, perhaps voters are not so "irrational" in casting ballots on the basis of party identification.

Furthermore, differences between the two parties may add support to the theory of legislative expense. Given Democratic control of Congress between 1960 and 1980, we would expect Democrats to have ordered more expensive programs than Republicans. If we review the domestic alternatives, we see that there are indeed clear differences between Democrats and Republicans. The Republicans have fewer legislative proposals, fewer large requests, fewer allocative policies, and slightly more new agenda items. The Democrats have more proposals, more executive orders, more large requests, more allocative policies, and greater first-year costs. These patterns, drawn from the preceding pages, are summarized in table 15. As before, the percentages flow from the 266 OMB cases. Thus, 73 percent of the Kennedy, Johnson, and Carter agendas focused on proposals, compared with only 43 percent of the Nixon and Ford agendas.

Table 15 suggests that Republicans and Democrats prefer different means to the policy ends. Specifically, Nixon and Ford selected alternatives that involved small-scale, low-cost initiatives; the Democrats opted for large-scale, high-expenditure proposals. Kennedy, Johnson, and Carter fit the traditional Democratic stereotype.

There are two potential explanations for the party differences. First, perhaps Nixon and Ford pursued smaller-scale and administrative programs because of their political goals. Perhaps Republicans prefer more limited programs regardless of political capital. In the same vein, perhaps Democrats have a natural preference for large-scale legislative requests. According to one OMB officer, there is at least some reason to support the argument.

> The President can have a tremendous impact on the kind of ideas that are brought forward. Through his personal style, he can encourage comprehensive programs or simple, single-purpose bills. It is clear that Johnson believed in the big-bang theory of policy-making, while Ford believed in the more limited evolution. In the Ford administration, aides were unwilling to bring the major programs forward; they anticipated the President and decided to wait for better times. Ford made it quite clear that he didn't want too many broad-aim programs; the government didn't have the money, and Ford didn't have the influence.

A second, more attractive explanation for party differences is political capital. Though goals are critical in the initial stages of the search for alternatives, capital is the primary factor in defining the scope of presidential requests. Goals shape the direction of agenda requests, while capital affects the size. Though Nixon and Ford may have had some preference for smaller-scale programs, given their political situation in Congress, neither President had much choice.

Thus, the better question is whether Republicans would change their legislative strategies under different political conditions. Did Nixon and Ford hold back large-scale programs for better times? Did they develop large-scale initiatives only to delay them in the face of congressional opposition? If

Table 15. Democrats versus Republicans

Policy Content	Democrats[a]	Republicans[b]
Proposals	70%	43%
Large programs	54	38
New Programs	62	64
Large-new programs	38	27
Small-new programs	18	37
Spending programs	55	31

[a] 185 cases.
[b] 81 cases.

so, we might question the impact of goals on party differences in scope. There is little doubt about Nixon's interest in large-scale initiatives. Welfare reform and revenue sharing are two examples of major programs drafted during his administration. Had Nixon faced a Republican majority in Congress, his agenda might have expanded rapidly. Proposals for special revenue sharing, executive branch reorganization, budget retrenchment, and energy independence all languished during the Nixon term. Though Nixon wanted major departures in the federal role, there was little support in the Democratic Congress. The case is less clear for Ford. Ford's long career in Congress was characterized by a commitment to limited programs. Yet, was Ford's strategy based on his ideology or on his position as the leader of a minority party? As President, Ford delayed several large-scale programs on the basis of his political support in Congress. As one assistant remarked,

> Had the economy cooled off and the President been elected in his own right we were prepared to announce at least three major packages: first, we were going to present a comprehensive energy package. Our 1975 effort was more a stopgap measure, and needed substantial additions. Second, we were going to move ahead on catastrophic health insurance; in fact, we were rethinking the entire national health insurance concept. Third, we were preparing a new crack at welfare reform. Welfare reform was still a hot topic, and we were moving on a new plan. The political and economic situation meant that we had to cool off for a couple of years. But it did not mean we were sitting idly by, waiting for government to get better on its own.

As noted earlier, a look at Reagan may help answer the goals-versus-capital debate. Facing the first Republican Senate in thirty years, Reagan submitted a series of large-scale requests. Though the Reagan agenda is conservative in purpose, it is large-scale in scope. Goals affected Reagan's decisions on the agenda content, but capital has determined the legislative packaging.

For both Democrats and Republicans, the search for alternatives is affected by the nature of the status quo. Nixon and Ford were forced toward new programs precisely because modification of the old ideas was contrary to their political goals; Reagan was forced toward large-scale budget revisions because of his perceptions of the economic crisis. Whereas Nixon, Ford, and Reagan were forced toward new departures, Kennedy, Johnson, and Carter could more easily opt for expansions of old programs—the status quo already included many of their policy goals. For the Democratic Presidents, it has been much easier to build on past successes—the New Deal and the Fair Deal laid the groundwork for the Kennedy, Johnson, and Carter agendas.

What can we expect from the Democrats and Republicans in the 1980s? On one level, we can expect increased constraint on the domestic alternatives. There will be fewer spending programs and more efforts to modify and reshape old initiatives. Reagan's election signaled a pattern already evident in the Carter aminstration. Along with Nixon and Ford, Carter had already started to cut back along many of the lines proposed by Reagan. Defense spending was expanding at least three years before 1980, with proportionate drops in domestic growth. On a second level, the Republicans cannot be expected to suddenly return to the heydays of passive management. At least for the next decade Republicans have a great deal of legislative work to do. Cutting spending, redirecting the federal role, and reducing regulation all require legislative actions. Though the substantive content of the programs will be philosophically different, the sheer quantity of legislative activity will not drop in the coming years. The directions change, but the tools do not.

Go or No Go

The dominant White House orientation is toward substantive action—Presidents want to act. Sometimes, however, Presidents make the decision not to act. Kennedy made a "no go" choice with civil rights in 1961, Ford with welfare reform in 1975, Carter with national health insurance in 1977. In each case, the President had selected a specific issue only to decide that substantive action was not immediately possible. In each case, the staffs agreed that the President wanted to act but felt restrained by political and economic circumstance. Thus, there are two major factors which lead to the "no go" choice.

First, Presidents and staffs are acutely aware of policy *costs,* which involve political, economic, and technical evaluations. According to a Johnson aide, "The President has to evaluate just how much he is willing to spend for each program. I don't mean just dollars. . . . The President has to look at the political costs: How much will he give up to get the particular bill? How much will he need to sacrifice to win? He also has to think about his time: How much will he need to draft the bill? How much will he waste on a losing cause?" Presidential capital has a dramatic impact on the search for alternatives. Legislative proposals are more expensive than vetoes; legislation is more expensive than administrative action; large programs cost more than small ones; new programs cost more than old ones; spending programs are more expensive both economically and politically than nonspending ones. Presidents are keenly aware of the costs. They set up evaluative screens to consider the potential impact of the available alternatives—costs become a primary hurdle in the choice of programs. Once again, we assume that Presidents want to identify a preferred alternative, an alternative that will attain the issue benefits at the least program costs. (We will return to that argument in chapter 6.)

Second, Presidents and staffs often must abandon an issue because an alternative simply cannot be found. Even when an issue involves high benefits, preferred alternatives may not be avalable. Economic conditions may preclude an allocative policy; political conditions may hinder a large-scale proposal. Even when an issue arrives with an alternative already attached, the President may not be able to justify the costs. Despite Nixon's preference for some form of welfare reform, by 1973 the preferred alternative was politically impossible. Despite Kennedy's preference for a legislative answer to civil rights, in 1961 the alternative demanded too much capital. Despite Carter's commitment to national health insurance, by 1977 the money was not available. In each case a preferred alternative could not be found.

In the preceding pages, we have examined a number of choices in the search for alternatives: proposals versus vetoes, large programs versus small, new programs versus old, spending options versus nonspending. In each distinction I have suggested that the opportunities for choice have become more constrained in the 1980s. Presidents are increasingly restricted in the search for acceptable alternatives. Adopting the theory of legislative expense, we might argue that Congress has raised the cost of presidential programs but limited the range of viable options. The administrative channel has been increasingly choked by congressional surveillance. The rise of legislative vetoes and burgeoning statutory limits have combined to foreclose executive action as an acceptable alternative. The spending channel has also been closed, as national pressures for reduced spending have grown. Presidents cannot afford to present high-expenditure programs in an atmosphere of increasing budgetary conflict. Yet, if the spending channel is winnowing, so is the nonspending option. The growing concern for regulatory reform places remarkable burdens on Presidents as they search for appropriate alternatives. Further, Presidents face renewed constraints on large-scale programs. With the failure of the Great Society, Presidents must gauge the size of new domestic initiatives against anticipated impact. In virtually every search for alternatives—whether large or small, new or old, spending or nonspending—Presidents are caught in an increasing no-win conflict. Some might argue that such cross-pressure leads to greater planning and more deliberate choice. In several respects, the argument carries weight. Yet, the purpose of comprehensive planning is to produce strong policy, regardless of the specific means. If potential options are foreclosed at the start of the search, Presidents must turn to the lesser of program evils. Instead of leading to careful analysis, the tightening of options may restrict the search for good policy.

6 selecting the alternatives

On 16 April 1976 candidate Jimmy Carter pledged his unequivocal support for national health insurance. His plan was to include new delivery systems and redistribution of health-care professionals. It would attempt to reduce barriers to early preventive care, and it was to be financed through payroll taxes and general revenues. The proposed plan not only provided for universal care but it demanded quality control and built-in cost ceilings.

Despite Carter's campaign promise, a firm legislative proposal did not appear on either the 1977 or the 1978 domestic agenda. The plan did not resurface until spring 1979, when it took the form of a series of health principles. When the outline finally emerged, it was limited to a small expansion of Medicare. The goal of universal coverage was no longer a cornerstone of the Carter agenda. The critical factor in the plan's evolution was cost. Shogan summarizes one typical discussion of costs from early 1977:

> Stuart Eizenstat, the President's chief staff adviser on domestic policy, was worried about money. He quickly offered his senior staff colleagues long-range estimates of the cost of some of President Carter's major promises—$10 billion for tax reform, $15 billion or so for welfare, maybe another $10 billion for national health insurance. All this, he pointed out, had to be reconciled with one of the most fundamental of all Carter's campaign pledges, to balance the budget by 1980. "That," Eizenstat said, "is going to be absolutely hard to do."
>
> Slouched in his chair, coatless and tieless, Hamilton Jordan suggested ingeniously, "Why don't you just talk him out of that, Stu?"
>
> Eizenstat winced, and most of the others laughed.
>
> "Talking the President out of balancing the budget is not one of the things I'd like to try to do," Jody Powell said (Shogan 1977, pp. 194-95).

According to the Carter staff, universal health insurance was dead on two counts. First, Carter was convinced that there was very little money available for a comprehensive plan. "We kept looking at the plans and

136

calculating the costs," one Carter health aide noted. "The costs kept rising, but the potential revenues kept falling. We felt we had to get some ceiling on health costs before we could go ahead with the health plan." Carter's perception of available funds was crucial. Second, regardless of the specific plan, few domestic aides believed national health insurance could survive a congressional test. Despite Ted Kennedy's personal enthusiasm for national health insurance, the Carter liaison team was concerned about the potential for success. As late as 1979 one legislative assistant argued that "national health insurance cannot pass. It couldn't pass today, and I don't think it could have passed in 1977. Congress was not in the mood to authorize a major new federal program in health."

By early 1977 Carter had decided to pursue hospital cost containment in lieu of national health insurance. Though there was an explicit linkage between the two items within the White House, it was not communicated to Congress. Hospital cost containment became the preferred *alternative* for the health *issue*. It allowed the President to present a substantive plan with low costs. What better way to minimize costs than by a cost containment bill? According to Stuart Eizenstat, "Carter's commitments to social justice are as strong and his accomplishments as meaningful as any past Democratic President."

> Jimmy Carter brought with him to the White House not simply great intelligence and diligence but strong Democratic commitments in the grand tradition I have evoked.
>
> But every President must face the reality he inherits; he must govern based on the facts and situations handed to him. He cannot recreate the 1960s when he must govern with the far different problems of the 1970s (Eizenstat 1979, p. 2).

Policy Costs

As Presidents search for specific alternatives to match the domestic issues, the main evaluative criteria rest on *costs*. This emphasis on costs may exist from the very beginning of the search. In 1977 Carter demanded a welfare plan with zero additional cost to the federal budget; cost was a principal criterion in the search for a preferred alternative. The cost consideration may also arise very late in the process, as the President considers competing solutions. Regardless of whether the discussion comes early or late, cost is the central tool for determining policy alternatives. According to the five White House staffs, three basic cost criteria act to screen policy alternatives: political, economic, and technical.

Political Costs. Presidents examine political costs at virtually every step in the policy process. They consider the potentials for congressional success; the cooperation of the bureaucracy, and public opinion. According to one Kennedy assistant,

> The first question was always, Will it fly on the Hill? It was important to make adjustments in our programs to meet potential resistance. Our liaison team was one of the best in recent history. Their judgments were central to our decision to go ahead or hold off. If liaison felt there were major problems, we generally reconsidered the bill. If liaison felt the problems could be handled, we generally moved ahead.

A Nixon aide concurred: "We were forced to consider the potential congressional reactions even if we didn't heed them. We didn't want to send legislation that had no chance of success, but we also didn't want to hold back on legislation that had an opportunity."

Congress is the most important factor in the calculation of political costs. Depending on the party composition and the political mood of Congress, the "price" of specific alternatives can vary greatly. "You spend a great deal of time just counting heads," a Ford liaison officer argued. "You have to be on guard for shifts in support. On one issue, you might be able to find the right balance of votes; on another issue on the same day, you might not be able to get lunch." For the staffs, congressional support equaled party seats; that was the first line for organizing support. As one Nixon aide noted, "You turn to your party members first. If we couldn't move our own people, we felt the opportunities were pretty slim." This is not to argue that the staffs considered each party member an automatic vote. Indeed, the staffs argued that the party tally could change for each successive issue. Rather, the staffs subscribed to a mild form of party discipline. According to one Johnson assistant, "We told the party members that they should seriously consider coming along on certain issues. It was in their best interest, as well as ours. The President has certain tools at his disposal to gain party support, not the least of which is to cut off the social channel."

The battle for congressional support is one reason why Presidents court congressional input on program development. Lyndon Johnson recognized the advantages and attempted to reduce his political costs by including Congress in the drafting of major initiatives:

> The trick was . . . to crack the wall of separation enough to give the Congress a feeling of participation in creating my bills without exposing my plans at the same time to advance congressional opposition before they even saw the light of day. It meant taking risks, but the risks were worth it.
>
> My experience in the NYA [National Youth Administration] taught me that when people have a hand in shaping projects, these projects are more likely to be successful than the ones simply handed down from the top. As Majority Leader I learned that the best guarantee to legislative success was a process by which the wishes and views of the members were obtained ahead of time, and, whenever possible, incorporated into the

early drafts of the bill. As President I went one step further. I insisted on congressional consultation at every single stage, beginning with the process of deciding what problems and issues to consider for my task forces right up to the drafting of the bills (in Kearns 1976, p. 232).

Johnson viewed the strategy as a method for cutting political costs. "It was much easier to win if we could bring the Congress in early," one Johnson legislative assistant reflected. "If we could forge some support before the programs were drafted, we were halfway there."

Economic Costs. With the increased fiscal pressure of the 1970s, economic costs have emerged as the most important factor in domestic choice. For both the Ford and Carter administrations, economic costs became the first question in the search for policy alternatives. As a Carter aide reflected, "The President made it quite clear that we were to consider the fiscal impact first. By 1978 economic costs were the most frequent reason for rejecting and redrafting potential programs. We were still concerned about workability and Congress, but the economic impact was the first and last test." According to Eizenstat,

> President Carter inherited an enormous budget deficit and a "stagflation" —both high inflation and high unemployment—from his two immediate predecessors of a kind unknown to Presidents Johnson and Kennedy.
>
> In 1965, the first full year of the Great Society and the outburst of new social programs it launched, the federal deficit was $1.6 billion. President Carter inherited a $66 billion deficit. The inflation rate in 1964 and 1965 was 1.5%—it averaged 8% for the three years before President Carter took office. No President can nor should be expected to do as much in that situation—not of our own making—as could be done under vastly better economic circumstances. Yet our nation's appetite for greater amounts of government services—most of it needed—remains undiminished. In an era of inflation the collective demands of our country exceed our capacity to satisfy them. We must thus prioritize as never before to satisfy the legitimate desires of those people and localities most in need (Eizenstat 1979, p. 3).

Economic costs were also important to Kennedy, Johnson, and Nixon, though to a lesser degree. Kennedy kept close track of the budget in his first year of office. Despite internal pressure to use increased spending to stimulate a recessionary economy, Kennedy steadfastly refused to inflate the budget. Nor would he propose a "quickie" tax cut in 1962. Yet, according to Sundquist, Kennedy's motivation was less economic than political.

> For years the Republicans had been painting the Democratic party as the party of reckless spending and inflation, and throughout the autumn Kennedy had done his best to neutralize that issue by speaking in clear tones of fiscal soundness. Now he had won by the narrowest of margins, with a mandate far from plain. As he saw it, his imperative duty in his first

weeks of office was to demonstrate to the nation—and especially the business community, which had given him substantial support and whose backing would be necessary in the future—that the Democratic party, under his leadership, was indeed fiscally responsible. Moreover, after his inaugural appeal to the people to ask what they could do for their country, not what their country could do for them, it would be anomalous to offer, in the next breath, a program of lower taxes and easy spending (Sundquist 1968, pp. 35-36).

The emphasis on a balanced budget continued until 1963, when Kennedy opted for a major tax cut. Yet, even then the administration was more concerned about the political costs. Kennedy was determined not to be the first President to top the $100 billion mark in the federal budget. As one Kennedy aide argued, "The $100 billion level did affect our decisions. We were approaching an election year and did not want to be the first over the top. It was nothing compared to Carter's budget, but Goldwater would have made it stick."

If there was any point when economic costs were virtually ignored as a guide to policy, it was in early 1965, at the start of Johnson's first full term. Still convinced of the need for economic stimulus, Johnson worried about not spending enough. "Remember," one LBJ aide remarked, "Johnson wanted a War on Poverty and a Great Society. If anything, he was concerned that the programs were too small. He wanted to make sure they were properly funded . . . even if that meant massive deficits." By late 1965 Johnson's economic advisors had begun to caution restraint. Whereas 1965 was characterized by excess, the final years of the Johnson administration were marked by restraint. As one aide remarked, "We didn't worry much about costs in the first year. It wasn't necessary. Our forecasts pointed toward a boom; the war was only starting to heat up." That attitude quickly changed. By mid-1966, economic costs had regained their importance in the evaluation of policy alternatives. According to one economic advisor, "We tried to persuade the President that it was time to cool off the economy. The long-awaited tax cut of 1964 had taken too long to pass. By the time it started to have an effect, the economy was already on fire. The recession of the early 1960s became the surge of the Vietnam War. By 1967 we got the President's ear and started to pull back."

Economic costs grew in importance during the Nixon administration. Though Nixon presented a series of expenditure programs in his 1969 agenda, economic conditions began to dictate restraint by 1971. As the economy soured, pressures on the budget accelerated. According to one Nixon economic assistant, "As we moved toward wage and price controls, we had to institute ceilings on the spending programs. The veto of the Hill-Burton Hospital Construction Act was intended to give notice that the budget was sacred territory." A Nixon domestic policy assistant offered his chronology of events:

> When the President was inaugurated, he offered us almost unlimited opportunities to use the budget as one tool of the New Federalism. Welfare reform and revenue sharing were both rather significant spending programs. By December 1969 we began to get a new set of messages from the economic staff. The President had opened the cookie jar and now was slapping our hands for digging in. By 1971 there was no point in staying. The economic group had taken over the helm. When I left, the budget was *the* determinative factor in the policy debate. If a program didn't pass the test, it was out.

Yet, if economic costs were merely important to Kennedy, Johnson, and Nixon, they were determinative for Ford and Carter. Both Presidents identified inflation as the top economic priority, and they focused on the deficit as one cause. Whereas Carter's 1977 agenda originally focused on unemployment—a decision that led to a series of allocative programs—Carter reversed directions within six months of inauguration. The growing problem of inflation placed economic costs at the top of the program criteria. It also increased the influence of OMB and the Council of Economic Advisers. As one Carter aide noted, "We had always asked for comment from OMB and CEA, but by 1978 they were generally asked first. The paper loop shifted to the economic teams; their responses received more initial attention from the President." The emphasis on inflation also led to a greater concern with the budget as a tool of economic restraint.

If economic costs have grown in importance, a major part of the explanation rests on increased budgetary conflict, which has centered on the tightening of economic resources. Just as low levels of presidential capital lead to greater concern about political costs, dwindling economic resources lead to a greater emphasis on expenditures. Part of the concern stems from White House perceptions of economic reality. Both Ford and Carter *believed* that inflation demanded a tighter budget. Yet, as one Carter aide remarked, "Five billion one way or another really won't have much impact on inflation. If the President wanted to spend the extra money, I doubt it would make much difference. It's when you talk about tens of billions that we get into trouble." Much of the contemporary economic conflict rests on the absence of increments. As Schick argues,

> A major explanation for the recent escalation in budget conflict is that increments are no longer available in sufficient amounts to cover both the built-in increase in the budget and claims for new programs. Nowadays, much of the budget battle revolves around future increments. Inasmuch as the current increment is already claimed by past commitments, the various interests maneuver to gain an advance commitment of future increments. This means that when the next year arrives, its normal increment has already been encumbered by past decisions, and it is necessary to buy budget peace by claiming another year's share. The predicament thus becomes self-perpetuating (Schick 1975, p. 57).

Why is there so little room for new expenditures? What happened to the increment? According to Charles Schultze, Carter's chairman of the Council of Economic Advisers, and his colleagues, "the answer is simple":

> First, in the space of ten short years, federal civilian expenditures as a percentage of GNP almost doubled; even if no new programs are added, the annual growth in existing expenditure programs now absorbs a much larger fraction of the growth in revenues than was the case ten years ago. Second, the American people and their political representatives have accepted a greatly broadened concept of the appropriate role of the federal government in dealing with the nation's social problems; there is a large backlog of unmet demands for new or sharply expanded federal programs addressed to those problems—assuming a share of local education finance, providing day care centers for children of working mothers, and financing a large part of the cost of environmental cleanup, to name but a few. Third, and paradoxically, over the same decade the nation has chosen to reduce federal income and excise taxes in a number of successive steps and by a large amount. In combination, these developments have radically altered the nature of the budgetary problem and have transformed the historical problem of fiscal drag into its opposite, the problem of "fiscal squeeze" (Schultze et al. 1971, pp. 397-98).

As Schultze, Fried, Rivlin, and Teeters conclude, instead of the fiscal drag foreseen fifteen years ago, "it appears increasingly difficult under existing tax rates to accommodate the fulfillment of admittedly high-priority national objectives." It is no coincidence that these conclusions affected the Carter agenda: Charles Schultze became Carter's top economic advisor, and his perception of the economic pressure had an important bearing on domestic programs throughout the Carter administration.

Though the recent concern for economic costs reflects real world pressures, the emphasis also involves presidential *perceptions*. Nixon, Ford, and Carter all subscribed to a tight budget as one solution to the inflation problem. Once again, as one Carter economic aide remarked, "There is very little difference between a budget deficit of $30 billion and [one of] $20 [billion]. The actual amounts have very little effect. It is the impression that seems to make the impact." A second aide agreed: "Containing the deficit is an important goal, but the image is critical. If the President had introduced a massive health plan, it would have opened the floodgates of backlogged legislation." Certainly, the President's ideology has an impact on perceptions of external events. One might argue that Nixon, Ford, and Carter were disposed to see inflation as a critical economic priority, that each was ideologically prepared to see fire when there was smoke. The argument carries some weight for Nixon and Ford, but it is partially refuted by Carter's early emphasis on unemployment. Like Kennedy and Johnson, Carter started his term with the traditional Democratic stimulus package. Unlike Kennedy and Johnson, Carter soon faced 10 percent inflation. According to the Carter staff, the shift of priorities was directly linked to economic conditions. As one Carter aide suggested,

> We have heard all the reports that the President was a conservative anyway, that he was a tight-fisted son of a bitch to begin with. It doesn't match the record. The economic stimulus plan was a typical Democratic program. The only problem was that inflation started to heat up again. I'd like to see Ted Kennedy in the office trying to square the old-line Democratic platform with the economic conditions. We had to change directions because of the actual conditions. . . . If you think about it, inflation ought to be a Democratic issue anyway. Inflation hurts people on fixed incomes and welfare. The guidelines don't go up as fast as the price index.

For most Presidents, including Reagan, the concern for economic costs reflects the impact of both reality and perception. There is ample objective evidence of the need for economic restraint in the past decade. Ford, Carter, and Reagan did not manufacture the inflationary spiral. There is also ample evidence of the increasing inflexibility in the federal budget. According to the Nixon, Ford, and Carter staffs, the "controllability" of the federal budget is a central factor in the decline of expenditure policy. The figures have received widespread attention in the White House, and they offer a convenient tool for explanations of the tight budget policies. "Just take a look at the budget figures," one Carter aide insisted. "Look at Johnson and Carter. The budget just doesn't have as much room as it once did." The figures on budget controllability deserve inspection, if only because the staff use them to justify choice. The percentage of budget controllability for the past fifteen years is summarized in table 16.

The figures support the Ford and Carter complaints about controllability; they are also misleading. In 1970 Nixon's budget controllability was 37 percent. That 37 percent involved approximately $73 billion. By 1980 Carter's budget controllability had dropped to 25 percent; adjusting for inflation, however, that 25 percent involved well over $80 billion. The percentage of controllability had dropped, but the dollar amount had increased. It is important to recognize that the controllability estimates have become a catchall for *perceptions* of fiscal constraint. Consider the views of one media observer:

> The Carter people have really pulled the wool over our eyes. They use that damn budget figure whenever someone asks why they haven't done X or Y. When you look at the actual figures, the Carter people have a considerable amount of leeway. They like to use those figures to explain their decisions to the liberal wing of the party. When the AFL-CIO walks in and asks about national health insurance, they tell them to look at the controllability.

Table 16. Budget Controllability

Year	Amount Controllable (billions of dollars)	Percentage Controllable
1967	66.4	41.8%
1968	73.4	41.1
1969	70.1	38.0
1970	73.3	37.3
1971	73.7	34.8
1972	81.3	35.0
1973	76.9	31.0
1974	78.4	29.1
1975	92.6	28.4
1976	102.8	28.1
1977	112.9	28.1
1978	121.9	27.0
1979	132.8	26.1
1980	140.8[a]	25.0[a]
1981	150.3[a]	24.4[a]

Source: The Budget of the United States Government, 1977, 1980.
Note: Figures are not available for 1961-66.
[a] Estimated.

The impact of economic costs on domestic choice cannot be minimized. Obviously, concern with economic costs leads to lower expenditure levels. Nixon, Ford, and Carter actively searched for "cheap" alternatives. Part of the concern was based on the economic realities—inflation was a pressing problem, and tight spending was an available solution. Yet, part of the concern evolved from the individual personalities. Ford had a longstanding familiarity with the budget from his service in the House. Once in the White House, he spent considerable time reviewing the line-items in the budget. Carter also emphasized budgetary detail—several aides reported that Carter often added the figures in the budget requests for accuracy. Regardless of presidential style, all three administrations invested considerable time in the budgetary process in the effort to restrain expenditures; alternatives had to meet cost criteria. "We learned a lesson from welfare reform," a Nixon aide remarked. "You can't take those figures in stone. You have to check the accuracy. We were burned on that issue and made an effort to nail down the figures on other programs." With the establishment of the Congressional Budget Office, both Ford and Carter became even more emphatic about accuracy. As one Carter assistant noted, "CBO can provide alternate statistics and budgets. Congress no longer takes the President's data as the final line." Yet, the White House is interested in more than accuracy. For Ford and Carter, the primary demand was for the greatest political benefit at the lowest economic cost. Both Presidents imposed strict limits on new expenditure programs, limits which became the first hurdle in the search for alternatives. According to one OMB officer,

More than any other time in history, Presidents are watching the budget as the main defense against economic pressure. They tend to view the budget both as a psychological tool for reducing inflation and as an opportunity to squeeze more out of the existing programs. If the programs cannot pass the cost test, they are not going to move. Even if the problem demands immediate relief, the cost criterion comes first.

Technical Costs and Workability. Beyond political and economic costs, Presidents have some interest in technical workability. According to a Carter aide, "Every President has to ask the question at some point. Every President has to make some estimate of the impact of the program. Unfortunately, it is often the last question asked, and even if there is a negative answer, it is often ignored." The question of technical workability generally falls to the departments or to lower-level White House staffs. Because of limits on internal resources, Presidents have very little opportunity to investigate workability. Instead, Presidents often simply assume that the alternatives will work. "Otherwise, why would the programs come up?" one Johnson assistant asked facetiously. "The staff naturally assumed that most of the programs will work as intended, that the problems will be both minor and fixable. The overwhelming evidence suggests that the confidence is misplaced, but the staff just doesn't have the time to check it out."

Even if the internal resources were available, the incentives to check workability rarely exist. Program effectiveness is not a particularly important political variable. One OMB assistant offered the following explanation:

> The people in the White House are there for such a short time. The pressure is on making some impact and getting some programs passed. There is not enough time or reward in thinking carefully about effectiveness and implementation. The emphasis is really on quantity, not quality. The President could never be reelected on the effectiveness theme. "We didn't do much, but it is all working very well." Do you think a President could win with that?

Questions of workability are also complicated by the lack of information. Even if the staff had the internal resources and political incentives, could they answer the question? How do we measure program effectiveness? Given the political nature of presidential programs, it is exceedingly difficult to estimate just what the program objectives are. Most federal programs are not designed to facilitate discussions of workability. According to Alice Rivlin, director of the Congressional Budget Office, one reason for the absence of systematic planning rests on the effect of "inadequate description of inputs and outputs and lack of information on the same individuals over time."

> Another is the failure thus far to organize social service systems to facilitate investigation of their effectiveness. Major deviations from the established pattern are rare and their effects are hard to disentangle from

the special circumstances that brought them about. Equally little has been learned from evaluations of federal government programs. The reasons are much the same. Headstart, Title I, model cities, and federal programs *could* have been designed to produce information on their effectiveness, but they were not (Rivlin 1971, p. 86).

Workability is even more difficult to predict for new programs. Presidents can estimate the impact of a social security increase or an expanded defense program, for the programs have been modified before. Presidents have more difficulty projecting the consequences of an untested welfare reform or urban renewal. As one Nixon welfare reform expert argued, "One of our major problems was that we couldn't check the validity of our advice from the departments. We didn't have enough information from trusted sources, and we didn't have enough background on the issues to distinguish bad advice from good." According to Martin Anderson, the Family Assistance Plan was undercut by poor information and unattainable goals—neither of which stopped the program from proceeding to the Hill.

> No one seemed to clearly comprehend that there was, in fact, no way out of the dilemma presented by the conflicting goals of reasonably high welfare payments, low tax rates, and low cost. To some it seemed that the plan was "such a good thing" that the possibility of it not being possible was never seriously considered. So Nixon sent the Family Assistance Plan, the version with the high marginal rates, to the Congress. The House of Representatives never did have the time to understand the complexities of the proposal and passed the bill (243 to 155). Subsequently, however, an understanding of the important and radical implications of Nixon's welfare reform plan began to spread, and by the time it reached the Senate Finance Committee enough members of that committee understood them well enough to ask the questions that destroyed it. . . .
>
> The saddest aspect of this humiliating defeat, from the viewpoint of the Republican Administration, was that it was totally unnecessary. Patricelli [then deputy undersecretary for policy at HEW] and other welfare experts from HEW were aware that the bill sent to the Congress contained defects that, if widely known, could cause its defeat. And they knew it when they sold the welfare reform plan to Nixon (Anderson 1978, pp. 143-44).

Part of Anderson's complaint may reflect his bitterness from the internal struggle over the substance of welfare reform—Moynihan had won, and Burns and Anderson had lost—yet, part reflects the realities of presidential choice. The White House simply did not have the necessary information or incentives to evaluate workability.

Despite the recent increase in congressional oversight and foresight, information on workability is still scarce. As a Kennedy aide argued, "We were not in the business of checking every detail for workability; that was a function of the executive branch. We were in business to make some changes. There were problems with Medicare and Aid to Education. But our purpose was to get the damn programs passed. We could not wait for the perfect programs." A Nixon welfare expert agreed: "We were widely criticized for sending up a flawed bill. However, we felt we had to move for some reform. Even after six months, we had not found the 'perfect' solution. If we hadn't moved when we did, we wouldn't have had a chance in Congress. As it was, we were still too late." Though Presidents certainly ask questions about program effectiveness, there is rarely more than passing reference to the problem. As one Carter aide noted, "You have to get off your butt and make some solid proposals. There is no time to wait for the ideal program. They just don't exist."

The absence of technical expertise and resources elevates the importance of the *available alternative*. Presidents have neither the incentives nor the resources to develop truly new alternatives. As one academic observer suggested, "The President is severely limited by the inability to explore the domestic options. Unless the President is truly knowledgeable, he has to rely on a very narrow range of alternatives, usually coming from the same departments and agencies. There is not enough time to examine that many new ideas and concepts; the President has to select from the available items."

The available alternative affected Nixon's attempt at welfare reform. According to M. Kenneth Bowler, an important set of conditions that "must be considered in attempting to explain why Nixon ended up proposing radical welfare reform included the immediate accessibility of an innovative course of action, the status of this proposal among recognized welfare experts, and the availability of information by which it could be evaluated."

> In other words, substantial research and theoretical work had been done in the income maintenance field. Innovative courses of action were available and visible. Furthermore, as a result of their research, writing and, in some cases, governmental service, some of the proponents of the different guaranteed income schemes . . . were now recognized by many as *the* "welfare experts" (Bowler 1974, pp. 61-62).

The available alternatives have considerable impact in the discussion of domestic priorities. "There you are," one Carter aide remarked, "looking for a specific program in, say, urban assistance. Once you begin your search, you will run into agencies which have specific programs already drafted. They have the figures and the sample bills; they may even have sponsors in Congress. It's hard to ignore them. They can save you a lot of time." At least in domestic policy, the available alternatives have three basic advantages in the search for specific programs.

First, the available alternatives generally arrive earlier than the competition. As the President and the staff begin the search for alternatives, they may face a variety of potential solutions. Some may be developed; others may not. With the pressure to move the domestic agenda as quickly as possible, the White House often adopts the strategy "first come, first served." According to a Johnson assistant, "The first ideas have the greatest chance of adoption. Think of the domestic agenda as a grain hopper. What goes in first will come out first. If a department has a program which seems to address a presidential issue, it is in their best interest to get the program to the President as soon as possible." In some cases, the available alternative may be attached to the issue when it enters the domestic process. When Kennedy selected medical care for the aged, Medicare was the available alternative; when Carter selected welfare reform, the Program for Better Jobs and Income was waiting. In most cases, Presidents can expect considerable help from the available alternatives. "Can you fault Nixon for grabbing at the Family Assistance Plan?" one legislative assistant asked. "The program was ready to go. Once they decided to use guaranteed income, HEW was ready. The computer had to be reset to generate new figures, but FAP was essentially available on day one." A congressional aide agreed:

> In the Nixon and Carter administrations, the deck was always stacked against anything but the old ideas. Both Presidents liked to see the programs down on paper—they wanted the pros and cons. Some of the most creative ideas were neglected because they weren't as far along. The really innovative programs need more time. Both Presidents turned to the tested solutions, the programs with the ready-made support.

As Presidents try to set the agenda early in the first year, available alternatives offer significant advantages.

Second, the available alternatives generate greater bureaucratic support. Derpartments and agencies often develop programs that resurface over time. These programs are well-documented and carefully drafted; they may reflect years of bureaucratic compromise and analysis. According to a former Nixon Domestic Council assistant, "Once Nixon opted for welfare reform, you could almost hear the cheers in HEW. They knew they had a plan ready to go; they had tremendous internal support; they had the computers. They also knew they had Daniel Patrick Moynihan in the White House to champion the program." Because of scarce internal resources, the President is often forced to rely on the executive branch for specific advice and detail. It is extremely difficult for the White House to refute unanimity within a department or agency. Thus, despite Nixon's distrust of the federal establishment, the near unanimous support within HEW and among welfare experts generated considerable confidence that the Family Assistance Plan would work.

Third, regardless of whether the available alternative is eventually accepted, it tends to frame the debate. The White House policy process often focuses on a single alternative as the basis for discussion. Though Presidents may encourage consideration of competing solutions, the process often centers on a single alternative and proceeds with variations on the theme. According to a Carter aide, "There aren't too many issues which involve multiple alternatives anyway. Take national health insurance. There are only so many basic approaches. You can reduce coverage and use either federal or private plans, but there are only one or two central concepts." According to the Carter staff, initial discussions of national health insurance began with the discussion of mandated private coverage versus universal public enrollment—the same debate that occupied the Truman administration in 1949. In 1979, the Carter decision still rested on a direct descendant of the Truman proposal. It was the available alternative. "We were haunted by the trail of past proposals," one Carter aide lamented. "We didn't have that much room to innovate."

This emphasis on the available alternatives responds to scarce decision-making resources. Scarcity of time leads the staff to search for detailed drafts; scarcity of information leads the staff to rely on executive branch data. "No White House aide can become an expert in the short time in office," a Nixon assistant suggested. "No one has enough time or stamina to keep working on truly new ideas. The staff has to rely on other experts. When a specific program comes up, the staff can evaluate its political impact, but there is not enough opportunity to create a set of truly innovative programs." In the effort to conserve resources, Presidents rely heavily on available alternatives; it is to their advantage. The incentives to create new solutions are rarely present in the domestic policy process.

The First Question

On 15 January 1975 Gerald Ford presented his first State of the Union address as President. In the address, Ford proposed a one-year $16-billion tax cut to stimulate employment: "Cutting taxes, now, is essential if we are to turn the economy around. A tax cut offers the best hope of creating more jobs. Unfortunately, it will increase the size of the budget deficit. Therefore, it is more important than ever that we take steps to control the growth of federal expenditures." In placing a ceiling on federal spending, Ford offered legislation to restrain the growth of a number of domestic programs. More important, Ford announced that "no new spending programs can be initiated this year, except for energy. Further, I will not hesitate to veto any new spending programs adopted by the Congress." Ford had decided that economic costs would be the first question asked about potential domestic alternatives. Though political costs remained as an important consideration, economic costs were given top priority in the domestic policy process. As one Ford assistant remarked, "The spending rule was applied to every new program. It was used against welfare reform and catastrophic health insurance, public works and emergency housing. It was sure as hell applied to the federal budget." During Ford's term, the first question asked of most programs was, How much does it cost?

Table 17. The First Question

	Percentage of Respondents Selecting		
President	Economic costs	Political costs	Workability
Kennedy	22%	68%	10%
Johnson	26	64	10
Nixon	60	31	9
Ford	84	11	5
Carter	72	24	5

Note: The staffs were asked to answer the following questions concerning the administration of which they were a part: When the administration looked at potential programs, what do you remember as the first question asked about the specific alternatives? did you ask about the economic costs? the congressional reaction? workability? There were 90 respondents.

The choice of the first question has an impact on the domestic agenda. The first question acts as an evaluative screen through which all potential alternatives must pass. It is a signal to the program staffs of the kinds of alternatives that are acceptable. In the Ford administration, the "no new spending" rule forced the agenda toward regulatory policy. It also elevated the importance of the budget as a tool for domestic choice. As one assistant remarked, "There were several programs that were held back to meet that requirement. Instead of bringing the ideas into the Oval Office, the staff began to back off. The decisions were being made at a much lower level. The staff started to anticipate the President at an earlier point. It kept his desk clear of expenditure programs, but that also isolated him from a full and open discussion of all options." A second Ford aide continued: "The planning staff was told not to bring the spending programs in. Only Caspar Weinberger [secretary of HEW] had the courage to propose another crack at welfare reform. And, even then, he barely survived."

In structuring discussions of potential alternatives, past Presidents have assigned different weights to political, economic, and technical costs. When the staffs were asked to describe the first questions in the domestic policy process, the importance of economic costs was evident. The responses from the five White House staffs are presented in table 17.

Two findings emerge from table 17. First, economic costs dominated the search for alternatives in the 1970s; second, workability was rarely the first question in the evaluation of potential programs.

Economic Costs. Economic costs currently control the search for domestic alternatives. Whereas both Kennedy and Johnson gave passing reference to economic costs, Nixon, Ford, and Carter turned to costs in the vast majority of domestic choices; economic costs were their top concern in the discussion of alternatives. The pressure should not decline for Reagan.

Aides in the Nixon, Ford, and Carter administrations blamed the pressure for low-cost programs on the economic environment. Inflation has been a persistent problem for Democrats and Republicans alike. Tight budgets have emerged as the preferred alternative. As noted before, however, the choice of economic costs as the first question reflects both reality and perception. Both Nixon and Ford were inclined to view economic costs as a natural focus of Republican policy. As one Ford assistant candidly remarked, "We were much more concerned about having to fight unemployment. It was unfamiliar ground. It was much more comfortable for us to be tackling inflation. That was the traditional Republican territory."

Would Nixon and Ford have turned to the economic criteria even under neutral economic conditions? Once again, it is difficult to disentangle the interaction between perceptions and reality. We know that Nixon originally pursued some expensive social programs. Welfare reform, mass transit, revenue sharing, health maintenance organizations, the SST prototype, and housing expansion all had high prices. One Nixon staffer said, "I think we would have continued to spend, but not to the same degree as the Democrats. We were moving toward a different kind of spending—more on the revenue sharing model—but I don't think we were ready to renounce money altogether. I believe the drop in expenditure programs involved a decline in federal revenues and inflation." It is also possible that Nixon and Ford set the inflation "threshold" at a lower level than did the Democrats. Whereas a 5 percent rate might have been acceptable to the Democrats, it was definitely unacceptable to the Republicans.

Unlike his Republican predecessors, Carter pointed directly at changing economic conditions. Carter's first-year agenda was in the mainstream of traditional Democratic programs. As one Carter aide angrily responded,

> It has been an unfair charge that Carter is somehow less of a Democrat. It's true he's not Ted Kennedy, but does Kennedy really represent the Democratic mainstream? We have been faced by terrible economic constraints and haven't had the opportunities that Lyndon Johnson had. Our economic-stimulus package was a true Democratic program, but we couldn't stick with it given the economic pressure.

Carter's first-year program included a number of standard Democratic programs: a guaranteed-income program; a $21 billion economic-stimulus package; a national no fault insurance plan; a Consumer Protection Agency; a Department of Education; an Alaska lands bill; comprehensive reform of the Taft-Hartley Labor Relations Act. Thus, at the start of the term, Carter moved in precisely the same directions as Kennedy and Johnson had. What changed was the inflation rate. Instead of the 1 or 2 percent levels of the early 1960s, Carter faced 7 percent in 1977 and 1978. With the rate of increase perched at 13 percent through 1979 and 20 percent in 1980, the pressure on economic costs increased dramatically. Ultimately, Carter's ideology may have led to an increased sensitivity to inflation as a primary economic concern. It definitely affected his choice of alternatives in coping with the inflationary spiral, choices which led to the heated primary campaign against Ted Kennedy.

Workability. Regardless of the year or the administration, workability is not a first concern. It is a disappointing finding for those presidential scholars who have called for greater systematic planning. According to one Johnson assistant, "There have never been incentives for more planning. Congress certainly wouldn't reward us for taking the time to carefully evaluate the programs. The press doesn't spend much time on "workability." If anything, the community wanted as much as we could give. Johnson was never asked to prove that the programs would work, nor did Congress seem particularly interested." The rest of the staffs generally agreed. Evaluation and planning have not received adequate support within either Congress or the bureaucracy. The emphasis is still on moving as quickly as possible. "We all believe there should be more planning," one Carter aide remarked. "The President has stressed the need for more caution. But when we fall behind, the President will impose a deadline. It is still a political system; and political systems are interested in results, not implementation." Accordingly, until the political incentives change, Presidents are not likely to express much interest in workability or effectiveness. When the incentives for careful planning increase, Presidents can be expected to allocate more scarce resources to the effort. As one Nixon aide argued, "What were the payoffs for planning? If we took too much time, we had no chance for passage. If we took too much of what you call energy, we lost ground on other projects. There is little interest in Washington for planning. Perhaps when oversight gains credibility in Congress, Presidents will find more time."

Conclusion

Costs are critical in the search for alternatives. As Presidents begin the effort to draft specific options for the domestic issues, costs form a series of what might be called evaluative screens. If the programs do not pass through the screens, the issue may remain unresolved. Whereas benefits are important in the selection of issues, costs are primary in the search for alternatives. The difference rests on scarce resources. As Presidents draft the domestic programs, they must consider the economic and political costs.

Unlike the selection of issues, the search for alternatives is characterized by conflict. It is precisely because alternatives involve specific commitments that the conflict appears. Issues do not involve a zero-sum game; alternatives do. That conflict has a variety of important implications for how Presidents decide. The conflict produces both competing staff coalitions and efforts at internal domination. As we shall see, domestic choice does not resemble the "rational" ideal. According to one Carter assistant, "Issues are important, but everyone remembers the programs. It's not what you say but what you do. Sometimes what we did was more the result of political struggle than careful thought."

Before turning to the decision-making structure, however, we will take a brief look at presidential priorities. Once Presidents select the issues and adopt specific alternatives, they assign priorities. Not surprisingly, the priorities reflect the potential for legislative success.

7 presidential priorities

In January 1976 Gerald Ford announced his proposal for a massive federal commitment to energy development. Popularly labeled the energy corporation, the program would have provided over $100 billion for both traditional and alternative sources of energy. The brainchild of Vice President Nelson Rockefeller, the proposal engendered immediate White House staff opposition. On the surface, the administration was committed to the concept of an energy-development fund. Yet, within the various program staffs and the energy agencies, there was determined opposition. Though there was support for the *issue* of energy development and an endorsement of a specific *alternative,* the energy corporation was never a presidential *priority.* It never reached the President's must list. As one Ford assistant suggested, "There was never any real pressure behind the bill. We knew it wouldn't pass and were content to let it fail. There was just no point to the bill—it was a big money program with no guarantee of success."

Accordingly, the energy corporation was never taken seriously on the Hill. Though the program was mentioned in Ford's 1976 and 1977 State of the Union addresses, it was never a Ford priority. As one legislative assistant remarked,

> The bill never had a chance. Even before Ford gave the go-ahead, there was tremendous antagonism within the staff. Only one person really supported it: Rockefeller. Only one person really wanted to testify: Rockefeller. There wasn't anyone in favor of the proposal outside of the VP's office. After Ford gave the go-ahead, there was absolute indifference. No one would push the bill; no one wanted to go to the Hill and trade. House members would call to ask about the energy corporation and the staff would answer "What energy corporation?" The departments were opposed, and the bill was dead before it was announced.

154

The President's Must List

Just what is the President's must list, and why is it important? From the staff viewpoint, the must list constitutes a shortened version of the legislative agenda and contains the critical priorities, the items that are considered crucial to the presidential program. In 1961, for instance, Kennedy offered twenty-five specific requests for legislative action; there was, however, little hope that all twenty-five would pass. "We didn't have enough capital," one aide reflected. "There was no way we could get it all. Instead, we felt some pressure to tell Congress which items were most important, which ones had to pass, which ones the President felt he had to have. Even then, it didn't make much difference—we didn't get much anyway." Aid to Education, Medicare, area redevelopment, manpower retraining, and youth employment all became part of Kennedy's must list, while agriculture, community-health facilities, saline-water conversion, food-surplus distribution, and water-pollution control were given lesser status.

All five presidential staffs recognized the value of the must list, though the administrations varied in their willingness to provide one. Former President Nixon summarized the value of priorities as follows:

> It is not enough simply to "manage," examining each set of choices in a philosophical vacuum. The President's central principles must be there, they must be consistent, and they must be clearly seen. His own staff, his Administration, Congress, the press and the public all need from him a clear indication of what he considers important; of his values, his priorities, and the directions in which he seeks to lead the nation and the world. Whether his direction is right or wrong, it is essential to the debate that it be visible, and that it bear a logical relationship to his other policies and programs (*Time,* 10 November 1980, p. 32).

Congress and the Demand for Priorities. Congress often demands some indications of presidential priorities. Just as Presidents face resource constraints, Congress must make choices on the legislative agenda. "The leaders get pretty hot about the President's priorities as the session closes up," one Johnson legislative assistant argued. "With less than two weeks left in a session, there is great tension over what will be considered and what will be left for next year. The leaders come in and ask what's important. They want to know what we want right now and what can wait." A second Johnson assistant concurred: "I'd guess that's where the pressure originates, but I wouldn't place it all on the Congress. Sure, they want to know what they can leave behind, but the President has to make some choices, too. Those last two or three weeks are pure hell. You have to make a decision on what comes first." Indeed, even a cursory reading of the *Congressional Record* for the last weeks of the session demonstrates the frenetic pace. Bills are considered and passed with remarkable speed. Yet, for all the activity, Congress must abandon many items.

According to the liaison staffs, the last moments of a session often involve the greatest opportunities for success. "It is really incredible," a Carter assistant remarked at the end of 1979. "You can beat your head against the Hill for a full year and still have everything come down to a vote in the last days of the session. If you can get your act together, it's the best time to get results." These opportunities often rest on the sheer confusion of the final days. Congress is inclined to wrap up the loose ends of the session, to dispose of the unfinished business. As one congressional observer argued, "The House and Senate do have some energy invested in finishing the term with a flurry. During an election year, there is good reason to go home with a full legislation sack."

Given the amount of business in the closing weeks of a congressional session, it is in the President's interest to offer some ranking of his priorities. Once again, the key is *competition*. In competing for scarce space, the President can push certain proposals ahead by giving them a high priority. In scheduling its agenda for the final surge, Congress must make choices, choices which are critical for the President's success.

The congressional demand for priorities cannot be ignored. According to one Ford assistant, "Some members will actually call you up and ask what you want. They will demand some indication of what they can or cannot delay, what will or will not be signed. If you don't respond, you can be in trouble. They may decide that nothing is important." Whatever the specific vehicle, Congress expects the President to provide direction on the top items. Nor is the demand for guidance restricted to the end of the session. Though rankings have an important impact on the final moments, Congress demands signals from the President throughout the term. As one liaison officer from the Ford administration suggested, "Congress needs time to digest what the President sends; time to come up with independent analysis; time to schedule hearings and markups. Unless the President gives some indication of what's truly important, the Congress will simply put the proposals in a queue."

Perhaps Carter suffered most from the absence of explicit priorities. In Carter's first eighteen months, congressional leaders repeatedly bemoaned the amount of legislation on the domestic agenda. As I noted in chapters 2 and 5, Carter did not send a particularly heavy slate of proposals; he trailed both of his Democratic colleagues in the absolute number of requests. Yet, the Carter agenda was perceived as massive by Congress. According to both congressional and media observers, Carter's problem centered on the lack of priorities. The bulk of Carter's domestic program moved to Congress without any indication of relative importance. At a time when Congress was trying to sort through an eight-year backlog of legislation, the absence of presidential priorities was a major problem. Hospital cost control was to be treated with the same urgency as offshore-oil safety; welfare reform was to be accepted with the same priority as strip-mine reclamation; energy was indistinguishable from election reforms. It was a significant miscalculation. As one media observer remarked, "Carter expected Congress to take each of his programs on face value; the simple fact that a program came from the White House was to be enough. Rather than rank his priorities in some meaningful fashion, Carter wanted Congress to do it all." The reaction was immediate. According to one former Nixon assistant, now a legislative aide in Congress,

> Most of the committees felt that Carter's attitude was both arrogant and inept. They expect the President to contribute to the legislative agenda, but not by asking for everything. If hospital cost containment can wait, the President should say so. If welfare reform has to come tomorrow, the President is welcome to give the signal. Instead, Carter sat up on his high horse and said, "Take all or nothing." Congress decided to take very little.

Like his timing of the domestic program, Carter's inexperience in national politics hampered his ability to use the institutional framework effectively. Following continued congressional complaints about the Carter agenda, Vice President Mondale pressed for greater attention to the formal executive agenda in order to give both the staff and Congress a guide to priorities.

Resources and the Need for Priorities. Priorities are central to the conservation of both internal and external resources. For the liaison staffs, the critical resource was presidential capital. "The President cannot expect Congress to act on every proposal," one Nixon assistant argued. "He must give them a lead on the top items. Otherwise, he will spread his momentum over too many issues." A second Nixon assistant agreed:

> When you look at the situation we faced, the need for priority-setting was even more important. We had a very slim electoral margin; we faced a hostile Democratic Congress; the executive branch was not particularly interested in our ideas. Without a firm statement of priorities, we could not focus our energy. That was the primary reason for the repeated reference to the Six Great Goals in 1971. It was an attempt to concentrate our political strength.

It is to the President's advantage to provide some statement of priorities. With increased competition for agenda space, the President must focus his scarce political support on the most valuable proposals — at least that is what the liaison staffs believe. As one Carter assistant apologized, "I don't mean to simplify a very complex process, but Congress no longer offers that many opportunities for the President to set the agenda. Unless the President gives Congress a firm list of priorities, the Congress will drift to other business. That was a lesson we learned quite early."

The rankings of presidential priorities are rarely explicit, that is, they are rarely ranked from one to ten. As one aide argued, "You don't want to tell them exactly what's first or last. They may take you too seriously. But you do want to let them know which ones are at the top. Always let them know what's important; never tell them what's not." Once again, Carter serves as an example. Though Carter was a Democratic President facing a Democratic Congress, the staff soon realized that the competition for congressional space was intense. As one former Johnson assistant argued,

> It was clear that the political environment had changed since 1967. We had the seats in Congress, but we didn't have much influence. The election had been too close, and there was a hefty backlog from the Nixon and Ford years. The biggest mistake we made in the early going was the failure to focus on a few items as the top priorities. We needed to demonstrate our ability to produce substantive results. Instead, we used a shotgun approach.

As Mondale pressed for an executive agenda, the importance of priorities began to rise. Welfare reform, energy, and hospital cost containment were to be taken first; urban assistance, reorganization, and electoral reform second. By the time the priorities were ranked, however, the early momentum was gone. It wasn't until 1978 that the Mondale agenda began to take hold. According to one outside observer, it was "too little too late."

> Congress was already confused. The Carter program had been too extensive and too disorganized. The first year was the most important moment for impact, and Carter wasted it trying to pull the program together. By the second year, the program was too disrupted to be drawn into some coherent form. The first year was the time for a "New Foundation." You announce the idea first, then present the programs.

Priority-setting is also important for the conservation of internal resources. Not only are priorities a signal to Congress and the executive branch but they direct internal staff commitments. As one Kennedy aide suggested, "Left to their own devices, the staff will take on too damn much. Each aide has some pet project. If the President doesn't lay down the law, the staff will waste too much time." From this standpoint, the staff might be viewed as a group of policy "entrepreneurs." The tendency for individual assistants to generate personal programs is natural; in fact, such advocacy is one method to gain prestige within the White House. Priority-setting is one method for reducing the impact of just such widespread advocacy. Though Presidents need to be wary of isolation, clear statements of domestic priorities can reduce the waste of internal resources. As we shall see, multiple advocacy is a very expensive decision-making style.

Transmitting the Must List. How is the must list communicated to the participants? We have already seen that congressional leaders may actively pursue statements of presidential priorities. According to the liaison staffs, the President's priorities are often relayed directly to the congressional leaders. "We always wanted to make sure they understood what we wanted," one Johnson assistant suggested. "We let them know which items came first and which ones could wait. The President had several items that he felt he had to have. I'm not saying highway beautification wasn't important, but that was way down the list. He could have lived without it."

The President may attempt to transmit the list through the press. Once again, the press is an *indirect* channel. From 1961 through 1969, for instance, both Kennedy and Johnson presented annual summaries of the legislative record. In 1967 the Johnson administration itemized a list of fifty-seven "gains" and eighteen items of "unfinished business." That list, published on 16 December 1967, was specifically intended to focus attention for the next session. According to a Johnson aide who worked on the release, "We wanted to make sure that Congress knew what we wanted in 1968. When the session opened, we wanted to have Congress already thinking about what they had missed." The list of eighteen items began with the tax surcharge and the Safe Streets Crime Control Act; it ended with the elected school board for the District of Columbia and highway beautification. For the Johnson staff, the order of "unfinished business" had specific meaning for the President. It was as close to a numerical ranking of priorities as the President was willing to go. "We tried to avoid those kinds of lists," one aide argued, "but it was true that the tax surcharge was much more important at that point than highways. Hell, we were trying to get the funds for a war in Vietnam and the Great Society. We were also trying to slow inflation—highways were not that important compared to the surcharge."

In 1969 Nixon discontinued the listing of legislative gains and losses. In part the decision reflected the absence of legislative success. Nixon had a very difficult first year—primarily because of the delays in presenting the domestic agenda. As one Nixon aide asked, "Why in God's name would we want to prepare such a list? We didn't have that much on the Hill, and we surely didn't have too many victories." This is not to suggest that there were no priorities. According to the Nixon liaison staff, cues were given to key congressional allies. Welfare reform was at the top, followed by revenue sharing, environment, crime, and reorganization. By 1973 welfare reform was no longer at the top; special revenue sharing had taken over the first spot. Eventually Nixon made his first-term priorities quite apparent in the 1971 "Six Great Goals" State of the Union message. In the speech, Nixon asked not "simply for new programs in the old framework, but to change the framework itself—to reform the entire structure of American government so we can make it again fully responsive to the needs and wishes of the American people." According to Nixon, the first of the Six Great Goals was already before Congress in the unfinished business of the first two years.

Regardless of the specific channel, the President is the chief conduit for the must list. Whether through contacts with individual representatives and senators or through the liaison staff, the President must be the primary source of the priorities.

The State of the Union Address. In all five administrations the State of the Union address was the central battleground for presidential priorities. As Kessel suggests,

> Experienced participants in executive politics certainly recognize these "cardinal decision-and-action forcing processes" for what they are. Cabinet members, White House aides, and others are quite aware of the significance of getting material included in the State of the Union message. Favorable mention of a policy gives visibility to it and confers presidential backing to the enterprise at one and the same time. Since there are obvious limits to the number of policies that can be thus favored, very real contests take place over control of this scarce resource. "The name of the game," we are told, "is Who Controls the Final Draft?" (Kessel 1972, p. 3).

The recent history of the State of the Union address certainly reinforces its value as a priority-setting device. At least since Theodore Roosevelt, Presidents have used the message as a statement of both foreign and domestic priorities.

The message is of primary importance to the White House staffs; it is *the* statement of legislative priorities. There is conflict over the positioning of requests within the address, over the length of sentences, over punctuation. A program has a higher priority if it is presented separately from the frequent "laundry lists": if it comes earlier in the domestic section of the message; or if it is mentioned in the introduction or conclusion of the address. As one former speech writer complained, "I've never seen such bickering between the various departments and staffs. Everyone had a favored sentence, and everyone wanted it presented first. When I got around to pulling together a final draft, it was next to impossible. They all stopped in to check the draft, to pencil in a correction here or there." Thus, it is not enough just to receive mention in the address: advocates want a clear statement of priorities. As the speech writer concluded, "They want to know that their program is at the top. They want to take the document to the Hill and point to the exact number of words. 'Look at this,' they will say, 'we had the top domestic request in the message.' Apparently, it is very important to them; otherwise they wouldn't fight so much. I'm sure it isn't lost on the President."

Moving onto the Must List

All five staffs recognized the importance of presidential priorities. Though the list is rarely written down or presented in an explicit numerical order, the staff knows which items are most important. (According to several assistants, that knowledge is a sign of proximity to the President. As one Kennedy aide argued, "There is always some sense of the top priorities. You know what's important and what isn't. The people who don't know just aren't that involved.") As the President's priorities shift and evolve over the term, certain items move onto the list and others move off. Several specific considerations force items up and down on the must list. Here, it is important to recognize that the must list is actually the *top of the agenda*. As Presidents set the domestic agenda, some items reach the top and others fall to the bottom. Thus, we are interested in how and why Presidents *rank* their domestic requests.

Legislative Potential. Not surprisingly, in the definition of top priorities the President and the staff emphasize programs that have a greater chance of legislative success. Like the search for alternatives, presidential priorities reflect the assessment of political costs. As one assistant remarked, "There are times when a bill is moving along and all that is really needed is a push from the President. In those cases, we will apply the pressure to secure action as quickly as possible." These assessments of legislative potential are reflected in the domestic priorities. According to a Nixon aide, "We watched the progress of key bills and programs. We often elevated the importance of a specific item because it was so close to passage; we sometimes demoted another because it was in the way."

According to the staffs, priorities are intimately tied to policy "windows"—a concept that emerges from Kingdon's (1978) research on transportation and health—that is, opportunities for legislative success open for very brief periods of time. According to a Ford assistant, "Sometimes, you have the potential for action in a rather brief time span. You might find a hearing or floor vote which could aid your effort. That instant could mean the difference between success and failure." One method of opening the window is to move an item onto the must list. "You'd be surprised at how much the mention of a program at a press conference can affect congressional reactions," a Kennedy aide remarked. "Congress does listen and will often respond to the President's request. If you can take advantage of the openings, the success rate will go up. It is as simple as that."

Policy windows involve the merging of political interests. Congress, the President, interest groups, and the executive branch may come together at a critical moment. That was the case for national health insurance in 1974. The Democrats had decided to produce a bill; organized labor was close to a compromise; Nixon had supported the concept of comprehensive coverage. The window opened briefly in the spring, but it closed with Nixon's resignation and labor's willingness to wait for the 1976 election. According to the staffs, the President's priorities are a powerful tool in such windows. As one Johnson aide suggested, "When the opportunity arises, the President has got to keep the pressure on. Mention the program in a press conference, make a televised address, use the phone. The President has got to make it absolutely clear that the program is a priority." Policy windows will usually open at the start of the term; with the passage of time, the windows start to close. As presidential capital dwindles, the opportunities decline. According to the staffs, presidential priorities become a primary weapon in the struggle for legislative progress. The decision to move an item to the top of the must list can speed legislative adoption; it can also open legislative windows. Though Presidents are limited in the timing of the domestic program, the use of priorities remains an area where expertise can have a dramatic impact.

Crisis. Beyond legislative windows, presidential priorities involve the perception of crisis. Presidents and staffs pay greater attention to problems that are perceived as demanding immediate attention. According to one liaison officer from the Kennedy-Johnson years, "Crisis often provides the momentary surge necessary for passage. If some event takes place which clearly promotes an issue, it is important to make the connection. Congress is much more responsive to crisis." Consider the impact of the Birmingham riots on Kennedy's civil rights legislation. Following a five-week demonstration in April 1963, violence brought civil rights to national attention. Kennedy responded to the crisis by dispatching the national guard to bases near Birmingham. Kennedy also decided to pursue immediate legislation. The crisis provided a "window" for substantive action, and civil rights legislation moved to the top of Kennedy's must list. As one Kennedy aide argued, "Birmingham was the driving force behind the legislation; it was the catalyst in the President's choice. Without Birmingham, I doubt that civil rights would have made it until 1965. It was that sensitive. Birmingham was frightening, but it was also important. If it hadn't happened, the President would have been forced to wait another two years." The crisis pressed civil rights toward the top of the President's domestic agenda. It not only affected the issue and the alternative but drove civil rights to the Kennedy must list.

Crisis also affected the Nixon agenda. Following the outbreak of the Yom Kippur War between Egypt and Israel on 6 October 1973, the Arab position on United States involvement hardened. By the end of October that opposition had turned into a full-scale oil embargo. Early projections forecast a 10 percent drop in imported oil reserves, but by mid-winter the figure had climbed. According to the Nixon administration, the oil embargo was the direct factor in subsequent energy legislation. Moreover, the oil crisis forced energy to the top of the domestic program. As one Nixon energy expert noted, "The Alaska pipeline, the 55-mile speed limit, daylight-saving time, and the energy independence program were all products of the OPEC action. We were not tuned into energy before 1972. For several reasons, we simply had not predicted the problem. The oil embargo changed the agenda dramatically." A second Nixon assistant agreed: "The oil embargo was the most important event of the entire administration. We were not prepared for the supply cut, nor were we prepared for the price increases. The oil embargo changed our priorities completely. Energy arrived and moved to the top."

That crisis atmosphere also affected the Carter energy priorities. Despite Carter's vigorous support of a comprehensive energy plan, the staff emphasized the impact of crisis as the key to success in 1979. Up to that point, the administration had not been notably successful with energy legislation. In fact, as one aide suggested, "We had gone nowhere. The legislation was unpopular in Congress, and almost universally rejected by the public. After three years of the moral equivalent of war, the program hadn't moved." The summer 1979 gas lines in California and the District of Columbia changed the perceptions. The gas lines, coupled with the November Iranian oil embargo, generated a wave of support for the energy plan. Although stand-by gasoline rationing had failed in the summer, it passed in early 1980; and although the windfall profits tax had stalled in summer, it moved in January.

The President's priorities reflect the perception of both costs and benefits. Presidents do not move items to the must list unless they are important, and they distinguish among even the important programs—some are more immediate than others. When Presidents are forced to present the must list, potential for success and crisis are critical factors.

Moving off the Must List

Once an item reaches the must list, it does not necessarily stay. Items are moved off the must list for a variety of reasons. Enactment automatically removes many priorities from the list; once a program is passed, administrative attention may shift to other items. Items also move off because of restricted space. Just as the President's agenda can contain only so many items, the list of top priorities can focus on only a limited number at any given moment. We have already seen that the domestic agenda is restricted by both internal and external resources; the must list is similarly limited. As one Johnson-Carter assistant put it,

> How many items can we deal with at one time? As far as the most important priorities go, we are fairly tight. Pushing a bill through Congress demands maximum effort, especially if there is a degree of opposition and controversy. When the President says a program is his first priority, it means that a number of other programs will have to wait until the legislative action is cleared. LBJ used to think of the agenda as a plate. It had to be kept full, but never piled too high. A serving of this and a serving of that, but never let the food spill off on the table.

Obviously, movement off the President's list of priorities is a signal of either frustration or displeasure. Frustration may center on the lack of congressional action. Welfare reform dropped from the Nixon list partially because of the heavy investment of presidential capital in a no-win situation; Aid to Education and Medicare dropped from the Kennedy list for similar reasons. Displeasure may stem from internal reevaluations. Urban assistance and real-wage insurance dropped from the Carter list in part because internal reviews of costs undermined support. The Carter staff eventually redrafted the bills with lower budgets or dropped them completely. As one urban affairs assistant argued, "Urban assistance had to be redrawn. Congress just wouldn't accept the bill. Publicly, we were very happy with the number of titles that passed. Privately, the most important components were left out."

The signal of declining interest may be transmitted to Congress via a liaison office request for legislative withdrawal. "That's always an option," one Kennedy aide argued, "but it is rarely used. If an item is dying in Congress, we usually don't have to commit euthanasia. It is somewhat embarrassing to ask that a proposal be dropped." The White House may stop talking about the priority. Congress does monitor presidential signals; if the President stops pressuring for action, Congress will sense the change. According to a media observer, "We knew that welfare reform was dead when Nixon stopped asking about it. Nixon no longer talked about it, and the staff was no longer interested. The bill just floated in Congress. It was a long-term decision, but the silence was conspicuous." There are also institutional opportunities for abandonment. If a proposal is not passed in a two-year Congress, that bill must be reintroduced for consideration in the next session. The President may drop a priority by merely deciding not to request new sponsorship. According to one OMB officer, "We watch the bills come and go. Some keep coming back year after year. You can tell what the President doesn't want by watching the items that don't come back. The President might decide to wait for a better opportunity or just abandon a bill completely."

Congressional Resistance. The most frequent explanation for change in priorities centered on congressional resistance. Just as potential success often moves items up the must list, the specter of failure often moves items off. "Most Presidents are unwilling to stick with a priority if there is no chance of passage," one OMB analyst argued. "At some point the White House must decide whether to continue a losing cause. If there is no further opportunity, the White House must either redraft the bill or let it die peacefully." According to the presidential staffs, congressional failure is a critical factor in the decision to reorder top priorities. Aid to Education, Medicare, welfare reform, and urban assistance are examples of the impact of the congressional environment on presidential priorities. Consider the Family Assistance Plan under Nixon. As one aide remarked,

> We sent the Family Assistance Plan to Congress in August 1969. We couldn't get a hearing until 1970. We were able to pass through the House that year, but the Senate would not budge. We went after them with everything we had, but they would not give in. We stayed with the plan as

long as possible. Finally, we had to give up; it was not going to pass regardless of how hard we pushed. We decided to put our energies into other programs. We had reached the wall on welfare reform and had to let it go.

Carter faced similar problems with his version of welfare reform. Like the FAP, Carter's Program for Better Jobs and Income (PBJI) was unable to pass. Despite significant investment of time and energy, the program stalled. One Carter assistant argued that "we were still interested in welfare reform, but we weren't going to get anything through Congress. By 1978 it was clear that it was not going to pass. We switched to a more basic income floor for the states. PBJI just wasn't going to make it." By 1979 the plan had dropped from Carter's must list. According to a Carter liaison assistant, "No one could justify spending much more time on the program. It was obvious Congress wasn't committed to the plan. Why bust a gut on a loser?" As we shall see, PBJI was also undermined by consistent problems with economic costs.

It is difficult to predict how long a President will stay with a losing priority. Welfare reform remained on Nixon's must list for three years. As one Johnson aide remarked, "You hammer at the proposal until it is fairly clear that there is no chance. If the program is truly important to the Chief Executive, you stay with it until it begins to block more important items. When Aid to Education started to affect civil rights, Kennedy had to start thinking about dropping it." One outside observer summarized the process succinctly:

> Most of us watch the agenda change very quickly. One day some issue will be very hot—the Congress will be interested, the President will be interested, even the bureaucracy will be interested. But in this town, nothing stays hot too long. The big guns map out the territory and stake their claims. It is not unusual for an idea to reach the boiling point overnight and then cool immediately. Often that cooling will clog the process. An issue will get caught in midstream, or should I say mid-steam?

Yet, whatever the initial level of concern, repeated failure eventually leads to abandonment. "None of us wanted to give up on Medicare," one Kennedy aide noted. "It was a very important part of the New Frontier. It simply became evident that it would not pass—that Wilbur Mills would not allow it out of committee. The President was still committed, but realistically we had to say uncle."

The liaison office is a critical participant in the decisions. The assessment of the potential for success affects movement both onto and off of the must list. However, as one liaison officer remarked, "It's not an awesome responsibility. You gauge the congressional process and make a recommendation. Either the program stands a chance or it doesn't. You look ahead for a year or so and look at the key obstacles. Are any members up for reelection? Can we make any trades?" The President must weigh the potential benefits against the political costs. For Aid to Education, the potential benefits still guaranteed a substantial commitment of resources. Even when Aid to Education became a liability, the liaison office continued the lobbying effort. Aid to education was a central theme of the domestic agenda and warranted considerable investments of presidential time, energy, and capital. Thus, more than any other choice, the decision to drop a priority involves some calculations of costs *and* benefits.

Increased Costs. Items also drop from the must list because of increased costs. Whether through congressional hearings or internal reviews, certain programs are subject to increased political, economic, or technical costs. With the emergence of the Congressional Budget Office as an independent source of information, the President increasingly has become subject to external analysis. As one Carter welfare expert argued, "Of course we watched CBO. Their review of PBJI was a big hit down here. Our figures were either very wrong or we had been misled. Congress is certainly no longer willing to take our analysis as the final word." Before CBO, competitive analysis was either unavailable or unheeded. Though OMB provides review of budgetary impact, it is not possible to analyze each proposal with respect to cost or workability. OMB and the President often must rely on the same departmental advice.

In 1969 not only did HEW's information dominate the White House process but it precluded any viable counteranalysis in Congress. The final downfall of Nixon's FAP involved a very limited series of case examples that undermined confidence in the basic figures. In 1977, CBO supplied the damning figures. Eventually, CBO acquired HEW's computer program and, in cooperation with HEW, began its own analysis. It took the CBO four months to penetrate Carter's welfare reform plan and to make its own estimates of the costs and the numbers of people involved. Whereas Carter had announced the cost at $2.8 billion, CBO projected the cost at $19.2 billion by 1982.

The Carter staff had received hints of the disparity in costs long before the CBO analysis was released in December 1977. In October 1977 Richard Nathan, a nationally respected welfare expert and former deputy secretary of HEW under Nixon, testified before the House Welfare Reform Subcommittee. In that testimony, Nathan suggested that the Carter figures were much bigger "by a magnitude of two or more in costs than they have said." The initial reaction in the White House was one of surprise. "Frankly, we couldn't understand the discrepancy," one Carter liaison assistant noted. "The hearings caused considerable rethinking on welfare reform. Then the CBO report came out. We started to think about how we might let the ship go down without too many casualties."

Cost considerations returned to undercut both urban assistance and real-wage insurance. Development of the urban assistance plan had taken over a year and had involved considerable efforts at internal compromise.

The program had been introduced as an omnibus bill, but it involved a variety of separate proposals. Though the administration had some success with the less controversial items, the major expenditure items floundered. According to one Carter liaison officer, "Congress refused to budge on the big budget items. They had already begun to slip into the cost-cutting frame of reference. We had to withdraw the program to scale it down." The real-wage insurance program involved a similar though more pronounced effort. Originally, the plan involved tax rebates to individuals who held income increases under Carter's 7-percent guidelines. With inflation running at 8 percent, the plan was expensive but affordable; however, as inflation continued to rise, the plan became more expensive. "Each half-percent increase in inflation meant several billions," one assistant argued. "Once inflation hit 8.5 percent, the real-wage program became too expensive." The plan was eventually dropped after a roller-coaster ride on the Carter must list. It was at the top in late 1978, off in January 1979, on in February, and off in March. The indecision involved the President's assessment of the importance of the issue versus its specific economic and political costs.

Once a program reaches the President's must list, there is a natural atrophy. The first moments of the term offer the greatest windows for impact. The longer an item remains, the more incentive to turn to other issues. The item is either abandoned altogether or simply demoted until a new window appears. "The longer that program is up there, the more opposition," a media observer argued. "The longer it stands as the highest priority, the more pressure against adoption. If it doesn't pass within a year or two, there are serious problems. Either the President hasn't paved the way properly or the opposition is simply too strong." Thus, if an issue does not "hit" within a relatively short period of time, it is undercut within the White House staff. For these staffs, windows open and close quickly. Just as a space shot may have only a few minutes to pierce a window into orbit, there are limits on presidential momentum.

Conclusion

Among items that reach the President's domestic agenda, certain items receive maximum presidential attention. According to the staffs, items move onto the must list as their potential for success increases. Items move off the list in response to rising costs or legislative failure.

Once an item reaches the top of the President's agenda, it stays until one of two events occurs: the program may pass, automatically making room for another priority—a first cousin or an unrelated program—or it may be deliberately abandoned by the President or the staff. If Congress fails to approve the item or if the program costs increase, the President must give serious consideration to removal. As we shall see in chapter 8, these decisions involve considerable staff conflict.

Presidential priorities provide one avenue for reducing the impact of increased domestic competition. Presidents cannot afford to focus on a wide range of issues, as Carter did, with little guidance on the relative standing of each. In an era of scarce presidential resources and growing congressional competition, Presidents must produce some indication of priorities. These rankings help Congress allocate agenda space, and they direct White House time and energy. More now than in the 1960s, Presidents must link legislative requests with explicit priorities; they cannot afford to waste resources.

8 presidential choice

The choice of domestic programs involves considerable pressure. Presidents want to maximize benefits while reducing costs; to conserve political capital while generating a legislative record; to move the agenda quickly without sacrificing good policy. The domestic policy process thus becomes a balancing act.

Carter's 1978 urban-assistance package is one example of the impact of process on the domestic agenda. Like most presidential priorities, the decision involved considerable conflict and uncertainty. Indeed, according to most accounts, choices were still being made less than an hour before the package was announced. According to one press report,

> The process—marked by lengthy debate, quarreling, lobbying and finally uneasy compromise—says much about the way public policy is made in a world of political and economic constraints. It says much about this President's decision-making. It demonstrates the limits to Presidential authority, and, cynics might say, why so many Government programs wind up not working.
>
> The program was as much political as substantive. It had a little something for everybody. There was fiscal relief for mayors, but not too much. There was direct funding for local neighborhood groups, but not without mayoral consent. There was a little incentive money to induce states to help their cities, but no penalties for those that did not.
>
> Ultimately, the plan was shaped greatly by lobbying, from mayors, governors, neighborhood advocates, businessmen and Federal bureaucrats. The influential and penny-pinching Office of Management and Budget broke out a fresh supply of wet blankets for the occasion. (Reinhold 1978, p. 1).

Carter was caught in a squeeze between ideology and reelection. Carter was highly skeptical about the government's ability to solve urban problems, but

169

he was also indebted to blacks, labor, and the poor for his electoral margin. Once Carter decided to move ahead with the issue, costs became the primary pressure on the alternatives. Yet, despite the seeming importance of the urban package, Carter was not directly involved in the decisions.

> The President's role in all this is unclear. While he was briefed periodically, it appears he did not see a full list of initiatives until just five days before the policy's unveiling. . . . He was handed a 178 page memorandum asking him to make scores of "yes/no" decisions. With each item was a recommendation from Mr. Eizenstat and the budget office. . . .
>
> "He likes to see things in writing—he gets briefed, reads carefully and makes decisions," said one aide, who asserted that the last-minute frenzy was not unusual in the White House. But to outsiders it was unnerving. "He just sits there alone and checks things off," said one high Administration official (Reinhold 1978, p. 1).

Carter liked to make decisions in the relative isolation of the Oval Office; he liked to see the choices in detailed memoranda. Did it make a difference?

One way to answer the question is to compare Kennedy, Johnson, and Ford with Nixon and Carter. According to the White House staffs, Kennedy, Johnson, and Ford generally preferred to make most decisions in person. All three settled policy disputes in the presence of the interested parties; all three made domestic decisions by facing the arguments in a relatively open setting. They used policy memoranda to focus decisions, but they dealt with the major issues in person. Nixon and Carter, however, preferred to make most decisions on paper. Both chose to tackle competing demands in decision memos; both made domestic decisions in the quiet of their private study; both avoided personal confrontations. One OMB officer summarized the difference between the Ford and Carter styles as follows:

> Ford and Carter were like night and day. Ford definitely wanted to meet the protagonists in a face-to-face discussion, no holds barred. If there was internal conflict, he wanted it out in the open, in the Oval Office, not in Congress. He felt that he could mediate most differences, and wanted to hear the opposing arguments in person. Carter, on the other hand, can't stand personal confrontations. Carter has set up a system which insulates him from the conflict. He does not want to waste his time listening to people fight. He wants to read the arguments and make a choice based on the pros and cons.

Does the choice between an in-person and an on-paper strategy make any difference? Several aides remarked that the on-paper approach may suppress good ideas. As one Nixon assistant noted, "If you can't get your idea on paper, you can't get it in to the President. We lost some good ideas because they weren't ready for a memo presentation." A Carter staffer agreed: "If you don't go through channels, the President simply won't listen. But hell, some programs just aren't ready for channels. The President actually refused to listen to some damn good ideas simply because they weren't committed to paper." One Carter aide related the story of a colleague who brought an idea to the President without first staffing it out: "Carter was so mad that he refused to look at the idea when it came back through on paper."

The on-paper approach may also disguise intensity. Whereas Kennedy, Johnson, and Ford were able to gauge the intensity of the combatants, neither Nixon nor Carter had the same advantage. According to one Carter aide, "Everybody looks the same on paper. Califano comes across as calm as Eizenstat. It is never like that in the real world. If Califano is angry and the President doesn't know, what's going to happen in Congress? The President has to find out about the potential opposition *before* he decides, not after." Though decision memos often contain lists of assistants either for or against an idea, there is no measure of intensity. To a great extent, the last aide to "pile on" ends up with the most influence. According to former President Ford,

> There can be conflicts, too, between different officials favoring different options. I myself liked to have a consensus developed before a problem came to my desk for decision, but then I reserved the right to go behind that consensus to find out what the differing views were in the process. In that way I got a feel as to whether it was just a weak compromise or whether it was a legitimate one that provided the best answer. You can have compromises that just destroy the arguments on either the right or the left, and that is a pretty poor policy. On the other hand, you can have a good consensus where things actually mesh (*Time,* 10 November 1980, p. 31).

If the on-paper strategy inhibits creativity and hides conflict, it saves vast amounts of presidential time and energy; it also protects secrecy. "There comes a point when the President has to fish or cut bait," one Nixon aide remarked. "You can go on debating forever, but the President has to reach a decision based on the facts, not . . . on the staffs. We learned our lesson when Moynihan sold the President on the Family Assistance Plan." Nixon's preference for the on-paper style evolved from both his personality and the welfare debate. The bulk of the decisions on welfare were forged in face-to-face conflict which often entered the Oval Office. By the end of the first three months, Nixon was already drifting toward the on-paper style. According to one aide, "He was tired of all the backbiting. He felt that Moynihan and Burns had cost him at least three months." Clearly, Nixon did not like dealing with the "players" in person. Indeed, when the decisions were finally made regarding welfare reform, Nixon could not face Arthur Burns to tell him of the choice. Despite Burns's heavy investment in the outcome and his personal loyalty, Nixon had Ehrlichman make the telephone call.

Three Models of Choice

The distinction between the in-person and on-paper styles is but a small part of each President's decision framework. It is nonetheless important. Unfortunately, presidential scholars have made only passing reference to White House decision-making. There have been a variety of studies on the *tools* of choice, but few on their application. When presidential scholars have examined decision-making, they have focused on foreign affairs, perhaps because the area is less complicated in terms of participants and outcomes. Graham Allison's (1971) study of the Cuban missile crisis remains the standard source on presidential choice and decision-making.

There are several reasons why we might study domestic decision-making. The decision structure determines who participates in the agenda choice. In 1978-80, for instance, the Mondale agenda ensured that the liberal wing of the Carter staff would have greater participation in the domestic program; it provided access for Mondale, Eizenstat, and the Domestic Policy Staff. According to one Mondale aide, "The most important fact about the agenda is that the Vice President gets the last crack at the contents. . . . He gets the memoranda before anyone else, and it comes back to him after everyone has signed off."

Moreover, the decision structure affects the number of ideas under consideration at any one point in time. We have already seen how the domestic policy process tends to focus on the available alternative. The on-paper style encourages that reliance. As one Johnson assistant notes, "There is no reason to ask for a comprehensive review of all potential options. There is no way the staff can find all of them; there is no way the President can review all of them; and out of all the potential alternatives, there are only a small number that are actually feasible." The decision structure can also inhibit multiple advocacy. Both Johnson and Carter demanded an annual canvass of potential programs. In the discussion of the results, however, Carter requested much greater detail. "He would not review a program unless it was properly prepared," one Carter assistant argued. "That obviously restricted the number of ideas that entered the White House."

Finally, the decision structure influences the timing of domestic choice. As we shall see, different decision frameworks demand different amounts of time. A rational model of presidential choice, for example, requires more time than a bargaining model. The rational framework also demands greater energy, information, and expertise—all scarce resources in any administration.

It has been ten years since Graham Allison published *Essence of Decision*. The organizational literature has grown rapidly in the ensuing years, but there is still no consensus on a general theory of organization, still no firm agreement on the definition of terms. There are, however, promising new developments which supplement and redirect Allison's emphasis. Allison offered three separate models to explain the Cuban missile crisis. Model I, called "rational actor," focused on what might be called the comprehensive, or rational, decision structure; Model II, "organizational process," centered on a behavior theory of presidential choice; and Model III, "governmental politics," involved Neustadt's (1960) bargaining theory of presidential power. All three models are still viable for the study of presidential choice. In the following discussion, however, I will retain the rational framework; combine Allison's models II and III; and add a third, rather unusual framework for comparison. I will concentrate on three distinct models of organizational choice—rational actor, behavioral, and "garbage can"—emphasizing both their organizational structure and their behavior.

Over the past two decades, many different labels have been used to describe presidential decision-making. At least a dozen major models of presidential choice and an equal number of attractive names have been produced: rational, quasi-rational, collegial, competitive, formalistic, hierarchical, root, branch, governmental politics, rational actor, bureaucratic, muddling-through, spokes-of-a-wheel, and wagons-in-a-circle. Fortunately, many of these models can be grouped under the three major models I will discuss. In the hope of returning to a semblance of clarity, I will use the original labels or those most frequently associated with the three major schools of decision-making.

Rational Actor. The rational-actor model emerges from the traditional school of organization theory and has received its strongest support in economic frameworks of choice. In its extreme, the rational model involves a full description of values and objectives, measured analysis, and a detailed analysis of costs and benefits. The key word here is *comprehensive*. Lest the requirements of the model be drawn too tightly for the presidential policy process, the rational model asks only that the majority of issues be identified; the majority of alternatives located; and explicit comparisons made between competing items. As Allison suggests,

> the power of the theory of rational action derives from its rigor—rigor purchased at the price of assumptions too heroic for many empirically oriented social scientists. The rigorous model of rational action maintains that rational choice consists of value-maximizing adaptation, within the context of a given payoff function, fixed alternatives, and consequences that are known (in one of three senses corresponding to certainty, risk, and uncertainty). But what guarantees that value-maximizing behavior within these parameters will in fact maximize the agent's values? Obviously, it would not, if the set of alternatives failed to include an option whose consequences ranked higher than any of the stated alternatives (Allison 1971, p. 31).

In the rational-actor model, conflict is resolved through analysis and persuasion; ideally, the "best" solution will always survive. The organizational structure for rational choice is generally both hierarchical and specialized. The organization must be prepared to staff the search for the widest range of ideas and alternatives.

The Behavioral Theory of the Firm. The behavioral model is culled directly from the Cyert and March (1963) analysis of the business firm. According to Cyert and March,

> [the] classic theory of an omniscient firm is inappropriate for a theory of the firm directed toward answering questions about microbehavior. Without denying the substantial abilities of organizations as problem-solving and decision-making institutions, we have suggested that a business firm is constrained by the uncertainty of its environment, the problems of maintaining a viable coalition, and the limitations on its capacity as a system for assembling, storing, and utilizing information. As a result, the theory . . . characterizes the firm as an *adaptively rational* system rather than an *omnisciently rational* system (p. 99).

The choice mechanism involves "satisficing": programs are selected such that all goals are satisfied to some degree. According to this behavioral model, all organizations continually face multiple, competing goals. Given conflicting demands, the firm tends to engage in a search for issues and alternatives that leaves no actor greatly dissatisfied. Bargaining is one method of settling conflict and was the basis for Allison's Model II. Cyert and March also allow for the rise of political coalitions within the organization:

> Let us view the organization as a coalition. It is a coalition of individuals, some of them organized into subcoalitions. In a business organization the coalition members include managers, workers, stockholders, suppliers, customers, lawyers, tax collectors, regulatory agencies, etc. In the governmental organization the members include administrators, workers, appointive officials, legislators, judges, clientele, interest group leaders, etc. (Cyert and March 1963, pp. 27, 30).

In the White House, the coalition members might include the President himself, the liaison officers, the domestic policy staff, economic advisors, OMB, the department chiefs, mid-level civil servants, and so on. Typically, differences between the various subcoalitions will be settled through bargaining. According to Neustadt, bargaining involves the power to persuade: "Underneath our images of Presidents-in-boots, astride decisions, are the half-observed realities of Presidents-in-sneakers, stirrups in hand, trying to induce particular department heads, or Congressmen or Senators, to climb aboard" (Neustadt 1966, p. 64).

The behavioral model allows for a wide degree of conflict. According to Cyert and March, "Basically we have argued that most organizations most of the time exist and thrive with considerable latent conflict of goals. Except at the level of nonoperational objectives, there is no internal consensus. The procedures for 'resolving' such conflict do not reduce all goals to a common dimension or even make them obviously internally consistent" (1963, p. 117). What if bargaining cannot resolve the conflict? Does the behavioral theory allow for multiple paths to conflict resolution? According to one Kennedy aide,

> Most of the time we just worked things out. Sometimes we would go out for dinner or lunch and hammer out some kind of compromise. There were times, however, when it came down to who carried the most weight. If you were a member of the strongest group, you got the most concessions. When a compromise couldn't be cut, the biggest coalition—no, the strongest coalition—would win. That was frustrating. Arguments didn't mean a damn if you were in the minority, unless that minority happened to include Jack Kennedy.

In the past, organizational theory has separated such activity into a distinct framework of its own, appropriately labeled the "political model," represented in Allison's Model III. In the political model, conflict is resolved through open confrontation and staff domination. For the purpose of model-building, however, political conflict can also be viewed as an activity within the general behavioral theory. For our purposes, the behavioral model encompasses two specific activities: *bargaining* and *domination.*

The line between bargaining and domination is sometimes blurred. Bargaining frequently collapses into warfare between competing factions; political domination often includes bargaining within the major coalitions. Both bargaining and domination can be considered potential methods for accommodating conflict in an "adaptively" rational organization. As we shall see, the shift from bargaining to domination is tied directly to declines in presidential time, energy, and capital. Yet, whether the decision style is bargaining or domination, the organizational structure remains stable. Standard operating procedures, avoidance of uncertainty, and organizational learning usually occur whether specific choices are resolved through bargaining or domination. *Presidents can and do behave differently within the same organizational system.* The context of each choice becomes critical for predicting presidential decision-making; as time, energy, and capital decline, domination should increase. As the organization "ages" over time, we can also expect increasing structure. The decision process will become more formal, and standard operating procedures will evolve.

The Garbage Can. The garbage-can theory of organizational choice, easily the most unusual of the three system models considered here, was developed by Cohen, March, and Olsen to deal with "organized anarchies."

> These are organizations—or decision situations—characterized by three properties. The first is problematic preferences. In the organization it is difficult to impute a set of preferences to the decision situation that

satisfies the standard consistency requirements for a theory of choice. The organization operates on the basis of a variety of inconsistent and ill-defined preferences. It can be described better as a loose collection of ideas than as a coherent structure; it discovers preferences through action more than it acts on the basis of preferences.

The second property is unclear technology. Although the organization manages to survive and even produce, its own processes are not understood by its members. It operates on the basis of simple trial-and-error procedures, the residue of learning from the accidents of past experience, and pragmatic inventions of necessity. The third property is fluid participation. Participants vary in the amount of time and effort they devote to different domains; involvement varies from one time to another. As a result, the boundaries of the organization are uncertain and changing; the audiences and decision makers for any particular kind of choice change capriciously (Cohen, March, and Olsen 1972, p. 1).

In the garbage-can model, decisions are the result of several independent "streams" within the organization: problems, solutions, participants, and energy. Ultimately, choices are made in three different ways: by resolution ("some choices resolve problems after some period of working on them"); by oversight (some choices are made quickly "without any attention to existing problems and with a minimum of time and energy"); and by flight ("the problems leave the choice, and thus it is now possible to make the decision").

As Lawrence Mohr suggests, the choice mechanism in the garbage can is "*strategic agglomeration,* i.e., a decision relative to a goal is rendered only if the latter happens to be under consideration when a choice on some other matter, call it the 'central choice,' is actually made" (1976, p. 631). Since there are a variety of problems, solutions, participants, and choice situations in constant movement through the organization, authoritative decisions are rarely made.

A certain amount of politics, bargaining, or rational analysis may take place, but these are not the behaviors with greatest importance for outcomes. Rather, the kinds of behavior that are typical and instrumental in the Garbage-can process of choice are going, coming, and waiting. For example, a new dean is to be selected. In the process, goals having to do with the hiring of women, neglect of social science departments, antiquated data processing facilities, student rights, pass-fail grading, weak athletic teams, falling enrollments, and interdisciplinary programs become attached to the choice as problems to be resolved. Rational attempts are made, but it is clear that there is not enough energy available to solve all of these problems in the context of this particular choice. Gradually, problems wander off voluntarily in search of other choices (Mohr 1976, p. 631).

Each choice situation acts as a "can," collecting "garbage" often unrelated to the issue at hand. In Congress, for instance, garbage cans may be created in the annual "Christmas tree" bills—continuing resolutions may stimulate amendments ranging from bans on abortion funding to new pork-barrel projects. As resources tighten, there are fewer and fewer opportunities for peaceful resolution of conflict—interests and alternatives flock to choice situations whenever they arise.

The Context of Choice

Many organizational scholars have argued that the decision structure is relatively stable over time, that a rational process will remain rational and a bargaining system will remain collegial. The assumption is rarely justified. The Presidency is not comparable to formal organizations in the private sector, particularly those organizations that have existed for decades. In organizing the White House, each President faces a novel situation. Offices must be staffed, lines of communication established, and working relationships defined. Contrary to the opinion of several members of Reagan's kitchen cabinet, the Presidency is not General Motors. Indeed the Presidency could resemble General Motors only if General Motors suddenly lost its key management personnel from the corporate board on down to the middle-management level. Unlike General Motors, the Reagan administration did not face formal operating procedures, clear networks of command, or organizational memory. Though the institutional features of the Presidency remain relatively stable from year to year, the wholesale replacement of top staff every four or eight years creates a remarkably dynamic organizational style. Thus, the President's decision style changes over time, just as any new organization changes and evolves over time. The major difference, however, is that the private organization is allowed to age and mature, while the Presidency is in constant flux.

In presidential choice, there is ample evidence of change. According to one OMB officer, "We normally see a change in how Presidents decide as the term wears on. At the beginning, there is a tendency to accept most new ideas. The President doesn't ask OMB for too much help. Toward the end of the first year, the tide begins to change." The President starts to rely on OMB for more information and advice; the first budget is formed; OMB becomes a mediator of bureaucratic disputes. A second OMB assistant agreed:

> The patterns are fairly logical. At the start of the term, there is plenty to go around. The President is looking for a domestic program and wants ideas. There is very little in-fighting on the issues . . . mainly because most ideas can be accommodated. However, as the Congress starts to hold back, the pressure increases; as the budget figures come in, the conflict grows. There just isn't as much to spread around.

The context of choice determines decision style. At the start of the term, there is a trend toward internal accommodation and cooperation, what we have called bargaining. According to a Johnson aide, "In 1965 we didn't have to choose. Virtually every idea that came up was turned into a substantive proposal. By 1966 it changed—Califano was brought in to clean house and make sure the programs made some sense." My assumption here is that the context—or situation—surrounding each domestic agenda decision is often in flux, creating a potentially different style for every choice. Decisions on welfare reform in January may involve collegial bargaining; decisions on health insurance in March may involve the struggle for domination. The key to understanding the domestic process thereby rests on the specific context of choice.

There are at least six specific situational determinants of presidential choice, several of which are drawn from Mohr's (1976) study of judicial policy-making. These six variables help us understand why Presidents drift toward the rational, behavioral, or garbage-can decision style. Moreover, we should also be able to distinguish between behaviors, particularly between bargaining and domination. The six variables and their relationships to the decision models are summarized in table 18. For now, it is important to note that the rational style demands the greatest commitment of presidential resources, while domination reacts to dwindling opportunities. A contextual model of presidential choice thereby helps predict decision style. Given differing levels of presidential resources, we can start to understand why most Presidents begin their terms with bargaining and end with domination.

Time and Energy. Time and energy have a predictable impact on choice. The rational model of decision-making demands a heavy commitment of both presidential time and energy; indeed, a frequent criticism of the rational model rests on the lack of available time and energy. The rational model makes certain assumptions about the amount of internal resources

Table 18. The Context of Choice

	Decision Model			
	Rational	Behavioral		Garbage Can
Contextual variable	Comprehensive search	Bargaining	Domination	Coming, going, waiting
Time and energy	high	moderate	low	high
Information and expertise	high	moderate	moderate	low
Capital	moderate-high	moderate	low	low
Goal compatibility	high	moderate	low	low
Consistency of participants	low	high	low	low
Presidential involvement	low	high	low	low

available for analysis and search, assumptions that do not match presidential reality. As one Carter aide argued, "When the President asks to see all the potential alternatives, it is an impossible request. Not only do we have to limit the range to the few that just might work but we have to cut back to save on time. The staff already has too much to do without attempting that kind of analysis—it involves too much time."

Within the behavioral model, the bargaining style requires more time than internal staff domination. Domination becomes the most convenient of all decision styles. Once the dominant coalition is established, there is a relatively stable commitment of time and energy. The coalition might have to resist internal challenges, but the demand for time is greatly reduced. As one Nixon aide remarked, "Whatever else Ehrlichman was, he was efficient. Along with Haldeman, [he] set up a tremendous system. The choices were handled with minimum conflict. If someone disagreed too frequently, there was a good chance that the someone would leave." A second Nixon assistant concurred: "The reason Ehrlichman eventually took over was that no one else was making the decisions. For the first six months of 1969 it was a real mess. Compromise demands a degree of presidential involvement. It also takes time. The Domestic Council was one way of reducing that conflict, especially when it became Ehrlichman's baby."

Like the rational model, the garbage-can model requires time. Once a garbage can is created, it takes a certain amount of time and energy to clear the field of participants and problems. Whether decisions are made by flight or by oversight, the garbage-can model clearly rests on an investment of time. Recall that the garbage-can framework involves "coming, going, and waiting." Those behaviors are intimately linked to the amount of time available for choice. Even a garbage ejection process demands a degree of effort; removing entrenched participants may be impossible. According to one Carter aide, "The President believed that setting deadlines was one way to push the process forward, but sometimes the deadlines slowed us down. Making the decisions on major programs involves time. If the President sets unreasonable deadlines, the mistakes will eventually follow."

Information and Expertise. The rational model also makes heavy demands on scarce presidential information and expertise. First, the information often does not exist. Despite a recent surge in program oversight, presidential information remains scarce. Nor has the White House become particularly specialized in comprehensive analysis. Second, most information entering the domestic policy process is biased by political perceptions. As one Johnson aide said, "We didn't want the raw data. The facts had to be placed in some context. We had to have information that was directly linked to the problems." Third, Presidents rarely have the expertise to engage in the rational ideal. Though Presidents often attempt to maximize resources, the decision system is not rational. One media observer offered the following observation:

There are many academics who prescribe the rational model for all the ills. They suggest that the President could make the choices more carefully, that the President could be more comprehensive. Unfortunately, the Presidency is a political office. There are many variables which simply do not yield to a comprehensive analysis—at least as I understand it. How do you assign a utility function to a poverty program? It's damn easy in defense—you can count missile-kill ratios—but it isn't as easy in domestic politics.

Bargaining can operate with less information, but it still requires a certain expertise. That is one lesson of Neustadt's work. According to a Ford aide, "Building an effective compromise involves considerable presidential effort. Unless the President can enter the bargaining fray and make the proper trades, the compromise will not work. If the President hasn't had any experience in that kind of give-and-take, the compromise will never take hold." Domination requires even less information. Though coalitions often attack using argument, success generally rests on position. Those individuals closest to the President have the greater internal power. As we shall see, internal influence is the result of several factors—expertise, control of scarce resources, persuasiveness. Yet, domination in and of itself does not demand information. It does, however, involve some expertise. "Mondale's rise within the Carter administration was definitely related to his experience in Washington," one media respondent noted. "He was virtually the only member of the top staff to have extensive federal experience, and it affected his stock in the White House. As Carter began to suffer, Mondale began to rise. He knew how to move the pieces."

The garbage can demands the least information and expertise. The system relies less on information than the ability to outlast the opposition. Since outcomes reflect the impact of comings and goings, the primary demand is for patience. Thus, neither information nor expertise is intrinsically related to success in the garbage can. Though the two resources may influence final decisions, they are not prerequisites for participation.

Capital. Presidential capital has a pronounced impact on decision-making. According to one Ford aide, "It has everything to do with decisions. What is the point of the so-called comprehensive analysis when you can't use the best alternative? Why bother with all the options when only one is politically possible?"

Both domination and the garbage can are encouraged by declining levels of presidential capital. As the opportunities for choice drop, there is an increase in internal conflict; as the agenda tightens, there is a natural tendency toward internal struggle. Johnson's first and second years are useful counterpoints. In 1965 the Johnson staff reported a high degree of consensus; there was very little in-fighting. As one Johnson aide remarked, "There was no need to get involved in heavy battles. There was no need for that kind of struggle.

At the start of 1965 Lyndon Johnson was Santa Claus, and the stocking was full. HEW wanted an expanded poverty program; they got it. Interior wanted a scenic rivers system; they got it." By 1966, however, the mood had changed. As the aide concluded,

> By 1966 Santa Claus was going broke. The programs were getting cut on the Hill. We couldn't get funding for rent supplements or Model Cities. Once it was clear that the sack was empty, there was an increase in the staff conflict. Groups broke off into separate teams, each pressuring for different projects. By 1967 Califano was losing control of the system. The war was getting all the candy, and there was a fight for the last few pieces.

There is a clear relationship between presidential capital and staff conflict: *as capital declines, conflict increases.* As one Nixon aide reported, "It is a hell of a lot easier to get along with your enemies when you both can be satisfied. When it turns to a game with winners and losers, the response is to drag out all the old weapons. There may be a truce at the beginning of the administration, but it is broken very quickly." Thus, both domination and the garbage can are tied to conflict. As conflict increases, the staff either engages in attempts at internal domination or collapses into organized anarchy.

The rational system demands the greatest amounts of capital in reserve. Under a comprehensive strategy, there must be enough capital to satisfy the range of potential alternatives. Though rational choice can produce relatively "cheap" alternatives, the system must have a store of capital in the event that the "best" alternative demands heavy amounts. Presidents obviously determine just what "best" means. It is usually defined by the choice of questions to be asked of potential programs: the President can set a series of screens through which all alternatives must pass. According to a Nixon aide, "There is a world of difference between saying you want the program that will work and the program that will pass. The program that will work best might not pass; the program that will pass might not work as well. If the President wants the very best program, he might not be able to get legislative acceptance. He will have the best program, but nowhere to go."

The bargaining model operates when the level of presidential capital is moderate. When the level of capital is high, there is little need to bargain—all coalitions can be satisfied. When the level of capital is low, the pressure towards domination is intense. According to a Johnson aide, "There is no problem making deals at the start of the term. As you move on toward the end, however, you can't listen to everyone, and you sure as hell can't make everyone happy." Since Presidents rarely face massive levels of capital, the major White House problem becomes maintaining internal peace. The problem obviously becomes more difficult as the capital steadily declines. As long as capital remains moderately high, there is an opportunity for accommodation; as it drops, the substance of compromise evaporates.

Goal Compatibility. The White House staff is not a single-minded entity; it is made up of individuals. The goals of the legislative liaison staff may be different from those of the Domestic Policy Staff; the goals of the Council of Economic Advisers may compete with those of OMB. The roles often produce internal conflict. According to a Carter liaison officer, "We sometimes found that the Domestic Policy Staff was unwilling to give. They had a different perspective on the congressional process. Our job was to pass the program, which often meant we had to change certain programs. The DPS often did not understand and would not cooperate."

The degree of goal compatibility has a direct bearing on decision styles. If the White House staffs agree on the goals, there is a greater opportunity for compromise on the alternatives. When goal compatibility is low, decisions by "flight" or domination can be expected. The dominant coalition might choose to exclude or isolate opponents. According to one Nixon assistant, "Moynihan's departure was a very important victory for Ehrlichman. Though Ehrlichman already had Nixon's ear, Moynihan was still a thorn in the side. There was an immediate relaxation of hostilities once Moynihan left."

Presidential staffs vary in their degree of goal agreement. In part, goal compatibility involves recruitment and length of service. Compare Kennedy with Nixon. As one Kennedy aide argued, "We had all been together in the Senate and knew how each worked. We got along fairly well. We understood what the main objectives were—Medicare, Aid to Education, unemployment, the Peace Corps. We never fought over the top items." The Kennedy staff was characterized by high goal compatibility. That was not the case in Nixon's first year. According to one Nixon aide, "We had Moynihan in one corner and Burns in the other. We had HEW on one side and OMB on the other. We had Finch versus Shultz; Shultz versus Burns; Burns versus Finch. I'm surprised we were able to do anything those first six months. It is a credit to Ehrlichman. He was the only one who tried to pull the staff together." By the end of the first year, Ehrlichman had taken the reins of the domestic policy process. Ehrlichman gained control in part through the domination of his opponents, in part through the departure of those whom one domestic aide called the "malcontents."

When goal compatibility is high, the tendency is to use a rational process; the staff can maximize the main goals. When compatibility is moderate, there is a certain pressure to compromise. There is enough opportunity for consensus to produce bargaining. When compatibility is low, the natural tendency is to fight. If the staff does not agree on even the most basic goals, there is little choice but to escalate the conflict or leave. Given the basic framework of the President's domestic agenda, goal compatibility is often in the moderate range. There is enough advocacy to prevent uniform agreement, enough agreement to avoid massive conflict.

Consistency of Participants. Consistency of participants can be broken down into two primary components: (1) the extent to which decision-making involves face-to-face contact, and (2) the extent to which participants remain for future decisions (see Mohr 1976). As one Johnson aide remarked, "It is somewhat easier to cut your opponent when he is not present. If you have to face your competition in the open, there is some incentive to be cordial." A Ford assistant agreed: "There is no payoff in destroying someone you have to work with everyday. These are the people you eat with and socialize with. If you slaughter someone in a meeting one day, you might not get an invitation to his party the next. The White House is a very social organization." These sentiments were echoed across the five administrations. One Kennedy aide argued that "we were all friends to some extent. We worked in the same building and under the same conditions. There were times when conflict broke out, but the usual tone was one of cooperation. There is something about the office that leads to some effort at compromise."

According to Mohr, consistency of participants may be the most important variable in the behavioral model:

> If consistency is high, there is great pressure to satisfice, at least in Western societies; it is difficult for participants to tolerate repeated loss of face, by oneself or by another, in any long-term face-to-face group. If consistency of participants is low, there are several possibilities. If at the same time the goals are incompatible, then Garbage-can and [domination] processes will predominate. In other words, when goals seem to be divergent at the outset, and when there are also no personal ties and no possibilities for trading on demands in future choices, the incentives are either to leave or fight. Low consistency of participants can also lead to Rational decision making, primarily when the goals of participants are compatible, as is the case with a jury (Mohr 1976, p. 635).

However, as Mohr concludes, "Whenever the consistency is greater than zero, a strong incentive to bargain is introduced. Even in groups that might otherwise be rational, consistency of participants undermines the maximization dynamic by allowing the otherwise latent goals of individuals to creep into the active demand set" (pp. 635-36). We would expect the consistency of participants in the White House generally to remain high. At least for the first two years staff turnover is fairly low. Yet, depending on the other contextual variables, the consistency of participants may have marginal impact on decision styles. Consistency is important, but it may be secondary when compared with capital or goal compatibility. One way to accommodate both high consistency and low goal compatibility is to remove the incompatible members.

Presidential Involvement. Presidents vary in their degree of involvement in the decision-making process. Eisenhower, for instance, was reluctant to engage in competitive management. Instead, he preferred a hidden-hand approach. Though Eisenhower was more involved in presidential management than previously believed (Greenstein 1979), his decision structure reflected a formalistic approach. Eisenhower did not want to be directly involved in staff conflict. As we have seen, both Nixon and Carter preferred a detached strategy. Reagan started his term with a similar approach, adopting what he called a "chairman of the board" strategy. It was an approach that emphasized presidential distance and maximum delegation.

The degree of presidential involvement has an impact on the decision-making structure. Presidential involvement acts as a signal to internal coalitions. Political domination is one product of low presidential involvement; staffs sense the opportunity for empire-building. Bargaining, however, demands a considerable investment of the President's own resources. According to one Nixon aide, "The main thrust behind Ehrlichman's rise was to provide some breathing room. Nixon just didn't want to become overly involved in the internal disputes. He wanted the arguments thrashed out *before* they reached his desk." By 1971 Ehrlichman had formed a dominant coalition which met Nixon's personal needs. In contrast, Ford started his term with a "collegial" approach. According to Ford's spokes-of-a-wheel style, arguments were to be settled through bargaining. As Ford quickly discovered, the system demanded maximum presidential involvement. According to one Ford aide, "The spokes bent and often broke, but the President was committed to the concept. It took a great deal of time to settle some of the conflicts, but he was willing to make the commitment."

While bargaining demands a degree of presidential effort, both the rational and the garbage-can frameworks can survive without direct supervision from the President. Indeed, the garbage-can system thrives on indifference. If there is a high degree of goal compatibility and sufficient resources, the rational model can exist under conditions of presidential disinterest. If there is considerable internal conflict, low consistency among participants, and presidential isolation, the "organized anarchies" will emerge.

Involvement ultimately reflects the President's personal style. As such, it is the one contextual variable which is directly linked to character and personality. Consider Bryce Harlow's portrait of past Presidents:

> Lyndon Johnson was the most forceful person in relationship to people that I have ever met or expect to meet. He could charm you, he could frighten you, he could buy you, he could seduce or induce, influence you in an incredible variety of ways that came to him automatically. And he could dominate you—and would dominate you one way or another. . . . You have to be mean to be a powerful man. But you also have to be compassionate and have those nice things. But you have to have the capability of being mean or nobody will pay any attention to you, and so Lyndon could be—believe you me—*mean*. He'd just sit in a committee room, and there'd be dust rising around him almost, just sitting there. . . .

Well, Gerald Ford is not good about jumping on people. It's something that's rather alien to him. He has a tremendously heavy streak of stubbornness, and if you try to press President Ford beyond a certain point, that Dutch in him comes right up to the top. And he just pats his feet and looks at you, and his lips get real thin, and he goes silent, and you have lost, and you can't do a thing about it whatso—it's like that. He turns off on you, he just turns off. But he doesn't whale at people. He doesn't "kick 'em around," as the saying goes. He's not a muleskinner. Lyndon was a muleskinner. Dwight D. Eisenhower was an army sergeant. He could eat you out. He could eat you out, son, like you'd never heard before. Oooh. It's just like looking into a Bessemer Furnace—these different personalities, you see. Harry Truman, oh, he was a good Missourian. He'd jump on people and just get mad, you know, and rise all kinds of Cain, and swear and everything, and carry on, and it'd all be gone. He didn't carry a grudge, didn't carry any malice in him. He was uncomplicated. It was like summer storms, cleaning up the air (PBS, "Every Four Years," transcript, January-February 1980, pp. 49-50).

Do Presidents have to be "mean" to be involved in the decision-making process? Probably not. Active participation can flow from many different personalities. Lyndon Johnson, Harry Truman, John Kennedy, and Gerald Ford had remarkably different personal styles, but all were involved to one degree or another in the domestic policy process. Therein lies the point: it is not necessarily the meanness or the calm but the *degree* of involvement that is important is forestalling staff conflict. Presidential participation—whether heavy-handed or gentle—must involve a steady signal of interest and oversight. The President must be willing to wade in and referee potential battles; the only way to do that is to attend the fights.

Predicting Presidential Styles. By now it should be apparent that each contextual variable has a different impact on the decision structure. Some are more important for a bargaining style; others are critical for rational choice. It also should be apparent that the variables interact—the level of one may affect the impact of another.

Information and expertise are essential for the rational model. Without high levels of these two internal resources, regardless of the other contextual variables, the rational framework will not work.

Capital is critical in the emergence of political domination. As capital declines, there is a marked increase in domination. According to one OMB officer, "The President and staff are going to be much happier at the beginning of the term than at the end. There is an esprit de corps at the start that generally disappears by the end. It is simply impossible to maintain a high level of comraderie when tough choices have to be made."

Capital and the consistency of participants are primary pressures in the garbage-can system. Once again, as capital declines, conflict increases;

as capital declines, the opportunities for accommodation drop. When capital is coupled with low levels of staff consistency, organized anarchies may evolve.

If there is one variable that affects all four decisions styles, it is goal compatibility. Moderate to high goal compatibility leads to efforts at bargaining and compromise; low goal compatibility leads to intense staff conflict. It is clear that goal compatibility has some impact in creating contingencies for the other five contextual variables. If goal compatibility is moderate to high, then dwindling capital may have less impact on domination. If goal compatibility is low, then capital may produce acute conflict. The impact of goal compatibility might lead Presidents to devote more attention to staff recruitment. The President must walk a fine line between the need for multiple advocacy and the problems of low compatibility. There may be such a thing as too much advocacy.

In a review of the six contextual variables, the Presidency must be seen as a highly dynamic institution. Generally, the presidential term starts with relatively high political capital, time, and energy and lesser levels of information, expertise, and goal compatibility. As the term progresses, the contextual picture changes. Capital, time, and energy begin to drop as the cycle of decreasing influence appears; information and expertise grow. As disaffected advisers depart, goal compatibility may actually increase. Presidential involvement, however, will usually be greater at the start of the term than at the end. Presidents have their own stores of resources, whether physical stamina or personal interest. As the term moves forward, Presidents will find less time for internal coalition building. Foreign policy may siphon off interest; the rise of dominant coalitions may even solve the need for presidential oversight. Consistency of participants will generally grow over the term, as routine methods of decision-making evolve. Yet, depending upon exits of unhappy advisers, consistency may be less important in predicting decisions styles. The primary point to stress is that for all contextual variables, the first year of the term is remarkably different from the rest of the term. There is a much greater opportunity for multiple advocacy in that first year than at any other point in time. Since there is a greater pool of presidential resources, the President can afford to encourage multiple advocacy.

The Presidency as an Organization

The Presidency will always involve a mixture of the three models of organizational choice. At times the office will resemble a garbage can, with streams of problems, solutions, and participants; decisions will be more accidental than planned. At other times it will resemble the ordered efficiency of the rational model, with attempts at comprehensive choice. Usually, however, the Presidency resembles the *behavioral* system: choices are the result of either bargaining or domination; structure increases over time.

Why the behavioral model instead of the garbage-can or rational framework? First, the contextual variables lead us to expect a behavioral framework. The President does not have the resources for a rational approach: information and expertise do not approach the levels demanded by rational choice; capital is rarely high enough; goal compatibility is usually moderate. The same holds true for the garbage can: the contextual variables simply do not match the needs of organized anarchies. Neither the goal compatibility nor consistency meets the contextual scheme. Rather, the President's resources, staff compatibility, and consistency fit the behavioral model closely. The context of choice leads us to expect either a bargaining or a domination style.

Second, the White House staffs consistently described the policy process in terms that fit the behavioral model. Bargaining was seen as prevalent in the early days of each administration; domination was perceived toward the end; structure developed over the term. At least six features of the domestic policy process fit the behavioral framework: (1) a variety of coalitions within the staff, (2) standard operating procedures, (3) avoidance of uncertainty, (4) problemistic search, (5) quasi resolution of conflict, and (6) a degree of what might be called organizational learning. We will consider the characteristics in order.

Coalitions. The White House staff is not a single arm of the President. Though there are many competing fiefdoms within the Executive Office of the President (EOP), we often neglect the impact of internal White House rivalries. We tend to view the President's personal staff as a unified body, united against the rest of the EOP and the bureaucracy. According to the staffs, there are a variety of factions within the White House alone; and within each coalition exists the potential for conflict. In legislative liaison, for instance, the House and Senate staffs may differ on legislative strategy; the tactics that persuade senators may be woefully inadequate to persuade House members.

Of the competing coalitions, the domestic policy staff generally has the greatest initial advantage in shaping the domestic agenda. In each of the five administrations, the domestic policy staff was given primary responsibility for drafting the President's program; it set the parameters of the internal discussion. According to the staffs, the domestic policy coalition gains additional strength from the departments. There is a marked pattern for the domestic policy staff to align with departments and agencies in a very potent executive coalition. Though the domestic policy staff often presents a common front, there are often disputes within the coalition. In 1977, for instance, there was internal feuding within Carter's Domestic Policy Staff over the relative status of welfare reform vis-à-vis national health insurance. National health insurance advocates wanted to reserve space for a comprehensive plan; welfare advocates wanted to move with the Program for Better Jobs and Income. Welfare reform won the debate.

Whether through bargaining or domination, coalitions mold the bulk of the President's agenda. Though most internal coalitions can find agreement on the broad goals of the agenda—reelection, historical achievement, and good policy—there is considerable conflict on the speciffic alternatives. This conflict sets the boundaries of the policy process. As one Johnson aide argued,

> There weren't many individuals within the White House. Everyone was identified by their office or department. Califano had some good ideas, but he was from the domestic policy staff; Wilbur Cohen had some decent programs, but he was from HEW. All the advice was colored by who belonged to what office and by who belonged to whom. The amount of power each one carried had an important effect on their weight with the President. One assistant would say that he had three departments and the policy staff behind him; another might argue that he had the House and Senate public welfare committees backing him. It was like a war game—each group moving their pieces around the board.

One way to appreciate the impact of internal coalitions is to examine Carter's mid-summer crisis of 1979. In early July Carter had scheduled a major energy address to follow his return from an economic summit in Japan. Gas lines were long, and fuel prices were rising. However, less than a week before his scheduled address, Carter abruptly canceled the speech and called for a "domestic summit" at Camp David. Carter eventually drafted what was to be a major domestic message, designed to mark the turning point in his administration. The message itself involved intense staff conflict: would the speech emphasize Pat Caddell's finding of mass "malaise" or Eizenstat's agenda for domestic change? Two coalitions formed, one pressing for a major change of style (Caddell) and one cautioning against overreaction to the drop in public approval (Eizenstat). Beyond the conflict over the Carter speech, major fighting occurred as Carter prepared a major Cabinet shake-up. On 17 July all White House staff and Cabinet members were asked for resignations.

Perhaps the most divisive Cabinet resignation involved HEW Secretary Califano. Earlier resignations were more routine, including the removal of Michael Blumenthal (Treasury) and Brock Adams (Transportation). But when the Jordan-Cadell-Powell coalition moved against Califano, there was a major battle. Neither Mondale nor Eizenstat supported the firing of the one-time Johnson aide. Eizenstat argued that Califano was a capable secretary, that despite difficulties, Califano was a valuable asset. Mondale was more emphatic. He argued that Califano was a strong secretary with a strong constituency. The decision to fire Califano involved dramatic conflict between the two coalitions and the victory of the "Georgia" coalition. Though Mondale and Eizenstat managed to tone down parts of the Carter address, their arguments were in the minority. In both domestic and economic policy, the liberal wing of the White House staff had lost a major battle.

Standard Operating Procedures. One method to minimize such conflict is to establish standard operating procedures (SOP). These SOPs are the "memory of the organization" and have emerged in at least the last five administrations. They reflect increased organizational structure. In each Presidency, the rules evolved as the term progressed; as conflict increased, so did standard operating procedures. This will happen again under Reagan. The SOPs were used to regulate staff performance and information. As one Nixon assistant argued, "We have to have some rules to manage the information coming in. There was just too much confusion in the first year, too much paper floating around. We needed a system to manage the incoming fire." All five staffs reported a drift toward standard operating procedures by the end of the first six months. "We definitely needed some kind of coordination," one Kennedy budget aide noted. "There was just too much moving through the White House. Before we came in, the problem was getting elected. Once we made it, the problem was getting started. By the end of the first year, we had to generate some organization to keep the system on track."

Carter's policy system developed in roughly the same pattern as those of his four predecessors. Though Carter moved rather quickly to relabel the Nixon Domestic Council to the Domestic Policy Staff, he did not establish the Presidential Domestic Policy Review System until 14 September 1977, nine months after his inauguration. Like his four predecessors, Carter soon discovered the need for standard operating procedures. During the first six months, the policy process produced significant amounts of confusion. As one Carter aide remarked, "Everyone seemed to converge on the President at once. We found the first choices to be relatively easy, but as the bills began to pile up, the conflict increased." The Presidential Domestic Policy Review System, recommended by the Carter reorganization project, focused on a hierarchy of four memoranda: issue-definition memoranda, response memoranda, decision memoranda, and final presidential directives. Unfortunately, the system did not arrive until September. By the time Carter's Domestic Policy Review System was in place, virtually half of the agenda was already before Congress. As one aide lamented, "It was a good idea, but it should have been ready on January 1, 1977. We could have used it to prevent some of the early mistakes."

Carter's Domestic Policy Review System was the direct descendant of the Executive Agenda, under the direction of Vice President Walter Mondale. The agenda made its first appearance in November 1976, during the transition. It was revealed to the senior staff immediately after Christmas, at St. Simons, the resort community off the Georgia coast.

> Each guest was given a copy of a twenty-nine page memorandum, ranging broadly over the next half year, along with a more detailed calendar that blocked out on a weekly basis a schedule of Presidential activities through the end of March. The stated purpose of this combined prospectus was to

"suggest a strategy for leadership during the crucial first few months of the Carter administration." The Mondale agenda incorporated recommendations from another planning memorandum ordered up by the President-elect, called "An Initial Working Paper on Political Strategy." This sixty-nine page document had been prepared by Patrick Caddell, pollster-in-chief for the Carter campaign, who had been asked by his victorious client to serve him in the White House as a political adviser outside of government (Shogan 1977, p. 109).

According to the Carter staff, the Mondale agenda received little internal attention during the first months. Though the agenda was circulated among the staff, it did not begin to rise in importance until late spring. According to one Carter domestic policy aide, "There were many who felt that the Mondale agenda was too inflexible. They just did not want to be told what to do on a minute-by-minute basis. One old politico kept complaining that he had been to kindergarten once." By April, Carter had committed several political errors—including the fifty-dollar tax rebate—and the need for some standard operating procedures increased. The agenda became a topic of considerable internal conflict. The draft Executive Agenda for the month of April 1977 is presented in table 19. Note the importance assigned to energy, welfare, tax reform, and health and the recurring emphasis on defense and the budget. According to the Carter aide who supplied the document, "There should be no question about the impact of the agenda on the domestic decision process. The agenda provides the structure for domestic choice; there is a distinct set of hurdles that each proposal must jump." Under Carter, the agenda became a permanent fixture of the policy process; it was prepared each January and was updated every three months.

This tour through the Carter system should highlight the importance of standard operating procedures. They constitute one response to the cycle of decreasing influence. As presidential capital drops, the need for careful choice increases. In this respect, SOPs are one indication of increasing effectiveness. Carter's decision to implement the Domestic Policy Review System reflected his growing awareness of organizational needs. The early mistakes led to the emphasis on a tighter domestic process. Like the four Presidents before him, Carter eventually moved toward a coordinating structure for domestic choice to reduce the impact of internal conflict. But also like them, he failed to adopt that structure in time to affect the early choices.

Avoidance of Uncertainty. In the behavioral model of choice, organizations try to avoid uncertainty whenever possible. Since the future cannot be easily predicted, organizations stay very much in the present: solve pressing problems first, avoid long-term planning, negotiate with the environment.

Table 19. Draft Executive Agenda, April 1977

Category	April 1-9	April 11-16	April 18-23	April 25-30
Special events	—	—	—	—
Diplomatic and defense events	Sadat; announce non-proliferation policy	Pan-American Day address	Khaddam; Jenkins	Hussein; economic summit
Budget	—	—	—	—
Economy	Review/ consultation on anti-inflation	Announce anti-inflation policy	Possible signing of stimulus package	Possible signing of stimulus package
Energy	Review policy	Review/ consultation on energy	Address to joint session of Congress	—
Welfare	Planning	Planning	Planning	Planning
Long-term: Tax reform Health	—	—	Health message	—
Reorganization	Sign Reorgani-zation Act	—	—	—
Other items	—	—	—	National Labor Relations Act reform
Controversial	—	Water projects	—	—

The White House does seek to avoid uncertainty. Accordingly, Presidents stay very much in the present, spending a great deal of time "firefighting." Rather than engage in long-range planning, the domestic policy process tends to focus on impending events and crises. As one Johnson assistant argued, "Just when we would get on top of one issue, a new problem would arise. We rarely had enough time to digest the new issues before we had to act. Most of what we did was fight brush fires. With the hot winds coming down from the Hill, they were damn hard to control." This emphasis on short-term problems is an accepted part of the domestic policy process; references to firefighting or "backstopping" recurred throughout the interviews.

Much of the President's time is devoted to dealing with the certainties of the present. One of the policy functions specifically stated in the formal creation of the Nixon Domestic Council was to provide rapid response to pressing issues. As Kessel notes, the "inclusion of this assignment was paradoxical; it *seemed* not to fit. The other tasks—information-gathering, clarification of options, determining priorities, and monitoring agency activity—followed an orderly sequence. But there, in the middle of the list, was an explicit reference to emergency activities." Ultimately, Kessel concludes, *"fire-engine chores are an inescapable part of life on the White House staff"*:

> Why should that be so? Part of the answer can be found in the two factors affecting administration behavior . . . : the complexity of the political environment and the fixed political calendar. In combination, they imply staying in touch with a large number of agencies, all of which must meet recurring deadlines. Consequently, special effort is often needed just to get things done on time. Often an emergency sequence is initiated by actions taken outside the White House (Kessel 1975, p. 95).

The firefighting role is a paradox only if we expect a rational system. Once we accept the "adaptive rationality" of the behavioral model, firefighting fits rather well.

The White House also attempts to create a stable environment. The adoption of standard operating procedures and legislative calendars is one way to reduce uncertainty. By using a strict timetable, the President lets other members of the environment know when his programs are coming. In that effort, the President also attempts to anticipate congressional reactions. That is certainly one reason behind the Nixon and Ford "watchlist." It was one way to reduce uncertainty. The legislative liaison office also attempts to negotiate with the environment. Liaison clearly tries to schedule the introduction of both friendly and hostile legislation, as well as to anticipate the movement of problem bills. For the White House, the emphasis rests on establishing communication with the environment; this emphasis involves the Public Liaison Office as well. As one Ford aide remarked, "Part of the problem is just knowing what's going on. I'd guess that I spend 40 percent of my time just tracking bills. I wanted my contacts to keep me posted and wanted to have some influence on when bills were going to break."

Problemistic Search. Problemistic search is a fundamental component of the behavioral model. The search for both issues and alternatives is directed and purposive. As Cyert and March argue,

> By problemistic search we mean search that is stimulated by a problem (usually a rather specific one) and is directed toward finding a solution to that problem. In a general way, problemistic search can be distinguished from curiosity and the search for understanding. [Problemistic search] is distinguished from the former because it has a goal, from the latter because it is interested in understanding only insofar as such understanding contributes to control. Problemistic search is engineering rather than pure science (1963, p. 121).

According to Cyert and March, problemistic search is characterized by three distinct patterns. First, *search is motivated:* it is stimulated by a problem and ends with a solution.

> A problem is recognized when the organization either fails to satisfy one or more of its goals or when such failure can be anticipated in the immediate future. So long as the problem is not solved, search will continue. The problem is solved either by discovering an alternative that satisfies the goals or by revising the goals to levels that make an available alternative acceptable. Solutions are also motivated to search for problems (Cyert and March 1963, p. 121).

Presidential search is motivated. In the Carter Domestic Policy Review System, the search for an alternative began *only* when an issue-definition memorandum had been approved by the President, that is, once a problem had been selected as a topic for action. As one Carter aide noted in 1979, "Usually we have to stop when we find an appropriate solution. The system does not provide for either review or oversight once the decision has been made. Nor is that the purpose. The system stops once a decision is completed."

According to the White House staffs, the search for alternatives usually reacts to the entrance of a problem. Though there are cases when solutions pursue problems, the domestic policy process is based on incoming fire. Given internal resource limits, the President has little incentive to keep a constant watch for multiple alternatives. Yet, precisely because resources begin to drop, there is greater concern for the quality of the programs. Presidents want the most for the "money." At the start of the term, Presidents are content with the "one problem/one solution" ideal. As the term wears on and opportunities decline, there is more emphasis on making careful choices. Unfortunately, as Presidents develop this increased awareness, they are constrained by the cycle of decreasing influence. Presidents make the bulk of choices when they are least able or experienced.

Second, *search is simple-minded:* it is generally limited to the "neighborhood" of the current alternatives. Even if the President is concerned about the quality of alternatives, there are a variety of incentives to rely on the available ideas. The simple logic of problemistic search is one visible explanation for the incremental nature of domestic policy. According to Cyert and March, the "neighborhood of existing policy rule inhibits the movement of the organization to radically new alternatives (except under circumstances of considerable search pressure). Such an inhibition may be explained either in terms of some underlying organizational assumptions of continuity in performance functions or in terms of the problems of adjustments required by radical shifts" (1963, p. 122). In the Presidency, the pressure on the available alternative rests on resource scarcity—the President and the staff do not have the time, information, expertise, or energy to conduct an exhaustive search for the "best" alternative. Instead, the President is all too often forced to rely on the product of organizational compromise. As we shall see, Presidents face what might be called the *cycle of decreasing discretion:* the closer the President moves toward drafting a specific program, the more he must rely on the executive branch and the White House organization. As one Carter aide reflected, "Frankly, the staff never has the necessary resources to engage in detailed analysis. The staff has to move and get the programs in as soon as possible. There is little time to produce truly innovative programs unless . . . (1) a department has already come up with something good or (2) someone in Congress has one ready to go." Or as a Nixon Domestic Council aide argued, "Most of us were very impressionable. We didn't know that much about the areas we were forced to work on; we hadn't had that much exposure to the program options. When we put out feelers for specific alternatives, we were at the mercy of whatever was already cooking. It's like asking your waiter what looks good tonight."

Third, *search is biased:* if a President is interested in large-scale initiatives, the search will produce large-scale initiatives; if the President wants a war on energy, he will receive a battle plan. As Cyert and March suggest, there are three different kinds of search bias: "(1) bias reflecting special training or experience of various parts of the organization, (2) bias reflecting the interaction of hopes and expectations, and (3) communication bias reflecting unresolved conflict within the organization" (1963, p. 122). All three biases exist in the domestic policy process. Certainly, the search for alternatives involves staff specialization. According to one Nixon aide, "After a period of time, you become accustomed to a particular style of program. We eventually became quite familiar with the block-grant concept and attempted to use it whenever possible." A Johnson assistant offered a similar opinion with respect to categorical grants:

> We had several people who were quite adept at the categorical grant as a tool of domestic policy. They knew how to draft the legislation and ensure implementation. By 1966 the categorical grant was the favorite of both LBJ and the domestic policy staff. But I wonder how often we took old bills that were lying around and simply changed the names and figures. There were standard models for drafting bills, and they cropped up throughout the Great Society.

Bias also arises from presidential hopes and expectations. As we have seen, Moynihan used Nixon's goal of historical achievement to sell the Family Assistance Plan. We have also seen how the White House has become particularly concerned about costs in the search for alternatives. The President and the staff set "evaluative screens" to limit the range of potential alternatives. For Ford and Carter, the primary screen involved economic costs. As one Carter aide noted, "We obviously try to anticipate the President's response. In the case of welfare reform, we did not present the whole range of options—some were too damn expensive. We had to rule some out at the very beginning."

Finally, the search for issues and alternatives often reflects unresolved internal conflict. One frequent source of conflict is the annual programming process. According to one Nixon aide, "One agency came up with the same program every year. We rejected the idea each year, but it would come back. The agency would lobby hard and lose, only to come back again next year." As the President attempts to draft a legislative program for each session, the conflict between the various White House coalitions grows. The programming process is a conduit for both ideas and infighting. As one speech writer remembered, "There is no more difficult task than to draft a State of the Union message in the last two years of a term. Everyone wants on board before the ship begins to sink. On the *Titantic* they all wanted off; in the White House they prefer to rearrange the chairs."

Quasi Resolution of Conflict. Veteran observers of presidential politics recognize that internal conflict is a way of life. As one reporter argued, "Conflict is not only prevalent, it is necessary. Those who suggest that the President ought to sit back and make his decisions by carefully weighing the pros and cons are only partially correct. In many respects, the President ought to encourage internal competition. I think FDR was right: the more people you have fighting to get the right idea, the greater chance of finding it." Yet, even if conflict produces stronger programs, it demands a measure of guidance. Conflict may be valuable for proponents of "multiple advocacy" but it is potentially destructive if left unchecked.

Contemporary Presidents have several methods for accommodating the day-to-day conflict in the domestic policy process. They can recruit a single-minded domestic staff. They can ignore conflict and drive it underground, acting as if it doesn't exist. But if Presidents want to use conflict to their advantage, they must adopt strategies that reduce the impact of the unbridled infighting. There are several techniques for handling White House conflict; the President's choice of one method over another will depend on the *context* of choice. Staff compatibility, consistency of participants, and presidential involvement each have an impact on the level of conflict. Given a moderate level of compatibility, consistency, and involvement, we can expect two major organizational responses to coalitional conflict.

Presidents can reduce conflict through internal *specialization.* Cyert and March call such specialization "local rationality":

> We assume that an organization factors its decision problems into subproblems and assigns the subproblems to subunits in the organization. From the point of view of organizational conflict, the importance of such local rationality is in the tendency for the individual subunits to deal with a limited set of problems and a limited set of goals. At the limit, this reduces to solving one problem in terms of only one goal (1963, p. 117).

Though presidential staffs do specialize, conflict is often accentuated by the flow of problems. Single responsibility is rarely delegated to one "locality" in the White House. The domestic policy staff is never given sole control over programs; OMB, CEA, liaison, the departments, and the President are also involved. Specialization reduces the resources needed for domestic choice, but it does not reduce the eventual conflict over the specific alternatives. Instead, specialization tends to delay the conflict until later in the process. The domestic policy staff is given some flexibility to select the preferred alternative; it is when a final decision must be made that the conflict grows.

Presidents can also reduce conflict through *sequential attention to goals:* they can attack one problem at a time. In the domestic policy process, sequential attention to goals is rather prevalent. This is not to argue that the staffs are unaware of what is occurring in the domestic system. Welfare advocates watch health; energy advocates follow reorganization. As one Kennedy aide remarked, "It is worth your while to keep posted on what's happening in other policy areas. If the President is putting the lid on education, you might have to present your program along different lines. It doesn't take that much effort to stay on top of the competing programs."

Sequential attention to goals occurs across the term. However, the transition into office holds the greatest opportunity for comparison of goals. During the Kennedy transition, for instance, top domestic aides met repeatedly with the President-elect in Palm Springs, Florida, to review the list of potential programs; immediately following the Kennedy assassination, LBJ met with his top staff on the range of options in domestic policy; Nixon met frequently with Arthur Burns at the Pierre Hotel in New York City to make preliminary choices on the domestic agenda. In each case, the President began the term with some effort at comparison; lists were composed and reviewed. Yet, even here, there is still evidence of sequential attention. According to one Kennedy aide, "Instead of taking the entire list and asking which ones were most important, we went down the list checking each item. Did we want to do area redevelopment? Yes or no? Next item. Did we want to do Medicare? Yes or no? Next item. Each program was reviewed as a somewhat separate proposal. There wasn't much discussion of an 'either/or' type. We didn't ask about area redevelopment *or* Medicare."

By the end of the term, sequential attention is the dominant strategy. As conflict increases and resources decline, the staffs report a greater emphasis on a "first come, first served" approach. To an extent, the domestic process involves a queue. One Ford assistant offered the following explanation of welfare reform.

> We explained to Weinberger that he would have to wait for welfare reform until at least 1977. First, we had to handle the economy. If we didn't get inflation under control, there would be no welfare reform. Second, we had to deal with welfare fraud. In a very immediate sense, the President wanted to tighten up the regulations and the rolls. If we didn't reduce waste, there would be no effort to build an income floor. Third, we had to reserve as much discretionary funding for energy. Above all

else, we had to come up with an energy package. After number one, two, and three, we told HEW that we might be willing to consider welfare reform. HEW had to wait its turn.

Once again, as presidential capital drops, there is a greater need for efforts at conflict management. Sequential attention to goals is only a small part of that attempt.

Ultimately, the President and staff can settle disputes by bargaining or by political warfare. The distinction between *bargaining* and *domination* is intimately linked to the context of choice summarized in table 18. Though all administrations will inevitably experience some elements of both styles, all five staffs pinpointed bargaining as the early preference, domination as the eventual necessity. "At some point you have to say enough is enough," one Johnson aide noted. "You have to make some effort to listen to all points of view, but there is a breaking point."

It is always difficult to distinguish between bargaining and domination. What might look like political warfare to one observer might look like nothing more than aggressive bargaining to another; what might look like forced exit to one might look like a career change to another. It is conceivable that there might be considerable bargaining within the dominant coalition. Thus, what might look like bargaining could be the artifact of a successful effort to establish a dominant coalition. Perhaps the best method to settle such confusion is to examine the basic context of each decision. The contextual variables in Nixon's first term confirm our observations of political domination: goal compatibility was low, presidential involvement was almost nonexistent, and capital was down. The contextual framework in Kennedy's term, however, reflected a more collegial style: goal compatibility was moderate, presidential involvement was high, capital was moderate, and consistency of participants was high.

Organizational Learning. Learning is the final characteristic of the behavioral model. It may also be the most important. As Cyert and March suggest,

> Organizations learn: to assume that organizations go through the same process of learning as do individual human beings seems unnecessarily naive, but organizations exhibit (as do other social institutions) adaptive behavior over time. Just as adaptations at the individual level depend upon phenomena of the human physiology, organizational adaptation uses individual members of the organization as instruments (1963, p. 123).

Organizations have considerable potential for change. In the Presidency, we would expect adaptation as resources ebb and flow. The President and the staff adapt with respect to issues and alternatives—they learn what will work and what won't, what is publicly acceptable and what isn't. They also develop strategies for dealing with an uncertain environment and increased staff conflict. It is this kind of learning that contributes to the cycle of increasing effectiveness. According to one Carter legislative aide, "It takes a while to figure out what will wash. We all thought that reorganization would be a hot topic, but it hasn't exactly excited anyone. After all the complaints about government size, we expected significant support, but it never came." The President and the staff certainly learn which policy areas offer the greatest political promise; they also learn which issues offer the greatest programmatic costs. As one Johnson assistant concluded, "Yes, we did learn during the term. We became more adept at moving the programs through Congress and became more skilled at implementation. We learned where our strengths were and where we had to tread lightly."

The President and the staff also develop considerable expertise in the search for issues and alternatives. The administration learns where to look for alternatives and where to turn for information. In both the Nixon and the Carter administrations, the staff began the term with a somewhat naive acceptance of bureaucratic advice. "We naturally assumed that HEW knew what was going on with welfare reform," one Carter aide reflected. "We accepted their estimates on the PBJI and took their draft bills. After we were burned on the Hill, we took their data with much more suspicion. You can bet that it affected our analysis of Califano's health plan."

According to Cyert and March, "When an organization discovers a solution to a problem by searching in a particular way, it will be more likely to search in that way in future problems of the same type; when an organization fails to find a solution by searching in a particular way, it will be less likely to search in that way in future problems" (1963, p. 124). That is generally the case in the presidential policy process. The President's preference for a particular style of policy formulation often rests on the record of the technique. In the Carter administration, the 1977 comprehensive energy plan emerged from a very isolated process—energy czar James Schlesinger was given primary responsibility for drafting the package. According to the Carter staff, the eventual legislative failure convinced the President to adopt the Domestic Policy Review System. "We could not afford to make those kinds of errors again," one aide remarked. "The program was good, but it was not popular, either inside or out of the EOP. No one had been brought in on the project; Congress was caught by surprise. We decided to move to the review system to prevent those kinds of problems again."

The President and the staff also learn to screen out preferred sources of ideas. As the term wears on, there is a greater emphasis on reaction. "We found more and more that what we did was fight fires," one Kennedy aide noted. "At the start of the term, we mostly looked to the Democratic party or the departments for help on the domestic program. By the second or third year, we had turned toward watching for potential damage from events. We started to concentrate on the drive for reelection and learned where the best ideas were." Ultimately, the President and the staff identify the sources of ideas that offer the greatest benefits. According to one Nixon aide, "By 1971, we were very cautious about the social service bureaucracy. We didn't want to use them for too many new ideas. We had lost welfare reform and weren't going far with restructuring HEW and HUD. We had to develop new sources of ideas."

Conclusion

In the domestic Presidency, policy is the result of organizational dynamics. The interaction between the institutional structure and staff activity produces issues, alternatives, and priorities. When conflict arises, coalitions either bargain or dominate. The perception of benefits and costs is certainly shaped by the decision structure. And the decision structure is tied to the context of each choice. The Presidency is most likely to resemble the behavioral model: goal compatibility is generally moderate, consistency is moderate to high, presidential resources are moderate to low. There is simply not enough information or expertise for rational choice, but there is a semblance of organization and staff order. There is little opportunity in the four short years for organized anarchies. In this respect, the President's decision style is closely related to the cycles of decreasing influence and of increasing effectiveness. The former produces growing conflict over time, which produces pressure for coalitional domination. The latter, however, leads to standard operating procedures and organizational learning. Theoretically, as effectiveness increases, Presidents should be better equipped to handle internal conflict, as well as to make "good policy." Once again, the start of a President's second term holds the greatest prospects that he will be making decisions under the most favorable circumstances.

The main characteristics of the behavioral model exist in most White House decisions. There is considerable coalitional activity; the staffs form competing centers of power and influence. Numerous SOPs arise as resources tighten. Efforts are made to avoid uncertainty through reliance on short-term planning. Problemistic search begins, but it usually stops at the first satisfactory alternative. Conflicts are resolved through sequential attention to goals. Finally, organizational learning affects the nature of presidential choice.

This view of the White House organization leads to the question of the President's own impact. What difference does the individual President make? Perhaps the best method to answer the question is to examine the *cycle of decreasing discretion*. As Presidents move through the process of domestic choice, the organizational dynamics become more important. Once the issues are selected, alternatives must be found. It is at this point that the organization gains its most dramatic impact. Presidents are forced to rely on the available alternatives; they are forced to turn to internal advice and information. Whereas Presidents have wide discretion in defining the agenda issues, they are constrained in the choice of specific programs. The limits on presidential resources lead to the search for standard operating procedures and efforts at internal compromise. The President receives a decision memorandum with a set of pros and cons, but he hardly has the resources to see whether there is anything more, whether the advantages actually exist, or whether the disadvantages are important. If the President becomes involved in the details of each choice, he will lose sight of the broader problems. If he remains aloof, he is at the mercy of his staff and the organization. The President sits at the end of a long funnel, without the time or the energy to enter the vast wasteland which molds presidential policy.

Internal domination may be an inevitable outcome of the White House decision process. Given the drop in presidential resources and the need to control internal conflict, the goal of multiple advocacy may be impossible. Presidents are caught between difficult cross-pressures. Presidents definitely want "good policy," but they also want immediate results. Perhaps the only way to be effective is to remove internal conflict. One congressional observer offered the following opinion: "While it is true that Presidents have to get a handle on infighting, they have to be willing to let it flourish. It is through that kind of conflict that the really innovative solutions arrive. Presidents have to be patient with the staffs. It may take more time to discover the solution, but it will be worth it. Of course, it's always easier said than done."

A contextual model of choice also raises questions for multiple advocacy. In this prescriptive framework, originally developed by Alexander George (1972), Presidents are asked to staff the White House with a variety of advocates of different stripes and persuasions. These advocates are to be supervised by an impartial secretariat and are to be equally girded for the internal debate. Resources are to be fairly divided among these multiple advocates, and a comprehensive discussion of pros and cons is the desired result. According to George, "Effective competition is usually necessary if the processes of bureaucratic politics within a complex organization are to produce the functional equivalent of a rational consideration of, and choice among, policy alternatives" (p. 761). Multiple advocacy thereby becomes the direct response to what Irving Janis (1972) calls "groupthink," a notorious disease in which groups of advisors formulate misguided decisions based on peer pressure. Unfortunately, multiple advocacy is a very expensive cure with high risks of conflict. According to a Ford assistant, "Multiple advocacy is very nice on paper. It just can't work in the White House. We don't have the time to make sure all the advisors have access to the President. This is not a daycare; it is survival of the fittest." Multiple advocacy requires maximum resources across the presidential term. It demands considerable time, presidential involvement, and organizational commitment. Further, without firm guidance, multiple advocacy has the dangerous potential to bloom into full-scale staff conflict. Multiple advocacy offers the assumption that winners will be gracious, and losers silent. That is an unwarranted assumption given the stakes of the game. This is not to argue that multiple advocacy cannot exist in the White House. There is some evidence that it does arise, particularly at the start of the presidential term—witness Moynihan and Burns in the battle over welfare reform in 1969—but as the term progresses, the opportunities and costs of multiple advocacy rise.

In the final analysis, presidential involvement may be the key to an effective staff system. Unless the President is willing to enter the decision process, the movement toward domination will ultimately appear. Whatever the standard operating procedures or the amount of organizational learning, there is a natural tendency for the staffs to engage in coalitional conflict. Without the President's assertion of authority, the conflict often leads to the exit of qualified advocates. Certainly, multiple advocacy is an important goal. The problem is how to achieve that goal given the constraints on presidential choice.

9 a no win presidency

> *Some days, I would sit in my office and ask myself just what the hell I was doing out there. I would try my damndest to figure it all out. We would spend months working out a program—ironing out all the problems as carefully as possible—only to be kicked down by Congress. Sometimes I would be on the verge of throwing it in, only to come back the next day to start all over again. It was, to put it mildly, a hell of a way to earn a living.*

These are not the comments of a disenchanted Carter aide or an angry Ford official nor those of a victim of Watergate or the infamous Johnson treatment. They are the words of a former Eisenhower assistant who worked with both a Democratic and a Republican Congress. Could the Presidency have changed so much since then?

There is always a tendency to look back in time for the "golden days," to remember Franklin Roosevelt's hundred days or Lyndon Johnson's legislative wizardry. We tend to obscure the failures. Yet, all thirty-nine past Presidents have encountered elements of what might be called the No Win Presidency. History is strewn with instances of presidential cross-pressures—from Jackson's battle over the federal bank to Wilson's struggle for the League of Nations. Yet, recently the cross-pressures have escalated. Congressional competition, complexity, and surveillance have increased. There has been a coinciding decline in the opportunities for presidential influence, with a basic change in the pool of available ideas. Now more than at any time in recent history, Presidents are caught in a stream of cross-pressures. The President is forced to balance the cycles of influence against the cycles of effectiveness, the goal of reelection against the goal of good policy. The President's resource base has not kept pace with the increased cost of presidential policy. Before I turn to the concept of a No Win Presidency, it should be useful to review the findings on the domestic agenda. Since it was the study of the agenda process that led to an interest in the No Win Presidency, it will be particularly important to highlight the main thrusts of this study.

A Brief Review

This has been a study of the President's domestic agenda—how it has evolved and how decisions are made. We have looked at timing, the sources of ideas and pressures, the search for alternatives, the definition of priorities, and the decision-making structure. Throughout the analysis, I have emphasized the impact of resources on the domestic agenda. According to the White House staffs, Presidents enter office with specific amounts of time, information, expertise, energy, and capital. These resources are expended and developed over time, creating within the domestic policy process a cycle of decreasing influence and a cycle of increasing effectiveness. These two cycles create obvious cross-pressures. Presidents must often choose between careful planning and congressional success. The only point at which both cycles are mutually compatible is at the start of the second term. Yet, even then, the two-term limitation leads to a rapid acceleration of decreasing influence. Again, Presidents face a no-win situation: they must either wait for stronger planning or take advantage of the first moments of the term.

These cycles create identifiable patterns in agenda choice which may help future Presidents cope with the No Win Presidency. We know, for instance, that the timing of agenda choice is highly structured. Despite our interest in the mythical "sense of timing," Presidents attempt to set the agenda early and repeat it often. Even Lyndon Johnson, the supposed master of timing, understood the importance of moving the agenda within the first moments of the term. In the effort, all Presidents face restrictions. The sheer readiness of specific alternatives has a major impact on timing. If the programs are not ready to go, there will be predictable delays compounded by levels of presidential and staff expertise. Moreover, there is substantial variation in timing within the first year. Some Presidents are fast, some slow. Nixon's 1969 agenda, for instance, was remarkably late, moving to Congress during the late summer and early fall; Kennedy's 1961 agenda was sent to Congress early in the first quarter following the inauguration. The differences in timing help to explain the differences in congressional passage. Nixon failed to capitalize on his brief honeymoon, preferring to focus on foreign affairs instead.

In our search for explanations of agenda choice, it is particularly useful to divide each domestic program into three separate components: (1) issues, which involve the definition of national needs; (2) alternatives, centering on the specific programs; and (3) priorities, which reflect the level of presidential interest and involvement. Our underlying assumptions are that each component has a different set of incentives and that all presidential choice is purposive. In the definition of issues, for instance, Presidents search for *benefits.* Presidents select those issues which help them achieve one of three goals: reelection, historical achievement, good policy. Over the past two decades there has been a slight increase in the emphasis on reelection, perhaps reflecting the slim electoral mandates given Nixon in 1968 and Carter in 1976. In the search for alternatives, Presidents must consider the *costs*—political, economic, and technical. In the past twenty years, the emphasis on the economic costs of potential programs has increased dramatically. Contemporary Presidents are much more concerned than were their predecessors about the budgetary impact of domestic alternatives. This concern seems to be a direct product of changing economic conditions and of the perception of inflation as the most important national problem. Finally, in the definition of priorities, Presidents tend to look at the potential for congressional success. In moving items onto and off the White House must list, Presidents respond to congressional delay, increasing costs, and the potential for defeat. Thus, Nixon's welfare reform, Ford's national health insurance, and Carter's real-wage insurance are all examples of programs that once occupied the must list, only to fall under presidential review.

Perhaps the most important findings of this study relate to the presidential decision-making structure. We have looked at three possible models of presidential choice, each with its own organizational structure and associated behaviors: (1) the rational model, (2) behavioral, and (3) garbage can. Adopting a contextual approach toward understanding presidential decisions, the behavioral model supplies the most valuable description of actual agenda activity. Presidential resources, staff compatibility, and the degree of presidential involvement all point toward bargaining and domination as the two major White House decision-making styles. As resources ebb and flow, Presidents consciously or subconsciously shift decision strategies. We can expect the staff system to move rather quickly from an early bargaining approach to staff conflict and domination. The pattern has appeared in each of the past five administrations—from Kennedy to Carter—and it should return with Reagan. Each administration started out with noble ideas of staff collegiality and ended with structured domination and conflict. Malcontents and minority coalitions were forced out, and a dominant coalition emerged. This model of organizational change has some implications for presidential reform. Since multiple advocacy puts heavy strains on the White House policy process, those who propose such a system must account for changing resources. The question is whether the gains of multiple advocacy would outweigh the heightened potential for severe internal conflict.

The Domestic Presidency

The domestic Presidency has changed dramatically over the past two decades. White House staffs complain of increasing constraint, decreasing success, and growing frustration. Though the structure of the domestic process remains fairly stable, the relationship between the President and Congress has undergone a marked evolution. Congress has finished a decade of internal reform; the political parties have withered; the basic issues that feed the policy gristmill have shifted; and there is a new atmosphere of surveillance on Capitol Hill. As one Carter aide remarked,

> This has become a no-win job. It involves a series of obstacles, one hurdle after another. Each problem is followed by a second, more difficult problem. We simply can't get closure on the issues. Energy and welfare reform seem so much more complex than Kennedy's Medicare or Johnson's Aid to Education. The office of the President has not changed much over the past decade—a new Office of Management and Budget, a new Domestic Council, but not too much else . . . not so much in formal terms, but in the way the President interacts with the rest of Washington and the nation. We have less flexibility today; there is more conflict. Congress seems more hostile and confused; the public is uncertain. I simply think that it is more difficult to succeed now than in 1960. Lyndon Johnson would be a very frustrated President.

The growth of this No Win Presidency is a 1970s phenomenon. It was kindled by a series of presidential misjudgments, most notably the War in Vietnam and Watergate, and was fueled by a string of congressional reactions, the most important of which were the War Powers Resolution and the Budget and Impoundment Control Act (see Greenstein 1978). It is reflected in the way the press covers the President, in the legislative process, and in an emerging string of one-term Presidents. Presidents are increasingly caught in a political vise. They are cross-pressured from a number of angles, with little opportunity for release. In domestic policy, the development of this No Win Presidency involves at least five separate trends, each with somewhat separate causes and effects. Separately the trends have created unique problems for the President; combined they have increased the cost of presidential policy. First, there has been a remarkable rise in the amount of congressional competition for scarce domestic agenda space. The explanation rests partly on the backlog of legislation left after the Nixon and Ford years, a backlog created by legislative stalemate, and partly on changes in the congressional environment. Congress has new sources of information, more technical expertise, larger staffs, and increased incentives for drafting its own agenda. The President no longer can rely on automatic access to the legislative calendar. Whether the President is a Democrat or a Republican, the congressional system increasingly provides active competition for agenda space. Second, the domestic policy process has continued to fragment, thereby increasing legislative complexity. The rise of subcommittee government in Congress has reinforced White House frustration—legislation must now pass through more stops on the road to enactment (see Patterson 1978). Though there are fewer single obstacles to passage in Congress, the number of active participants and claimants has spiraled. The growth of complexity has limited the President's ability to influence outcomes and has increased the problems of White House liaison. Third, Presidents now face a significant drop in their potential influence in Congress. The White House can no longer rely on the President's party to produce the margin of support in either Congress or the electorate. The parties have been drowned out in the nominating process, and they have lost considerable cohesion in Congress. Despite Carter's substantial congressional majorities in 1977—which rivaled Lyndon Johnson's 1965 margins—Carter was unable to secure passage of his domestic program. Party is falling as the "gold standard" of presidential influence. Fourth, Presidents must now operate in an environment of increasing surveillance. The mood of public distrust has not abated in the post-Watergate era, nor has Congress relaxed its oversight of presidential choice. Presidents are currently limited by the tools of congressional oversight—not the least of which is the legislative veto. Fifth, and perhaps most important, the domestic issues have changed. The issues may not be more difficult in 1980, but they transcend the familiar coalitions and jurisdictions. Carter's energy plan, welfare reform, and hospital-cost containment all failed to fit the traditional political framework. Unlike the issues of Kennedy and Johnson years, the new domestic issues have few active constituents; there are few natural allies, and there is no shortage of enemies. The changes in the "pool of issues" reflect an increase in what King (1978) calls the "atomization" of politics. As federal resources decline, Presidents increasingly must build their legislative coalitions "in the sand." The price of domestic policy success has gone up, while presidential influence has not.

Increased Competition. Not so long ago Presidents could rely on "star billing" for the domestic agenda. The party leadership faithfully waited for the President's program; Congress patiently reserved space for the President's legislative agenda. By the mid-1970s, however, the presidential star had dimmed. Carter could no longer expect automatic attention for his domestic agenda—the amount of competition had increased. Congress had little time for the new President; there was a massive backlog of legislation from the Nixon and Ford vetoes. After eight years of Republican rule, Congress had its own unfinished business. The President, not Congress, would be the rubber stamp. Carter's Congressional Liaison Office became painfully aware of the problem. As one assistant lamented, "Congress had its own priorities in 1977, and there was precious little room for our program. There were literally hundreds of bills left over from the Ford administration. Ford had vetoed so many damn bills that there was barely any time for Carter's legislation. There was too much demand and not enough supply."

Much of the 1977 competition was the result of a very simple move in liberal strategy in 1974, during the final days of the Nixon administration. Rather than compromise with a crippled administration, congressional activists decided to pull back on the agenda in anticipation of a midterm landslide. Following the Nixon resignation and the Ford pardon, congressional Democrats felt confident of electing a "veto-proof" Congress. Though the 1974 elections increased congressional majorities, the Democrats fell short of their goal. Few predicted Ford's heavy reliance on the veto—sixty-six separate vetoes in two years—nor did they anticipate Ford's success in sustaining those vetoes on the House and Senate floor. Thus, by 1977 congressional Democrats had a long list of delayed priorities which had precedence over the Carter agenda.

But the Carter experience was more than a temporary phenomenon. Several trends suggest that Presidents will have to endure competition for many years to come. There are more incentives for competition, more resources for policy initiation, and less reverence for the wisdom of presidential planning. Ronald Reagan can anticipate no shortage of congressional activism, whether from the Democratic House or the Republican Senate.

Throughout the 1970 reform period, Congress has attempted to restore the balance between the two branches. Much of the post-Watergate effort centered on rebuilding competition with the President. This reform pressure was far more than a reaction to the Nixon Presidency. As one Carter aide suggested, Congress has become committed to a greater role in the domestic policy process:

> I think one of our most significant mistakes was not involving Congress in the planning process—in energy or health, for instance. I think we misread the reform era as mainly a reaction to the Nixon administration and Watergate. It was more than that: Congress wanted to have a say in the development of legislation. Congress was blamed for much of what went wrong with the Great Society and Vietnam. Most of the members had been pretty ignorant of what was involved with the programs. If they were going to take the heat for national mistakes—you know, increased spending, inflation, the war—why not take part in the planning?

The Budget and Impoundment Control Act of 1974, the War Powers Resolution, the rise of the legislative veto, and the growth in congressional oversight all signal a growing competition for political power. The congressional reform effort encouraged more competition, if only by spreading internal power to a larger number of policy "entrepreneurs." Since advertising and credit-taking are recognized paths to reelection, and since the responsibility for initiation now rests with a larger number of congressional actors, Presidents cannot expect a dramatic drop in the competition for agenda space.

Changes in the composition of Congress also has contributed to the domestic competition. As older members have been replaced, the emphasis on legislation has grown. The last four elections all introduced large transfusions of "new blood" into both houses of Congress—ninety-two freshmen in the House in 1974, eighteen freshmen in the Senate in 1980. Regardless of party, these changes have brought to Congress a greater legislative interest and a coinciding expansion of competition. According to a Carter liaison officer, "A lot of these new members want to make their mark with bills. They want to go home and show how powerful they are. That makes it more difficult for us. They clog up the system, and we end up negotiating with freshmen." The 1980 election does not spell great change in the activist bias of Congress. The new Republican members of both the House and Senate are likely to be as interested in initiation as were their liberal predecessors.

Beyond the changes in the balance of power and membership, Congress has also increased the basic resources of competition. The creation of the Congressional Budget Office (CBO), coupled with the expansion of the Congressional Research Service and the General Accounting Office, has added to the legislative information base. Assuming that information is one ingredient of initiation, Congress has increased both the quantity and the quality of the supply. The Congressional Budget Office, in particular, has become an important source of competing information, whether against the President or the executive branch. Under its mandate, CBO has broad powers of analysis and review. It has become a valuable source of preliminary staff work on potential congressional programs. Furthermore, Congress has more than doubled the number of staff members in the House and Senate. Personal staffs as well as committee staffs have steadily expanded. This influx of new staff eventually leads to a greater emphasis on policy initiation—legislators increasingly use the staffs to develop new ideas, and the staffs are more than willing to comply. The personalized nature of the new staff system provides ample incentives for committee and subcommittee chairmen to hire activists, whether liberal or conservative. These staffs in turn see rewards in the initiation of major programs that compete directly with presidential priorities. As Congress has expanded its information base, it has increased its capability to use that information for policy competition. Congress now has both the will and the expertise to challenge the President's domestic leadership.

Did the 1980 election change the competitive nature of Congress? Is Congress more likely to cooperate with the President? Preliminary indications suggest that Republicans are just as likely to challenge their President as are Democrats. After two decades of minority status, the new Senate majority cannot be expected blindly to follow the lead of their new President. Senators Garn, Thurmond, Hatch, Domenici, Hatfield, and Percy have their own ideas, which will compete with the Reagan agenda. Nor is the Republican congressional party likely to demonstrate much more cohesion than the Democrats. It is composed of dissimilar interests and ideas which will also heighten the competition for scarce agenda space.

Increased Complexity. Carter's first moments in office were characterized by confusion; neither Carter nor his staff was prepared for the transition from Georgia politics to national policy. The problem rested in part on Carter's relative inexperience. Yet, Carter was also faced with very real changes in the domestic policy process. In the eight short years following

Lyndon Johnson's Presidency the policy process had become much more complex. The rise of subcommittee government in Congress, coupled with the emergence of a new set of domestic issues, created a greater level of complexity. According to former President Ford,

> We went on a wild nightmare of reforms, and we really messed up the way Congress effectively works. You could run down a list of things that have been done under the title of reform, and they all look good, but the net result is that the Congress has really lost its capability to respond. I think all the so-called reforms since the late 1960s ought to be reviewed to see whether or not they have been counterproductive (PBS, "Every Four Years," transcript, January-February 1980, p. 30).

Even Johnson, with all his legislative skills, would have been confused by the new complexity.

According to Dodd and Schott (1979), the rise of subcommittee government took place in three distinct waves. First, from 1947 to the present there has been an increased reliance on subcommittees to conduct legislative business. Faced with a rise in the congressional workload, chairmen had little choice but to farm out a number of chores to the subcommittees. Second, during the same period, there was a steady growth in the absolute number of subcommittees: in 1945 there were 130 House and Senate subcommittees; by 1977 there were 267. This proliferation contributes to legislative complexity and jurisdictional confusion. As one Carter aide argued,

> Take a good look at comprehensive energy. Look at how many stops it had to make in Congress. There was a great deal of committee interest, but more important was the number of *sub*committees who took some action. From our standpoint, it was just too complicated. It takes a real effort just to know where the legislation is, when the decisions are going to be made, and what needs to be done. There was a drop in our ability to influence outcomes in that kind of fragmented system.

The third wave of subcommittee government involved grants of formal autonomy. The Legislative Reorganization Act of 1970, the Hansen Committee reforms, and the "Subcommittee Bill of Rights" each extended the power and influence of the congressional subcommittees. Of the reforms, the Bill of Rights was the single most important source of complexity. Subcommittees were given formal jurisdictions; prompt referral of bills was guaranteed; staffs and budgets were mandated; and subcommittees were created for all House committees with more than twenty members. The immediate impact was to dilute the power of the Ways and Means Committee, but in the long run, subcommittees gained a sizable margin of power in directing the legislative process. Though House members recognized the potential for subcommittee confusion, they steadfastly refused to redraw jurisdictional lines. The result was increased subcommittee power plus greater policy confusion. If committee government had been only moderately complex, subcommittee government promised new levels of frustration.

Much of the subcommittee confusion stems from jurisdictional gerrymandering. The President's domestic program is now subject to a greater number of cross-cutting demands. With the advent of split and joint referrals in the House, Presidents can expect major legislation to fall prey to multiple pressures. In the case of Carter's welfare reform, for instance, the jurisdictional complexity heightened liaison headaches and reduced the prospects of success. When Nixon originally proposed welfare reform in 1969, the White House liaison staff was primarily concerned about securing *committee* support. "Our strategy was to move the Family Assistance Plan past the two or three major obstacles in each House," one Nixon aide remembered. "it was mainly a problem of staffing the process and providing some timing pressure. We were concentrating at the committee level. If there was subcommittee interest, we preferred to aggregate to the larger levels." By 1977, however, the rise of subcommittee government had complicated an already fractionalized process. The number of congressional claimants had increased, and the battle for welfare reform was joined at both the committee and the subcommittee level. According to a Carter liaison aide,

> The welfare-reform legislation was most difficult in the House. Disregarding our problems with the bill, we had a lot of trouble coordinating the lobbying effort. We had help from the departments, but on a bill like that the President has to supply the whip. The problem was in finding the horses. That bill moved to four committees in the House alone—Ways and Means, Agriculture, Education and Labor, and a special ad hoc committee on welfare reform. Within at least three of the committees, we had to deal with subcommittees—subcommittees on the budget impact as well as the legislative substance. We just didn't have the manpower. Neither did the departments. Now you tell me, how does the White House influence those kind of decisions in that many committees? How should we design a system to have maximum input?

The rise in subcommittee government complicated an already intricate domestic process. The path to enactment has shifted since 1960; there are more side trips and dead ends. Moreover, subcommittee government has been fueled by the increased use of split and joint referral of bills. Split referral means breaking a bill into its many different parts and moving the parts to separate committees. Prior to 1975 the House did not allow split referral. With its adoption, the House merely added to internal confusion. Bills are now giant puzzles to be broken down and pieced back together later.

Obviously, subcommittee government is not all pain for the President. There are fewer single obstacles to the President's agenda. Carter did not have to deal with an entrenched House Rules Committee as Kennedy did, nor did Carter have to persuade a reluctant House Ways and Means chairman as Johnson did. But despite fewer blockades, Carter ran into more participants. The power of one chairman or committee to forestall legislative action fell between 1960 and 1980, but the power of many smaller coalitions increased.

The greater number of access points leads to a new brand of legislative stalemate: inaction caused by the process itself. With the dispersion of congressional power, Presidents are increasingly limited in their ability to concentrate influence at key decision points. There are simply fewer opportunities for intense lobbying. Presidential influence is often a blunt instrument—the new congressional policy process demands a surgeon's skill. According to one Carter aide, "The big question is where to put your energy. Which committee is the best to work with? Which subcommittee is going to cause the most damage? We try to work with the Speaker and the Majority Leader, but the process is so mixed up. Too many chiefs. . . . " The paradox is clear: Congress has diluted the power of single committee chairmen to impede progress but increased the complexity of the legislative process. Congress has removed one major obstacle but has developed many smaller hurdles. The 1980 elections only complicated the process further. The Reagan administration must now deal with a Democratic majority in the House and a new Republican majority in the Senate. The staff changes, committee restructuring, and legislative turnover in the Senate serve to confuse an already complex system. Now more than ever, the President needs to understand the system.

Declining Influence. The post-Watergate period has witnessed a steady drop in the President's potential influence over domestic policy. Once again, a primary explanation rests on subcommittee government and the dispersion of congressional power. There are fewer opportunities for the kind of personalized leadership made famous by Lyndon Johnson; there are more actors with congressional influence in direct competition with the President's domestic agenda. As one Johnson assistant reflected, "In 1965, there were maybe ten or twelve people who you needed to corral in the House and Senate. Without those people, you were in for a tough time. Now, I'd put that figure upwards of one hundred. Believe it, there are so many people who have a shot at derailing a bill that the President has to double his effort for even routine decisions." The erosion of congressional parties only compounds the problem. Once the gold standard of presidential influence, parties have been the major victims of the dispersion of House and Senate power. Presidents can not rely on party as the one potent route to success. Carter's sizable Democratic majorities did not guarantee more than fleeting consideration. Unlike Johnson in 1965, Carter was unable to convert his party numbers into firm support. As Gerald Ford suggests,

> I loved the Congress, and I have nothing but the warmest feelings toward the House of Representatives. I developed many friends, Democrats and Republicans. It's a great institution. It's the finest legislative body in the world. But I think its effectiveness, its capability of doing the job, has degenerated in the last five or ten years, for a variety of reasons. And the net result is that it has developed certain characteristics that are detrimental in doing the job that's needed and necessary to solve some of our

problems. . . . The Congress has disintegrated from the position of responsibility and how it can operate. No longer do we have the capability of the Speaker of the House, or the minority leader, to get their troops, so to speak, to follow the Democratic Party policy, on the one hand, or the Republican Party policy on the other. They go off in 10 different directions. They seem to follow the public surveys rather than party philosophy. And the net result is no leader in the Congress, Democrat or Republican, can say, "My party is going to follow this party position." They just can't get the troops to do what I think the public wants them to do under our two-party system (PBS, "Every Four Years," transcript, January-February 1980, p. 36).

Of the five most recent Presidents, Lyndon Johnson is often viewed as the most effective legislative leader. Stories abound of Johnson's ability to sway even the most reluctant ally. Much of the image is myth. Contrary to his reputation as a legislative master, Johnson's success was closely tied to the massive Democratic majorities that swept into office on the 1964 coattails. Johnson's style was uniquely personalized, but there were limits to its actual impact. Johnson would have had considerable problems in the post-Watergate Presidency. His personalized leadership would be much less effective today. The potentials for Johnson's kind of leadership have dropped, partially in response to the erosion of the congressional parties. As one Carter aide joked, "It is easy to be a star quarterback when you've got great receivers, when every ball you throw up is caught. When Johnson was President, he had a pretty disciplined team. Now the Democrats are offsides on almost every play; the receivers have hands of iron and want to run their own patterns." Or, as Jack Valenti argues, what makes things "so different from the Eisenhower days is the balkanization and fracturing of the Congress."

> I have always considered myself a liberal Democrat but I am having some difficulty now holding that description because the liberal reformers have ruptured the Congress, in my judgment. In the old days, only a decade ago, the president could sit with the leaders of the Congress, and negotiate a deal to try to lift the quality of life in this country and then count on the leadership to deliver the votes required to put that program into effect. When Eisenhower was president in those halcyon days that now seem like ten light years ago, two men made him look very good, two Democrats, Sam Rayburn who ran the House, and Lyndon Johnson who ran the Senate. Between them they could deliver the votes. . . . You can't do that anymore (Valenti 1980, pp. 7-8).

The increased number of actors that have influence in the domestic process means that the number of individuals that the President must persuade has increased. No longer can the President turn to the Majority leader to whip congressional support. The opportunities for persuasion have fallen sharply, if only because the President is one actor among many. This problem is compounded by the changing role of the congressional parties. Presidents must be wary of relying on the parties to provide the base of support. Gone are the days of strong party leaders and powerful committee chairmen. The parties are no longer in the business of mustering support for the President's agenda. The recent electoral problems of House Majority Leader Jim Wright, House Whip John Brademas, and a score of committee chairmen may lead to even less time devoted to party leadership. These declines in party leadership do not spell the end of the congressional parties. The party leadership in both the House and the Senate has been reinforced in the post-reform period. The Speaker of the House has greater influence over committee assignments, legislative referral, and scheduling; we can expect a similar regeneration for the Senate Republicans. Yet, the parties will never return as the once omnipotent managers of the legislative process. Bills now originate from a myriad of sources; decisions proceed on many levels. Today, the most important party function may be to *coordinate* the legislative process, not to mobilize blocs of votes on key issues. Party is still the basis of presidential capital; it still supplies the foundation of White House influence in Congress. Therein lies an important facet of the No Win Presidency. Parties now provide only a shallow base of influence in the legislative process. Presidents must still turn to the parties, but the parties no longer supply the whip.

Increased Surveillance. Presidents now operate in a vastly altered political environment—an environment of surveillance. Congress, the press, and the public all maintain a degree of distrust and suspicion. At least three specific trends offer little hope for change in the atmosphere of surveillance.

First, Congress seems ever ready to impose statutory constraints on the President's domestic discretion. Starting with the Budget and Impoundment Control Act of 1974, Congress has shown a willingness to apply legislative sanctions to the President's domestic agenda. For example, Congress increasingly relies on the legislative veto to supply oversight of executive-branch implementation. From 1970 to 1977 there was a threefold increase in the number of bills containing some form of the legislative veto. Despite presidential protests, Congress continues to use the veto to ensure proper administration. This statutory surveillance has made its mark on the presidential policy process. According to one Carter domestic aide, "The aura here is of congressional suspicion. They don't trust much of anything we do. Whatever our intentions, Congress suspects the worse. We are at a disadvantage from the start." A second Carter aide continued, "It's not all bad for Congress to take a close look at our programs. What has become a problem is the assumption that the President will always mislead. We have swung full circle from the 1960s. Then everything the President did was good. Now everything seems to be bad."

A second source of surveillance originates with the press. The media is far less likely to shelter the President or his staff in the post-Watergate era; honeymoons are destined to be short as Presidents are examined under the white-hot glare of constant attention. The phases of the press relationship seem more pronounced today. Carter summarized his problems with the media as follows:

> One of my biggest disappointments was the irresponsibility of the media. I think that's a natural reaction of a President who is involved in literally months of study, preparation, the evolution of an idea or a program, its presentation to the Congress, and then to have it either ignored, or the analysis of it, at least in the President's perhaps biased opinion, distorted. But I think this is something we have to live with. And my own belief is that the openness of government is an advantage, and the inquisitiveness of the news media is an important facet of American life. I think there's too much of an aftermath of Watergate, where many members of the media feel that most public officials, Presidents, members of Congress, governors, mayors, are untrustworthy and that their word of honor is doubtful, and that their good intentions are not to be trusted (PBS, "Every Four Years," transcript, January-February 1980, pp. 40-41).

Obviously, media coverage has its benefits. Presidents can structure the news to their advantage, and incumbency is a powerful electoral tool abetted by media coverage. What is important is the way media surveillance has changed the presidential policy process. It creates yet another no-win situation as the potentials for presidential influence are reduced. "How can the President work with Congress under that kind of hounding," one Ford liaison officer asked. "Every little detail is likely to end up in tomorrow's paper. The level of innuendo is incredible. What we need is a nice, quiet environment in which to work. Instead, we are under constant surveillance."

The increasing congressional and media surveillance are compounded by a third, more pervasive trend: the increasing level of public distrust of the Presidency. Contrary to expectations, public cynicism has not declined as we have moved further away from Watergate. Indeed, public distrust continues its slow boil. The public cynicism has two important impacts on the presidential policy process. First, it limits the President's ability to convert public approval into congressional support. Given the steep declines in public approval over the term of office, it is increasingly difficult for the White House to use public support in the legislative struggle. Indeed, Presidents are actually encouraged to separate their congressional fortunes from the volatile roller coaster of public opinion. It is difficult to predict whether Reagan will be able to stem the rapid drop in public approval experienced by Nixon, Ford, and Carter. Future Presidents may have to become accustomed to continued public dissatisfaction.

The second impact of public distrust is a curious electoral cycle. Public distrust reinforces the level of congressional and media surveillance, which in turn may increase public distrust. It is a difficult circle to break. Instead of providing the intended emphasis on "good policy," this surveillance may actually provoke more presidential concern with reelection. Like House members, Presidents may fixate on achieving mandates for their second terms. Declining levels of public support may increase the courtship of a second term, raising the conflict between the dual goals of reelection and "good policy." Moreover, high public distrust may heighten the search for "outsiders" to fill the Presidency. We elected two such outsiders in 1976 and 1980. Unfortunately, these outsiders are more likely to lack experience in federal policy, which merely accelerates the cycle.

The Changing Issues. Along with changes in competition, complexity, and surveillance, the basic issues have shifted over the 1970s. Energy; welfare reform; hospital cost containment; social security financing; government ethics; the Lockheed, Chrysler, and New York City bankruptcies—all are remarkably different from the issues of the 1960s. Whereas Johnson could secure his goals of good policy and reelection simultaneously with Medicare or the War on Poverty, the 1970s produced a new set of domestic issues that refuse to fit into the New Deal-Great Society framework, refuse to bend to the prevailing congressional or bureaucratic jurisdictions. Given ever-declining federal resources, these new issues break across the old coalitions, pitting former allies against each other—cities against cities, states against states.

Unlike the Kennedy and Johnson programs, the Carter agenda did not arrive with a ready base of constituents—energy, welfare reform, and social security financing were all "orphans" in the domestic policy process. The Carter issues signaled the rise of a number of "constituentless" issues to the national agenda. Which major coalitions backed the comprehensive energy program? Which groups supported hospital cost containment? Where was the natural base of support for welfare reform? All three issues moved to Congress with little interest-group support, minimal public concern, and active bureaucratic resistance. Of the 1977 Carter issues, only the fifty-dollar tax rebate had significant public support. Of the 1978 proposals, only youth employment and urban assistance elicited a New Deal response.

Did Carter naively pick these constituentless issues from the shelf, or was there a basic change in the "pool of available ideas?" According to a Carter Domestic Policy Staff aide, the answer rests on a change in the kinds of ideas that currently circulate through government:

> We are entering a period of very difficult choices for the President and Congress. The issues we have to deal with are no longer as easy to support as they used to be. We have entered a period of resource shortages which require a firm governmental response. Gas rationing is not exactly the kind of issue to ride to reelection, but the President has to take it on. We are also in a period of extreme pressure on federal funding; of choices between B-1 bombers and hospital equipment, between an MX missile and inner-city redevelopment. We have to make very hard choices now.

Maybe we are also in a period of one-term Presidents. There were very few issues that we could have selected that would have helped us in the campaign. Most have involved some level of public sacrifice, and all we see ahead of us is more of the same.

The change in the pool of domestic issues is the direct result of increasing shortages in natural and fiscal resources. The energy crisis has brought forecasts of sustained periods of rising prices and shortages. The Iraq-Iran War that began in 1980 is only one sign of the U.S. vulnerability in the battle for oil. The energy crisis, with its coinciding inflationary pressure, places greater stress on federal fiscal resources. Nor is there currently a shortage of claimants for budget support. Cities are concerned about a dwindling tax base; states are worried about continued tax-cutting; senators want more defense spending; blacks want more jobs; the steel and auto industries want import controls and tax incentives. Many of the new issues involve intense political conflict which cannot be managed in the old legislative framework.

Changes in the issue pool are complicated by the jurisdictional confusion in Congress. Energy and welfare have yet to fit into the prevailing congressional mold. In 1977 both programs were referred to multiple committees, with special ad hoc arrangements in the House. The nature of the issues involved a tangled web of legislative review, which eventually increased the time needed for passage. The absence of constitutencies made the Carter agenda that much more difficult to handle. Since energy was a fairly recent issue, Congress was ill-prepared for speedy deliberation, but welfare reform has been around since 1969. This is not to absolve the Carter administration of tactical errors and misjudgments. Yet, the jurisdictional confusion only raised the price of policy. How does personalized leadership work in an ad hoc energy committee? How does liaison handle split and joint referral in a fragmented House? As one Carter aide angrily remarked,

> Energy is not the kind of program you expose to intense vote trading. It is a very complicated issue which has to be thought out carefully. You cannot allow it to be opened up on the floor. The President is not as free to compromise on these kinds of issues. It is not as through we can afford to engage in a prolonged amending process. Either the program is allowed to work, or not. You cannot let the House sink its hungry teeth into these kinds of programs.

Perhaps the most important change in domestic issues rests on the disintegration of stable political coalitions. Neither Carter nor Reagan could turn to a consistent base of support; a new coalition had to be constructed for each issue. As King notes, politics has become "atomized"; coalitions are both fleeting and instable:

> The ideas of the New Deal are no longer the ideas around which American politics is organized; but no new public philosophy has emerged to take

their place. Power in Congress is even more widely dispersed than it used to be; the conservative coalition is much less prominent than it was. The old party machines and bosses have largely gone; nothing has replaced them. There are far more interest and issue groups than there used to be; the great majority of them lack internal cohesion. Within the federal government in Washington, the old "iron triangle" (coalitions of a sort) have given way to much more amorphous issue networks, to the description of which a simple Euclidean geometry is no longer appropriate. Even among the electorate, the voting blocs of the 1930s and 1940s have been gradually eroded by time; only the blacks remain. To the words suggestive of disintegration, of breaking up . . . we should clearly add "atomization." American politics have become to a high degree, atomized (King 1978, pp. 390-91).

Has the Reagan election changed the atomization? Power in Congress remains dispersed, the parties are still in disarray, interest groups continue to expand, money grows as a power in elections. Moreover, the issues that now dominate the pool of ideas seem more intractable than ever. Like Ford and Carter before him, Reagan remains caught in a No Win Presidency.

The Price of Policy. Thus far, we haved talked of five rather separate trends which have contributed to a No Win Presidency in domestic affairs. Together the increased competition and complexity, declining influence, pervasive surveillance, and change in the available issues have steadily increased the price of policy. Presidents must now pay more for domestic programs. Presidents must be more careful about timing, as well as about the selection of "winnable" issues and alternatives. While the price of policy has risen, the President's resource base has not. Presidents no longer have the resources to expend on "educating" the public; they no longer have the time to spend on a full search for new ideas and programs. If anything, the President's resource base has dwindled over the 1970s. The cost of presidential policy has grown, while the President's ability to influence outcomes has declined. It is a remarkable no-win position.

Winning the No Win Presidency

What can Presidents do to win the domestic No Win Presidency? How can a Carter or a Reagan survive in the stream of cross-pressures? To answer such questions, it is essential to define the desired outcomes. What do we want in future administrations? successful legislative strategists or careful program administrators? Presidents who will educate the public on critical issues or Presidents who search for "doable" programs? Not all choices involve such clear-cut distinctions. Perhaps we can have both reelectable Presidents and protection of the national interest; perhaps we can have careful planning and congressional success. For our purposes, however, it is useful to draw these sharp dichotomies. Presidents and their staffs view choices in these terms, and so shall we. Indeed, one of the end products of the No Win Presidency is that Presidents must make such decisions. Given changes in congressional complexity and competition, Presidents must often sacrifice careful planning in the search for legislative enactment; given changes in the opportunities for influence and the pool of issues, Presidents must often choose between reelection and good policy. At least in the next few pages, we will assume that Presidents are interested *only* in legislative success, reelection, and doable programs. How then should Presidents behave? Eight recommendations arise from the No Win Presidency, many of which will seem contrary to the conventional wisdom, since the conventional wisdom often ignores the structure of incentives that face Presidents at the start of the term.

1. Move it or lose it. Easily the most important response to the No Win Presidency is "move it or lose it." At the start of their administrations, Presidents face a very simple choice created by the dual cycles of decreasing influence and increasing effectiveness. With the growth in congressional competition and complexity, Presidents cannot wait for a comprehensive review of domestic issues and alternatives. There is not enough time, information, or energy. If Presidents are to take advantage of what little resources they have, the domestic agenda must move quickly.

The "move or lose it" approach is a response to a double bind. First, Presidents face a new set of legislative issues. If Presidents hope to utilize what little honeymoon they have, and if they continue to select constituentless issues—energy, welfare reform, and social security financing are all examples—they must move the agenda early and repeat it often. Second, these are precisely the kinds of issues that take the most time to develop. In the case of energy and hospital cost control, neither the information nor the expertise existed when the issues first surfaced. According to a Carter official, the absence of ready alternatives slowed the policy process for the very issues that had to move fast:

> We did not come into office with a handful of already developed programs. If anything, we had a set of ideas that took more than their share of time. There was no set of experts working on hospital cost containment when we came in, and energy was a mess. We had to start the programs all over from scratch. We were the ones who had to canvass the executive branch for ideas. We were also the ones that had to look for some potential solutions. Nothing was tied up and ready to go when we came in.

In adopting a "move it or lose it" strategy, Presidents must accept potential flaws in the legislative package. Presidents and their staffs do not have the time to evaluate a comprehensive set of alternatives, nor do they have the resources to develop novel ideas. In drafting the domestic agenda, Presidents are forced to search for the available alternatives. That is what both Nixon and Carter did with regard to welfare reform; indeed, Carter benefited directly from Nixon's earlier effort: Carter's welfare reform struck a familiar chord in Congress, for it was remarkably similar to Nixon's 1969 Family Assistance Plan.

2. Learning must wait. Presidential scholars often argue that the first year of the first term is a time for learning, that Presidents ought to spend the early days acquainting themselves with the office. The No Win Presidency argues to the contrary. Presidents do not have the time to further their education once in office. They are more successful if they adopt an on-the-job-training strategy. As Presidents enter office for the first term, they face many unfamiliar tasks and issues. One strategy for coping is to develop an information base and build greater expertise. Yet, given the cycle of decreasing influence, Presidents are encouraged to postpone the learning process. Since increased congressional competition and complexity demand a quick White House response, learning must wait.

In this dilemma, Presidents must ask whether the risks of waiting outweigh the potential for policy mistakes, whether hastily packaged programs violate the search for good policy. Though we want our Presidents to learn and unlearn once they enter office, the increased complexity and competition of Congress offer the President and the staff a very difficult choice. The President can present the domestic agenda quickly, take the gamble that the programs will work, and accept the potential flaws or take the resources to develop careful alternatives that may not pass. Assuming that Presidents are interested in legislative success and reelection, it should be no surprise that the "move it or lose it" strategy is the most attractive option.

3. Take the first alternative. As Presidents engage in the search for domestic alternatives, they set certain requirements for adoption. Presidents increasingly demand that new programs have zero fiscal costs—Carter's 1978 urban-assistance package is an example. Presidents also require at least some potential for passage and minimal workability. The distribution of these requirements affects the final programs. Yet, often there is more than one solution for a domestic problem. How many options should the President review before adopting a specific program? How many alternatives should a given search produce? In the No Win Presidency, the answer is one. In the search for domestic alternatives, Presidents are encouraged to take the first alternative which meets the search criteria; once that first alternative is found, the search for other options should be abandoned.

Taking the first alternative has several implications for the national policy process. The first alternative is usually better prepared, better staffed, and more popular within the executive branch; however, it is not always the best alternative. The first alternative may reflect years of incremental compromise and adjustment; it may involve the least unpopular of all options. Acceptance of the first alternative generally undermines the search for innovation. Presidents do have a choice in designing the search for alternatives.

They can emphasize an extensive, broad-gauged search or a more limited, short-term approach. Though political scientists often urge the comprehensive strategy, the No Win Presidency emphasizes a "neighborhood" search, that is, a search for alternatives in the general region of past decisions, but only until the first one that fits the search criteria is found.

Why accept this first alternative? Because to do otherwise expends scarce resources. Since the first alternative often involves the most extensive compromise and political support, Presidents ultimately save internal time and energy. Though the first alternative may not embody the "best" solution, it usually involves the greatest potential for passage and implementation, hence less capital. There is always the potential for failure in such a short-term approach. However, the first alternative offers an opportunity for cutting decision-making costs, while increasing legislative success.

4. No innovations. Political scientists spend a certain amount of energy on the "President Proposes, Congress Disposes" issue. Students are asked to find the source of major legislative innovations and to assess credit or blame. Long tally sheets are produced to support the importance of one branch or the other. In several respects, the exercise is of little value in terms of the domestic Presidency. First, Presidents are increasingly restricted in the amount of innovation they can produce. It is to the President's advantage to borrow, steal, coopt, and appropriate ideas from Congress. The cost of innovation has risen steadily over the past decade, leaving Presidents with little incentive to create new ideas. Presidents are encouraged to take the available programs, not the novel solutions. Second, the increased competition and complexity make presidential innovation politically costly. In the development of new ideas, Presidents lose precious time which is better spent pursuing the available ideas. Finally, given constraints on presidential information and expertise, one might question any President's ability to create new ideas. Innovation demands both information and expertise, which are in short supply at the start of any term.

Our textbook expectation that Presidents ought to innovate is in direct conflict with the No Win Presidency. Presidents hardly have the resources to engage in widespread innovation. The search for the novel program is futile if that program will not pass. Contrary to textbook demands, Presidents have little incentive to develop new ideas at least until the second term. If Presidents are successful in their drive to reelection, the goal of good policy may be given greater play in the second term. In the first term, however, Presidents are advised to hold off on innovation; to take as much from the pool of available ideas and wait for better opportunities. In the second term Presidents may have more opportunity, but even then it may be too late. Under the two-term limitation, Presidents have little time to follow through on innovation. Though there is more freedom for new ideas, there is less potential for success. The cycle of decreasing influence accelerates during the second term, leaving the President an early lame duck.

5. *Avoid details.* In the No Win Presidency, Presidents must decide how to distribute time, information, expertise, energy, and capital. Presidents must decide how much of their personal time and energy to invest in the policy process; how much of their expertise to expend on domestic affairs. The No Win Presidency encourages a "no details" approach to allocating these personal resources. One of the several errors of the early Carter administration resulted from the President's own desire to become immersed in the details of policy. Carter wanted to delve into the specifics of each agenda choice; to review the budget for accuracy, not substance. Given Carter's personality and background, his interest in the details of policy was not surprising; however, it conflicted with the demands of the No Win Presidency. Carter's misplaced interest wasted scarce resources and left the staff to its own devices. It left the domestic agenda without broad guidance.

The No Win Presidency places a premium on presidential distance from the details of policy formulation. Since internal resources are limited, it is to the President's advantage to leave the substance of legislation to his staff. The President must supply the general guidance; the staff must provide the specialization. Carter could have left the details to the staff. One Carter aide complained that "the President shouldn't spend his time adding and subtracting budget figures. He's got to stand back and take a broader focus." Though Carter was roundly criticized for his interest in detail, there may be reason for an increased focus on legislative specifics. Given the increasing complexity of legislation, Carter's concern may not have been misplaced. In major legislation like welfare reform or national health insurance, the detail becomes remarkably important. The calculation of benefit-formulas can commit billions in federal funds, while affecting incentives for public behavior. In 1970, for instance, it was the original benefit-formula that undermined Nixon's welfare reform. Yet, regardless of the impact of detail, the No Win Presidency encourages generalization; specialization is for the staff and the departments, not for the President.

6. *Reelection comes first.* The domestic policy process has always been political. Presidents are exposed to considerable pressure as they choose among competing issues and alternatives. As national resources drop, the process will only become more intense. Scholars frequently lament this political nature of presidential policy. Some go as far as to suggest that Presidents should be insulated from at least the electoral pressure through the adoption of a single, six-year term. Others support a return to "responsible parties" as a method of protection from single-interest groups. Regardless of the strategy, these scholars hope to free the President from the choice between reelection and good policy. Unfortunately, under the current framework, Presidents have little choice but to emphasize reelection first. If good policy follows, that is a bonus.

As Presidents survey their territory following the first inauguration, most are struck by the remarkably short time frame. At best, they have eight very short years to make some impact on the federal system. One primary reason behind the "move or lose it" and "no innovation" strategies is the simple erosion of time. Presidents must move their programs quickly if they are to compete within the legislative process. Presidents will inevitably hit snags in the domestic agenda—a key committee will balk, a department will stall for time, funds may be withheld, implementation may fail, bureaucrats may engage in sabotage. A single four-year term is just too short. It has thus become the wisdom of politics that the President must return, that the second four-year term offers the best chance for impact. The White House threat of reelection is one lever on the federal gears even when the President does not intend to stand for a second term. Thus, when Reagan announced that he would treat his first term as his only term, he may have foreclosed a potent source of influence within the national policy process.

Regardless of the normative implications, reelection must be the President's top priority in the first term. In and of itself the goal is not necessarily negative. Yet, as I have noted, recent changes in the pool of domestic issues may have heightened the conflict between reelection and good policy. In 1961 Kennedy's drive for reelection and the search for good policy seemed compatible. Aid to Education, Medicare, area redevelopment, and tax reform all not only addressed substantive national needs but boosted public approval. By 1977 the shift in the pool of issues had created greater tension between the two goals. Energy, welfare reform, hospital cost containment, and social security financing were not particularly popular issues, especially for Democrats. Although good policy is a noble presidential goal, it is of little value if the President cannot return for a second term. Carter's demand for national sacrifice on energy will be of little solace during the next four years in Plains, Georgia.

7. No Cabinet government. Presidents inevitably enter office with a call for Cabinet government. Nixon, Carter, and Reagan all announced their Cabinet appointees with the usual fanfare. These officials were to be the backbone of the policy process. They would run the federal government like General Motors. Nixon, Carter, and Reagan each intended to be the first President actually to follow through. Both Nixon and Carter eventually abandoned Cabinet government. By February 1981 Reagan had already deviated from the goal of full Cabinet government, creating an "executive Cabinet," comprising a small number of key Cabinet officers.

Cabinet government looks very strong on paper. The President is free to proceed with the more important problems, while the Cabinet provides the proper advice and information. Cabinet government releases the President to concentrate on more demanding issues and eliminates the need for large White House staffs. Since the Cabinet supplies both advice and implementation, there is little need for a White House policy staff. On the surface, Cabinet government is relatively inexpensive; in reality, it places heavy demands on the President and absorbs heavy amounts of White House resources. As one Ford assistant argued,

> There is a lot of interest in Cabinet government in Washington. My thinking is that it is often a waste of time. . . . If anything, the White House has to spend too much time just monitoring what's going on in the Cabinet. The people who keep agitating for the Cabinet just don't understand what happens to the Cabinet officers. They go over to the departments, and before you know it, they belong to the executive branch. And you know, that's exactly the way it should be. They should represent the views of their departments to the President. You can't expect them not to. What you don't want to do is kiss them goodbye and hope they'll do the job. That just isn't how organizations work. What the White House should do is run the foreign and domestic process and make sure that the departments follow suit.

A Carter Domestic Policy Staff aide offered a similar argument: "Cabinet government has some very good ideas for giving the Cabinet more responsibility. But it is also pretty damn naive as to what actually happens in formulating policy. Policy has to flow down from the President, not from the Cabinet. Those people work for the President, not vice versa."

Presidents certainly need help from the Cabinet. There is a marked shortage of White House information and expertise, which can be supplemented from the departments. Moreover, Presidents must rely on the executive branch for the bulk of domestic ideas and alternatives. Yet, Cabinet government has very high risks and generally low payoffs. Presidents cannot afford to cut the Cabinet free to propose legislation which is eventually accountable to the White House. Nor can Presidents ignore the potential problems of bureaucratic capture. Instead of using the Cabinet as the sole source of policy, the rise of the No Win Presidency encourages tighter reins. With increased competition from Congress, Presidents cannot afford equal competition from the Cabinet. With declining influence and increasing complexity, Presidents must make careful use of their resources. The concern with potential conflict between White House staffs and the Cabinet, between the President's program and the departmental agendas, must take precedence over the potential advantages of Cabinet government. Until competition and complexity decline, Presidents must make the important decisions themselves.

8. Beware the spokes of the wheel. Presidents must also be careful about too much internal delegation. The President's staff is not simply an extension of the Chief Executive. Each member of the White House staff is a potential advocate; each member is likely to have some desire for influence. Whatever their specific goals—whether ambition, loyalty, or good policy—staff members have ample opportunity to influence domestic outcomes. The staff prepares the option papers for the President; the staff decides what constitutes a viable alternative. If the President chooses from options A, B, and C, it is the staff that decides not to present D, E, or F.

The President who enters office with the expectation that the staff can be left alone under delegated authority is making a critical mistake. The President cannot afford to let the staff drift toward internal domination, nor can he gamble that the power vacuum will be filled by qualified assistants. Without firm presidential involvement, the decline in White House resources eventually produces conflict. It is a fact of organizational behavior. The President who adopts a "chairman of the board" approach is destined for a measure of staff infighting. What goes on outside the board room becomes critical to effective policy-making. The President must be prepared to watch the staff—to mediate conflict. Though the staff serves at the President's disposal, the domestic policy process builds remarkable tension and conflict. Thus, it is to the President's advantage to become involved in the day-to-day exchanges between key White House entrepreneurs. There is no question that the internal conflict ultimately affects the President, whether in the discussion of issues and alternatives or in the exit of qualified lieutenants.

Once again, however, Presidents are caught in a no-win situation. Presidents often do not have the resources to engage in careful surveillance of their own staff system. Earlier I argued that Presidents should avoid details. Can I now argue that Presidents should spend time mediating conflict? In several respects, the rise of the No Win Presidency suggests that domination is not necessarily bad, particularly if the President selects and supports the dominant coalition. Presidents, like their staffs, are limited by time and information. Presidents rarely have the resources to engage in the careful movement of the staff chessmen. Can Presidents referee staff conflict while also tackling the myriad problems that surface in the policy process? In a direct contradiction of multiple advocacy, the No Win Presidency encourages an early rise of a dominant internal coalition. Presidents must watch the staff, but how? With or without the President's consent, dominant coalitions emerge. John Ehrlichman's rise to power under Nixon is a prime example. Though domination does not serve the goal of multiple advocacy, it is one tool of resource management. The exit of disenchanted aides is not particularly negative under high resource constraints; it saves both time and energy and reduces public displays of internal conflict. Like Cabinet government, multiple advocacy is strong on paper but very expensive in reality.

Most of the ideas I have just discussed run contrary to notions of strong management and good policy. I have recommended that Presidents move quickly without particular regard for the content of domestic programs; that they avoid innovation and take the first available alternatives in an effort to save time. I have even argued that domination is not all bad. Throughout this discussion, I have assumed that Presidents are only interested in legislative success, reelection, and doable legislation. I will turn to that assumption in a

moment. For now, it is important to recognize that regardless of my recommendations, the No Win Presidency encourages precisely those behaviors
that public observers find most objectionable. We want Presidents who care
about programs, who look beyond reelection and short-term gain, who search
for new ideas and programs, who encourage internal debate. Unfortunately,
the current system does not supply the needed incentives. The long-term
solution to the domestic No Win Presidency must involve an attempt to
change presidential rewards. Instead of penalizing Presidents for learning, we
might encourage them to take their time in building programs; instead of
criticizing Presidents for political naiveté, we might allow a greater period of
on-the-job training.

Converting to a Winnable Presidency

Perhaps the most important lesson of this study is that Presidents
face a new set of domestic problems in the 1980s. Presidents must cope with
fixed limits on internal and external resources as well as on both the timing
and the size of the domestic agenda. Further, there are firm boundaries on the
definition of issues and the search for alternatives, as well as ample competition from Congress. Complexity has increased, while influence has dropped.
Despite all the advice we can muster, Presidents are still mired in a No Win
Presidency. Thus, it becomes even more important to look at what Presidents
can bring into office with them. Since Presidents can have little impact on the
new constraints on domestic policy, the information and expertise they bring
to office become crucial.

In contrast to our earlier assumption about presidential goals, we
now assume that Presidents are interested in more than a simple blend of
success and reelection. Presidents do not enter office to fail, nor do they
deliberately create poor policy. Presidents endeavor to minimize errors and
maximize impact, regardless of whether that helps or hinders reelection.
Presidents want both reelection and good policy, both influence and effectiveness. Much of our advice to Presidents on winning the No Win Presidency still
stands. It is still important to move the agenda early; it is still difficult to
innovate; learning is still an on-the-job dilemma. Yet, Presidents are not
powerless to mitigate the impact of no-win pressures. The greater each President's information and expertise upon entering office, the greater the potential
for converting the No Win Presidency into a winnable Presidency.

My interest is not in the structural reform of the Presidency. Calls
for a six-year term, major reorganization of the executive branch, or multiple
Presidents are interesting topics, but they are of little help to contemporary
Presidents. Nor do the reforms seem likely in the near future. Rather, my aim
is to suggest ways for Presidents to convert a No Win Presidency into a more
manageable, winnable Presidency. In this regard, I will make four simple

recommendations to incoming Presidents: plan ahead, hire expertise, set priorities, and don't be an amateur.

Plan Ahead. Over the past decade, presidential campaigns have become much longer. States struggle over the first caucus dates; candidates gear up for campaigns two years in advance. Many contemporary observers criticize the sheer length of the campaigns, and at least one of the major parties has attempted to shorten the nomination season. Though we might agree that such length has negative consequences for democratic ideals, the campaign offers an important opportunity for advance planning. Presidents can gain a head start on the "move it or lose it" pressure by allocating a portion of their campaign resources for learning. Since Presidents have little time for learning once in office, they are encouraged to use the campaign as a time for preparing the domestic agenda. In the past, however, such advance planning has not been rewarded.

First, there seems to be a stigma attached to policy planning during political campaigns. In 1976 Carter's serious advance-planning effort was often misinterpreted as a sign of overconfidence. According to one Carter aide, "The planning team had to be kept quiet and under wraps. We didn't want the public to get the impression that we thought the election was in the bag. That kind of arrogance could have cost us the election." A second Carter assistant echoed the concern:

> After the convention, we had a twenty-point lead over Ford. Naturally, we started to think about November and the transition. We wanted to start planning for the 1977 agenda. The effort was quashed very quickly. There was a feeling that the planning effort would become too political, that Ford would get wind of just how sure we were and make that an issue. As it was, the planning staff was kept hidden in Atlanta. American voters seem to like underdogs, especially if the favorite is a bully.

That isolation of the Carter policy team limited its impact during the post-election transition. It also engendered considerable staff feuding. Presidents have to handle many problems in the campaign, not the least of which is simply getting elected. Though advance planning is often given a measure of support, the first priority rests on winning the election. Policy planning becomes expendable. Rather than being viewed as a necessary prerequisite, advance planning is viewed with suspicion. We want our candidates to concentrate on the issues, but we don't want them to be too specific.

A second problem for advance planning is the lack of resources. With the advent of the Federal Election Campaign Act in 1971 and limits on both spending and contributions, candidates are forced to weigh the advantages of campaigning against those of planning. It is an easy choice in the current financial framework. One reason why the Carter planning effort fell short of its goal was that the campaign staff felt resources could be better allocated to winning the election. The planning office, under the direction of

Jack Watson, was often criticized from within the Carter campaign for its isolation from the immediate struggle. Campaign aides argued that the policy staff was not contributing enough to the drive for election. Three years after the 1976 campaign, a Carter aide offered the following question: "What good is a planning team if the President isn't elected? We had to put all of our energies into the campaign, not into the transition. Specific planning could wait until we had won. I understand the need for planning, but it is secondary in the campaign. First things first." A Carter planning assistant voiced a rather different opinion:

> The campaign staff had the run of the shop during the last months of the election. They will probably tell you that the election had to come first. Well, they are only half right. Mr. Carter won. After that, what did we have? We were slow in developing specific programs and lost our edge at the start of the term. So what did the campaign staff accomplish? We won the election but weren't prepared to lead.

If Presidents are to prepare for domestic planning during the campaign, they must be given the incentives. Several formal changes might encourage more advance planning. The Federal Election Campaign Act could easily be amended to grant an overage on spending limits specifically for policy planning. The concept of overage is neither new nor novel. Currently, the Federal Election Commission grants overages for presidential fund-raising as well as for the cost of complying with spending disclosure. It is a small step to recommend an exemption on spending limits for money earmarked for a policy planning staff. Though the Federal Election Commission would have to restrict the definition of a policy staff, such an overage is not unworkable. A second, more attractive option is to grant public financing directly for planning. This would not be a simple overage, but a separate financing effort. Candidates would not have to choose between campaigning and planning. Granting of such special funds would help remove the stigma of advance planning, while encouraging all candidates to allocate funds for policy analysis. Since the federal government currently provides the President-elect with transition funding, it is but a small jump to similar funding during the campaign.

The final pressure for advance planning must, however, come from the candidates themselves. Candidates need to recognize just how limited the President's resources are. The campaign offers a rare opportunity to develop ideas and increase information. By allocating campaign resources to the planning effort, candidates would gain a head start on the cross-pressures of office. A formal planning effort in each campaign would provide strong incentives for converting the No Win Presidency into a more winnable Presidency. Candidates should be encouraged to look beyond their short-term political needs to decide how they will cope with the first days of office. Until candidates realize the limits of the three-month transition, advance planning will not gain in value and importance.

Hire Expertise. One of the most interesting findings of this study has been the importance of staff, particularly that relatively small group of aides who work within the White House office. Though the average staff numbers between five hundred and one thousand, the "inner circle" of aides who interact with the President is much smaller. Proximity to the President is the key to both internal influence and effectiveness. The inner circle acts as a powerful screen for ideas and is primarily responsible for shaping the domestic agenda.

Despite the importance of the White House staff, Presidents spend remarkably little time in the appointment process. In the past, Presidents have stressed rather limited criteria in selecting the top hundred-odd White House aides. First, Presidents have usually gauged loyalty; in fact, loyalty often is more important than ability. Loyalty is certainly a key factor in the relative influence of top aides. Haldeman, Cheney, Powell, Jordan, and Meese all had long been associates of their respective Presidents. It was no surprise that each gained a measure of influence within the White House. Second, Presidents have often attempted to reward service. Much of the Carter upper echelon had served the President in some respect in Georgia or in the campaign. Their positions in earlier battles assured them of spots in the President's inner circle. For staffs of candidates with limited federal service, the campaign becomes the primary proving ground. Both Nixon and Carter relied heavily on their campaign organization to provide key advisors. According to one of the more experienced Nixon aides, "Many of the Nixon appointees were little more than advertising men in the 1968 campaign. Half of the staff had received their first contact with national issues as advance men . . . in backwater towns and cities." These two criteria—loyalty and service—all too frequently overshadow a third potential screen: expertise. Though Presidents always want experienced aides, if the expertise does not arrive cloaked in loyalty or service, it is often overlooked. Expertise is of secondary concern in the White House talent search. Thus, an initial recommendation on staffing is that Presidents actively search for expertise. It is a scarce resource which can be dramatically increased by the simple selection of qualified aides. A second recommendation deals with lower-level staffs.

In selecting staff, Presidents generally concentrate on the top of the organizational chart. The President's chief of staff, press secretary, personal counsel, budget director, National Security Council, and domestic policy advisor all receive more attention than the lower-level staff. However, one lesson of the No Win Presidency rests on the potential influence of the lower-level staff. The deputy assistant for energy policy on the Domestic Policy Staff often has considerable impact on final outcomes. Though Presidents do not consciously neglect the search for qualified lower-level aides, the pressures of the first days often require that these appointments be left to others. Thus, the domestic policy advisor selects his own assistants, who in turn select their assistants, who in turn select their deputies. This delegated appointment process serves to further the development of potential internal coalitions and to minimize the search for expertise. This is a critical mistake in at least two specific White House offices: the Congressional Liaison Office and the Office of Management and Budget. Not only should Presidents become more involved in the appointment process for these two staffs but they should lessen the importance of loyalty and service among selection criteria. These positions are not "plums" to be given out for long-term friendship; they are positions with considerable impact on the domestic agenda.

Why are the Congressional Liaison Office and OMB so important in the policy process? Because these two offices face *outward* from the Presidency. Liaison and OMB are the key buffers between the White House, Congress, and the executive branch. By recruiting expertise into these two offices, Presidents can reduce the impact of the No Win Presidency. By appointing a strong staff to legislative liaison, the President can reduce the impact of congressional complexity and increase his own ability to compete for scarce agenda space. By appointing an equally strong staff to OMB, the President can increase the opportunities for new ideas, coordination, and information. By making appointments on the basis of expertise, the President eventually can link up with greater sources of information and expertise. In short, expertise produces expertise. Despite their relative importance, both offices are often neglected in the appointment process. And of the two, liaison is most often ignored in the presidential talent process. While Presidents recognize the value of liaison, they tend to underestimate the impact of their liaison appointments. Liaison is too often considered to be the home for the political hacks, when in fact it is a critical window to the Capitol.

Legislative liaison provides one of the more perplexing problems in the No Win Presidency. Liaison is the main lobbying arm of the White House, but it has a tarnished reputation among the inner circle. Both Nixon and Carter needlessly undercut liaison through lack of support. Yet, even had these two Presidents actively encouraged liaison, the lessons of the 1960s no longer apply to Congress and lobbying. Given the limited number of staff in legislative liaison, it is increasingly difficult to mount a successful lobbying campaign. With increased competition in Congress, liaison needs two basic resources for influence: (1) a staff who understands the recent changes of in Congress. and (2) an increase in the number of aides who make up that staff. Whatever other problems Carter's 1977 liaison team had, it lacked a basic knowledge about the legislative process itself. Aides did not understand changing congressional needs, nor did they fully perceive the impact of recent reforms. By the end of 1977 the liaison office had abandoned its issue-oriented lobbying strategy in favor of an individual-member approach: instead of concentrating on key actors on energy policy, for instance, the Carter staff switched to the assignment of specific senators and representatives to each liaison official. Whether such an approach offers much hope for any administration is not clear. As it is currently constituted, White House legislative liaison is not equipped to compete within Congress. Regardless of strategy, future liaison staffs many find themselves overwhelmed by congressional activism. During the 1970s, congressional complexity increased rapidly, with vast expansions of staff and information. During the same period, the size of the legislative liaison staff has remained static. With a White House liaison staff of only a dozen assistants, the President cannot expect to cope given the dispersion of power in Congress. Even with help from the various departmental liaison offices, the White House staff is outgunned on Capitol Hill.

The Office of Management and Budget also is a focus for presidential concern. At the start of the first term, OMB stands as the single most important source of information within the Executive Office of the President. It is the clearing house of executive-branch requests, budget analysis, and program planning. Of all the President's resources, OMB has the longest memory for domestic policy. If any organization can provide scarce information in the early days of an administration, OMB can. Yet, is is precisely at the start of the term that the White House is most suspicious of OMB. As one Carter aide remarked, "OMB is a very conservative institution. The staff is tight-fisted, penny-pinching, and widely viewed as a bunch of nay-sayers. That is exactly the opposite of what the President needs at the start of the term." As the administration ages, the President becomes more friendly toward OMB. As resources drop, OMB nay-saying becomes essential. OMB becomes a prized buffer between the President and the executive branch. Unfortunately, too often OMB is ignored until the resources drop. Though OMB has a store of both information and expertise, Presidents have tended to discount the agency until later in the term. By appointing qualified aides to OMB, particularly deep within the structure, the President can establish a linkage to the OMB memory.

Set Priorities. Scarcely three weeks after Carter's surprising defeat by Ronald Reagan, Hamilton Jordan was asked what he might do differently if he could go back in time. His answer was simple:

> If I look back at one thing, I would say that we made a mistake in the first two or three years—the first two years of the administration by not establishing public priorities for three or four major issues. Instead we came to Washington and we jumped on all of the issues that were, were and are, important to our people. And out of that, I think, oftentimes came a sense that there was not a clear understanding of what the administration was all about ("Meet the Press," transcript, 23 November 1980, p. 3).

The lack of explicit priorities in the Carter administration had at least three major effects. First, as Jordan admitted, there was little clarity in the communication of priorities to the American public. Instead of galvanizing support on two or three major national needs, the Carter administration proceeded on a number of fronts. There was a crisis in health care costs, a crisis in energy, a crisis in government ethics and reorganization, a crisis in welfare. As one Carter aide remarked, "I don't doubt the public was a little confused. So were many of us on the inside. We just tried too much." Second, and perhaps more important, the lack of priorities meant unnecessary waste of the President's own time and energy. That was in part Carter's own problem—he wanted to be in on the details of the major decision. Unfortunately, without firm direction from the Oval Office, the White House staff moved on a wide range of fronts. Resources were spread too thinly for effective choice. Third, the lack of priorities needlessly compounded Carter's congressional problems. Facing a backlog of unfinished legislation from the Nixon and Ford years, Congress demanded some indication of the President's priorities. When that guidance was not forthcoming, Congress had to piece together a domestic agenda with minimal White House impact. Carter's limited political capital was squandered on a variety of agenda requests when it might have been concentrated on the top of the list.

The lesson from the Carter administration is simple: rather than take a shotgun approach during the transition and the first months, Presidents ought to target their scarce resources on a limited number of critical topics. This would allow them to meet the "move it or lose it" strategy while producing reasonably careful choices. Moreover, given increased congressional competition, priority-setting would offer a clear signal to Congress on the President's agenda. While Congress digests and attacks these few top priorities, the President can move forward with a second wave of agenda requests. The staff would have time to become acclimated to their new positions and would be encouraged to learn. At the same time, the President could work to generate public support on a set of programs that could stand as the foundation for future elections. At the very least, priority-setting offers the potential for balancing the goals of good policy against the demands of the political environment. Nor is priority-setting a particularly difficult chore. What it demands is firm guidance from the President and clear signals to the Congress and public.

No Amateurs. In both 1976 and 1980, political scientists witnessed a change in the recruitment patterns for Presidents. Prior to 1976 there was a stable link between service in the Senate and movement to the White House. The bulk of Presidents and candidates came from national political institutions. In 1976 Jimmy Carter entered office after a single term as governor of Georgia. In 1980 Ronald Reagan was elected President after two terms as governor of California. Nineteen eighty offered the first contest of governors in fifty years.

Throughout this study I have emphasized the impact of expertise. In addition to affecting the timing of the domestic agenda, expertise influences the selection of issues and alternatives and the evolution of the decision-making structure. Expertise is the most important resource that varies directly with the individual President. It is far more than a simple summary of past occupations: it is the sum total of the President's learning prior to election. Richard Nixon, for instance, had considerable federal experience before his victory in 1968. He had been a member of Congress, a senator, a Vice-President, even a federal bureaucrat. However, Nixon's primary interest was in foreign affairs. When he turned to domestic issues in 1969, he was unwilling to assume command of the policy process. Despite his extensive experience, he had limited expertise in domestic affairs.

Our concern with amateurs flows from the recent change in recruitment patterns. In theory, senators, House members, and Vice Presidents should have a greater understanding of the national policy process than governors or other state officials. Though expertise involves more than office-holding, we would expect national political figures to have greater exposure to the legislative process than state or local officials. Because of the nature of governmental service, however, such comparisons are fraught with bias. Regardless of prior position, our concern is with the nature of each individual's learning. A governor of Georgia cannot gain vast exposure to national policy whatever the day-to-day problems. Though Carter learned about management styles and staff coordination, he could not learn much about the federal system. Georgia is a far distance from Washington.

The same problem applies to Ronald Reagan, though to a lesser degree. Despite campaign advertisements to the contrary, California is not a microcosm of the United States. What worked in California does not necessarily work in Washington. Reagan's experience was more relevant to national politics than Carter's, but even in California the governor's office is remarkably different from the Presidency. Reagan's experience in California did not prepare him to assume control of the executive machinery, nor did it expose him to the congressional policy process. Reagan's experience as governor does have advantages—few senators have the management training to control the executive office. In recruiting our Presidents, however, we are faced with a difficult choice: do we want Presidents who know how to run an executive office or Presidents who know how the federal system works? The post-Watergate distrust has led to a preference for "outsiders" as President. The success of both the Carter and Reagan campaigns reflects an effort to capture these elements of public unhappiness. Yet, the selection of governors as potential Presidents creates a circularity in the public distrust-recruitment linkage. Public support for outsiders may eventually create even greater demands for outsiders. Since Carter's limited experience in Georgia eventually undermined his performance as President, the selection of another outsider to fill his spot indicates a circular system. Reagan's 1980 campaign appealed to public dissatisfaction with insiders, thereby creating increased pressure on Reagan to produce quick results. If Reagan does not succeed, we can expect even greater pressure for an outsider in 1984.

Conclusion

Throughout this book, I have emphasized the importance of the President's agenda. It determines the distribution of political benefits; it is a signal to the Congress and the public of national needs; it carries the President's vision of the past and the future.

Unfortunately, agenda-setting is often haphazard. Under intense pressure to send the agenda quickly, Presidents frequently neglect comparisons of competing programs. The agenda is often more a product of sleepless nights or accidents than one of systematic evaluation. Moreover, in the current political environment, Presidents are encouraged to adopt the "move it or lose it" approach. Domestic agenda-setting has become a vicious circle: each failure breeds greater pressure for action, which in turn leads to more failure. At some point the circle must be broken—whether through advance planning, greater expertise, or systematic priority-setting.

Ultimately, the structure of incentives must be changed. Presidents must be rewarded for patience, not haste; for planning, not short-term success. What is needed is a fundamental change in how we view the policy process. Unless the Congress, the public, the media, even political scientists are willing to wait for careful policy, the President must respond to our impatience.

10 the Reagan experience

I'm just not going to spend a lot of political capital solving some other guy's problem in 2010.

David Stockman

Presidents have always been torn between their place in history and public approval, between legacies and landslides. Forced to balance short-term political rewards against long-term policy achievement, they are pols and prophets at the same time.

Few understood this fragile balance better than David Stockman, Reagan's Budget Director from 1981 to 1985. From the very beginning of the term, Stockman saw the potential for lasting change, provided that the President acted quickly to avoid a GOP economic Dunkirk. Recall his transition warning: "If bold policies are not swiftly, deftly, and courageously implemented in the first six months, Washington will quickly become engulfed in political disorder commensurate with the surrounding economic disarray. A golden opportunity for permanent conservative policy revision and political realignment could be thoroughly dissipated before the Reagan administration is even up to speed."

Alas, much as Stockman talked as a prophet of long-term change, he was very much a short-term pol, resorting as he later admitted to "accounting gimmicks, evasions, half-truths and downright dishonesty" to propel budget and tax cuts through a reluctant Congress (quoted in Ullman 1986, p. 322). Driven by his nightmares of political catastrophe, Stockman moved at near light speed to package a new budget before Washington (and Reagan's own Cabinet secretaries) could organize against him, changing the underlying economic assumptions one moment, reprogramming the OMB computers the next, calculating a new bottom line the next. As he later admitted, "We were doing the whole budget-cutting exercise so frenetically. In other words, you were juggling details, pushing people, and going from one session to another, trying to cut housing programs here and rural electric there, and we were doing it so fast, we didn't know where we were ending up for sure" (quoted in the *Atlantic*, December 1981).

Thus did the agenda-setting process shape the final proposals themselves. Frantic decisions by a frenzied budget director produced frenetic proposals: revisions of Carter's budget by early March, a foredoomed Social Security cut by April, and deep budget and tax cuts by summer. More important for understanding the Reagan domestic agenda, almost all of Stockman's policy ideas were designed for instant impact even if that meant long-term disaster. Budget savings would take effect immediately; programs would be changed overnight; taxes would be cut in one fell swoop. No one stopped to ask whether these measures would work.

Nevertheless, the Reagan agenda achieved instant impact, driving Democratic alternatives off the legislative calendar in its advance. Despite the Senate's unanimous rejection of Stockman's Social Security package (see Light 1985), Reagan's budget and tax cuts emerged virtually intact after a long summer of bargaining and close votes.

The only problem was that the budget and tax cuts failed to reduce the deficit. Instead of a promised balanced budget by 1984, the federal government continued to pile one huge deficit upon another. As Stockman later admitted, "The reason we did it wrong—not wrong, but less than the optimum—was that we said, Hey we have to get a budget out fast. And when you decide to put a program of this breadth and depth out fast, you can only do so much. We were working on a twenty or twenty-five day time frame, and we didn't think it all the way through. We didn't add up all the numbers" (quoted in the *Atlantic*, December 1981).

Ten years later, Bush's Budget Director, Richard Darman, would blame the continuing deficit crisis on Stockman's "now-now-ism," perhaps forgetting that he had been Reagan's Deputy Chief of Staff at the time. "It may be apt to view all this metaphorically as a set of children's games: the budget as Cookie Monster; its future threatened by hidden PACMEN; its path a journey through Wonderland," Stockman's friend and former colleague wrote in his first Budget Director's message. "But at some point, it is appropriate to put games aside—*at least for a while*. At some point, there is an obligation to be serious. At some point, partisan posturing must yield to the responsibility to govern."

To be fair, however, Stockman was neither the first Budget Director to go short-term, nor would he be the last. In fact, even as Darman chastised the Reagan administration and Congress for its "short-term-itis," Bush was under fire for what one columnist called "bow-wow-ism," that is, for chasing after each new public complaint—drugs, flag burning, the savings and loan crisis— without any sense of direction. Much as Stockman brought a new sophistication to agenda-setting, using every trick in the book plus some, he hardly deserves all the blame implied in Darman's sardonic message. One could easily argue, for example, that the contest between prophecy and politics was much more intense prior to the Twenty-second Amendment, before Presidents were limited to two terms in office.

More to the point of this chapter, Stockman was merely playing his part in what has been a thirty-year erosion of long-term thinking in the Presidency. Simply put, the incentives and constraints that Presidents now face are overwhelmingly directed to short-term goals. They are increasingly pols, and pols only. Indeed, my data suggest that Reagan's year of greatest legislative achievement, 1981, was built almost entirely on short-term policy proposals designed to pay out quickly, whether politically or economically. The No Win Presidency described in chapter 9 has fallen way to the Short-Term Presidency.

Agenda-Setting in the Reagan White House

The place to start describing the Short-Term Presidency is with Reagan's agenda-setting process. Much as his eight years were billed as the "Reagan Revolution," Reagan's agenda actually fit rather well with the patterns established by his five predecessors.

In fact, in his zeal to hit the ground running in 1981, Reagan followed at least seven of the eight new rules listed in chapter 9 (pages 217–25).

- As noted above, by drafting his budget revisions and tax proposals as quickly as possible, Reagan accepted the need to "move it or lose it."

- By making these key budget and tax decisions long before his Cabinet secretaries had been appointed and confirmed, Reagan acknowledged that learning must wait.

- By embracing Stockman's unique vision of what those proposals should look like, a vision kept in his back pocket, Reagan took the first alternative, whether right or wrong.

- By leaving the finer points to the midnight machinations of his harried Budget Director, Reagan avoided details, a pattern he followed throughout his term.

- By appointing a troika of aides—Edwin Meese, James Baker, and Michael Deaver—to run the White House, Reagan avoided the spokes of the wheel.

- By establishing Cabinet councils organized around distinct policy areas—economics, national security, domestic policy—Reagan avoided at least some of the perils of traditional Cabinet government.

• By establishing a public affairs operation unparalleled in White House history, there can be little question that reelection came first in the Reagan White House.

Although Reagan was the first President to master the rules of the No Win Presidency, he did violate at least one of the rules—no innovations (see page 220). With deficits still mounting a decade later, Reagan's decision to adopt an untested innovation called "supply side" economics ranks as his single greatest policy mistake.

The Focusing Skill. Not only did Reagan follow the unconventional rules of the No Win Presidency, he adopted at least three of the four strategies listed in chapter 9 for converting the No Win Presidency into a more effective enterprise (pages 225–32).

• By launching a carefully coordinated transition operation in the summer of 1980, Reagan clearly opted to plan ahead. With his most trusted confidant, Meese, in charge, the effort paid off in Reagan's 1981 legislative success. (As noted below, despite his intense transition planning, he was later in making his first appointments than Carter, Nixon, or Kennedy.)

• By hiring a seasoned team of White House aides, most significantly James Baker and his deputy Richard Darman, and an equally talented team of legislative lobbyists, Reagan established the value of hiring expertise. Whether he was willing to listen to that expertise, particularly in the internal struggles with the far less seasoned Meese, is again open to question. At least in the beginning, however, expertise appeared to win out.

• By concentrating on a handful of legislative initiatives, dropping failures like the 1981 Social Security package as quickly as possible, Reagan sanctioned the need to set priorities. His tax and budget cuts were *the* only item of business in 1981, focusing congressional attention to an extent not known since Lyndon Johnson's drive for the Great Society in 1965.

As ex-governor of California, Reagan shared many of Carter's problems as an ex-governor of Georgia. Yet, what set Reagan apart from Carter was his willingness to set priorities. By focusing attention on two priorities his first year, Reagan drew an immediate contrast with Carter, who spent his first year chasing after almost two dozen.

Indeed, Reagan offers proof positive that legislative success often turns on the ability to focus congressional attention on specific proposals. It is not enough merely to present a list of pet projects to Congress and wait. Presidents must make some effort to tell Congress where they want to spend their capital.

In turn, Congress pays at least some attention to what Presidents say and how they say it. If a President launches a major legislative initiative, but never talks about it, Congress will get the message. If, however, a President launches a bill, say an omnibus budget measure, and talks of nothing else, Congress will also take note. All things being equal, Congress will move on the bill the President cares about, particularly if the President has a reasonable number of votes in Congress and public support back home in the districts.

Obviously, lobbying skill is no substitute for hard capital—that is, seats in Congress and popularity back in the home districts. As George Edwards has demonstrated in an exhaustive analysis, "Legislative skills are not at the core of presidential leadership of Congress. . . . Their utility is at the margins, in exploiting rather than creating opportunities for change" (Edwards 1989, p. 185). Lyndon Johnson said as much when he observed, "You can tell a man to go to hell, but you can't make him go," a phrase that seemed to be "particularly apt," he wrote in his memoirs, "when I found myself in a struggle with the House or Senate. I would start to speak out . . . and remember that no matter how many times I told the Congress to do something, I could never force it to act" (Johnson 1971, p. 461).

However, without some effort to focus its attention, Congress will drift aimlessly from one presidential proposal to the next with no way to determine what proposals come first, setting the legislative agenda on the basis of anything but the President's wishes. As such, the President's ability to focus attention may be an important *intervening* skill, increasing the value of the initial political capital. Just as a new car buyer can get a better deal by jawboning, arm-twisting, and knowing the facts, so, too, can a President get a better deal by focusing congressional attention. No matter what the President's starting resources, the focusing skill can help the President make the most of the opportunities. It may be a skill that operates at the margins, as Edwards rightly notes, but the margins are where many of the President's priorities are won—from Johnson's War on Poverty to Carter's War on Energy.

Consider the 1981 budget and tax fights as an example. Reagan used at least four tactics to make sure Congress knew exactly what he wanted.

Communication. With four major addresses on the budget and tax cuts during June, July, and August, Reagan plied his skill at personal and political communication. Indeed, his July 27 message on the tax cut may have been the single most effective televised speech in history. Although the White House orchestrated much of the public response, Congress could hardly ignore the flood of phone calls and telegrams from their constituents. On the day after the message, the congressional switchboard handled 33,000 calls, double the normal load. "I have never seen anything like this in my life, to be perfectly truthful. What is the authority for this? Does this mean that any time the president of the United States is interested in a piece of legislation, he merely sends it over? You do not have any regard for the process, for open hearings, discussion as to who it affects, or what it does to the economy," said the Speaker of the House after losing the first key vote in June. "Do we have the right to legislate?"

Personal Amenities. Washington was and still is a very social city, a fact well appreciated by Reagan and his social staff. Tickets to State dinners, seats in the President's box at the Kennedy Center for the Performing Arts, invitations to the executive compound at Camp David, and special access to the White House rarely change votes in Congress, but they most certainly can make it easier to vote with the President on close issues. As former Vice-President Hubert Humphrey once argued, "You've got to know what makes 'em tick, you've got to know their wives, you've got to know their families, you've got to know their backgrounds. You know, I used to say Johnson was a personal FBI. The son of a gun was incredible, but so was Kennedy, and so in a sense was Ford."

Vote-Trading. Far more important than seats at the Kennedy Center are pet projects back home. Reagan exchanged sugar price supports for budget cuts in June, peanut price supports for tax cuts in July. One member of Congress traded his vote on the tax cut to win a White House promise not to close a military base in his district plus a $37-million grant to help clean up the accident at the Three Mile Island nuclear power plant. Members from natural gas states won presidential promises for a veto on any windfall profits tax on gas companies. As David McCurdy, one of the Democrats who traded his vote, explained at the time: "It's accessibility. . . . You like to know you have access and I feel I have more so now. The president said he would remember I have three military bases in my district. I just want to know that if we come to a crunch over that, they're going to remember me."

Arm-Twisting. When all else failed—public persuasion, perks, and vote-trading—Reagan was always willing to twist an arm. Unlike Lyndon Johnson, who was the great intimidator, Reagan preferred to leave the twisting to his lieutenants. In one application, prominent conservative campaign funders were asked to apply pressure to their fundees. In another, key corporate leaders from back home were asked to call upon their representatives to demand the right vote. Ultimately, arm-twisting helps to explain why only three Republicans voted against the President during the key budget and tax votes in June, July, and August.

Much as these tools of focusing helped Reagan set the legislative agenda that first year, they pale in comparison to the simple fact that he had enough Republicans and conservative Democrats to forge a working majority in the House. That, plus his enormous personal popularity, meant Reagan's focusing skills could be put to good use (see Light 1989 for a more detailed description of the focusing skill and its role in presidential influence).

The Reagan Agenda

The question, then, is where Reagan spent his capital. As noted earlier, he was not remarkably different from his immediate predecessors in trying to fit his political resources to a legislative agenda. Even as he stretched his capital through effective focusing, Reagan had limited purchasing power in Congress. In spite of his majority in the Senate, House Democrats held a 242–189 edge in 1980, 268–167 in 1983, 253–182 in 1985, and 260–175 in 1987. Only Ford worked with fewer fellow partisans.

This is not to argue that Reagan was merely a repeat of Nixon or Ford. At least for the first Congress in 1981–82, he had enough capital to purchase more than his two Republican predecessors, Nixon and Ford. As a result, Reagan was able to concentrate on legislation, not administration, as his policy vehicle. Indeed, throughout his eight years in office, Reagan issued the smallest number of executive orders, 381, among the six Presidents, averaging just 48 per year. In contrast, Carter issued an average of 79 per year, Kennedy 70, Johnson 64, Nixon 63, and Ford 61.

Nor is this to argue that Reagan ignored the President's vast administrative options—appointments, executive orders, informal reorganizations, etc. He was extremely effective in using his appointment powers to shape the courts and control the executive agencies, and, although he issued fewer total executive orders than his peers, those he did issue were remarkably powerful. His executive orders establishing a cradle-to-grave review of regulations, for example, constituted the most determined attempt in recent history to control the federal bureaucracy. Rather, he was able to use the legislative channel more aggressively than either Nixon or Ford, largely because he had sympathetic partisans in the Senate and House to work with.

Yet, even with a working majority in the House, Reagan had less capital than his three Democratic predecessors, Kennedy, Johnson, and Carter, all of whom worked with much larger accounts on Capitol Hill. It is not surprising, therefore, that Reagan exercised his veto power so often, particularly after losing 26 House Republican seats and his working majority in the 1982 mid-term elections. All totaled, Reagan exercised 78 vetoes, or 10 per year, roughly the same number as Kennedy, Johnson, and Carter *combined*. Only Ford had a higher average per year, 33, largely because he had no working capital in Congress at all.

The notion that political capital shapes the President's policy pro-

Table 20. Reagan Requests for Legislation, 1981–89

Term	Year	Total Requests	Repeats*
Reagan I	1981	8	0
	1982	7	1
	1983	11	3
	1984	4	5
Reagan II	1985	0	7
	1986	0	5
	1987	0	5
	1988	0	4

Source: State of the Union and Inaugural messages coupled with Congressional Quarterly Almanac for each year.
*Repeats from previous State of the Union addresses.

posals is confirmed in table 20, which summarizes the overall Reagan agenda (see table 2, page 42, for the Kennedy-Carter data).

As table 20 suggests, Reagan trails his Democratic predecessors in total proposals per year. No matter his focusing skill, Senate Republican majority, personal popularity, or considerable social grace, Reagan could only do so much, particularly working within the bounds of the No Win Presidency.

Before turning to the table in detail, however, it is important to note that the Reagan data do not come from the same source as the Kennedy-Carter data. Much as I hoped to duplicate the coding process I used in 1980 to identify the Kennedy-Carter proposals, the raw materials were no longer available. Recall that the Kennedy-Carter list is drawn from all legislation (1) cleared "i/a," or "in accord" with the President's program, by the Office of Management and Budget and (2) mentioned in the President's State of the Union message.

Unfortunately, access to the needed OMB records was an innocent victim of the 1981 Reagan assassination attempt. Along with heightened security around the White House and Old Executive Office Building, the Secret Service also decided to close the new Executive Office Building and its small public library to the public. More to the point, even those who gained entry to the library could no longer find the clearance records. If the records and the tracking system that produced them still exist, they will not be open to curious researchers until the Reagan presidential library opens sometime later in this decade.

Thus, in adding the Reagan agenda to this book, I had to rebuild the clearance records by hand, using an entirely different set of materials, guessing somewhat at the President's agenda priorities. Using the university library as my source, I defined the Reagan agenda to include any legislation that was (1) mentioned in either the Inaugural address or subsequent State of the Union messages and (2) later formally introduced as a legislative initiative recorded by Congressional Quarterly's yearly Almanac.

As a result, there are limits to comparisons between the five Presidents and Reagan. First, I may have underestimated the size of the Reagan agenda by counting proposals only after they were introduced. Because Stockman's Social Security plan was never formally introduced, for example, it does not show up as a proposal.

Second, I may have underestimated size again by counting proposals only after they were assembled in legislative packages. Reagan's 1981 budget package was outlined as seven broad goals in his Inaugural address and was eventually presented to Congress as a single omnibus proposal. Therefore, it only shows up as seven proposals in my count of the 1981 agenda when, in reality, it contained hundreds of specific ideas. This is less of a problem than it might seem at first blush, for the OMB clearance records have been equally broad in recording initiatives like civil rights, aid to education, welfare reform, revenue sharing, and the various forms of deregulation as single initiatives in their respective administrations, too.

Third, by relying on *Congressional Quarterly,* I put great faith in its staff to have included every Reagan proposal somewhere in the *Almanac.* Given the 40,000 bills, public and private, introduced in the House and Senate from 1981 to 1988, surely *Congressional Quarterly* must have missed a few. Again, the problem is a potential undercount in the Reagan agenda. Again, however, this is less of a problem than it may seem. Some of the 40,000 are duplicates; others involve concerns of private citizens; and still others are joint resolutions of one kind or another. The President's proposals are the least likely to be missed among all the bills *Congressional Quarterly* covered.

The potential undercount notwithstanding, the Reagan data appear solid, if not perfectly comparable to that for Kennedy-Carter. Readers are wise, however, to reread my original caution on page 10. These new data should be viewed more as illustrations of a theory than as absolute proof of specific conclusions, too.

Caveat noted, table 20 offers some interesting insights on the timing and content of the Reagan agenda.

First, Reagan's agenda is the *smallest* in recent experience, averaging four proposals per year over the eight-year term. Reagan's agenda looks even smaller considering the fact that seven of his eight first-year proposals appeared in the same omnibus budget resolution. Looking only at the first term, Reagan averages seven proposals per year, still slightly below both Nixon and Ford.

Despite this surprisingly low number of proposals, it would be a mistake to characterize Reagan's agenda as anything but activist. The fact that he had so few proposals is a logical consequence of his decision to set careful priorities. Whereas Carter's twenty-one separate proposals were often ignored, Reagan's two omnibus proposals dominated the legislative calendar. In addition, Reagan's omnibus budget and tax bills contained a wide range of separate initiatives—the budget package included cuts in virtually every program account, while the tax bill reduced corporate and individual rates, changed the rules for depreciation of capital investments (accelerated tax depreciation), and indexed the tax code to eliminate so-called bracket creep.

Thus, even though Reagan was the most conservative President in a half century, he clearly understood that he could not achieve his policy aims by merely maintaining the status quo, for, by 1981 that status quo was a Democratic creation. He had to adopt a legislative agenda that paralleled the activism of his Democratic predecessors.

Second, Reagan's agenda is the *latest*, peaking in the third, not first, year of the term. Reagan's third-year surge is not led by the social agenda, however, but by a mix of the old and new, large and small: a Social Security rescue plan alongside the first call for tax simplification, reauthorization of the Civil Rights Commission side-by-side with tuition tax credits and child support enforcement. In many ways, Reagan's third year is fairly similar to most other President's first years.

Again, one reason is the emphasis on the budget and tax cuts as Reagan's sole priorities in the first year. There is no question that Reagan always wanted a school prayer amendment, a line item veto, a balanced budget amendment, tuition tax credits for private schools, and an anti-abortion amendment. That he waited to ask Congress to move on his social agenda until the third and fourth years is a testament to his political patience. Had he offered those five items the first year, when all on the conservative right-wing wanted them most, Reagan's timing would look much more normal, shifting as follows: first year, 13; second, 7; third, 7; fourth, 3. In this case, moving the social agenda early would have meant losing the budget and tax cuts, perhaps demonstrating that setting priorities may be the more important prescription for presidential success in the No Win Presidency.

Third, Reagan's agenda is the most *repetitive* of the six, with the second term consisting entirely of repeats from his first four years, including tax reform (first offered in 1983), urban enterprise zones (1982), the line item veto (1984), prayer in school (1984), and the continuing efforts to cut the federal budget using many of the tried but unpassed proposals from 1981.

With the 1988 presidential campaign underway almost immediately after his second inaugural, his White House in almost constant turmoil, his executive appointees establishing new turnover records, and the Senate lost to the Democrats in 1986, Reagan had precious little to propose and almost no chance of legislative success. In fact, according to table 20, Reagan had no new ideas after 1984. Instead of the outpouring of innovation Neustadt predicts in a President's fifth and sixth years in office (see page 40), Reagan's entire second term consisted of proposals from his first, in large measure because of the failure of the budget and tax cuts. Although he played a significant role in the tax reform that passed Congress in 1986, Reagan was nongermane, so to speak, his final two years. Preoccupied with $200 billion deficits each year, neither Congress nor the President had much freedom to add new issues to the agenda.

More significantly, by the start of his second term Reagan had lost much of the political capital that had once fueled his legislative agenda. Despite an overwhelming victory over former Vice-President Walter Mondale in the

244 / the president's agenda

Table 21. Presidential Requests for Legislation: New Programs versus Old Programs, Kennedy to Reagan*

President	New Programs		Old Programs		Percent New Programs
	Total	Average per Year	Total	Average per Year	
Kennedy/Johnson	33	8	20	5	62%
Johnson	55	14	36	9	60
Nixon	46	12	19	5	71
Ford	6	3	10	5	44
Carter	25	6	16	4	61
Reagan	18	2	12	2	60

*Does not include repeats.

Table 22. Presidential Requests for Legislation: Large Programs versus Small Programs, Kennedy to Reagan

President	Large Programs		Small Programs		Percent Large Programs
	Total	Average per Year	Total	Average per Year	
Kennedy/Johnson	28	7	25	6	53%
Johnson	50	12	41	10	55
Nixon	23	4	42	7	35
Ford	8	4	8	4	50
Carter	22	6	19	5	54
Reagan	13	2	17	2	43

1984 campaign, and continued personal popularity, the public was increasingly critical of the Reagan policy agenda. Carrying a growing list of scandals, including the Iran-Contra arms-for-hostages deal, Reagan lost his Republican Senate majority in 1986. And, with Democrats lining up in droves for the 1988 campaign, Reagan was, for all intents and purposes, a lame duck by his seventh year in office. In retrospect, Reagan's dual decision to move quickly and set priorities proved the wise path.

Size and Scope. Reagan's broad strategy becomes much clearer in tables 21 and 22, which compare the number of new/old and large/small proposals on the Reagan agenda (see tables 11 and 12, pages 120 and 123 for the Kennedy-Carter comparisons). Recall that all policy proposals are not created equal. As Mark Peterson suggests in his recent study of Congress and the Presidency, "If we are to understand fully the processes by which the President and Congress make legislative choices, and if we are to evaluate the policy-making capacity of both institutions, including giving meaning to the notion of presidential 'success,' then it is essential that careful efforts be made to distinguish among various kinds of policy initiatives" (Peterson 1990, pp. 237–38).

Here, I assume that Congress can tell the difference between a small request and a large one—that is, between highway beautification (small) and civil rights (large) under Johnson, daylight savings time (small) and a national minimum income (large) under Nixon, a White House Office of Consumer Affairs (small) and a Department of Energy (large) under Carter, and urban enterprise zones (small) and tax reform (large) under Reagan. Just as it costs more to get a President's bill through Congress than to veto one, so, too, does it cost more to get a large or new proposal through than a small or old one. Thinking big costs more.

Also recall that new proposals involve departures from the status quo to either expand or reduce the government's role in society. Finally, note that the general coding rule on new proposals is *not* to give the President the benefit of the doubt. Even if a proposal contains an especially novel idea, it must be classified as an old initiative if the overall weight of the initiative falls within the boundary of existing ideas. Thus, the following tables may generally understate the number of new ideas on the Reagan agenda, just as they may understate the number of new ideas on the Kennedy-Carter agendas.

The tables suggest the challenges in studying the Reagan domestic agenda. Looking at the percentage of his agenda devoted to large and new proposals, he looks more like a Democrat than a Nixon or Ford, but looking at the raw numbers, he looks passive by comparison.

Legislative packaging may explain the difference. Reagan's budget package, for example, touched virtually every entitlement program on the books, established new user fees for dozens of government services, reduced federal contributions to a host of spending programs (school lunches, student aid, and housing finance), and proposed the consolidation of 77 categorical programs in social, education, and health services into five block grants. Thus, had each item in the omnibus budget been presented as a separate proposal through the normal OMB clearance process, Reagan's first year agenda might well be the most active since Johnson.

Presented as a single legislative package—albeit one of the longest bills ever considered by Congress—the agenda looks more limited. These packaging decisions notwithstanding, six of Reagan's first eight proposals (or 75 percent) were new ideas, suggesting again that Reagan understood the need to get his new ideas into the process as quickly as possible. Presenting the new ideas fast was hardly unique to Reagan, however. Thirteen of Kennedy's first 25 proposals were new (52 percent); as were 20 of Johnson's first 34, 1965–66 (59 percent), 13 of Nixon's first 17 (77 percent); 12 of Carter's first 21 (57 percent). New ideas may be the heart and soul of any President's honeymoon, but may be even more so for Republicans with limited political capital.

Table 23. The Reagan Agenda: Large/Small versus New/Old Programs, by Congress

Congress	Large/New	Large/Old	Small/New	Small/Old
1981–82	6	0	5	4
1983–84	5	2	2	6
1985–86	0	0	0	0
1987–88	0	0	0	0
Total Reagan	11	2	7	10
Percent	36%	6%	23%	33%

Nor is this to argue that Reagan's agenda was entirely new. Like most of his predecessors, Regan proposed a fair share of reauthorizations and extensions, what Richard Rose calls "inheritances" in his study of British policy (1989). However, to the extent possible, Reagan held the necessary evils to small, not large, expansions—more money for environmental protection following the Gorsuch-Burford scandal, an extension of revenue sharing. In fact, of Reagan's twelve old initiatives, only two were large-scale—the 1983 Social Security compromise built from the ashes of Stockman's initial disaster (see page 256), and a sweeping revision of the criminal statutes which actually originated in the Senate, not the White House.

The Nonincremental Agenda. Reagan's overall focus on large-scale proposals is clear in table 23, which breaks his agenda into incremental (small/old, large/old, small/new) versus nonincremental (large/new) proposals. Nonincremental proposals such as Johnson's Medicare, Nixon's welfare reform, Carter's civil service reform, and Reagan's budget cuts involve a much greater commitment of presidential time, energy, and capital, costing much more than large/old, small/new, or small/old proposals.

Bluntly put, dramatic change in the status quo is never cheap. As Paul Schulman argues, "No barrier is more essential for nonincremental policy to breach and overcome permanently than the penchant for thinking small. Overcoming this trait is a major necessity in developing the imagination and receptivity closely associated with organizational innovation" (1975, p. 1357). (Although small/new proposals are not considered nonincremental, they are hardly incremental adjustments either. Therefore, it is useful to keep the various types of incremental, or not-nonincremental, proposals separate in table 23.)

Using the Apollo space program as his example, Schulman argues that nonincremental programs are "distinguished by their demand for comprehensive rather than incremental decisions, synoptic rather than piecemeal outlooks and vision. These policies are characterized by an indivisibility in the political commitment and resources they require for success. . . . This class of nonincremental, indivisible policies is perhaps small but is nonetheless significant. It consists of large-scale undertakings commanding major shares of the

Table 24. Presidential Requests for Legislation: Democrats versus Republicans versus Reagan, 1961–89

Policy Difference	Democrats (Kennedy, Johnson, and Carter)	Republicans (Nixon and Ford)	Reagan Only
Large/New Programs	38%	27%	36%
Small/New Programs	18	37	23
Large/Old Programs	22	11	6
Small/Old Programs	23	25	33

Democratic sample = 185 cases
Republican sample = 81 cases
Reagan sample = 30 cases

public budget" (p. 1355). Kennedy could hardly ask for the money to get a space crew to the moon without asking for the money to get them back.

As table 23 suggests, Reagan did his share of thinking big during the first two years of his term, averaging roughly the same number of nonincremental proposals as his three Democratic predecessors. Although not every piece of the 1981 budget package was large—his proposed work requirement for welfare recipients, while important, is coded as a small/new proposal—the cumulative impact of his omnibus budget bill was undeniably nonincremental.

When considered as a single collection of proposals, Reagan's 1981 agenda may have been the most significant presidential initiative since the Great Society, akin to Roosevelt's first Hundred Days in both reversing past federal programs and changing the prevailing constituencies of government. Unlike the distributive and redistributive agendas of the 1960s and 1970s, which sought to grant benefits to new publics, the Reagan agenda was mostly *de*distributive in that it sought to take away old benefits once provided to millions of lower- and middle-class Americans. On the national security agenda, in contrast, Reagan's defense build-up was anything but new, continuing an expansion begun under Carter in 1979.

Thus, more than the two Republicans before him, Reagan can be considered a nonincremental President. Indeed, his 1981 performance dispels any lingering notion that there is a Republican style of agenda-setting. As table 24 shows, 11 of his 30 proposals (36 percent) were large/new, compared to 38 percent for Kennedy, Johnson, and Carter, and 27 percent for Nixon and Ford.

The most interesting finding in table 24 may be the fact that Reagan falls so far behind his Republican peers in small/new initiatives, resembling the Democrats again. Reagan was simply more able to afford larger scale ideas. Table 24 also confirms Reagan's success in limiting old ideas to the smallest scale possible. Reagan had the lowest percentage of large/old initiatives among the six Presidents and the highest percentage of small/old. Again, Reagan kept these necessary evils to a minimum.

For those who still believe Republicans are naturally passive, the lessons from these past four tables are simple: (1) Presidents will propose to the level they can afford and (2) the shape of the status quo will determine how many new ideas are needed. As long as the status quo reflects fifty years of Democratic legislation—from the New Deal to the Great Society—Republican Presidents can be expected to pursue change. And when armed with enough political capital, they will seek legislation first, if only because executive orders and other administrative maneuvers can be so easily swept aside with the next administration.

(Further, legislation also provides the occasional opportunity for innovations the President may not have even considered, offering a free ride of sorts for congressional ideas. In 1981, for example, Senate Republicans amended Reagan's tax cut to require indexation of the tax brackets to inflation. That single reform meant that the federal government would *not* grow by $30–60 billion a year over the next decade, eliminating a traditional source of funding for Democratic programs like Medicare and veterans benefits.)

Conclusion: The Two Reagans

In many ways, these tables show two Ronald Reagans: one who set the agenda with speed and focus in 1981, the other who became steadily more passive with the passage of time and political fortune; one who battled to hard-fought victory on his top priorities in 1981, the other who could barely get Congress's attention, let alone a floor victory, from 1982 onward.

The question is what happened? One answer is that Reagan always had a tenuous grip in the House. During the first year in office, he was able to hold liberal Northern Republicans who would have normally voted against his agenda, while drawing conservative Southern Democrats, "Boll Weevils," who might have voted with him anyway. It was an exceedingly fragile coalition, not just because the Boll Weevils came under increasing pressure from the House Democratic leadership, but because the liberal Northern Republicans had to run for reelection in 1982.

Moreover, in spite of the naming of a National Commission on Social Security Reform, Stockman's 1981 Social Security disaster simply would not die, providing cannon fodder for the 1982 midterm elections. What had started out as a quick-and-dirty way for Stockman to repair what he already knew was a budget hemorrhage eventually cost the President his working House majority.

A second answer is that Reagan could not hold back on his social agenda forever. Sooner or later, the ideologues who had helped elect him would demand their place on the calendar. By waiting on abortion, school prayer, and tuition tax credits for the first year, Reagan was able to keep Congress focused on the public's prevailing concerns about the economy. With those issues on the agenda in 1983–84, Reagan's always fragile legislative base was irreparably fragmented. As more and more right-wing Republicans pleaded with Reagan "to be Reagan," the prospects for legislative focus faded.

A third answer is the failure of the budget and tax cuts. As noted earlier, having promised a balanced budget by 1984, Reagan paid a high legislative price for his growing deficits. Even though Democrats remained unable to create an alternative budget of their own, Reagan's agenda became mired in the same bitterness that pervaded the rest of the legislative process. As Democrats blamed Republicans, House members blamed Senators, governors blamed mayors, and virtually everyone blamed the President, the entire governmental process seemed stymied by a lack of direction.

A fourth answer is Reagan himself. From the very beginning of the term, he was more interested in broad themes than the nitty-gritty of legislation. However, as his political capital dwindled with the natural passage of time, he became even more detached from the legislative process. Facing increasing turnover among his Cabinet secretaries and key staff—turnover that hit its peak in the fifth year of the administration—Reagan's White House operation began to falter, and the agenda with it.

Ultimately, Reagan may be remembered most for that one first year in office, a year of brilliant legislative maneuvers with less-than-brilliant budgetary results. Despite his oft-stated intention to reshape government, Reagan and his key lieutenants fashioned a legislative agenda with a surprisingly high number of short-term proposals. As chapter 11 will argue, Reagan may have been both creator and victim of political trends that have made it much more difficult to marry long-term intentions to long-term proposals.

In this regard, there may have been *three* Reagans, one who spent his first year in office pursuing proposals timed for immediate impact, the second who spent the next three years developing and launching a relatively large number of proposals designed for lasting change, and the third who spent the rest of his administration watching most of those proposals languish in Congress. Unfortunately for Reagan, by the time he was able to match his long-term intentions to long-term proposals, he had little political capital left to invest.

11 short-term-itis

How Reagan surprised us in 1981. Few expected him to handle Congress or the public so easily; few expected him to so fully exercise the persuasive powers of the Presidency. After Vietnam and Watergate, the Presidency had seemed weakened beyond repair.

Many Presidency scholars, myself certainly included, predicted Reagan would fall prey to the divided parties, special interests, and public distrust that emerged from nearly twenty years of build-ups, break-ins, and breakdowns. Forced to balance reelection against good policy, Reagan would quickly discover that the price of domestic policy success had gone up, while his influence had not.

My own prediction, recorded first in the 1981 edition of this book, was that Reagan was destined for failure, largely because of a No Win Presidency: "Presidents no longer have the resources to expend on 'educating' the public; they no longer have the time to spend on a full search for new ideas and programs. If anything, the President's resource base has dwindled over the 1970s. The cost of presidential policy has grown, while the President's ability to influence outcomes has declined. It is a remarkable no-win position."

I was not the only pessimist in the academic community, however. Geoffrey Hodgson titled his 1980 book *All Things to All Men: The False Promise of the Modern American President,* Anthony King wrote in 1978 of political "coalitions in the sand," Hugh Heclo and Lester Solomon described *The Illusion of Presidential Government* in 1981, and Louis Koenig's 1981 edition of his popular textbook, *The Chief Executive,* began with the following assessment of "The Diminished Presidency":

> The Presidency of Carter was destined by forces well beyond his control to be considerably less than the presidencies of the Roosevelts, Johnson and others of the twentieth century. The definite prospect is that Carter's successor, Ronald

250

Reagan, and even his successor, will be afflicted by the same forces, no matter how substantial their political talents may be (p. 2).

Despite our collective gloom, no scholar was as bleak about the future of the Presidency as former Carter counselor Lloyd Cutler. Writing in the fall 1980 issue of *Foreign Affairs*, Cutler blamed Carter's failure on the Founding Fathers:

In parliamentary terms, one might say that under the U.S. Constitution, it is not now feasible to "form a government." The separation of powers between the legislative and executive branches, whatever its merits in 1793, has become a structure that almost guarantees stalemate today. As we wonder why we are having such a difficult time making decisions we all know must be made, and projecting our power and leadership, we should reflect on whether this is one big reason (p. 12).

Obviously, we were all wrong to a degree. Reagan proved that a President can succeed on Capitol Hill, in large part by paying attention to the new rules of agenda-setting: "move it or lose it," no amateurs, avoid details, set priorities. Reagan also demonstrated that a President can bridge the separation of powers by focusing congressional attention on a handful of ideas and by exercising the full powers of the Presidency, including, as Stockman admitted, gimmicks, evasions, half-truths, and downright dishonesty. As for Cutler's call for a constitutional convention, Reagan clearly demonstrated that a President can form a government, especially by hitting the ground running.

The question, therefore, is not so much whether Reagan was able to form a government, but what kind of government he formed. As we shall shortly see, Reagan may have succeeded his first year by adding a new rule to the No Win Presidency: go short in the opening quarter. Facing a set of first-year economic and social problems that would have been difficult to solve even with carefully crafted long-term proposals, Reagan opted instead for a series of short-term cuts, caps, and accounting gimmicks.

However, as Reagan's honeymoon wore off, the cuts, caps, and accounting gimmicks were easily removed, breached, and ignored. Had Reagan's first-year agenda focused instead on the underlying structure of the American welfare state—the statutes, benefit formulas, and annual cost-of-living adjustments embedded in much of the domestic budget—1981 might have produced a very different legacy, indeed.

This is not to suggest that Reagan was consumed by short-term intentions. Quite the contrary. He held very strong beliefs about taxes, spending, and the proper role of government. With "No New Taxes" as his rallying cry, Reagan espoused one of the most uncompromising ideologies in recent presidential history.

Given the rhetoric of revolution, it may seem all the more surprising that the administration failed to craft a revolutionary set of first-year proposals to match. Despite several notable long-term initiatives in later years—taxes, welfare reform, and a new version of Nixon's New Federalism—the Reagan agenda had an overall thrust toward legislation timed for immediate returns.

While there is little doubt that a President as conservative as Reagan would want to do significant "weed cutting" at the start of the term, there is a difference between *weed cutting* and *weed pulling*. The fact that Reagan and his Budget Director opted for quick, if deep, cuts meant they would have to cut again and again over time to realize the President's broad plan of limited government. After all, weeds always grow back.

In retrospect, the decision to opt for short-term proposals reflected a series of both tactical and strategic problems early in the Reagan administration.

On the one hand, Stockman had little time to consider lasting reforms in America's "permanent government," not with a budget due in three weeks. Such a package would have taken months to develop, let alone pass in a single omnibus bill. Thus the best Stockman could do was cut and paste, keeping track of the running total on the back of an envelope. "I just wish there were more hours in the day or that we didn't have to do this so fast," Stockman admitted at the time. "I have these stacks of briefing books and I've got to make decisions about specific options. . . . I don't have time, trying to put this whole package together in three weeks, so you just start making snap judgments" (quoted in the *Atlantic,* December, 1981).

Moreover, a first-year package laden with more permanent reform might have faced endless delays in the congressional authorizing committees. Unlike Carter, who spent his first two years trying to figure out which committee was responsible for his omnibus energy package, Reagan was right to worry about how to secure passage of anything in a highly fragmented Congress.

On the other hand, there were few ready proposals to be found on Capitol Hill, especially for a President as conservative as Reagan. Unlike Kennedy, who could borrow and steal an entire legislative agenda from his Democratic colleagues in 1961, Reagan had no such option twenty years later. The lack of a House or Senate majority in the years *before* Reagan's election may have foredoomed his agenda to short-term proposals in the first years *after.*

Even had there been a Republican majority in Congress, it would likely not have been the kind to be of use to such a conservative President. Yet, coming into office as the consummate outsider, and a former governor to boot, Reagan had few detailed alternatives of his own. Absent an "adoptable" Republican agenda on Capitol Hill, the best the new administration could do was draw upon conservative think-tanks for overly broad recommendations, hardly a substitute for fully developed legislation in reserve.

Finally, even had there been a deep Republican agenda at the ready, it was not clear that Reagan had the political capital for a package of first-year reforms. Despite Reagan's working majority of quasi-Republicans and "Boll Weevil" Southern Democrats in the House, it was a fragile coalition at best. Perhaps an assortment of short-term cuts was all he could afford. In this regard, dismantling or repealing programs is a very different task from "zeroing out," or sharply cutting, the budget in a given fiscal year. The former raises even greater constituency counter-pressure than budget cuts, greater legislative review, and greater risk of delay. Hard as liberals fought to stop the Reagan budget and tax package, at least their programs would live to fight another day.

Ultimately, however, Reagan's first-year agenda reflected his own distaste for detail. Ignoring the sometimes painful process of translating broadly sculpted intentions into highly specific proposals, Reagan left the fine print to his Budget Director and Congress. In this regard, Reagan may have avoided details too much. Left to his own devices, Stockman drifted toward short-term proposals. While some might rightly argue that Reagan achieved his aim of limited government through creation of a persistent budget crisis, surely that is not what he originally intended. As Stockman also admitted,

> we should have designed those pieces to be more compatible. But the pieces were moving on independent tracks—the tax program, where we were going on spending, and the defense program, which was just a bunch of numbers written on a piece of paper. And it didn't quite mesh. That's what happened. But, you see, for about a month and a half we got away with that because of the novelty of all these budget reductions (quoted in the *Atlantic*, 1981).

The Short-Term Agenda

Reagan did not have to go short-term, however. Striking fast does not mean striking fast *only with short-term proposals*. Lyndon Johnson struck fast with a deep agenda of long-term reforms, including Medicare; Nixon struck somewhat later in his first year with welfare reform. In fact, first-year proposals can be designed to change the underlying structure of government or to pay off a short-term campaign promise, to test an important long-term experiment or to repair a tear in the President's coalition.

That the Reagan agenda might contain more short-term proposals than long is hardly a surprise given the basic changes in the Presidency highlighted in this and other books. There is considerable agreement among political scientists, for example, that Presidents have been "going public" more often lately, as Samuel Kernell argues, "displaying exceptional sensitivity to the breezes that blow into Washington." According to Kernell, going public has inevitable policy consequences:

> There is a compelling rationale for suspecting that the more presidents rest their leadership on going public, the more volatile policy outcomes in Washington will be. The public can be assumed to be more fickle in its assessments of politicians and policies than will be a stable community of Washington elites, whose business it is to make informed judgments. As the former becomes more important and the latter less, political relations will be more easily disrupted (1986, p. 233).

By itself, however, going public does not necessarily mean that the President's agenda will be more short-term than long. Rather, going public may cement the reciprocal relationship between public opinion and presidential policy, each one reinforcing the other over time. The more volatile the public, the more volatile the policy, and vice versa—a vicious circle that may eventually corrode the President's ability to think much beyond the next three months, let alone three decades. According to Dennis Simon and Charles Ostrom, Jr., the President faces a dilemma between improving the quality of outcomes (long-term) or engaging in high politics (short-term):

> The long-term approach will direct the president's actions and energies toward the solution of principal problems of the day. . . . To the extent that such attempts fail to solve problems, the president's resource reservoir will become increasingly shallow as the vicious circle begins to undermine his influence on the policy process. This explains the attractiveness of the short-term approach. The president is relatively unconstrained in relying upon political drama and will welcome the bursts in support which actions on the political stage trigger. However, the impact of such actions are short-lived and, by themselves, can do little but provide bumps and wiggles on the downward course of approval. Therein lies the dilemma (1985, pp. 65–66).

Assuming such trade-offs exist, it seems reasonable to test the Reagan agenda for differences between short-term and long-term policy.

Intentions, Proposals, and Consequences

Reagan was hardly the first American President to make choices among short-term and long-term proposals. Every President from George Washington to George Bush has faced similar tension. It is inherent in the very structure of the Presidency.

Nor was Reagan the first President to offer short-term proposals. He had two hundred years of precedent. Indeed, many, if not all of America's celebrated long-term domestic programs—Social Security, Medicare, unemployment compensation, the interstate highway system, wilderness preservation—carry some element of short-term politics. The growing power of the "gray lobby" no doubt crossed Lyndon Johnson's mind as he signed Medicare into law.

Rather, Reagan may have inherited a Presidency less capable of converting long-term intentions into long-term proposals. And, as the last half of this chapter will suggest, he surely left a Presidency even weaker. It has always been one thing for a President to intend long-term impact, quite another to draft and secure passage of long-term legislative proposals, and still another to assure successful implementation that produces the intended long-term results.

What makes the current era different, however, is that public patience for long-term programs may have worn thin, the proposals themselves may not be readily available, and the prospects for successful implementation

Table 25. Intentions versus Proposals

	Intention	
	Short-term	Long-term
Short-term	I. 1981 Social Security Rescue	II. 1981 Budget and Tax Package
Proposal		
Long-term	III. 1974 National Health Insurance	IV. 1983 Social Security Rescue

Table 26. Proposals versus Consequences

	Proposal	
	Short-term	Long-term
Short-term	I. 1981 Accelerated Tax Depreciation	II. 1977 Social Security Rescue
Consequence		
Long-term	III. 1981 Budget and Tax Package	IV. 1983 Social Security Rescue

may have been severely weakened. Intentions notwithstanding, today's President may simply be less able to go long-term.

This distinction among intentions, proposals, and consequences is central to understanding the Reagan agenda. Simply put, long-term intentions do not necessarily lead to either long-term legislation or ultimate long-term success. Indeed, the American policy landscape is littered with well-intended programs that failed to produce the desired long-term consequences—the War on Poverty, Model Cities, the War on Drugs, energy conservation, and so on. Some failed because the problems were too tough; others because the legislation was poorly drafted; still others because the world failed to perform as predicted.

Consider at least two places where long-term intentions can go astray. First, the President may be able to either locate or develop a long-term proposal to match. Second, the proposal itself may fail to work as designed, whether because of unfavorable external conditions or bureaucratic opposition. These two potential failures are summarized in tables 25 and 26.

The examples found in cells II and III of each table may well constitute a unique class of presidential policy decisions, for they show "disconnects" between intentions and proposals, or proposals and consequences. In short, they indicate policy failures of one kind or another—errors in forecasting, design, and/or implementation.

Reagan's 1981 budget and tax package emerges in each table as a policy disconnect, first as a failure to link long-term intention with a long-term proposal, next as a failure to match a short-term proposal to the *intended* long-term consequence. In contrast, Reagan's 1983 Social Security reform emerges in both tables as a successful match, first as a long-term intention tied to a long-term proposal, next as a long-term proposal that yields a long-term consequence.

Ironically, Carter's 1977 Social Security proposal actually laid the groundwork for Reagan's eventual success. Much as Carter promised at the time that his proposal would make Social Security safe for seventy-five years, the final rescue plan could not survive the hyperinflation of the late 1970s. The margins of economic error were simply too tight.

As a result, Social Security entered its second funding crisis in as many administrations three years later, in 1981. As table 25 suggests, however, Reagan's first pass at reform was anything but long-term. In the frantic search for budget savings, Stockman used the crisis to propose an immediate 25 percent cut in benefits and a so-called permanent delay in the annual cost-of-living allowance, in effect giving less than seven months notice to those who had planned to retire in 1982. Not surprisingly, this hasty marriage of short-term intention to short-term proposal was rejected 96–0 by the Senate, thereby creating the momentum for a third try at reform in 1983.

The most interesting case in the two tables may involve Nixon's 1974 national health insurance proposal, one of several familiar cases of short-term intentions that produced long-term proposals and/or consequences. Struggling to distract a Democratic Congress from the Watergate crisis, Nixon offered national health insurance in a last-second bargain to save his Presidency. Perhaps a short-term proposal would have attracted greater congressional interest.

As it was, Democrats refused Nixon's invitation, convinced that the 1976 elections would produce a Democratic victor, and, thereby, a stronger proposal. Alas for the nation's 37 million uninsured, this, too, was a failed strategy. By the time Carter entered office, health care inflation was accelerating so rapidly that national insurance was no longer affordable.

However interesting these policy failures, the question is not whether Presidents and their staffs sometimes make mistakes. Nor is it whether the policy process sometimes mismatches intentions to proposals or proposals to consequences. All in all, most short-term intentions convert easily into short-term proposals and short-term consequences. And, at least until the late 1970s, most long-term intentions converted smoothly into long-term proposals and long-term consequences.

Rather, the question is whether the prospects for long-term policy have decreased over the past three decades. Since (1) presidential intentions are very difficult to interpret—rare indeed is the press secretary who proclaims from the outset that a legislative priority is insignificant or limited—and (2) consequences may be beyond White House influence, proposals become the logical place to look for any increase in short-term thinking. Moreover, proposals are the glue that binds intentions to consequences. Without a proposal of some kind, intentions remain just that, intentions.

Making decisions for this book about what constitutes a short-term or long-term proposal is no small task, particularly since many proposals contain elements of both. The challenge is to make reasonable judgment calls based on the legislative specifics—first, whether the legislation itself was structured for immediate or longer-term impact, and, second, whether there is suggestive evidence that the proposal was designed for immediate political pay-outs. Remembering that the focus is on specific legislative proposals, not intentions or consequences, the following examples may help illustrate the broad categories.

> *Short-term:* postal rate increases, Kennedy's area redevelopment, juvenile crime control, accelerated public works, water projects, Carter's hospital cost control, the windfall profits tax, emergency strike controls, special revenue sharing, stand-by gas rationing, cuts in food stamps and Aid to Families with Dependent Children, Social Security reform (1981), and Reagan's acceleration of the 1980 Disability Insurance review.

> *Long-term:* Hatch Act reform (civil service political participation) Medicare, civil rights, clean water, Alaska Lands Protection, Clean Air Act, indigent legal aid, Social Security reform (1977 and 1983), airline, banking, and transportation deregulation, Nixon's Family Assistance Plan, Carter's Program for Better Jobs and Income, and Reagan's welfare demonstration projects, catastrophic health insurance, the balanced budget and school prayer amendments, and establishment of a Department of Veterans Affairs, and the proposed dismantling of the Departments of Energy and Education.

This is not to suggest that long-term proposals such as Medicare and civil rights do not carry any short-term effects. Nor is this to suggest that short-term proposals cannot become "immortal," as many government programs do. Rather, the judgment calls must be based on the weight of the legislative record at the launch of the proposal—for example, was the legislation timed for immediate impact, does the bill involve changes in the basic statute, does it lead toward more lasting reform?

Ultimately, such judgments are best treated as rough clues to potential trends in the President's agenda. However, even accepting the potential for disagreement over the specific examples offered above, the data presented in table 27 suggest that the President's agenda may be moving short-term. Looking back to Kennedy-Johnson (1961–65), Nixon's first and only full term (1969–73), Carter (1977–81), and Reagan (1981–89), the percentage of short-term proposals has risen by a third.

Table 27. Presidential Requests for Legislation: Short-term versus Long-term Proposals, Kennedy, Nixon, Carter, and Reagan

President	Year	Short-term	Long-term
Kennedy	1961	11	14
	1962	7	9
	1963	2	4
(Johnson)	1964	3	3
Total		23	30
Percent		43%	57%
Nixon I	1969	6	11
	1970	4	8
	1971	4	4
	1972	1	2
Total		15	25
Percent		38%	62%
Carter	1977	6	15
	1978	6	2
	1979	4	4
	1980	3	1
Total		19	22
Percent		46%	54%
Reagan*	1981	7	1
	1982	3	4
	1983	4	7
	1984	3	1
Total		17	13
Percent		57%	43%

*Reagan had no additional legislative requests in 1985–88.

The Short-Term Agenda

Imperfect though the data, table 27 suggests several patterns in the nature of presidential policy proposals.

A Difference in Decades? First, Reagan and Carter had a greater proportion of short-term proposals than either Kennedy or Nixon. Seven of Reagan's first eight proposals are defined as short-term, again not because the 1981 budget and tax cuts failed to exert long-term effects, but because the specific proposals were designed for immediate political and budgetary returns, a conclusion clearly supported by Stockman's own history of events.

Reagan may have been equally short-term in the administrative Presidency. His regulatory review process generally succeeded more in delaying than preventing new rules, while his management initiatives focused primarily on short-term productivity savings. Even in implementing legislation left over from the final days of the Carter administration, Reagan and his team focused on instant payoffs.

Implementation of the 1980 Social Security Disability Amendments is a case in point. Originally designed to remove a relatively small number of ineligible recipients from the benefit rolls, thereby saving a modest $10 million, the Reagan administration accelerated the program and increased the targets, fueled in part by a General Accounting Office (GAO) report that showed a possible $2 billion in savings. As Martha Derthick summarizes the history:

> Vowing that "a new management team" would "weed out" all of the ineligible recipients cited by the GAO, the Reagan administration—with support from the new findings and in its zeal to maximize budget savings—projected savings from the disability review totaling $3.45 billion in six years (1981–86). This was a complete departure from the earlier estimate of a mere $10 million net in four years (1982–85). Further, the SSA elected to begin the review right away, in the spring of 1981, rather than on January 1, 1982, as the law contemplated. The effect of these changes was to alter the spirit of the undertaking. What had been conceived by Congress in 1980 was a deliberate invigoration of a review procedure that had been too feeble to have much effect. What was set in motion in 1981 was more like a purge (1990, p. 36).

Ironically, just like the budget and tax cuts, the Reagan disability initiative failed. Individuals removed from the roles immediately appealed their cases upward through SSA and into the federal courts, tying up thousands upon thousands of hours that might have been used by the phalanx of new Reagan judges on other issues.

As to the consequences of this short-term endeavor, the plaintiffs almost always won, rendering the earlier savings moot. Ultimately, according to Derthick, the cause of the failure was in "performing on a much larger scale and at a faster pace procedures that were well established. But therein lies much of the explanation: under extraordinary circumstances, the pitfalls of ordinary procedures were magnified and dramatized" (p. 37).

Where Reagan was definitely *not* short-term was in his judicial appointments. By their very nature, of course, judicial appointments exert a lasting impact. In this regard, Reagan and his key staff took great care to select nominees who supported the President's long-term agenda. Although time will tell just how effective that strategy will be, the Reagan imprint emerged almost immediately in civil rights. This was a long-term intention matched to long-term appointees who began pursuing Reagan's judicial agenda immediately, an apparent match of intentions to proposals (nominees) to consequences (judicial opinions).

The Reagan Strategy. Second, Reagan offered the bulk of his short-term proposals in the first year, exactly the opposite of Kennedy, Nixon, and Carter. This may well be the most important finding of the entire short-term/long-term discussion. As noted earlier, Reagan may have had little choice—there was no long-term agenda waiting for his arrival, no ready stock of long-term conservative proposals.

Unfortunately for Reagan, by the time his long-term proposals came "on line," his political capital was gone. Thus, what remains of the administration is largely what passed in 1981. Although Reagan can claim some credit for tax simplification and welfare reform in his second term, he did not have the political support—nor, for that matter, a continued Senate majority—to shape outcomes as he had five or six years before.

Reagan's decision to strike fast with short-term proposals stands in direct contrast to Kennedy, Nixon, and Carter's decision to move their long-term proposals first. It may be that these three simply had the luxury of holding their short-term proposals for later in the term as a way of preparing for reelection. Perhaps they felt less need to pay off their supporters quickly because their coalitions were built on somewhat stronger party loyalties. Perhaps they also felt less "what-have-you-done-for-me-lately" pressure from the public.

It also appears that Carter became more short-term over time in part because his staff finally convinced him that American politics had changed. Facing a potential nomination fight with Ted Kennedy, Carter may have realized that the party could no longer deliver automatic renomination in 1980. And, having spent his first year making one political mistake after another, Carter may have also recognized the need to present programs that both Congress and the public might like. Moreover, as budgetary pressure increased with the hyperinflation of the late 1970s, Carter hardly had the dollars to go long-term. Indeed, his 1977 hospital cost containment proposal was designed to deal with that short-term problem as a first step toward a long-term national health insurance program.

It is equally possible that the public expectations toward the President were fundamentally changed by Reagan's image-based campaign strategies in 1980, thereby shortening his own honeymoon. After asking repeatedly whether voters were better off after four years of Carter, perhaps Reagan had to deliver faster. Although Reagan could have used his enormous first year popularity for long-term ideas such as a balanced budget amendment instead of the budget and tax cuts, he may have been limited by the agreements he had to make in building an electoral coalition. Going short-term on policy may have become part and parcel of going public in the No Win Presidency.

Finally, to be fair to Reagan, there was no guarantee that Congress would have enacted a long-term agenda in 1981. His window of opportunity may have been so narrow that only quick-hitting proposals could survive. As Carter learned in 1977, long-term proposals can absorb tremendous amounts of congressional time and energy, clogging key committees and subcommittees. Reagan's focus on short-term budget and tax changes may have been the only route to legislative success—while committees were involved in the debate, they had fewer options to delay through lengthy hearings on long-term impacts.

A Rising Tide? Third, the percentage of short-term proposals rises slightly over the four Presidencies, starting at 45 percent under Kennedy, falling to 38 percent under Nixon, then moving back up to 46 percent under Carter and 57 percent under Reagan. The recent pattern appears to continue through the first two years of the Bush Presidency with (1) a legislative agenda composed almost entirely of short-term proposals—the savings and loan bailout, crime, drugs, another budget crisis, and flag burning—and (2) the promised long-term agenda on education and environment still in development by the 1990 midterm elections. The question is whether this is a trend or merely a passing phenomenon, the artifact of temporary budgetary and political volatility. As we shall see shortly, the evidence would suggest more a trend than a passing problem.

The Size and Scope of Short-Term Policy

Ultimately, these data are not particularly significant in any statistical sense until they are combined in tables 28–29 with the earlier measures of size and scope.

The combination of the three policy differences—large/small, new/old, and short-term/long-term—is particularly important for understanding where Presidents invest their capital. It might be, for example, that Presidents only go short on the old issues, reserving their long-term vision for the new pro-

Table 28. Presidential Requests for Legislation: New/Short-term versus New/Long-term, Kennedy, Nixon, Carter, and Reagan

President	New/Short-Term		New/Long-Term	
	Total	Percent	Total	Percent
Kennedy	11	33%	22	67%
Nixon I	7	28	18	72
Carter	12	48	13	52
Reagan	9	50	9	50

Table 29. Presidential Requests for Legislation: Large/Short-term versus Large/Long-term, Kennedy, Nixon, Carter, and Reagan

President	Large/Short-Term		Large/Long-Term	
	Total	Percent	Total	Percent
Kennedy	13	46%	15	54%
Nixon I	2	14	14	86
Carter	10	45	12	55
Reagan	5	39	8	61

posals. It might also be that Presidents go short only on the small items, reserving their long-range ideas for the large opportunities.

According to these tables, neither argument is true. Kennedy and Nixon both used their nonincremental opportunities for long-term policy, while Carter and Reagan were much more likely to go short. As a proportion of their agendas, Carter and Reagan both offered roughly twice as much new/short-term policy as Kennedy and Nixon. Again, however, the key difference between Carter and Reagan is the timing of the short-term proposals. Of Carter's 1977 new proposals, only two of twelve were short-term; of Reagan's 1981 new proposals, five of six were short-term.

Table 29 is more difficult to interpret. Roughly half of Kennedy, Carter, and Reagan's large proposals were long-term, compared to 86 percent of Nixon's. One explanation is that the size of a President's short- and long-term initiatives is not always subject to choice. When old ideas hit the agenda—for example, the two recent Social Security financing crises—the President has little option but to go long.

However, Nixon's agenda also reflected pure political reality: he simply did not have the political capital to secure passage of his program, whether short- or long-term, large or small, new or old. Facing such limited legislative prospects, Nixon may have simply been in the business of developing proposals for his second term, showing the public that he was, indeed, a great thinker, even as he asked his campaign team to win by the biggest landslide possible.

One might even argue that Nixon's long-term agenda reflected his obsession with a place in history. In this regard, the content of his policy agenda may have been just another manifestation of the same psychological impulse that led to the secret White House taping system. Just as Nixon wanted a perfect historical record for the future, perhaps he also wanted the perfect policy agenda.

Intriguing though this hypothesis, it pales in comparison to the simple political realities of the Nixon agenda. Believing that 1972 would produce a landslide realignment on the order of 1932, Nixon's long-term policy agenda may have reflected nothing more than his own judgment that the second term would present ample opportunity for legislative achievement.

Ultimately, it is table 30 that raises the greatest questions about the

Table 30. Presidential Requests for Legislation: New-Large/Short-term versus New-Large/Long-term, Kennedy, Nixon, Carter, and Reagan

President	New-Large/Short-Term		New-Large/Long-Term	
	Total	Percent	Total	Percent
Kennedy	4	21%	15	79%
Nixon I	1	8	11	92
Carter	8	50	8	50
Reagan	5	45	6	55

Carter and Reagan eras. Comparing the mix of short- and long-term on each President's nonincremental agenda, table 30 suggests that Kennedy and Nixon operated in a very different policy period from Carter and Reagan. Whereas Kennedy and Nixon averaged only one short-term nonincremental proposal out of five, Carter and Reagan averaged one out of two.

As above, however, there are timing differences between Carter and Reagan, with all five of Reagan's new-large/*short-term* proposals arriving on Capitol Hill *before* his first new-large/*long-term* request. In contrast, six of Carter's first seven new-large proposals were long-term, perhaps explaining why Congress was choked by his agenda.

Short-term-itis

Despite the limitations in the data presented above, there is ample corroborating evidence that contemporary Presidents are moving toward more short-term policy. Although Reagan moved his short-term agenda quickly for many reasons—most notably, Stockman's three-week timetable and the lack of available long-term proposals—future Presidents will also find it difficult to launch a long-term agenda. Even if the public somehow becomes less fickle, it is no longer clear that government can either generate the basic ideas or sustain effective implementation.

Indeed, this disinvestment in the government's policy planning capacity may be one of the most important long-term consequences of the Reagan Presidency, a disinvestment that affects both Democrats and Republicans alike. As Stockman learned, it may take as much analysis and planning to dismantle a program as it does to create one. In casting about for proposals at the start of the term, tomorrow's Presidents and their assortment of policy entrepreneurs face three trends that limit the prospects for long-term proposals:

Number One. The political culture bracketing the President's agenda is increasingly one of impatience, characterized by declining long-term attachments to the political system and shallow investments in the electoral process. When coupled with a general disengagement from civic life, the erosion of party identification among younger Americans in general, and the baby-boom generation in particular, an environment in which Presidents have very few incentives for addressing long-term policy issues evolves. Although studies of the national mood are risky, it is clear that Presidents do pay attention to swings in public commitment.

Number Two. It is no longer clear that the policy system can supply the basic ingredients of a long-term agenda. The sources of ideas that fueled the President's agenda in the 1950s and 1960s either no longer exist or have been weakened significantly, and cannot be replaced by the proliferation of "boutique" interest groups—the highly specialized organizations that have blossomed in recent years. Moreover, disinvestment in planning and evaluative capacity in government has reduced the President's ability to develop policy with long-term horizons. The lost ability to understand how programs work has a clear impact on the President's ability both to develop policy proposals and to sell them to Congress and the public.

Number Three. Even if Presidents pursue a long-term policy agenda, it is increasingly unlikely that it will be successfully implemented. And if implementation is unlikely, presidential entrepreneurs are wise to focus on the short-term.

Ironically, many of these constraints were self-inflicted by past Presidents, reflecting efforts to gain control of the executive branch. As the National Commission on the Public Service (Volcker Commission) argued in 1989, two decades of pay freezes, "bureaucrat bashing," budget crises, political turnover, and an ever-tightening noose of internal regulation may have so demoralized the career work force that Presidents cannot be sure that even the shortest-term policies will be successfully implemented.

The Stream of Politics

The stream of politics clearly shapes the President's agenda and is the primary source of the political capital that Presidents spend on their domestic agendas. However, in addition to seats in Congress and short-term public approval, those who study presidential policy must consider what John Kingdon calls the national mood. As Kingdon defines the concept,

> People in and around government sense a national mood. They are comfortable describing its content, and believe that they know when the mood shifts. The idea goes by different names—the national mood, the climate in the country, changes in public opinion, or broad social movements. But common to all of these labels is the notion that a rather large number of people out in the country are thinking along certain common lines, that this national mood changes from one time to another in discernible ways, and that these changes in mood or climate have important impacts on policy agendas and policy outcomes (1984, p. 153).

Although Kingdon's general focus is on the rise and fall of issues, his definition might be stretched to cover the public's *patience for change,* patience rooted in longer-term civic attachments to the political system. To the extent individuals have stable connections to public life, they may be more patient about the President's policy agenda. To the extent they view their interactions with the system as fleeting and unreliable, they will be much less tolerant of delay.

Under this broader definition of the national mood, the decline in party identification among all Americans in general, and among the baby-boom electorate in particular, would have a profound impact on the kinds of policies Presidents prefer, for it would weaken attachments and increase public fascination with immediate outcomes. According to Morris Fiorina, a first facet of this decomposition involves the declining impact of party identification "as a variable that influences—indeed, that at one time *structured*—the voting decision. . . . The ties that bound in the past seem to bind less tightly today." Fiorina continues:

> A second facet of party decomposition is the decline in the importance of parties as organizations. Ignoring such older "reforms" as civil service, consider that the spread of direct primaries and open caucuses has stripped the parties of much of their power over nominations. Public financing and political action committees, or PACs, have lessened the financial importance of the parties. Active political participation by a large, leisured middle class dwarfs the manpower resources of the parties. Television provides cheap information. Increasingly, the parties grow irrelevant to the conduct of political campaigns (1981, p. 203–4).

As Fiorina notes, these two trends reinforce each other: "If the parties are perceived as irrelevant, candidates and their backers organize alternatives that compete for political resources, and this competition further weakens the existing party organizations, which further encourages independence among candidates and their backers, and so on" (p. 204). Political scientists now talk about a permanent dealignment in party identification.

More troubling for future Presidents, the decline in party attachments is most apparent among the voters who will dominate the political culture over the coming two decades: the 75 million baby boomers born between 1946 and 1964. As Helmut Norpoth and Jerrold Rusk note in their exhaustive analysis of the overall drop in party identification from 1964 to 1980,

> Younger voters were more inclined to abandon their partisan ties than were older voters, and the sharpest decline—using the partisanship of previous new voters as a benchmark—occurred among those voters who became eligible to vote in this period of change. Indeed, this group, together with the group of voters who had entered the electorate in the 1950s and early 1960s, contributed nearly 75 percent to the decline in partisanship in the American electorate (1982, pp. 535–36).

Consider, for example, the erosion of party attachments among high school students in the class of 1965, a class that has been studied closely by political scientists. After interviewing the same students in 1965 and 1973, for example, M. Kent Jennings and Richard Niemi concluded that roughly 40 percent had changed their party identification—e.g., from Democrat or Republican to independent—while almost 70 percent had changed the strength of their commitment—e.g., from strong Democrat to weak Democrat or leaning independent. Only 24 percent of those who had said they were strong Democrats in 1965 were still strong Democrats in 1973; only 32 percent who had said they were strong Republicans were still strong Republicans (1981).

After interviewing these students again in 1982, Jennings and his new coauthor Gregory Markus found party identification had stabilized at a lower level than originally predicted, with large numbers of these baby boomers still positioned in the independent, leaning, or weak identification categories. Although these respondents were somewhat less volatile over the 1976–82 period, they were stabilized at a much lower level of partisanship than their parents. As Jennings and Markus conclude, the class of '65 "began their adult political lives strikingly less committed to political parties than were their parents, and they have remained less committed for nearly two decades" (1984, p. 1015).

Thus, despite some evidence of "hardening" in party identification by 1982, 44 percent of the class of '65 remained independents of one kind or another, with only 15 percent strongly identifying as either Democrats or Republicans, numbers which have led some election scholars to conclude that independents were more likely to remain "loyal" than partisans. Yet, by definition, in saying they were independents, these baby boomers were declaring their lack of identification and attachment. Indeed, just about the only generational "unit," or subgroup, that had moved closer to a strong party attachment was the relatively small number of Vietnam War protestors, who became decidedly more Democratic over the 1973–82 period.

Thus, as the huge baby-boom generation takes its place as the dominant age cohort in politics, Presidents can expect little long-term loyalty. Not only do baby boomers often identify themselves as independents and party loyalists at one and the same time, they tend to view the political parties as irrelevant to their own voting decisions. "Increasingly, the image of the parties is just nothingness," Martin Wattenberg argues (1984, p. 120). Split ticket voting rises with each election, turnout declines, voting decisions come later and later in the campaign, and interest drops further, all betraying growing shallowness in commitment. The separation is even more pronounced within the baby boom where political decisions are made on the basis of limited information and shortened time horizons.

Indeed, the baby boomers may have changed the very definition of party loyalty. Party identification today is much less a statement of life-long commitment and much more a running tally of issues and images, a summary of what voters did in the most recent election, a product of policy preferences, not vice versa, a dependent variable in the voting equation. "They are a person's accumulated evaluations from previous elections," write Charles Franklin and John Jackson of party loyalties, "and are dependent upon the events and actions of political leaders during these elections and during subsequent terms in office. In this way, each campaign leaves its imprint, or residue, on individual identifications" (1983, p. 968). In such a retrospective system, voters would be reluctant to invest in long-term policy promises, particularly if they had no confidence in the ability of government or specific politicians to deliver.

Ultimately, however, these political attitudes are but a small part of the overall geography of public opinion a President faces in building a policy agenda. Basic life style changes may be far more important in understanding the fragile balance of presidential policy than the erosion of party identification.

The fact that the baby boomers have redefined traditional social roles like parenthood, work, and marriage may not automatically spring to mind as important indicators for those who study presidential policy. Nevertheless, the baby boom's political separation can be seen as but one element of a broader societal separation from traditional social roles. According to Joseph Veroff, Elizabeth Douvan, and Richard Kulka, a comparison of social attachments in 1956 and 1976 speaks to "a general loosening of people's social integration, a reduction in the meaning and satisfaction they find in assuming and performing roles in a social organization. Asked to define themselves, our 1976 respondents allude less often to positions they fill, roles they perform, compared to respondents in 1957" (1981, pp. 474–75). In many ways, party identification was merely one more role or connection that Americans in general, and again baby boomers in particular, left behind in the 1970s and 1980s.

The Stream of Proposals

This culture of impatience is not the only obstacle to long-term policy, however. Even if the President's entrepreneurs decided to fight the public volatility, they would need access to long-term thinking inside government. After all, policy proposals do not spring full blown from the President's imagination. As Kingdon notes, they are incubated deep within the primeval "soup" of executive and congressional politics:

> Many ideas are possible in principle, and float around in a "policy primeval soup" in which specialists try out their ideas in a variety of ways—bill introductions, speeches, testimony, papers, and conversation. In that consideration, proposals are floated, come into contact with one another, are revised and combined with one another, and floated again. But the proposals that survive to the status of serious consideration meet several criteria, including their technical feasibility, their fit with dominant values and the current national mood, their budgetary workability, and the political support or opposition they might experience. Thus the selection system narrows the set of conceivable proposals and selects from that large set a short list of proposals that is actually available for serious consideration (pp. 20–21).

Unfortunately, that policy soup is not quite as rich as it once was, at least for presidential tastes, that is.

The Sources of Ideas. One way to appreciate the increasing incentives for short-term policy is to examine the condition of potential sources of long-term ideas. We already know, for example, that Presidents rarely enter their first campaigns with fully developed legislative proposals. More often, they borrow, steal, coopt, and copy already existing proposals. According to the White House staff I interviewed in the late 1970s, Presidents draw the bulk of their ideas from Congress, events, and the executive branch, leaving the platform, campaign promises, and interest groups far behind.

Indeed, White House staff mention Congress as a source of ideas twice as often as the party platform and three times as often as the President's own campaign promises (see page 86). Stealing ideas from Congress is a time-honored practice for new administrations, one which was used by Kennedy to populate an entire domestic legislative agenda. So is pulling ideas up from the executive agencies.

Much as interest groups fuel the congressional agenda, Presidential staff rarely mention groups as a direct source of proposals. Nor do they say much about think tanks, although admittedly my original interviews were conducted before Reagan and the Heritage Foundation found each other. To reach the President's agenda, it appears that interest groups must first test their ideas in Congress or win sponsorship within the agencies. And if Congress and the agencies are unable to play this mediating role, it is not clear that interest groups have an alternative channel into the Oval Office.

Start with Congress and what Burdette Loomis calls *The New American Politician* (1988). As the book's subtitle aptly suggests, ambition and entrepreneurship have changed the face of political life, limiting the President's access to tested long-term policy alternatives.

At one level, the reforms of the 1970s increased the visibility of individual members of Congress, as well as their ability to develop their own policy agendas. With huge expansions in staff support, each member became a separate "enterprise," unaccountable to all but the voters back home, and, even then, each member held enormous incumbency advantages that virtually assured re-election every time out.

At another level, the individual entrepreneurship that so characterizes the contemporary Congress actually works against the development of ready long-term proposals for an incoming President. As Loomis suggests, "The very fragmentation of the Congress allows ambitious politicians to strive, almost continually, for one new position or another. Like building enterprises or seeking publicity, moving up, even incrementally, offers politicians the sense that they are accomplishing something, in the absence of more concrete evidence. Again, the entrepreneurial style often invites talented politicians to turn away from substantive accomplishment in pursuit of more accessible goals" (p. 232).

The impact of these new entrepreneurs is clear in the congressional staff agencies, too. At GAO (the General Accounting Office), for example, where 5,000 auditors, evaluators, and policy analysts work on issues of natural resources, accounting and financial management, defense and national security, program evaluation, human services, and general government, over 85 percent of today's work is done under requests from committees and individual members of Congress, up from roughly 35 percent two decades ago.

More important perhaps, Congress has been infected by the same turnover crisis that now debilitates the executive branch, albeit not among its members but its staffs. Although congressional scholars have yet to tackle the issue of staff turnover, it is clear that the 1980s witnessed a wave of retirements and a general decline in the age and experience of senior legislative staff, particularly in the Senate where the natural "greening" of the staff was accelerated by two party changes, from Democrat to Republican in 1980 and Republican to Democrat in 1986.

Now to the executive branch. Again, Presidents face two kinds of problems in building a long-term policy agenda. First, basic changes in the presidential appointments process have made it increasingly difficult both to recruit and to retain top level political staff, which, in turn, limits the President's access to long-term perspectives in the senior civil service just below.

While there are numerous differences over the past five presidential transitions, each President-elect has been later than his predecessor on major appointments and policy proposals, with George Bush setting all time records for tardiness in the appointment of both Cabinet and sub-Cabinet officials. Kennedy took just over two months on average to fill his top positions in 1960–61, Nixon took roughly three-and-a-half in 1968–69, Carter four-and-a-half, Reagan a bit over five in 1980–81, and Bush eight months plus (see MacKenzie, 1990, pp. 30–35).

Although Bush suffered in part because of the "exhaustion" of his potential recruiting base after eight years of Republican control of the Presidency, the 1978 Ethics in Government Act deserves some of the blame for bringing a new layer of review and paperwork to an already burdensome process. As G. Calvin Mackenzie concludes,

> The more rigorous financial disclosure and conflict of interest requirements of the past decade are an important new hurdle in the recruiting process. They are confusing, frightening, and often costly. They raise a widespread specter of public embarrassment and give pause to people who might otherwise willingly endure financial and personal sacrifices to serve their country. No one familiar with the presidential appointments process could possibly argue that the laws have no effect on recruiting (1987, p. 88).

Not only are presidential appointees arriving in place later and later in the term, they are staying for a shorter and shorter time in their original job. The incentive for presidential appointees, whose average *time-in-position* has declined over the past three decades to an average of twenty-two months in Reagan's first term, is clear: make a quick hit and get out.

Given an explosion in the number of jobs now subject to presidential appointment—up from 71 Cabinet jobs under Franklin Roosevelt to 290 in 1985; up from several hundred sub-Cabinet and noncareer senior civil service slots under Roosevelt to 2,500 in 1985—the greater challenge for Presidents lies in merely reducing the number of vacancies in a department or agency, keeping the lines of communication open both upward and downward. As I have argued elsewhere, "The political-career nexus can be easily severed by simply leaving the bottom band of appointments unfilled. Whether the strategy is deliberate or simply the product of the sheer number of positions to be filled, the result is a lack of leadership" (1987, p. 163). And, I might now add, a loss of access to long-term policy support.

The second problem in the executive branch involves the general decline in policy input from the senior civil service, and a further estrangement from the long-range perspective it provides. During the fifteen years between Nixon's second term and the end of Reagan's first, according to Joel Aberbach and Bert Rockman, senior civil servants and congressional party leaders alike saw themselves as having lost influence over policy, perhaps because the connections between civil servants and their traditional allies on Capitol Hill and in the interest groups no longer exist. Noting that "the *supply* of analysis *in* government depends on cultural and structural factors that value and sustain analytic input," Aberbach and Rockman also suggest that the kinds of problems facing the nation may crowd out the very analysis needed to develop effective solutions (1989, p. 299).

More to the point of this chapter, even as senior civil servants reported less effectiveness in finding alternative avenues, or "end runs," for their policy views (largely because of tighter White House surveillance), Cabinet secretaries reported a net gain in their influence despite the turnover problems discussed above. This substitution of influence from a relatively stable set of actors—civil servants and party leaders—for influence from relatively unstable players—Cabinet secretaries—suggests the erosion of another of the traditional buffers against short-term policy.

Further thinning of the civil service buffer is also suggested by declining morale among career civil servants. Not only is there a widespread sense of demoralization and a sense of drift, the failure of federal pay to keep pace with private sector compensation has produced a palpable frustration at the highest levels of government. As the National Commission on the Public Service (Volcker Commission) reports, "The resulting erosion in the quality of America's public service is difficult to measure; there are still many examples of excellence among those who carry out the nation's business at home and abroad. Nevertheless, it is evident that public service is neither as attractive as it once was nor as effective in meeting perceived needs" (1989, p. 2).

The Disinvestment in Planning. The weakening of the President's traditional sources of policy ideas is further exacerbated by the general disinvestment in analysis and planning across the federal government. According to Walter Williams,

> Ronald Reagan launched an eight-year war on policy information and analysis and more broadly on the institutional capacity of the executive branch; he won. The most ideological president in memory, certain of the rightness of his policies without needing facts and figures, became the first modern anti-analytic president. His unconcern with or distaste for expert policy information, analysis and advice led to the destruction of much of the institutional analytic capacity built up in the executive branch in the postwar period as Reagan cut deeply into the personnel, budgets, and influence of analytic and evaluation units (1990, p. x).

A decade of personnel cuts has left offices of program evaluation with limited resources to participate in long-range policy development, while the evisceration of government data bases under the Reagan administration has left future evaluators and analysts without many of the tools to ply their trade. Thus, according to Aberbach and Rockman, the Reagan Revolution had an inevitable impact on analysis:

> Two decades ago, at least in the U.S., policy analysis could be viewed as a means for energizing comprehensive change as a way of breaking through structures that resisted nonincremental change. The irony is that the powerful ideas of the present political leadership, arguably, have induced nonincremental change. The results, further, have induced *crashing the boards* strategies for dealing with the perceived, but politically sensitive, budgetary crisis left as the residue. That appears, for the time being at least, to have pushed policy analysis into the background as decision makers struggle with the new politics of deadlines and limits (1989, pp. 299–300).

This is not the book to tell the story of the decline in the federal government's evaluation capacity. Suffice it to say that both the number and scope of studies has changed dramatically. According to the General Accounting Office, resources for program evaluation declined from 1980 to 1984, with reductions in total full-time personnel and budget. Not only were the *number* of evaluation units reduced in government, the *kind* of evaluations produced in those units narrowed significantly. "In general, low-cost, short-turn-around, internal studies and non-technical reports—usually initiated at the request of top agency officials or program managers—increased in number and as a proportion of all studies"; GAO concluded, "larger, longer, externally conducted studies and more technical reports showed the opposite trend" (1987, p. 2).

In 1980, for example, 180 units in government engaged in some form of program evaluation; by 1984, the number was down to 133. During the same period, fiscal resources were cut by 37 percent (in constant 1980 dollars), even as total agency budgets increased 4 percent overall. Thus, even though the Department of Health and Human Services still maintained an Office of Planning and Evaluation, the number of staff had been cut from 300-plus to 150. As GAO speculated at the time, the resulting reduction in "product" quality across government was unmistakable:

> Short, low-cost, non-technical studies cannot typically present strong information on program results. Therefore, since technically adequate, well-disseminated evaluations informing on program results are likely to require relatively large investments of funding and staff resources, that information is likely to be much reduced in the future. The evidence from this report suggests that findings from both large and small studies have become less easily available for use by the Congress and the public (p. 4).

As suspected, these trends did not abate in Reagan's second term, leading GAO to express its concern to the next President in a specially prepared transition briefing document: "With few exceptions, we have found that both program evaluation and data collection capabilities have been gravely eroded in the executive branch" (1988, p. 1). Unfortunately, by the time the report was released, more units had disappeared. In the new Department of Veterans Affairs, for example, the Office of Program Planning and Evaluation had been swallowed whole by the new Assistant Secretary for Veterans Liaison, hardly the place where one would expect a focus on independent and objective research.

More important perhaps, the disinvestment in data collection continued unabated in Reagan's second term, signaling lasting damage to program evaluation. Without the basic information to evaluate programs, government is effectively blinded to the future, thereby stopping efforts to prevent problems and focusing policy analysts and presidential appointees on what they can see best, the short-term. By curtailing information *collection,* Presidents are denied the results of information *analysis.*

One lever for many of these delays and cutbacks was the 1980 Paperwork Reduction Act, which empowered the Office of Management and Budget to establish a clearance process for every information collection request. In one celebrated example, OMB used the act to delay a series of studies at the Centers for Disease Control, leading the authors of a House report to conclude that "OMB has delayed, impeded, and thwarted governmental research efforts designed to answer public demands for information on serious public health questions" (U.S. House of Representatives, 1986, p. 3).

Whatever one thinks of the Paperwork Reduction Act and its use in delaying past environmental and health studies, its significance to the presidential policy process cannot be minimized. Designed to increase the President's control over information, the act has had the unintended effect of reducing presidential access to research data across government, research which might fuel a long-term policy agenda. Again, GAO provides the documentation. According to a detailed study of the paperwork review process, "We found that some agencies have stopped collecting some data because of difficulties in the clearance process. For these agencies, OMB's review has had a chilling effect on the likely availability of data. This effect has been pronounced for new collections and for research-oriented collections" (1989, p. 64).

The Prospects for Implementation

Even facing the culture of impatience and the limited sources of long-term ideas, the President's entrepreneurs might still pursue a long-term policy but for the declining prospects for successful implementation.

Assume for a moment that Presidents and their staffs are quasi-rational beings. They survey the world around them, assess the rewards for short-term policy, the costs of developing long-term alternatives, the likely impacts on public approval and their place in history, and act accordingly. One part of this calculation would involve some estimate of the likelihood of success in Congress, where they would face much greater odds against large-scale, long-term proposals. Another part would involve an estimate of the likelihood of successful *and* timely implementation of their ideas.

Simply put, Presidents rarely invest in ideas with no chance of either legislative passage or executive implementation. This said, it seems clear to me that the prospects for success have declined. As noted above, there is more competition for scarce agenda space in Congress, more crowding out by budgetary politics, and less interest in long-term issues among the legislative entrepreneurs. There is also more risk on the road to final passage as more members show their willingness to "do it on the floor," as Steven Smith puts it (1989). The bottom line for Presidents is increased institutional volatility.

More to the point of the following discussion, even if Presidents saw a reasonable probability of legislative passage, the escalating appointee turnover and vacancies severely limit the prospects for successful implementation. Moreover, not only has there been an expansion in monitoring capacity within the executive branch almost as a substitute for implementation, there has been a decade long disinvestment in program management resources, both of which further undermine the implementation odds. By its very nature, of course, long-term policy demands the greatest level of confidence in executive branch implementation, for the yield may not come until years after the President has left.

The New Monitors. Few trends in public management have been more pronounced than the decade-long shift toward a new monitoring philosophy in executive administration, a philosophy which focuses on the twin goals of increased accountability and political risk management.

Spurred by the Housing and Urban Development fiasco, the trillion-dollar savings and loan crisis, and emerging problems in the Pension Benefit Guaranty Corporation, never before have Congress and the President invested so much in the executive branch's capacity to monitor and police itself. Among the statutes enacted since 1978 to combat general fraud, waste, and abuse are the Inspector General Act of 1978, the General Accounting Office Act of 1980, the Paperwork Reduction Act of 1980, the Federal Managers Financial Integrity Act of 1982, and the Program Fraud and Civil Remedies Act of 1984.

As a result, the new vocabulary of implementation in Washington is filled with words like "vulnerability assessments," "internal controls," "performance auditing," and "financial integrity." Despite a lack of money and staff to fully apply the statutes, and a persistent reluctance to invest in a new accounting system to replace the four hundred or so antiquated, uncoordinated systems across government, there can be little doubt that the new monitoring philosophy has affected the way departments and agencies view implementation.

Much as Congress and the President, indeed many in the Washington community of auditors and overseers, see this assortment of statutes as a spur to greater accountability, one unintended result has been a new fear among program implementors regarding the short-term risks of a "gotcha" audit. Because much of the monitoring capacity involves highly visible, independent audits and investigations by Congress, the Inspectors General, or GAO, program managers have become increasingly risk averse as their departments and agencies have added new layers of review to an already time-consuming implementation process. Presidents who assess the prospects for successful implementation of long-term programs must take this growing timidity into account.

More important, many of the resources, limited as they are, for enforcing these monitoring statutes have been drawn from program and management offices alike. Simply put, the rise of the new monitors in government may have actually increased the likelihood that they will find the very fraud, waste, and abuse they have been tasked to find.

Not all of the new monitoring has come from legislative statutes like the Inspector General Act of 1978, the Ethics in Government Act of 1978, or the Paperwork Reduction Act of 1980. Some was initiated by the President and OMB. Under Executive Orders 12291 and 12498, Reagan created a cradle-to-grave regulatory agenda-setting process, which requires clearance of every agency initiative that *might* eventually lead to a rule-making process. This controversial review system centralized White House control of administrative discretion to a degree not thought possible when then-President Ford inaugurated the first effort to keep track of major rules.

Some of this oversight is clearly warranted by duplication across agencies and cost. However, even the most ardent supporter of regulatory review acknowledges the continuing problems of delay, whether in complying with OMB's extensive internal paperwork (an ironic byproduct of the effort to reduce external paperwork) or the negotiations often necessitated to achieve permission to proceed.

One result of the increasing delay has been a growing tendency of Congress and the courts to set deadlines for agency action, which, in turn, often leads to what legal scholar Harold Bruff calls a game of administrative chicken: "Agencies have the formal responsibility to meet deadlines and are therefore vulnerable to threats of delay. At the same time, agencies can withhold their own submissions to [OMB] until a deadline nears, and press for immediate review. Indeed, if an agency is tardy enough, it may escape review entirely" (1989, p. 568). This battle over who controls agency discretion may well be the single most important issue facing Presidency scholars today, for it counterposes the President's need to exercise greater control over executive branch agenda-setting with the agencies' need for greater flexibility to assure implementation.

Like the wave of accountability statutes outlined above, this new regulatory monitoring carries a cost in delay even for the President's own programs. Implementation of Reagan's Job Training Partnership Act, for example, was slowed by the review process as the Department of Labor struggled to establish a legislatively mandated evaluation plan that did not violate OMB's interpretation of the Paperwork Reduction Act. This may be as close to a curious inversion as Presidency scholars can get these days: a review process likely established to prevent agencies from moving too quickly on environmental and health policy stands in the way of implementing one of the President's few domestic policy achievements.

The Disinvestment in Management. Alongside the rise in monitoring, the past decade also witnessed a general disinvestment in government's ability to manage programs once they are started. This disinvestment affects the President's agenda in two basic ways.

First, government becomes more vulnerable to the kinds of crises that drive short-term policy. According to Comptroller General Charles Bowsher, for example, the failure to invest in better regulatory systems and personnel training led to the savings and loan disaster, while antiquated computers and recruitment problems at the Internal Revenue Service annually account for $100 billion in lost revenue.

Second, disinvestment weakens confidence among policy entrepreneurs that long-term policy can be successful. Again consider the personnel and funding demands of the monitoring units themselves. Net reductions in personnel offices, for example, merely increase the delays programs face in filling vacancies. Net reductions in procurement offices merely increase the time needed to let contracts. The loss of two or three full-time slots due to "agency absorption"—the term used to describe the across-the-board reductions required by the start-up costs of new programs or unspecified budget cuts—even in huge agencies like the Department of Veterans Affairs can mean a significant backlog in operating assistance.

The cutbacks in managerial capacity are well illustrated at OMB, where the management side of the agency has withered over time. According to

Ronald Moe, the number of staff lines devoted to management have declined from 224 in 1970 to 111 in 1980 to 47 in 1988. As Moe concludes,

> The staff of the management side of the old BOB [Bureau of the Budget] had once been an elite corps of civil service generalists committed to protecting the institutional interests of the President and increasing the capacity of agency management to perform its missions. As the 1970s progressed, however, the staff withered, management functions were transferred to budget analysts, and organizational issues gradually ceased to be considered relevant to the management portfolio. During the 1980s, OMB systematically subordinated its remaining budgetary and financial systems priorities (1990, p. 134).

Some of the old management positions were simply retrenched permanently; others were converted into slots on the budget side of OMB. Regardless of the disposition, the weakened management capacity illustrates the broad theme of this paper: Presidents may be wise to invest in short-term policy, not only because of electoral pressures and a dwindling supply of long-term proposals, but because of the declining probability that any long-term policy can be successfully implemented, whether in its first year or its tenth.

The No Win Presidency at Plus Ten Years

In the final analysis, much as Presidents might hope otherwise, the No Win Presidency still exists. However, on top of the weakened parties, the interest group fragmentation, the growing policy complexity, and the increased surveillance, this chapter has cataloged a set of new pressures that make winning the No Win Presidency even more difficult. Perhaps Bush was right to ignore, or at the very least submerge, the domestic agenda his first two years. It is not clear that he had the internal resources to develop one had he wanted to.

What is still unclear is whether there is some need for drastic reform of the kind Lloyd Cutler and his Committee for a Constitutional System advocate. For now, I suspect that such a long-term proposal would have little chance in the short-term world of contemporary presidential-congressional relations. Presidents are still wise, of course, to do the advance planning, hiring of expertise, and priority-setting recommended in chapter nine, just as the American public will be wise to select Presidents with substantial Washington experience.

Whether future Presidents ought to follow Reagan's example and go short in the first year is less clear. If it was a place in history that Reagan wanted, he earned it through a legacy of continuing deficits and what Walter Williams calls the anti-analytic Presidency. In winning his war against the traditional sources of ideas, Reagan may have ensured that his successors will have little choice but to go short-term, too. It is hardly the shining achievement he must have wanted.

12 the derivative presidency

The 1990s have not been particularly kind to the President's agenda. Already predisposed by career to favor foreign policy and hemmed in by his "no new taxes" pledge, George Bush barely had a domestic agenda at all, and Clinton's first-term agenda was only briefly more ambitious. Easily characterized as a hodgepodge of unconnected ideas of mostly incremental intent, it was so widely belittled that it eventually prompted a two-part *New York Times* story titled "How a Presidency Was Defined by the Thousand Parts of Its Sum."

This is not to suggest that neither President ever thought big. But even acknowledging the occasional nonincremental proposal in each administration, including the North American Free Trade Agreement under Bush and national health care and federal welfare reform under Clinton, the 1990s hardly confirm the President's agenda as a central instrument of national policy making.

On the contrary, the President's agenda appears to be shrinking, increasingly dismissed as merely one of many inputs in structuring the national debate. It is as if the President's agenda of the 1960s has been exposed to some invisible force, irradiated, so to speak, by a political process that somehow altered its basic genetic structure as an action-creating device. Like the hero of the science fiction classic *The Incredible Shrinking Man*, the President may be slowly fading from sight as a significant force in setting the legislative agenda. Although Presidents can still engage in heroic battles with the spiders of public policy, there is only so much they can do with stick pins and paper clips.

Some political scientists argue that this shrinking is appropriate. They rightly caution that America has expected too much from the President's agenda and that scholars have placed too much emphasis on the President's role in directing legislative traffic. No one has made this cautionary case more effectively than Charles O. Jones. "Focusing exclusively on the presidency

277

can lead to a seriously distorted picture of how the national government does its work," he writes in his award-winning *The Presidency in a Separated System.* "The plain fact is that the United States does not have a presidential system. It has a *separated* system" (1994, p. 2). For Jones, the President's role in setting the domestic agenda varies with each occupant's resources, advantages, and strategic position. Some Presidents will enter office with more opportunity, some with less, but all will be bound by the checks and balances established by the Founders. To expect the President's agenda to remain dominant year in and year out is to ignore the normal ebb and flow of power built into the very fiber of the office.

Jones is not the only political scientist to argue for perspective, however. He has been joined by a host of colleagues, from presidential historians such as Stephen Skowronek (1993) to rational choice researchers such as Jon Bond and Richard Fleisher (1990) and sophisticated number crunchers such as George Edwards and B. Dan Wood. Edwards and Wood argue, for example, that Presidents mostly operate in a "reactive mode," setting their agendas in response to earlier signaling by the media and world events. "This is to be expected," the two researchers conclude, "because presidents have limited institutional resources and do not desire to be influential on all issues. As risk averse actors, however, they are ever watchful and respond when other institutions deem an issue worthy of greater consideration" (1996, p. 26).

None of these scholars suggests that the President's agenda is irrelevant, of course. Bond and Fleisher conclude, for example, that "the president's greatest influence over policy comes from the agenda he pursues and the way it is packaged" (p. 230), while Jones certainly notes the President's significant voice in setting the agenda, albeit one of many voices (p. 181). Moreover, regardless of how an idea reaches the President's agenda, there is no question that the agenda matters. As Edwards and Andrew Barrett argue after completing their exhaustive analysis of 268 presidential proposals covering a forty-year period from 1951 to 1992, "the president is very successful in obtaining agenda space for his potentially significant legislative proposals. . . . Once on the agenda, 40 percent of presidential initiatives become law, nearly twice the rate of congressional initiatives" (1998, p. 19).

Rather, the recent trend in presidential scholarship is toward a more balanced approach that views the President's agenda as part of a larger policy-making puzzle in which Congress, the media, interest groups, and the courts all struggle to gain the dominant hand in deciding which issues get resolved and which linger on. Reaching the President's agenda is a large step toward winning eventual legislative passage, but is hardly the last or only step to success.

The President's agenda still exists, of course. As we shall shortly see, Bush averaged five proposals a year in his one term, while Clinton averaged just over eight in his first term. And the President's agenda clearly still influences the national debate, with North American Free Trade Agreement

(NAFTA), education reform, family medical leave, national service, and managed care obvious examples. Nevertheless, as we shall also shortly see, there has been a steady erosion of bold, new ideas on the President's agenda. Looking back over the eight Presidents since Eisenhower, Bush set a modern record in the proportion of old ideas on his agenda, followed closely by Clinton. Bush also set a modern record in the proportion of small ideas on his agenda.

Before turning to this "derivative" Presidency in more detail, it is important to update this book's earlier findings on the cycles and rules that shape the President's agenda. In a sentence, the President's agenda is still buffeted by the same pressures and still governed by the same rules that affected the agenda from 1960 to 1989. If anything, the pressures are more pronounced and the rules more inviolable today than they were when this book went to press in 1980. Presidents have never been under greater pressure to move it or lose it, yet they have never been more vulnerable to making the mistakes that come with inexperience. Facing an ever more impatient public and shorter news cycles, Presidents continue to believe they have no time to waste and that they simply cannot afford to learn. They must set their agendas early and repeat them often if they are to have much of a chance for impact, or at least that is what they believe.

Unfortunately, there is no evidence that Presidents are entering office any more prepared for the work they must do. Locked in a tight three-way contest with an incumbent President and third-party rebel Ross Perot, candidate Clinton invested little time or energy preparing to become President Clinton. He had no preelection transition planning operation and wasted much of his three-month transition on a frustrating Cabinet search (see Jones, 1998, for an analysis of the presidential transitions as governing events). As Elizabeth Drew concluded, Clinton "hit the ground standing" (1994, p. 3).

Setting the Agenda in the Post-Reagan Era

There is no question that Bill Clinton heard the clock ticking as he set his agenda in the first days of his first term. He started off with a flurry of initiatives, revealing a tendency to overload the agenda that would haunt the administration throughout the first four years. He also made a number of mistakes attributable to his naivete as a Washington outsider. He quickly became embroiled, for example, in a controversy surrounding gays in the military and earned an early reputation for indecisiveness as he struggled to appoint a diverse Cabinet. He also demonstrated an enormous tolerance for endless debate, which heightened the sense that the administration was losing time. Only weeks into his Presidency, Clinton's staff was complaining of burnout (see Drew, 1994).

Whatever Clinton's personal style, his agenda was shaped by the two countervailing cycles identified early in this book. Just as it had done to

Presidents from Kennedy to Reagan, the cycle of decreasing influence continued to exert its force in constraining the Bush and Clinton agendas, most evident in the erosion of party seats in mid-term elections. Republicans lost nine seats in the House and one in the Senate in the 1990 off-year elections, further strengthening an already impressive Democratic majority in the House, while Democrats lost a whopping fifty-two seats in the House and nine in the Senate in the 1994 election, giving Republicans their first two-house majority in four decades. Although Presidents and Congress can still govern when divided by party (see Mayhew, 1991, for the proof), the predictable loss of party seats in the Bush and Clinton first terms merely amplified the pressure to move quickly.

Although party seats remain the gold standard of a President's political capital, the Bush/Clinton years suggest that public approval may be increasingly irrelevant to agenda influence. Twenty years ago, the trends in public approval seemed mostly immutable. Presidents started their terms at the peak of their approval and slid steadily downward. But for an occasional bump due to a foreign policy crisis, approval seemed to be governed by a coalition-of-minorities phenomenon. Each decision angered some small number of presidential enthusiasts, slowly eroding approval in each successive poll.

Having held for every President since 1960, the trend changed direction under both Bush and Clinton. Bush had the roughest ride. His approval ratings started out at barely 50 percent, rose steadily for the next two years to the 70 percent range, fell twenty points in the wake of the 1990 mid-term elections, rose again to unprecedented heights after the Gulf War, and fell again by nearly fifty points as the economy slowed prior to the 1992 election. His approval was so volatile that it is not clear how he could have harnessed it as a source of legislative advantage, nor is it clear how such instability could have helped the President convince Congress of either the inevitability of his success or the rightness of his cause.

Clinton's ratings followed a more orderly course, but again in the opposite direction from previous Presidents. Having won the Presidency by a plurality of just 43 percent, his approval started out in the mid 50 percent range, fell by roughly twenty points, then began a slow but steady saw-tooth rise back into the mid 50 percent range by 1996. His approval continued upward through 1997 and early 1998, rising even despite allegations regarding his relationship with White House intern Monica Lewinsky. By February 1998, Clinton's approval stood at 71 percent, a gain of nine points over a single month. According to a panel survey by The Pew Research Center for the People & The Press, one fifth of the President's new supporters were drawn to his side by his State of the Union address and another sixth by his ability to do his job despite the sex scandal. Among all respondents, roughly half said they did not like the President personally, but 70 percent liked his policies (Pew Research Center, 1998a, p. 1).

If Bush's roller coaster ratings reflected a mix of good luck (the Gulf War) and bad timing (a mild economic slowdown), Clinton's steady rise reflected an unrelenting effort to cultivate public sympathy. "The Clinton administration is the ultimate example of the public presidency," writes Edwards, "one based on a perpetual campaign to obtain the support of the American people and fed by public opinion polls, focus groups, and public relations memos. Within the White House the political consultants who ran Clinton's presidential campaign have had a presence and influence that has not been seen before" (1996, p. 234; see also Lawrence Jacobs and Robert Shapiro, 1994).

Although Clinton was hardly the first President to "go public," as Samuel Kernell (1993) calls the strategy, he easily eclipsed his predecessors in the intensity of his efforts. No President has ever spent more time, energy, and dollars seeking to understand and influence public opinion. He simply never stopped campaigning, launching a massive media campaign almost a year before he actually announced his bid for reelection. Although the campaign fundraising needed for the effort eventually created its own scandal, Clinton's high public approval appeared to insulate him from the Senate investigation. Americans became convinced that "everybody does it," "it" being questionable fundraising practices, and seemed ever ready to give the popular President the benefit of the doubt.

The question is not whether Clinton was able to raise his approval ratings through sheer will alone. Absent a strong economy and growing public optimism about the future (see Pew Research Center, 1998b), no amount of going public would likely have made an impact. The economy made the 1997 budget and tax agreement possible, which in turn allowed Clinton to claim credit for having finally balanced the budget. Rather, the question is whether that approval translated into the kind of political capital that enhances legislative success.

Here, the answer is more problematic. Clinton's highly popular 1998 State of the Union message, which clearly lifted his approval rating, was pronounced dead on arrival by the Republican Congress. The White House sex scandal may not have mattered to the American public, but it most certainly mattered to a Republican Congress.

It is entirely possible, of course, that going public cheapens the public approval it creates. Approval created through constant campaigning may not equal approval earned through presidential performance. "Popularity is like ice cream," suggests Kernell, "in that the more of it one consumes, the less satisfying the next helping will be. Beyond some point, the value of additional increments of support will diminish sharply" (p. 201). Although Kernell rightly argues that the point of diminishing returns will vary with a President's leadership style and transient political circumstances, the point of diminishing returns is also tightly linked to party support on Capitol Hill. Party seats remain the gold standard for presidential agenda-setting. Short-term gains in presidential approval can make the influence of those seats more liquid perhaps, but it cannot convert a Republican seat into a Democratic seat unless that approval creates coattails in the next election.

The impact of party seats is apparent in two ways. First, unified government increases the odds that the President's agenda will dominate the legislative agenda. To paraphrase Edwards and Barrett, when Presidents belong to the majority party in Congress, their fellow partisans are more willing to defer to them in both setting the congressional agenda and coming to consensus on shared ideas. Second, unified government increases the odds that the President's initiatives will actually pass. When the President and Congress are from the same party, according to Edwards and Barrett's data, 52 percent of the President's initiatives and only 16 percent of congressional initiatives become law. When the President and Congress are from different parties, the numbers even out, 27 percent for the President and 25 percent for Congress. In this regard, Clinton's downfall came in the 1994 mid-term election when Democrats squandered their majority.

If the cycle of decreasing influence still holds roughly where it was marked in the first edition of this book, the cycle of increasing effectiveness has gotten more pronounced. Presidents may not have more to learn per se, but they have much more difficulty finding and appointing their fellow students. Much of the problem resides in the presidential appointments process, in which the number of jobs and increasing scrutiny have combined to generate staggering delays in filling the top jobs. Never have there been so many jobs to fill in such short a time under such close inspection. G. Calvin Mackenzie summarizes the difficulty with cold precision:

> The number of PAS (presidential appointment requiring Senate confirmation) positions continues to grow. Because of the complex responsibilities that fall on the holders of those positions, recruiters must find appointees with special expertise and experience. The principal components of the appointments process — ethics and personal background checks, FBI investigations, and Senate confirmation — are elaborate and time-consuming. The low esteem of public service, the lack of funds for bold new programs, and persistent low government salaries deter many talented people from accepting or even considering a presidential appointment. Aggressive senators and jugular-seeking reporters and columnists terrify others (1996, p. 67).

It is no surprise that delays have increased with each passing administration. In 1961, for example, Kennedy's first full slate of appointees was confirmed by the Senate and sworn into office just two months after inauguration. Eight years later, Nixon's first full slate was in office three and a half months after inauguration. Eight years later still, Carter's first full slate was in office five months after inauguration. All respectable numbers, perhaps. But by 1989, Bush's first full slate was in office eight months after inauguration. And four years later, Clinton's first full slate was in office eight and a half months later. Given that a presidential term lasts just forty-eight months, forty-five of which occur before the next election when the President can still act with confidence, the loss of nearly one-fifth of an administration to delays in the appointments process is no small tax on the agenda-setting process. The Clinton delays were particularly troublesome given the party in power. Unlike Bush, who was able to carry Reagan holdovers comfortably into his new term, Clinton inherited the Presidency after twelve years of Republican rule. Perhaps more than any President covered by this book, Clinton needed to get his people into office quickly.

That he failed reflected a mixture of organizational confusion and Clinton's campaign promise to have a Cabinet that looked like a cross-section of America. Having made no effort to inventory the top jobs and start collecting resumes during the campaign, Clinton started from scratch in November. Stumbling immediately with the nomination of several candidates who had failed to pay Social Security taxes for their household help, the Clinton personnel process became a nightmare of endless cross-checking. According to Mackenzie, Janet Reno's nomination as Attorney General involved more than two hundred phone calls, not including the traditional FBI field investigation. Once burned on the proposed nominations of Zoe Baird and Kimba Wood, twice shy became a rallying cry as the personnel team searched for anything that might embarrass the President.

Clinton was not the only President to encounter appointments problems, of course. Bush lost precious days early by fighting for the appointment of Texas senator John Tower as his secretary of defense. Nevertheless, Clinton seemed to have more problems as new standards emerged in his search for a diverse Cabinet. The question of whether a nominee had paid Social Security taxes for nannies and maids had never been a concern before 1993, but it quickly emerged as Clinton nominated several high profile women for the Cabinet. As Clinton later remarked in an interview with CNN's Larry King, "That had never been an issue before. And all of a sudden it was a big issue and the press was pillorying people that had the problem, and it was a problem. And so we had to get that worked out. I don't think it will ever happen again now because now there are fairly clear rules." Presumably, potential candidates for senior posts also took note of the travail and began following the law.

These organizational problems were complicated by the sheer number of positions to be filled. Presidents have never had more helpers in government. By 1992, there were roughly 3,000 political positions open for occupancy in the federal hierarchy, including 1,000 appointees subject to Senate confirmation, another 600 noncareer positions in the Senior Executive Service, and 1,500 personal and confidential assistants under Schedule C of the federal personnel code. Just identifying the top jobs is no small task, let alone finding qualified individuals ready to sacrifice all semblance of privacy to compete for the post.

Adding to the parallel growth at the senior and middle levels of the career civil service, this "thickening" of the federal hierarchy not only complicates the presidential appointments process, but undermines the flow of information up and down the chain of command. At the very top of the federal hierarchy, the number of senior executives, political and career, grew form roughly 450 in 1960 to nearly 2,400 by 1997. Where there were ten department secretaries in 1960, there were fourteen by 1997; where there were fifteen under secretaries in 1960, there were forty-one in 1997; where there were eighty-seven assistant secretaries, there were 212 in 1997.

The problem with the thickening of government is not just in the absolute number of political and career executives. It is also in how those numbers sort into layer upon layer of management interposed between the President and the front lines of government. Where there were just seventeen layers of senior managers, political and career, at the very top of the federal hierarchy in 1960, there were forty-nine layers of senior managers in government at the start of 1997. These included a vast assortment of new titles in between the department secretaries, deputy secretaries, under secretaries, assistant secretaries, and administrators. Where no department had had a chief of staff to the secretary in 1960, thirteen out of fourteen had them by 1997; where no department had had an associate deputy secretary in 1960, eight had them by 1997; and where no department had had a deputy assistant assistant secretary in 1960, thirteen had them by 1997.

The thickening is not restricted to the Cabinet departments and federal agencies, however. The White House staff became taller and wider, too. In 1960, the White House staff consisted of one chief of staff, one principal deputy assistant to the President, six deputy assistants to the President, twenty special assistants, and one deputy special assistant. In 1997, it was comprised of one chief of staff, two deputy chiefs of staff, eighteen assistants to the President, thirty-two deputy assistants to the President, nineteen special assistants, and thirty-four deputy, associate, and assistant special assistants. Similar thickening occurred in the Office of Management and Budget, which grew from just three layers (director, deputy director, and assistant director) to eight (director, principal deputy director, deputy director for management, executive associate directors, associate directors, deputy associate directors, assistant directors, and deputy assistant directors) by 1993. The Office of the Vice President, which did not even exist in 1960, eventually grew to include the requisite shadow staff (chief of staff, deputy chief of staff, assistants to the Vice President, deputy assistants to the Vice President, special assistants, and deputy/associate/assistant special assistants of one kind and another).

What does this thickening do to the cycle of increasing effectiveness? In theory, more helpers should produce more information and access, which in turn should accelerate learning. In reality, I believe just the opposite occurs. Information must travel through more channels before reaching the President and senior staff, thereby delaying and possibly distorting the learning that would have otherwise occurred. No matter how loose the organizational culture, and the Clinton culture was as loose and pliable as any administration in modern times, information still gets misconstrued by hierarchy. Having essential information six layers down in the Department of Justice instead of three means it must travel further and suffer more distortion to reach its destination.

Moreover, high turnover rates among the President's top appointees, who now average just eighteen months in office before moving up or out, creates the very real possibility that there are multiple learning curves in an administration, each one starting anew. In contrast to my original conceptualization of the cycle, which imagined an administration getting smarter and more effective over time, it may be that an administration gets more effective, suffers inevitable turnover of talented staffers, and starts learning all over.

The only stable fixtures in such a volatile cycle would be the President, the Vice President, and their spouses. Although promoting staff from within as vacancies occur would certainly ease the effectiveness deficit, the learning opportunities that occur early in an administration are arguably more intense and telling, meaning that senior appointees who learn how Washington works in the early moments of an administration may be virtually irreplaceable no matter how talented their lieutenants may be. Such concerns clearly motivated Clinton to ask his old campaign consultants and first-term confidants, James Carville and Paul Begala, to return to the White House in the wake of the 1998 intern scandal. The one person who had not learned the right lessons during the first term, apparently, was the President himself.

The Derivative Presidency

The cycles of decreasing influence and increasing effectiveness clearly made their mark on the Bush and Clinton agendas. Although each faced a somewhat different constellation of resources and opportunities, they were both sharply constrained by the political realities. As table 31 shows, the Bush and Clinton agendas followed familiar patterns established by their predecessors.

Consider Bush first. Facing a Democratic Congress and staggering budget deficits created in large part from the 1981 Reagan/Bush tax cuts and subsequent defense build-up, Bush offered a modest agenda of mostly small-scale proposals. In absolute numbers, Bush offered just as many first-year proposals as Reagan had. But, as we shall shortly see, once past the raw totals, Bush was a much more modest agenda-setter.

His first cut at deficit reduction was hardly Reaganesque, for example. Speaking before a joint session of Congress only two weeks after his inauguration, Bush hit the deficit theme early and often, urging Congress to make a "very substantial cut" in the deficit, while renewing long-standing

Table 31. Requests for Legislation, All Years

President	Year	Total Requests	Total Repeats
Kennedy	1961	25	0
	1962	16	8
	1963	6	12
Johnson I	1964	6	11
Johnson II	1965	34	4
	1966	24	7
	1967	19	8
	1968	14	12
Nixon I	1969	17	0
	1970	12	9
	1971	8	12
	1972	3	14
Nixon II	1973	20	3
	1974	5	11
Ford	1975	10	3
	1976	6	7
Carter	1977	21	0
	1978	8	3
	1979	8	5
	1980	4	7
Reagan I	1981	8	0
	1982	7	1
	1983	11	3
	1984	4	5
Reagan II	1985	0	7
	1986	0	5
	1987	0	5
	1988	0	4
Bush	1989	8	0
	1990	7	5
	1991	6	6
	1992	4	5
Clinton I	1993	17	0
	1994	5	5
	1995	5	5
	1996	6	9

Reagan proposals for a line-item veto and a balanced budget amendment. Alongside a broad call for public school choice, he offered a long list of small spending sweeteners to cultivate public support, including more money for NASA, the National Science Foundation, Medicaid, the war on drugs, and adoption, while repeating his campaign call for a cut in the capital gains tax. Even when packaged together in an omnibus budget package, the Bush budget cuts and spending increases fell well below the threshold of significance to be included in the President's agenda under the coding rules for this book. It was hardly the stuff of which the Reagan-like revolutions are made. Most of the ideas were lost in the turmoil surrounding the forced resignation of Speaker Jim Wright and the campaign to repeal the catastrophic health insurance plan enacted only the year before (see Light, 1995, for a summary of the disastrous debate).

Once past the first year, Bush drifted steadily downward in agenda activity. Although Bush agreed to a $500 billion package of budget cuts and tax increases, thereby violating his "no-new-taxes" promise and sealing his ultimate defeat in the 1992 campaign, his agenda was hardly inspiring. His 1990 State of the Union was a mostly dreary summary of old ideas and modest tweaking of existing programs, including a small spending increase for Head Start and "global change research," a proposal to elevate the Environmental Protection Agency to Cabinet status, and a rapid-fire list of general issues for consideration: clean air, child care, educational excellence, crime, drugs, the farm bill, transportation policy, and urban enterprise zones. It is only by a generous linking of the general to the specific that the Bush second year agenda reached the modest total of seven. Buried in the speech was a single sentence, though, alluding to the need to "bring the staggering costs of health care under control." Although Bush never fully engaged the issue, the growing crisis in costs would eventually produce Clinton's most significant agenda item, national health care.

Nothing in Bush's third and fourth years changed the overall portrait. But for a small proposal to eliminate political action committees, which was mostly offered as an alternative to a comprehensive campaign finance reform moving forward in the Senate, and a very large and controversial endorsement for what he called the Mexican free trade agreement, the Bush agenda remained limited. Although Bush's 1991 State of the Union message did contain the obligatory laundry list of small-scale proposals, the ideas were buried in a speech that focused on the coming war with Iraq. Nothing else seemed to matter at the moment.

Clinton's first year in office could not have been more different from Bush's. Clinton lived for domestic policy innovation, priding himself on his intellectual and physical endurance. Unfortunately for his staff, Clinton was also indecisive. Aides devoted enormous time and energy that went nowhere. Although Clinton was able to pull a fairly significant number of ideas through his tangled first-year process, the staff was clearly being worn down. "Clinton's pace and his appetite for work, his proclivity toward talking long and working late and holding meetings at all hours and on weekends, had a nearly ruinous effect on some aides' lives," writes Elizabeth Drew of Clinton's first year in office. "As early as February, one aide remarked privately, 'I'm not sure how long I can take this.'. . . Harried Presidential aides were typically scheduled to attend wall-to-wall meetings — with the President or otherwise — with little time to think. And then spontaneous meetings would be added. When the President was in the White House, his top aides knew that their schedules were meaningless" (1994, pp. 97–98).

The effect on the agenda is telling. After sending seventeen proposals to Congress in his first year, including an economic stimulus package, a deficit cutting plan, campaign finance reform, and health care, and following a heavy push for NAFTA, Clinton's second year was a grand disappointment. Despite his growing public approval and continued Democratic support, the second year brought just five new proposals. It was the smallest second year agenda of any President in thirty years, smaller even than those of Nixon, Ford, Reagan, or Bush.

Clinton had started his second year hoping for much more. After all, he began his 1994 State of the Union message by celebrating the end of gridlock. Thanking Congress for giving the American public "the most successful teamwork between a President and a Congress in thirty years," Clinton called upon Congress to act on his three top priorities: health care, welfare reform, and crime. Congress not only did not act on the three, the rancorous debate over health care clogged the legislative agenda for months. The indictment of House Ways and Means Chairman Dan Rostenkowski on charges of embezzlement and fraud was no small part of the problem — he stepped aside from his chairmanship just as his powerful committee began marking up the Clinton health care plan.

It is not clear that the Clinton agenda-setting process could have produced more proposals even if there had been clear sailing. Clinton's heavy investment in health care reform, coupled with his personal style and limited political capital, worked against a larger agenda. All totaled, he averaged just eight proposals per year, just slightly above the number during Ford's abbreviated, highly limited term. His agenda looked as if he were in a divided government, a complaint sometimes echoed in the liberal wings of the Democratic party where Clinton was often criticized for being on some issues more Republican than the Republicans.

Like Bush before him, Clinton could do nothing in his third or fourth year to change the portrait, largely because he was now facing divided government in reality. Anticipating a tough reelection fight, Clinton began campaigning early in 1995. He decided early on in the campaign that he would have to run against both parties in Congress, attacking the Republicans for being too harsh and his own Democrats for being too liberal. By "triangulating" against both ends of the ideological spectrum, he won an additional 6.2 percent of the popular vote, rendering him the first President in history to win both terms by plurality votes.

It is when the Bush and Clinton agendas are sorted by the size (large or small) and scope (new or old) of proposals, not the sheer number, that the Clinton program comes into greater focus. Clinton's agenda, while often involving large-scale efforts, was mostly directed toward tinkering with existing programs. It may have included a longer list of proposals, but it mimicked Bush's earlier focus on fine-tuning. Whether their programs were big or small, both Presidents devoted the bulk of their agenda space to modifications of the status quo, not to entirely new departures in national policy. Putting the Bush and Clinton agendas together, one can easily make the case that the President's agenda has become derivative in nature. That imagined bridge to the twenty-first century that candidate Clinton used to such great effect in his reelection campaign appears to have been made mostly of old boards held together by rusty nails.

Weighing the Bush and Clinton Agendas

Before describing the "derivative Presidency" in more detail, it is first important to examine size and scope separately. Recall that size involves a simple judgment about the overall breadth of a given idea. Large ideas generally affect more people, cost more money, and generate more controversy. As such, they create greater disruption in the policy process, demand more attention, and tend to take up more time on the legislative calendar than smaller ideas.

Recall also that scope involves a judgment about the overall impact of a given idea on the status quo. The central question is whether a given proposal reinforces or departs from the prevailing wisdom about how to solve a set of policy problems. New ideas challenge that wisdom by proposing significant departures from the way things are, while old ideas tend to reinforce the prevailing wisdom through slight modifications in one direction or the other around the mean. A proposal to tighten Medicare eligibility or cut the NASA budget, for example, could be defined as new or old depending upon its intention. A significant retrenchment in Medicare or an end to the civilian space program would be considered new programs. But merely trying to get to the moon more efficiently is not necessarily a breach with the prevailing wisdom governing the effort.

Size. As table 32 shows, Bush and Clinton tracked their six predecessors in the relative size of their proposals. The Bush agenda does weigh in as the lightest of any President studied, but the relatively low proportion of large proposals is easily explained by the policy exhaustion that his administration confronted as the budget deficits continued to mount. Having won the Presidency as the heir apparent to the Reagan Revolution, Bush could hardly have been expected to reverse course. Indeed, compared to the final four years of the Reagan administration, during which no proposals of any kind were offered, Bush's agenda seemed like a blast of intensity. Lacking the "going public" skills of Reagan, Bush had little hope of reconstructing the conservative coalition of Republicans and Southern Democrats that had proven essential to the 1981 victories. Nor was his a Presidency to ignite passions.

In a similar vein, Clinton emerges as only slightly less committed to large-scale programs than his Democratic predecessors. Almost half of his proposals can be categorized as large-scale, including national service, family and medical leave, welfare reform, gun control, motor voter registration, and health care. Although his agenda repeated two of the four large proposals on

Table 32. Presidential Requests for Legislation:
Large Programs Versus Small Programs

President	Large Programs		Small Programs		Percentage Large Programs
	Total	Yearly Average	Total	Yearly Average	
Kennedy/Johnson	28	7	25	6	53%
Johnson	50	12	41	10	55
Nixon	23	4	42	7	35
Ford	8	4	8	4	50
Carter	22	6	19	5	54
Reagan	13	2	17	2	43
Bush	4	1	21	5	19
Clinton	16	4	17	4	48

the Bush agenda, NAFTA and deficit reduction, Clinton's program was much broader in scope, driven in part by a long list of congressional proposals-in-waiting such as the Family and Medical Leave Act, which were ready for the picking on inauguration day. The Clinton agenda may have only outnumbered Bush in the total number of proposals by a margin of thirty-three to twenty-six, but it included a much higher proportion of large initiatives.

It is important to note, however, that the bulk of Clinton's large proposals came in the first two years, when he still had a Democratic Congress. Fourteen of the twenty-two items forwarded to Congress in 1993 and 1994 were large, compared to just two of eleven in 1995 and 1996. Once Democrats lost control of Congress, Clinton switched to an incremental approach, reducing the size of his legislative proposals while pursuing his policy goals through executive orders whenever possible. "We developed a process by necessity in the wake of the '94 elections where we had to spend a lot more time focusing on executive action," Clinton's Domestic Policy Council director told the *New York Times* in late 1997. "And I think, you know, we have the drill down now."

That process also involved a long list of small-scale ideas, including calls for mandatory school uniforms, guaranteed hospital overnights for new mothers, cellular telephones for citizen crime-watch patrols, a national registry of sex offenders, safety locks for hand guns, the television V-chip, and a national tutoring initiative. Although few of the ideas ever reached the President's legislative agenda, they did create a sense of activism, albeit activism of limited range. His reputation for small ideas eventually prompted House Minority Leader Richard Gephart to complain in 1997 of leaders who "seem enamored with small ideas that nibble around the edges of big problems."

Notwithstanding this later focus on micro-policy, Clinton's first months produced the same kind of activist agenda one might have expected from any Democratic President who modeled himself on John Kennedy. Clinton's national health care package can be criticized on many counts, not the least of which that it was cumbersome, over-designed, and poorly explained. But it cannot be criticized for being unambitious. The 1,342 page bill had just about everything imaginable: a new federal system for managing health care costs, expanded benefits for millions of Americans, a complicated financing structure, and enough administrative thickening to baffle all but the most sophisticated public administrator.

What may cause some observers to underestimate the size of the agenda is the mix of ideas, for alongside the traditionally Democratic ideas such as his fairly predictable economic stimulus package, Clinton added a number of arguably Republican proposals to craft a first-term agenda that resembled those presented by Kennedy, Johnson, and Carter. At least in terms of size, Clinton's agenda had the heft of those of his predecessors, with his national service a virtual carbon copy of Kennedy's Peace Corps, his national health care plan just as ambitious, if not more so, than Johnson's Medicare plan, and his call for welfare reform on a par with Nixon's negative income tax.

Scope. It is on the scope of the agenda where both Bush and Clinton look very different from their predecessors. As table 33 shows, neither agenda comes even close to the 50 percent mark in total new ideas.

First, consider Bush again. His agenda is best described as a collection of fine tunings in the general support of already established ideas. His administration marked a high tide in what Jones calls co-partisanship, which is neither bipartisanship nor nonpartisanship, but a blend of self-interested action at both ends of Pennsylvania Avenue. According to Jones, co-partisanship "refers to a situation in which each political party has independent sources of power to the extent that (1) the power will be used to participate broadly in the policy process (including initiating proposals), and (2) negotiation carries rewards for both sides" (1991, p. 53). Central to a President's success is conciliation, not challenge; cooperation, not conflict. Bush adopted a conciliatory style from the very beginning, extending his hand to his friends in the "loyal opposition" in his Inaugural Address:

> I am putting out my hand to you, Mr. Speaker. I am putting out my hand to you, Mr. Majority Leader. For this is the thing. This is the age of the offered hand. And we can't turn back clocks, and I don't want to. But when our fathers were young, Mr. Speaker, our differences ended at the water's edge. And we don't wish to turn back time, but when our mothers were young, Mr. Majority Leader, the Congress and the Executive were capable of working together to produce a budget on which this nation could live. Let us negotiate soon — and hard. But in the end, let us produce.

This is hardly the kind of language one would expect from a President about to challenge the prevailing wisdom or create a revolution. The political circumstances would not have allowed otherwise. "Bush did not have a mandate," writes Jones, "lacking a marriage, there was no honeymoon;

**Table 33. Presidential Requests for Legislation:
New Programs Versus Old Programs**

President	New Programs		Old Programs		Percentage New Programs
	Total	Yearly Average	Total	Yearly Average	
Kennedy/Johnson	33	8	20	5	62%
Johnson	55	14	36	9	60
Nixon	46	12	19	5	71
Ford	6	3	10	5	44
Carter	25	6	16	4	61
Reagan	18	2	12	2	60
Bush	7	2	18	4	28
Clinton	12	3	21	5	36

power had already fled; therefore, influence was unlikely to cycle down . . . "
(1991, p. 53). Bush clearly intended not to rock the policy boat, offering
instead a long list of relatively limited adjustments in what had come before,
making his very much a "been there, done that" approach. In all, only seven of
Bush's twenty-five proposals could be declared new ideas, and they were
equally spread out over his four years.

Clinton was hardly different. Although he had a much higher proportion of large-scale proposals than Bush, he was only slightly more likely to
challenge the prevailing wisdom. His list of old ideas included an expanded
Earned Income Tax Credit, reauthorization of the Safe Drinking Water and
Clean Water Acts, immigration reform, an increase in the minimum wage,
reinventing government, and a host of small adjustments to existing programs.

Take reinventing government as one example. Much as the administration would argue that its vision for making government work was new,
Vice President Gore's reinventing package actually owes a fair amount of its
intellectual energy to none other than Richard Nixon. It was Nixon who first
argued that the problem in government is good people trapped in bad systems.
It was also Nixon who first recommended giving federal employees more
freedom to do their jobs. Although the Clinton administration took this "liberation management" to a more visible level, it was Nixon who began the effort
(see Light, 1997). By way of illustration, compare the following paragraphs
drawn from Nixon's 1971 message creating the Office of Management and
Budget and the opening of Gore's 1994 reinventing government report:

> Good people cannot do good things with bad mechanisms. But bad mecha-
> nisms can frustrate even the noblest aims. That is why so many public
> servants — of both political parties, of high rank and low, in both the legislative
> and executive branches — are often disenchanted with government these days.

> The federal government is filled with good people trapped in bad systems;
> budget systems, personnel systems, procurement systems, financial man-

agement systems. When we blame the people and impose more controls, we make the systems worse.

Although the two rationales are virtually indistinguishable, Nixon (paragraph one above) and Gore (paragraph two) came to very different remedies. Nixon drew heavily from the scientific management movement in proposing mergers of departments and greater central coordination, while Gore pushed for greater decentralization. Even here, however, Gore was hardly the first to argue for decentralization. Kennedy, Johnson, and Nixon all believed in some degree of what I have called liberation management, whether through the creation of government corporations (Comsat, Amtrak, Postal Service) or block grants and revenue sharing (Nixon).

At least in terms of government management reform, there is truly nothing new under the sun. As I argue, "there is not too little management reform in government, but too much. Contrary to conventional wisdom, Congress and the presidency have had little trouble passing reform measures over the years, moving almost effortlessly from one reform philosophy to another and back again, rarely questioning the contradictions and consequences of each separate act. If government is not getting better, it is most certainly not for a lack of legislation" (1997, p. 1). In this regard, it is difficult to find a single management reform that could be coded as a new idea. Thus, Clinton's lobbying reform is best viewed as an extension, albeit a large-scale extension, of the well established "watchful eye" approach to improving government conduct.

Putting Size and Scope Together. The derivative nature of recent agenda-setting is particularly clear once size and scope are combined into a single measure of policy impact. As table 34 shows, Bush and Clinton set new marks in the percent of agenda space devoted to small-old initiatives.

Bush emerges in the data as the consummate micro-President. Almost two-thirds of his agenda falls into the "small-old" category. His was clearly an agenda designed not to offend. His drift toward small-scale ideas was obvious in the first year, where half of his agenda was small-old. As Barbara Sinclair wrote at the time, his was to be a modest Presidency, built around a "kinder, gentler" agenda. "Facing a Congress firmly in the control of the opposition party, unable credibly to claim a policy mandate, and constrained by the big deficit, Bush proposed a modest legislative agenda. . . . For congressional Democrats, circumstances also dictated a strategy weighted toward compromise. Congressional Democrats did not fear Bush electorally; they did not believe he had a policy mandate that superseded their own. Yet Bush possessed the veto, and Democrats knew that mustering the two-thirds needed to override would seldom be possible" (1991, pp. 160–61).

Although co-partisanship was most certainly involved in Bush's drift toward small-old ideas, it does not so easily explain Clinton's agenda. Consider Clinton's first two years as an example. Although seven of his nine

Table 34. Large/Small Programs versus New/Old Programs

President	Large-New		Large-Old		Small-New		Small-Old	
	N	%	N	%	N	%	N	%
Kennedy/Johnson	19	36%	14	26%	9	17%	11	21%
Johnson	35	39	20	22	15	17	21	23
Nixon	18	28	5	8	28	43	14	22
Ford	4	25	4	25	2	13	6	39
Carter	16	39	6	15	9	22	10	24
Reagan	11	36	2	6	7	23	10	33
Bush	3	12	1	4	5	20	16	64
Clinton	9	27	7	21	3	9	14	42

new-large proposals came in the first year and all nine had been presented by the end of his second, Clinton's first two years also produced seven of his fourteen small-old ideas. Proportionally, Clinton's brief moment of unified government tended to invite bigger, bolder ideas. But in absolute numbers, his first two years also produced an almost equal number of conciliatory ideas. Even acknowledging that half of Clinton's small-old ideas came in 1995 and 1996, where he confronted the same divided government that had so constrained Bush, the co-partisanship explanation goes only so far in explaining why a President's agenda would move so far toward the small-old category. After all, Nixon faced a divided government and generated a very high percentage of small-new ideas. Much as one might credit Nixon's domestic policy adviser, Daniel Patrick Moynihan, for the innovativeness, Nixon and Reagan both dealt with divided government by being bolder.

Indeed, much as Clinton liked to compare himself to Kennedy, his first-term agenda actually turned out to look much more like the one presented by Gerald Ford. The two Presidents have almost identical percentages in all four categories of table 34: large-new proposals (25 percent to 27 percent), large-old (25 percent to 21 percent), small-new (13 percent to 9 percent), and small-old (39 percent to 42 percent). Despite their very different political circumstances, not the least of which were 116 more House seats working in Clinton's favor, the two Presidents ended up with remarkably simple derivative agendas.

Explaining the Rise of the Micro-Agenda

It is not surprising that Gerald Ford was so focused on old policy: his political prospects seemed to suggest no other course. It is the recent rise of derivative policy even under more favorable political conditions that remains unclear. Consider five competing explanations.

A first possibility is that intra-party politics is dictating the changing agenda composition. It could be, for example, that Republican and Democratic Presidents alike must move relatively far to their parties' extremes to win their first nomination, but must adopt a more conciliatory style to win the general election. As the party nomination process has become more polarized in recent years, the President's agenda may have become an increasingly important tool for reconciliation. The polarization would explain why both Bush and Clinton had such high percentages of small-old ideas. Having leaned hard to the right and left to win their first inaugurations, they may have used their agendas to restore political equilibrium in their first terms.

This highly polarized nomination process might also produce candidates who are more disposed toward conciliation. Although Bush's rise to the Presidency had more to do with the electoral politics that led Reagan to put him on the ticket in 1980 than with his special talents as a conciliator, he seemed perfect for the political environment, not to mention the co-partisanship, of the late 1980s. Consider how one senior official interviewed by Jones described the Bush agenda-setting style:

> The policy presidency of George Bush is reactive, not quite passive, anything but proactive. His instinct when it comes to issues is to say: "Let's let things germinate." Not, there's a problem, we better solve it; or, there might be a problem, let's do something before it becomes a problem. . . . Maybe the problem will go away. Maybe it will turn out to be less severe than we thought. If it does turn out to be worse and the time has come to act, then I'm perfectly comfortable looking at the alternatives and making a decision. It is not that I'm reactive because I don't want to deal with this [problem] (quoted in Jones, 1991, p. 59).

Although Clinton showed a greater willingness to take bold policy positions in years one and two of his Presidency, he hardly emerges as a more effective decision maker than Bush. Perhaps the electoral process is producing a kind of President much more willing to go with the flow, or so to speak.

A second possibility is that the Reagan Revolution so fundamentally altered the political and economic context that the President's agenda was changed for the foreseeable future. Reagan's immediate goal may have been a tighter federal budget and lower taxes, but his long-term goal was a lesser federal role in American life. The absence of a single initiative in his entire second term is quite compatible with that smaller federal presence. Given a choice between offering something old, as both Bush and Clinton did, or nothing at all, Reagan chose the latter option.

Table 35 offers one portrait of the "Reagan Effect." By reducing expectations of the Presidency as an engine for change, Reagan may have shrunk the agenda for his successors. Before his first inauguration, the percentage of old ideas stood at 47 percent; after, it stood at 63 percent.

A third, highly related possibility is that the budget deficit caused the drift toward old ideas. Reducing the deficit was a prominent theme of the Bush and Clinton agendas, and costs were always central to the agenda-setting

Table 35. Presidential Requests for Legislation, Pre- and Post-1981

Policy Difference	Pre-1981	Post-1981
Large-New	35%	26%
Small-New	24	17
Large-Old	18	11
Small-Old	23	46

Note: Pre-Reagan sample = 266 cases (Kennedy, Johnson, Nixon, Ford, Carter); Post-Reagan sample = 85 cases (Reagan, Bush, Clinton).

process. Both Presidents spent enormous time and energy trying to solve the budget deficit, and cost was always at the center of the agenda-setting process.

There is no question that the budget deficit constrained presidential decisions in the post-1981 period. The first months of the Clinton administration involved almost nothing else. Advisers fought over everything from the size of the problem to the balance between budget cuts and revenue enhancers, the new euphemism for tax increases. For his part, Clinton showed his characteristic indecisiveness. "The dynamic is inside himself," White House adviser George Stephanopoulos said of the fighting:

> There is always a tension between wanting to get this big program and knowing you have to reduce the deficit and get future growth and also make investments. It's a conflict among several sides of him: the part of him that's committed to children's programs and investing in jobs and highways; the part of him that knew the middle class had gotten screwed in the 1980s, that the middle-class tax cut was an important symbol; the part of him that's cut spending time and again in Arkansas but also the part of him that knows the intense pain caused by each cut; the part of him that understands the role of Wall Street and the part of him that knows that ordinary people have been screwed by those sources (in Drew, 1994, p. 64).

It remains to be seen whether the new-found budget surpluses in the late 1990s will change the dynamic. It is unlikely that the final two years of the Clinton administration will provide a definitive answer.

A fourth possibility for explaining the derivative Presidency is that the American welfare state has simply played itself out. After decades of steady expansion involving new twists and old fine-tunings, there may be no more room for innovation.

Such a conclusion is not incompatible with the leading research on both innovation and agenda-setting. The leading scholars of public sector innovation have long argued that most new ideas are combinations of old stuff. "Such programs are imperfect combinations of bits and pieces," write Martin Levin and Bryna Sanger of innovation. "Their character — that which makes them innovative — very often evolves over time through trial and error. The source of innovation is often old stuff — old stuff being used in new ways.

Indeed, often the innovation itself is simply the novel combination of familiar elements" (1992, p. 89). John Kingdon makes a similar argument; everything has its antecedents, he notes. "If alternatives change not by mutation but by recombination, there will always be familiar elements in the new combinations. And if the softening up process is as critical as we have claimed, it would be exceedingly surprising if wholly new ideas suddenly appeared on the scene in the policy primeval soup and immediately received a serious hearing" (1984, p. 141).

What if the recombinations became so familiar, so inbred, that innovation simply disappeared? Could there come a time in the expansion of a given policy arena where the status quo is so dominant that no new ideas are possible? Simply put, could a welfare state of the kind invented and expanded during this century eventually become a "black hole" of anti-innovation?

One can only speculate here, but muse for a moment about how the New Deal would fare if coded under the new-old, large-small criteria. Even a cursory review of Franklin Roosevelt's first-term suggests that his agenda contained a very high proportion of large-new proposals. How else would one categorize the Civilian Conservation Corps, the Agriculture Adjustment Administration, the Federal Deposit Insurance Corporation, the Securities and Exchange Commission, the Federal Emergency Relief Administration, the Works Progress Administration, the Tennessee Valley Authority, Social Security, and the National Industrial Recovery Act?

Assuming for a moment that Roosevelt's first-term agenda contained, say, 90 percent large-new proposals, the 1960s and 1970s would fit quite nicely as the mid-point of a long-term innovation cycle that would naturally play out by the 1990s. At some point in such a cycle, even new combinations of old ideas would lose their novelty as the universe of options folds in on itself in a celebration of minor expansions and contractions around defending a well-established status quo. Thus did Clinton celebrate the discovery of a budget surplus with a call to "save Social Security first."

A fifth possibility for explaining the derivative agenda is that the budget is being replaced by demographic destiny as the central constraint on the President's agenda. Clinton did not put Social Security at the top of his legislative agenda because he wanted to enshrine a New Deal flagship, but because the program is scheduled to run out of money in 2029. That budget surplus Clinton heralded in early 1998 was largely the product of cross-subsidies from the growing Old Age and Survivors Insurance trust fund, which has swelled with baby boom payroll taxes. Subtract the trust fund reserves from the deficit calculations and the federal government is still borrowing hundreds of billions to stay solvent. Presidents will be dealing with the baby boom for the next thirty years, trying desperately to make the old policy regime fit an aging America, to say nothing about satisfying an American Association of Retired Persons with a projected 50 million members by 2010.

This is not the book to resolve the causes of the derivative Presidency. Suffice it to say that there is very little in this discussion that would lead a President to think that the prospects are good for radical policy ideas. Nor, at least for the time being, do Americans seem to want more. The economy is sound and the national mood optimistic, even as cynicism toward politics remains high. Given their views of government's inability to do the right thing, Americans would likely oppose a raft of large-new ideas as unwarranted by the current conditions.

The problem, of course, is that conditions change. Whether Americans would rise to enthusiastic support for a policy revolution in the wake of the current devaluing of the Presidency is not clear. If Americans cannot trust government in sunny economic times, how will they view their democracy when the clouds return?

The No Win Presidency at Twenty Plus Years

Nothing in this chapter suggests an easing of the No Win Presidency. Presidents remain under great pressure to move it or lose it, even as their learning curves appear to lengthen with the thickening of government and the staggering delays in the presidential appointments process. The belief that learning can wait remains one of the great paradoxes of the modern Presidency. Presidents remain at their peak influence when they are at their lowest knowledge.

Perhaps it is just as well that the President's agenda has drifted toward smaller and older ideas: at least they are safer. The long-term effects of mistakes are lessened. If only the nation could figure out a way to give Presidents their maximum influence when they are the most knowledgeable about their work. That might help reverse the incredible shrinking of the agenda.

the interview sample

This research is based on interviews with 126 past and present White House officials. I completed the bulk of the interviews between January and March 1979. However, when questions arose in the analysis of the interviews, follow-up interviews were often necessary in order to settle confusion. Indeed, I called a small number of respondents several times after the original interview.

The total number of completed interviews was 126. Originally, I contacted over 170 past and present aides; the response rate was approximately 70 percent. In addition to the staffs, I interviewed 13 media observers. These respondents helped confirm some of the more unusual interview findings. Their responses, however, are not included in any of the tables.

Of the 126 interviews, I completed 69 by telephone and 57 in person. There was virtually no difference between the two methods in terms of the length of the interviews or, more important, in terms of the quality of the interviews. The telephone approach had several advantages. Clearly, telephone interviewing is much less expensive: each telephone interview cost approximately ten dollars, while each in-person contact cost upwards of twenty dollars. Telephone interviewing also can save considerable time. For one thing, telephone interviews are less likely to be interrupted. And if the respondent is not available, one can move on to the next interview quite easily. In the face-to-face situation, late appointments are a frequent problem. In the final analysis, quality must be the primary consideration.

In selecting potential respondents, I focused on five specific groups of "informants": (1) legislative liaison, (2) domestic policy staff, (3) OMB, (4) economic policy staff, and (5) the President's personal staff. I made no attempt to create a weighted sample. Rather, I was more concerned about talking with informed individuals. A brief summary of the sample follows:

Total interviews requested	172		
Total interviews completed	126		
Legislative liaison	18		
Domestic policy staff	45		
OMB	18		
Economic policy staff	13		
President's personal staff	32		
Media	13		
Total follow-up interviews	42	Average interview	50 minutes
		Longest	150 minutes
Total telephone interviews	69	Shortest	10 minutes
Total in-person interviews	57		

APPENDIX B

the questionnaire

I used a standard questionnaire for all respondents. However, each interview involved a great deal of unstructured material. Since the questionnaire involved only five questions, there was considerable time for the discussion of specific cases. I made every attempt to conduct the interviews in a conversational tone. Though I took notes during each interview, I made an effort to set the interview in an informal framework. Even when I asked the structured questions, I tried to present them more as a feature of the conversation than as part of the questionnaire. In the bulk of interviews, I presented the five questions in order. Regardless of question order, each item involved the opportunity for probes. The structured questions are summarized below:

1. Generally speaking, how would you define presidential capital? In specific, how would you define it for the domestic agenda?
2. What would you say were the most important programs of the _____ administration?
3. What would you say were the main reasons why the President selected _____ as a top issue concern?
4. Generally speaking, what would you say were the most important sources of ideas for the domestic agenda?
5. When the administration looked at potential programs, what do you remember as the first question asked about the specific alternative? Did you ask about the economic costs? the congressional reaction? workability?

APPENDIX C

coding

The coding of both the interviews and the OMB data was quite simple and direct. Most of the interview data involved straightforward categories; the bulk of the OMB classifications involved simple distinctions. However, in an effort to confirm reliability, several of the more difficult items were checkcoded. Question 3 from the interview data (see Appendix B) and the new/old distinction from the OMB data were each checked for reliability. Since these two distinctions involved the greatest potential problems, the associated intecoder reliability might be seen as a *minimum* level of reliability for all other questions.

Reliability was assessed through a very simple procedure. A sample of thirty items from each data set was drawn for evaluation. Subsequently, a checkcoder was instructed as to the specific distinctions involved in each code. The checkcoder then reviewed the data. For both data sets, reliability was defined as the number of cases *in agreement*. Reliability equaled 84 percent in the interview data; 87 percent in the OMB data. These reliability figures apply only to question 4 from the interview data (see Appendix B) and the new/old distinction from the OMB data. However, the reliability figures lend some confidence to both data sets. The figures are well within acceptable levels, particularly given the somewhat difficult nature of the specific codes.

bibliography

Aberbach and Rockman. "On the Rise, the Transformation, and the Decline of Analysis in Government." *Governance* 2 (1989): 293–314.

Allison, Graham T. *Essence of Decision: Explaining the Cuban Missile Crisis.* Boston: Little, Brown, 1971.

Anderson, Martin. *Welfare: The Political Economy of Welfare Reform in the United States.* Stanford, Calif.: Hoover Institution Press, 1978.

Barber, James David. *The Presidential Character: Predicting Performance in the White House.* Englewood Cliffs, N.J.: Prentice-Hall, 1972.

Bowler, M. Kenneth. *The Nixon Guaranteed Income Proposal: Substance and Process in Policy Change.* Cambridge, Mass.: Ballinger, 1974.

Bruff, Howard. "Presidential Management of Agency Rulemaking." *George Washington University Law Review* 57 (1989): 281–318.

Burke, Vee J., and Vincent Burke. *Nixon's Good Deed: Welfare Reform.* New York: Columbia University Press, 1974.

Campbell, John C. "The Old People Boom and Japanese Policy Making." Paper delivered at the American Political Science Association Meetings, 1978, New York.

Carey, William. "Presidential Staffing in the Sixties and Seventies." *Public Administration Review* 29 (1969): 450–58.

Cobb, R. W., and C. D. Elder. *Participation in American Politics: The Dynamics of Agenda-Building.* Baltimore: Johns Hopkins University Press, 1972.

Cohen, Michael D., James G. March, and J. P. Olsen. "A Garbage Can Model of Organizational Choice." *Administrative Science Quarterly* 17 (1972): 1–25.

Cronin, Thomas E. "Presidents as Chief Executives." In *The Presidency Reappraised,* ed. Rexford G. Tugwell and Thomas E. Cronin. New York: Praeger, 1974.

———. *The State of the Presidency.* Boston: Little, Brown, 1975.

Cutler, Lloyd. "To Form a Government." *Foreign Affairs* 59 (1980): 126–43.

Cyert, Richard M., and James G. March. *A Behavioral Theory of the Firm.* Englewood Cliffs, N.J.: Prentice-Hall, 1963.

Davis, Eric L. "Legislative Liaison in the Carter Administration." *Political Science Quarterly* 95 (1979): 287–302.

Derthick, Martha. *Agency under Stress: The Social Security Administration in American Government.* Washington, D.C.: Brookings Institution, 1990.

Dodd, Lawrence C., and Richard L. Schott. *Congress and the Administrative State.* New York: Wiley, 1979.

Edwards, George. *Presidential Influence in Congress.* San Francisco: W. H. Freeman, 1980.

———. *At the Margins: Presidential Leadership of Congress.* New Haven, Conn.: Yale University Press, 1989.

Edwards, George, with Alec M. Gallup. *Presidential Approval: A Sourcebook.* Baltimore: Johns Hopkins University Press, 1990.

Eizenstat, Stuart E. "Remarks." Presented at the Women's National Democratic Club, 4 January 1979.

303

Fenno, Richard F. *Home Style: House Members in Their Districts.* Boston: Little, Brown, 1978.

Fiorina, Morris. *Retrospective Voting in American National Elections.* New Haven, Conn.: Yale University Press, 1981.

Fishel, Jeffrey. "From Campaign Promise to Presidential Performance: The First Two (and ½) Years of the Carter Presidency." Paper presented at the Woodrow Wilson International Center for Scholars, Washington, D.C., 20 June 1979.

Franklin, Charles, and John Jackson. "The Dynamics of Party Identification." *American Political Science Review* 77 (1983): 957–73.

George, Alexander. "The Case for Multiple Advocacy in Foreign Policy." *American Political Science Review* 66 (1972): 751–95.

Greenstein, Fred I. "Change and Continuity in the Modern Presidency." In *The New American Political System,* ed. Anthony King. Washington, D.C.: The American Enterprise Institute, 1978.

Grogan, Fred L. "Candidate Promises and Presidential Performance, 1964–1972." Paper delivered at the Midwest Political Science Association Meetings, 1977, Chicago.

Heclo, Hugh, and Lester Solomon. *The Illusion of Presidential Government.* Boulder, Colo.: Westview Press, 1981.

Hodgson, Geoffrey. *All Things to All Men: The False Promise of the Modern Presidency.* New York: Harper and Row, 1980.

Hughes, Emmet J. *The Ordeal of Power: A Political Memoir of the Eisenhower Years.* New York: Atheneum, 1963.

Janis, Irving L. *Victims of Groupthink: A Psychological Study of Foreign-Policy Decisions and Fiascoes.* Boston: Houghton, Mifflin, 1972.

Jennings, M. Kent, and Gregory Markus. "Partisan Orientations over the Long Haul: Results from the Three-Wave Political Socialization Panel Study." *American Political Science Review* 78 (1984): 1000–1018.

Jennings, M. Kent, and Richard Niemi. *Generations and Politics: A Panel Study of Young Adults and Their Parents.* Princeton: Princeton University Press, 1981.

Johnson, Lyndon B. *The Vantage Point: Perspectives of the Presidency, 1963–1969.* New York: Holt, Rinehart, and Winston, 1971.

Kearns, Doris. *Lyndon Johnson and the American Dream.* New York: Harper and Row, 1976.

Kernell, Samuel. *Going Public: New Strategies of Presidential Leadership.* Washington, D.C.: Congressional Quarterly Press, 1986.

Kernell, S., Peter W. Sperlich, and Aaron Wildavsky. "Public Support for Presidents." In *Perspectives on the Presidency,* ed. Aaron Wildavsky. Boston: Little, Brown, 1975.

Kessel, John H. *The Domestic Presidency: Decision-Making in the White House.* Boston: Duxbury Press, 1975.

———. "The Parameters of Presidential Politics." Paper delivered at the American Political Science Association Meetings, 1972, New York.

King, Anthony. "The American Polity in the Late 1970s: Building Coalitions in the Sand." In *The New American Political System,* ed. Anthony King. Washington, D.C.: The American Enterprise Institute, 1978.

Kingdon, John. *Agendas, Alternatives, and Public Policy.* Boston: Little, Brown, 1984.

———. "Pre-Decision Public Policy Processes." Grant proposal to the National Science Foundation, 1978.

Koenig, Louis. *The Chief Executive.* 4th ed. New York: Harcourt, Brace, Jovanovich, 1981.

Light, Paul. *Artful Work: The Politics of Social Security Reform.* New York: Random House, 1985.

———. "The Focusing Skill and Presidential Influence in Congress." In C. Deering, *Congressional Politics.* Chicago: Dorsey Press, 1989.

———. "When Worlds Collide: The Political-Career Nexus." In *The In-and-Outers: Presidential Appointees and Transient Government in Washington,* ed. G. Calvin Mackenzie. Baltimore: Johns Hopkins University Press, 1987.

Loomis, Burdette. *The New American Politics: Ambition, Entrepreneurship, and the Changing Face of Political Life.* New York: Basic Books, 1988.

Lowi, Theodore J. "American Business, Public Policy, Case-Studies and Political Theory." *World Politics* 16 (1964): 677–715.

Mackenzie, G. Calvin. " 'If You Want to Play, You've Got to Pay': Ethics Regulation and the Presidential Appointments System, 1964–1984." In *The In-and-Outers: Presidential Appointees and Transient Government in Washington,* ed. G. Calvin Mackenzie. Baltimore: Johns Hopkins University Press, 1987.

McPherson, Harry. *A Political Education.* Boston: Little, Brown, 1972.

Mayhew, David R. *Congress: The Electoral Connection.* New Haven, Conn.: Yale University Press, 1974.

Moe, Ronald. "Traditional Organizational Principles and the Managerial Presidency: From Phoenix to Ashes." *Public Administration Review* 50 (1990): 129–40.

Mohr, Lawrence B. "Organizations, Decisions, and Courts." *Law and Society Review* 10 (1976): 621–42.

Nathan, Richard P. *The Plot that Failed: Nixon and the Administrative Presidency.* New York: Wiley, 1975.

National Broadcasting Corporation. "Meet the Press," transcript, 23 November 1980. Washington, D.C.: Kelley Press, 1980.

National Commission on the Public Service. *Leadership for America.* Washington, D.C.: National Commission on the Public Service, 1989.

Neustadt, Richard E. "Presidency and Legislation: The Growth of Central Clearance." *American Political Science Review* 48 (1954): 641–47.

———. *Presidential Power: The Politics of Leadership.* New York: Wiley, 1960.

———. "White House and Whitehall." *The Public Interest* 14 (1966): 55–69.

Norpoth, Helmut, and Jerrold Rusk. "Partisan Dealignment in the American Electorate: Itemizing the Deductions." *American Political Science Review* 76 (1982): 522–37.

Patterson, Samuel C. "The Semi-Sovereign Congress." In *The New American Political System,* ed. Anthony King. Washington, D.C.: The American Enterprise Institute, 1978.

Peabody, Robert I., Norman J. Ornstein, and D. W. Rohde. "The United States Senate as a Presidential Incubator: Many Are Called but Few Are Chosen." *Political Science Quarterly* 91 (1976): 237–58.

Pomper, Gerald. *Elections in America.* New York: Dodd, Mead, 1968.

Price, Ray. *With Nixon.* New York: Viking, 1977.

Public Broadcasting System. "Every Four Years," transcript, January–February 1980. Philadelphia: WHYY, 1980.

Public Papers of the Presidents of the United States. Washington, D.C.: U.S. Government Printing Office, 1963, 1965.

Reedy, George. *The Twilight of the Presidency.* New York: World, 1970.

Reichley, A. James. *Conservatives in an Age of Change: The Nixon and Ford Administrations.* Washington, D.C.: Brookings Institution, 1981.

Reinhold, Robert. "How Urban Policy Gets Made—Very Carefully." *New York Times,* 2 April 1978.

Rivlin, Alice. *Systematic Thinking for Social Action.* Washington, D.C.: Brookings Institution, 1971.

Rose, Richard. *Inheritance before Choice in Public Policy.* Studies in Public Policy Number 180. Glasgow, Scotland: University of Strathclyde, 1989.

Schattschneider, E. E. *The Semi-Sovereign People.* New York: Holt, Rinehart, and Winston, 1960.

Schick, Allen. "The Battle of the Budget." *Proceedings of the Academy of Political Science* 32 (1975): 51–70.

———. *Congress and Money: Budgeting, Spending, and Taxing.* Washington, D.C.: The Urban Institute, 1980.

Schlesinger, Arthur M., Jr. *A Thousand Days: John F. Kennedy in the White House.* Boston: Houghton, Mifflin, 1965.

Schramm, Sarah S. "The Politics of Executive Orders: Presidential Activism and Restraint." Paper delivered at the Midwest Political Science Association Meetings, 1977, Chicago.

Schulman, Paul. "Nonincremental Policy Making: Notes toward an Alternative Paradigm." *American Political Science Review* 69 (1975): 1354–70.

Schultze, Charles L., E. R. Fried, Alice Rivlin, and N. H. Teeters. *Setting National Priorities: The 1972 Budget.* Washington, D.C.: Brookings Institution, 1971.

Shogan, Robert. *Promises to Keep: Carter's First Hundred Days.* New York: Thomas Crowell, 1977.

Simon, Dennis, and Charles Ostrom, Jr. "The President and Public Support: A Strategic Perspective." In *The Presidency and Public Policy Making,* ed. G. Edwards, S. Shull, and N. Thomas. Pittsburgh: University of Pittsburgh Press, 1985.

Smith, Steven. *Call to Order: Floor Politics in the House and Senate.* Washington, D.C.: Brookings Institution, 1989.

Sorenson, Theodore C. *Decision-Making in the White House: The Olive Branch or the Arrows.* New York: Columbia University Press, 1963.

Sperlich, Peter W. "Bargaining and Overload: An Essay on *Presidential Power.*" In *Perspectives on the Presidency,* ed. Aaron Wildavsky. Boston: Little, Brown, 1975.

Sundquist, James L. *Politics and Policy: The Eisenhower, Kennedy, and Johnson Years.* Washington, D.C.: Brookings Institution, 1968.

Ullmann, Owen. *Stockman: The Man, the Myth, the Future.* New York: Donald Fine, 1986.

U.S. General Accounting Office. *Federal Evaluation: Fewer Units, Reduced Resources, Different Studies from 1980.* GAO/PEMD-87-9. January 1987.

———. *Paperwork Reduction: Mixed Effects on Agency Decision Processes and Data Availability.* GAO/PEMD-89-20. September 1989.

———. *Program Evaluation Issues.* Transition Series, GAO/OCG-89-8TR. November 1988.

U.S. House of Representatives, Committee on Energy and Commerce, Subcommittee on

Oversight and Investigations. *OMB Review of CDC Research: Impact of the Paperwork Reduction Act.* Washington, D.C.: U.S. Government Printing Office, 1986.

Valenti, Jack. *A Very Human President.* New York: Norton, 1975.

———. "The President as Political Leader." In *The Virginia Papers on the Presidency,* ed. Kenneth W. Thompson, vol. 4, pp. 1–29. Lanham, Md.: University Press, 1980.

Veroff, Joseph, Elizabeth Douvan, and Richard Kulka. *The Inner American: A Self-Portrait from 1957–1976.* New York: Basic Books, 1981.

Walker, Jack L. "Setting the Agenda in the U.S. Senate: A Theory of Problem Selection." *British Journal of Political Science* 7 (1977): 423–45.

Wattenberg, Martin. *The Decline of American Political Parties, 1952–1980.* Cambridge, Mass.: Harvard University Press, 1984.

Wayne, Stephen J. *The Legislative Presidency.* New York: Harper and Row, 1978.

Williams, Walter. *Mismanaging America: The Rise of the Anti-Analytic Presidency.* Lawrence: University of Kansas Press, 1990.

Wood, Robert. "When Government Works." *The Public Interest* 18 (1970): 39–51.

Additional References

Bond, Jon R., and Fleisher, Richard. *The President in the Legislative Arena.* Chicago: University of Chicago Press, 1990.

Drew, Elizabeth. *On the Edge: The Clinton Presidency.* New York: Simon & Schuster, 1994.

Edwards, George C., III. "Frustration and Folly: Bill Clinton and the Public Presidency." In *The Clinton Presidency: First Appraisals,* ed. C. Campbell and B. Rockman. Chatham, N.J.: Chatham House, 1996.

Edwards, George C., III, and Barrett, Andrew. "Presidential Agenda Setting in Congress." Unpublished paper, 1998.

Edwards, George C., III, and Wood, B. Dan. "Who Uses Whom? The President, the Media, and the Public Agenda." Paper prepared for the Midwest Political Science Association meetings, Chicago, 1997.

Jacobs, Lawrence R., and Shapiro, Robert Y. "Disorganized Democracy: The Institutionalization of Polling and Public Opinion Analysis during the Kennedy, Johnson, and Nixon Presidencies." Paper delivered at the American Political Science Association meetings, New York, 1994.

Jones, Charles O. *The Presidency in a Separated System.* Washington, D.C.: Brookings Institution, 1994.

Jones, Charles O. "Meeting Low Expectations: Strategy and Prospects of the Bush Presidency." In *The Bush Presidency: First Appraisals,* ed. C. Campbell and B. Rockman. Chatham, N.J.: Chatham House, 1991.

Jones, Charles O. *Passages to the Presidency: From Campaigning to Governing.* Washington, D.C.: Brookings Institution, 1998.

Kernell, Samuel. *Going Public: New Strategies of Presidential Leadership,* 2d ed. Washington, D.C.: CQ Press, 1993.

Levin, Martin, and Sanger, Bryna. "Using Old Stuff in New Ways: Innovation as a Case of

Evolutionary Thinking." *Journal of Policy Analysis and Management* 11 (1992): 88–115.

Light, Paul C. *Still Artful Work: The Continuing Politics of Social Security Reform.* New York: McGraw-Hill, 1995.

———. *Thickening Government: Federal Hierarchy and the Diffusion of Accountability.* Washington, D.C.: Brookings Institution, 1995.

———. *The Tides of Reform: Making Government Work, 1945–1995.* New Haven: Yale University Press, 1997.

Mackenzie, G. Calvin. "The Clinton Presidency." In *Obstacle Course: The Report of the Twentieth Century Fund Task Force on the Presidential Appointments Process.* New York: Twentieth Century Fund, 1996.

The Pew Research Center for The People & The Press. *Deconstructing Distrust: How Americans View Government.* Washington, D.C.: Pew Research Center, March 9, 1998.

———. *Popular Policies and Unpopular Press Lift Clinton Ratings.* Washington, D.C.: Pew Research Center, February 6, 1998.

Sinclair, Barbara. "Bush and the 101st Congress." In *The Bush Presidency: First Appraisals,* ed. C. Campbell and B. Rockman. Chatham, N.J.: Chatham House, 1991.

Skowronek, Stephen. *The Politics Presidents Make: Leadership from John Adams to George Bush.* Cambridge: Belknap Press, Harvard University Press, 1993.

index

Library of Congress Cataloging-in-Publication Data
Light, Paul Charles.
    The president's agenda : domestic policy choice from Kennedy to
Clinton / Paul C. Light. — 3rd ed.
        p.   cm.
    Includes bibliographical references and index.
    ISBN 0-8018-6065-2 (alk. paper). — ISBN 0-8018-6066-0 (pbk. :
alk. paper)
    1. Presidents—United States.   2. United States—Politics and
government—20th century.   3. United States—Economic policy.
4. United States—Social policy.   5. Policy sciences.
JK518.L472   1999
320'.6'0973—dc21   98-34586
                                                                            CIP